FREE DVD

FREE DVD

From Stress to Success DVD from Trivium Test Prep

Dear Customer,

Thank you for purchasing from Trivium Test Prep! Whether you're looking to join the military, get into college, or advance your career, we're honored to be a part of your journey.

To show our appreciation (and to help you relieve a little of that test-prep stress), we're offering a **FREE** *PTCB Essential Test Tips DVD** by Trivium Test Prep. Our DVD includes 35 test preparation strategies that will help keep you calm and collected before and during your big exam. All we ask is that you email us your feedback and describe your experience with our product. Amazing, awful, or just so-so: we want to hear what you have to say!

To receive your **FREE** *PTCB Essential Test Tips DVD*, please email us at 5star@triviumtestprep.com. Include "Free 5 Star" in the subject line and the following information in your email:

1. The title of the product you purchased.
2. Your rating from 1 – 5 (with 5 being the best).
3. Your feedback about the product, including how our materials helped you meet your goals and ways in which we can improve our products.
4. Your full name and shipping address so we can send your **FREE** *PTCB Essential Test Tips DVD*.

If you have any questions or concerns please feel free to contact us directly at 5star@triviumtestprep.com.

Thank you, and good luck with your studies!

* Please note that the free DVD is <u>not included</u> with this book. To receive the free DVD, please follow the instructions above.

PTCB EXAM STUDY GUIDE 2017–2018

Test Prep and Practice Test Questions for the Pharmacy Technician Certification Board Examination

TABLE OF CONTENTS

Online Resources i

Introduction iii
WHAT IS A PHARMACY TECHNICIAN?..iii
NATIONAL CERTIFICATION.....................vii

1 Pharmacology........................ 1
THE PRINCIPLES OF
PHARMACOLOGY 1
AN INTRODUCTION TO MEDICAL
TERMINOLOGY........................... 14
SYSTEMS PHARMACOLOGY 26
PHARMACY ABBREVIATIONS............... 116

2 Assisting the Pharmacist ... 123
AMBULATORY (COMMUNITY)
PHARMACY.............................. 123
INSTITUTIONAL (HOSPITAL)
PHARMACY............................. 162
PHARMACY AUTOMATION 167
INVESTIGATIONAL DRUG DATA 169

3 Pharmacy Law & Ethics 171
HISTORY.................................. 171
CONTROLLED DRUGS 188

4 Administration &
Management of
the Pharmacy 211
MEDICATION ERRORS........................... 211
REFERENCE MATERIALS....................... 228
HAZARDOUS MATERIALS AND SAFETY
IN THE WORKPLACE............................. 233
INVENTORY 247

5 Compounding
Pharmaceuticals 259
NON-STERILE COMPOUNDING........... 260
STERILE COMPOUNDING 270

6 Pharmacy Math 287
FUNDAMENTALS OF PHARMACY
MATH 287
FRACTIONS AND DECIMALS 293
RATIO, PROPORTIONS, AND
PERCENTAGE........................... 297
LIQUID MEASURES 300
CONCENTRATIONS................................. 301
DILUTIONS 306
ADMIXTURE CALCULATIONS 320
BUSINESS MATH 329

7 Practice Test........................ 339
ANSWER KEY 349

ONLINE RESOURCES

To help you fully prepare for your Pharmacy Technician Certification Exam, Ascencia includes online resources with the purchase of this study guide.

PRACTICE TEST

In addition to the practice test included in this book, we also offer an online exam. Since many exams today are computer based, getting to practice your test-taking skills on the computer is a great way to prepare.

FLASH CARDS

A convenient supplement to this study guide, Ascencia's flash cards enable you to review important terms easily on your computer or smartphone.

CHEAT SHEETS

Review the core skills you need to master the exam with easy-to-read Cheat Sheets.

FROM STRESS TO SUCCESS

Watch From Stress to Success, a brief but insightful YouTube video that offers the tips, tricks, and secrets experts use to score higher on the exam.

REVIEWS

Leave a review, send us helpful feedback, or sign up for Ascencia promotions—including free books!

Access these materials at:

www.ascenciatestprep.com/ptcb-online-resources

INTRODUCTION: BECOMING A CERTIFIED PHARMACY TECHNICIAN

Congratulations on your choice to become a Certified Pharmacy Technician! Pharmacy technicians play an essential role in the practice of pharmacy and are vital for its future as an evolving field. Because of the growing responsibilities of the pharmacy technician, becoming certified signifies that the pharmacy technician has achieved the competence necessary to become a trusted member of the pharmacy team. It also helps the pharmacy technician stay up to date with the continuing education crucial to the progressive field of pharmacy technology. This guide will introduce you to the essential skills that are required to pass the certification exam. In this chapter, we will review the different roles and responsibilities of pharmacy technicians, what the Pharmacy Technician Certification Board (PTCB) is, and present and future opportunities available for certified pharmacy technicians.

What Is a Pharmacy Technician?

Pharmacy technicians are a fundamental part of the pharmacy practice. As a pharmacy technician, you will be responsible for assisting the pharmacist. Almost anything that does not require the professional judgment of the pharmacist can be done by the technician. Under the direct supervision of a pharmacist, pharmacy technicians assist patients, interact with physicians and nurses, are responsible for the administrative responsibilities of the pharmacy, and help prepare prescriptions and compounded medications. Pharmacists rely on pharmacy technicians to fulfill the technical and production aspects of the pharmacy so they can focus more on patient care such as patient counseling activities and safe dispensing of medications.

Qualifications

Starting in the mid-1990s, with the advancement of pharmacy technology and the growth of managed care, an urgent need for competent pharmacy technicians arose. At that time, the most basic qualifications for pharmacy technicians were that they be at least eighteen years of age with a high school diploma or GED and a clear criminal record, with no felonies or drug-related offenses. As the pharmacist's responsibilities grew, pharmacy technicians required more specific skill sets to help reduce errors and free up pharmacists to focus on patient care. In response, more pharmacies offered incentives for pharmacy technicians to voluntarily become certified through the PTCB. This, in turn, increased their knowledge and abilities, giving pharmacy technicians credibility and recognition for their skills.

As pharmacy technology advanced into the twenty-first century, many state boards of pharmacy made **national certification** a requirement following the completion of pharmacy technician programs at **vocational schools** or **on-the-job-training**. National certification is required by many states to prove that the technician has the necessary level of skill and knowledge to perform his or her duties. Maintaining certification also requires reassessment through continuing education (CE) hours.

As of 2016, forty-five states and the District of Columbia also require pharmacy technicians to be **registered** through their state department of health. Registration is granted by the government and requires an individual to be licensed to practice an occupation in that particular state. The technician must prove that he or she has attained the proper minimum requirements needed to perform the occupation safely. Failure to comply with these requirements could result in suspension or revocation of the technician's license.

Common Responsibilities of Pharmacy Technicians

Being a pharmacy technician requires a strong code of ethics. Pharmacy personnel are trusted professionals, and patients rely on the pharmacy staff to deliver a safe, high-quality product. **Professionalism**, or the competence expected of the professional, puts patients at ease; they know that pharmacy staff will take all precautions necessary to ensure the correct medication is being dispensed.

Communication skills are extremely important in pharmacy. Besides the patient, pharmacy technicians interact with physicians, nurses, and other staff to meet the patient's needs. Whether it be calling the physician's office for a refill or preparing an intravenous (IV) admixture, addressing any questions or concerns can be the difference between helping and hurting a patient. **Safety** should always come first.

Other roles and responsibilities of the pharmacy technician depend on the healthcare facility where she or he is employed. Pharmacy technicians are responsible for a multitude of tasks that may change at the pharmacist's discretion. In a retail pharmacy, a pharmacy technician must assist both customers and the pharmacist. Pharmacy technicians may receive a prescription from a patient, input the prescription information into the computer, fill the medication, call physicians' offices for refills, work with insurance companies, order medications, inventory the pharmacy, handle cash, and do housekeeping.

In ambulatory pharmacies, pharmacy technicians work more closely with the nurses and staff and less with the patient. The pharmacy technician may be required to unit-dose and fill medication orders, prepare IV admixtures, enter data, deliver medications to the nursing floors, stock automated dispensing machines, do inventory, and order medications.

As pharmacy technology progresses, so do the roles and responsibilities of pharmacy technicians. **Continuing education**, or ongoing education related directly to pharmacy, helps to ensure the pharmacy technician develops intellectually as new opportunities arise.

HEALTHCARE SETTINGS

Healthcare settings for pharmacy technicians continue to progress as new opportunities arise. The two most common settings for the pharmacy technician are **community**, or retail pharmacy and **ambulatory**, or hospital pharmacy. However, there are a number of other settings where pharmacy technicians are needed.

In the past decade, **managed care** has become a growing institution in healthcare. Pharmacy technicians take on a more administrative role when working in managed care. Their medical knowledge has made them an indispensable part of the team in finding cost-effective ways to deliver quality care through prescription benefit management (PBM). Many pharmacy technicians who work in managed care work in **call center** environments. They may help patients find cost-effective solutions to high prescription costs, schedule appointments for medication therapy management (MTM), or assist in **medication compliance** if a patient is having trouble taking his or her medication regularly.

Nuclear medicine, which requires working with radiopharmaceuticals, is a more advanced role of the pharmacy technician. Some facilities that work with radiopharmaceuticals, such as **cancer treatment centers**, prefer technicians who have experience or have been certified to work in nuclear medicine due to the high health risk from radioactive chemicals. Nuclear medicine technicians must adhere to specific guidelines to avoid contamination.

With the growing older population in the United States, many IV medications are dispensed at home. If a patient is on **hospice** end-of-life care or **home healthcare**, pharmacy technicians can prepare and deliver an IV infusion from a centralized location, and a nurse can administer the medication from the comfort of home. Some **rehabilitation** and **long-term care** facilities have in-house pharmacies to better assist patients, while others work with local pharmaceutical companies or nationally accredited companies to deliver medications to facilities.

The companies will unit-dose patient-specific medications in blister packs or make patient-specific IV admixtures to dispense medications more efficiently.

FUTURE OF PHARMACY TECHNOLOGY

The future of pharmacy technology is very promising. As computer technology advances, so do the pharmacy technician's roles and responsibilities. There are now a number of fields experienced pharmacy technicians can enter to take on new and interesting responsibilities.

Telepharmacy is an exciting advancement in healthcare. With telepharmacy, telecommunications allows patients to receive pharmaceutical care in cases when they may not be able to have direct contact with a pharmacist. In telepharmacy, hospitals employ pharmacists who work remotely, inputting medication orders overnight. This cuts costs since the pharmacy is not required to stay open 24 hours a day. As educational requirements improve, telepharmacy opportunities are now being offered to highly qualified pharmacy technicians as well. The medication order is entered, and the pharmacist verifies the order when completed. In rural areas, some hospitals have also allowed pharmacy technicians to work independently in the pharmacy; working remotely, a pharmacist verifies the technician's work by reviewing images of the fill process.

As pharmacy technicians become more qualified and better educated, many are trusted to work in quality assurance to assist in developing methods to promote better **patient safety**. Some pharmacy technicians, alongside pharmacists, help train employees through seminars on medication safety and implement standards within the healthcare facility to avoid medication errors.

As requirements to become a pharmacy technician become more stringent, many state boards of pharmacy are requiring training through a vocational school. Consequently, there is a need for **educators** to teach these classes. Experienced pharmacy technicians can also become trainers at pharmaceutical companies for new hires and continuing education.

Being a **pharmaceutical sales representative** in the past used to require a bachelor's degree in pharmacy. Now, with higher educational standards for pharmacy technicians, these opportunities are open to them as well. Sales representatives promote medications and medical devices to healthcare professionals; employees must be well versed in the product they are advertising.

Pharmacy informatics focuses on medication-related data and knowledge within healthcare systems. It includes implementation, analysis, use, and storage of patient care and health outcomes. Although a career in informatics may require certain computer certifications and other degrees, there is a stark need for training in pharmacy software as new technologies develop. Growth in this field is exceptional; many employment opportunities are emerging.

National Certification

As explained above, national certification is now becoming a requirement of most state boards of pharmacy to ensure that the pharmacy technician has a strong knowledge base. This chapter will provide an overview of the Pharmacy Technician Certification Board (PTCB) and the skill sets needed to pass the Pharmacy Technician Certification Exam (PTCE).

The PTCB's **Pharmacy Technician Certification Exam (PTCE)** is accredited by the National Commission for Certifying Agencies (NCCA). To schedule a test, you must first get authorization from the PTCB showing you have met all the pre-qualifications. The pre-qualifications are explained in the PTCB Code of Conduct shown at the end of this chapter. After you receive authorization and pay the $129 test fee, you can schedule a test online or by phone with Pearson-VUE Professional Testing Centers. When you arrive at the center, be sure to have photo identification to prove your identity. The testing center may also collect your palm vein image digitally for verification and to protect the integrity of the test. No personal items are allowed in the testing area; you will be assigned a locker to secure your items while you test. When you enter the testing area, an employee will sign you in to a computer workstation and hand you any other materials permitted only for testing purposes. You are monitored at all times while taking the test and cannot communicate with other test-takers. Any disruptive or fraudulent behavior can cause termination of testing.

The PTCE is a computer-generated multiple-choice exam that contains ninety questions. Of the ninety questions, eighty questions are scored and ten questions are unscored. There are four possible answers for each question, but only one is correct. The exam takes 2 hours. A score of 1400/1600 or better is required to pass the exam. The range of possible scores is between 1000 and 1600 and is based off of the Modified Angoff method of testing. You will officially know if you passed the test within 1 to 3 weeks after you take the exam. Within 6 weeks, you will be sent an official certificate and wallet card stating you are a certified pharmacy technician.

WHAT IS THE PTCB?

The main governing organization for the Pharmacy Technician Certification Exam (PTCE) is the **Pharmacy Technician Certification Board (PTCB)**. The PTCB was created in 1995 by leaders in both the American Society of Health Systems Pharmacists (ASHP) and the American Pharmacist Association (APA). These leaders, realizing the need for a better way to educate pharmacy technicians on the skill sets essential to their profession, created a board of advisors who initiated a testing system that assesses the knowledge and abilities needed to perform pharmacy technician work responsibilities.

By passing the PTCE, pharmacy technicians are nationally accredited and receive the title of a Certified Pharmacy Technician, or CPhT. This accreditation proves to employers that its holder's knowledge will be beneficial to their company. The skill sets tested on the exam specifically correspond to required knowledge for performing technical and production duties in the pharmacy.

WHAT YOU NEED TO KNOW TO PASS THE PTCE

To pass the PTCE, the PTCB requires knowledge of specific subjects related to work as a pharmacy technician. The subjects and the percentage of each subject that will be on the test are listed below:

Pharmacology (13.75%): brand and generic names of pharmaceuticals, therapeutic equivalence, strength/dose, dosage forms, physical appearance, routes of administration, duration of drug therapy, drug interactions, common and severe/adverse side effects, allergies, therapeutic contraindications, dosage and indication of legend, OTC medications, herbal and dietary supplements

Pharmacy Law and Ethics (12.50%): storage, handling, and disposal of hazardous substances; hazardous substance exposure (including prevention and treatment); controlled substance transfer regulations; controlled substance documentation for receiving, ordering, returning, loss/theft, and destruction; formula to verify the validity of DEA numbers, record keeping, documentation, and record retention; restricted drug programs and related prescription processing requirements; professional standards related to HIPAA; requirements for consultation; recalls; infection control; professional standards; reconciliation between state and federal laws; facility, equipment, and supply requirements

Medication Safety (12.50%): error prevention strategies, patient package insert and medication guide requirements, look-alike/sound-alike medications, high-alert/high-risk medications, common safety strategies, issues that require pharmacist intervention

Sterile and Non-Sterile Compounding (8.75%): infection control, handling and disposal requirements, product stability, equipment and supplies, sterile compounding process, non-sterile compounding process

Quality Assurance (7.50%): quality assurance practices and inventory control, infection control documentation, risk management guidelines and regulations, production, efficacy and customer satisfaction measures

Medication Order Entry and Fill Process (17.50%): order entry; intake, interpretation, and data entry; calculate doses required; fill process; labeling requirements; packaging requirements; dispensing process

Inventory Management (8.75%): define NDC, lot numbers, expiration dates, formulary product list, ordering and receiving, storage and removal

Billing and Reimbursement (8.75%): reimbursement policy and plans, third-party resolution, third-party reimbursement, healthcare reimbursement, coordination of benefits

Information System Usage and Application (10.00%): pharmacy-related computer applications, databases, documentation management, inventory reports, override reports, diversion reports, patient adherence, risk factors, drug allergies, side effects, electronic medical records

Pharmacy Math and Calculations: dispersed throughout other subject areas including inventory, compounding, billing and reimbursement, order entry and fill process, and pharmacology

AFTER THE PTCE

After you pass the PTCE, you will receive your certification by mail. To keep your certification current, you will be required to re-certify every 2 years. Because CPhTs are expanding their roles to better support pharmacists, changes have taken place in 2015 and 2016. Since 2015, CPhTs have been required to submit pharmacy technician-specific continuing education (CE) hours. For reinstatement, pharmacy technicians must submit 20 CE hours. Of the 20 CE hours, 2 CE hours must be in pharmacy law, and 1 CE hour must be in patient safety. As of January 1, 2016, only 10 of the total 20 CE hours may be accredited by passing a college-based equivalent course with a grade of "C." Certificate holders must also pay a reinstatement fee every 2 years.

Depending on your state, you may also be required to re-register every 2 years. Registration is state specific, and it is important to check with your state board of pharmacy and/or department of health to determine the requirements for re-registration in your state. Most states require their own set of CE hours and a re-registration fee.

Due to the professional standards of working in a pharmacy, drug-related offenses and felonies as well as other disciplinary issues may cause suspension and revocation of your license and certification. Remember that you are a trusted professional and must abide by a set of ethical standards. When you become PTCB certified, you will take an oath to uphold the PTCB Code of Conduct.

The Code of Conduct follows:

PTCB is dedicated to providing and implementing appropriate standards designed to serve pharmacy technicians, employers, pharmacists, and patients. First and foremost, PTCB certificants and candidates give priority to the health interests and protection of the public, and act in a manner that promotes integrity and reflects positively on the work of pharmacy technicians, consistent with appropriate ethical and legal standards.

As pharmacy technicians, and under the supervision of a licensed pharmacist, PTCB certificants and candidates have the obligation to: maintain high standards of integrity and conduct; accept responsibility for their actions; continually seek to improve their performance in the workplace; practice with fairness and honesty; and, encourage others to act in an ethical manner consistent with the standards and responsibilities set forth below. Pharmacy technicians assist pharmacists in dispensing medications and remain accountable to supervising pharmacists with regard to all pharmacy activities, and will act consistent with all applicable laws and regulations.

A. Responsibilities Relating to Legal Requirements.

Each certificant/candidate must:

1. Act consistent with all legal requirements relating to pharmacy technician practice, including Federal, State, and local laws and regulations.

2. Refrain from any behavior that violates legal or ethical standards, including all criminal laws, Federal laws and agency regulations, and State laws and regulatory agency rules.

B. Responsibilities to PTCB/Compliance with Organizational Policies and Rules.

Each certificant/candidate must:

1. Act consistent with all applicable PTCB Policies and requirements.

2. Provide accurate, truthful, and complete information to PTCB.

3. Maintain the security and confidentiality of PTCB Examination information and materials, including the prevention of unauthorized disclosure of test items and format and other confidential information.

4. Cooperate with PTCB concerning conduct review matters, including the submission of all required information in a timely, truthful, and accurate manner.

5. Report to PTCB apparent violations of this Code upon a reasonable and clear factual basis.

C. Responsibilities to the Public and Employers.

Each certificant/candidate must:

1. Deliver competent, safe, and appropriate pharmacy and related services.

2. Recognize practice limitations and provide services only when qualified and authorized by a supervising pharmacist and consistent with applicable laws and regulations. The certificant/candidate is responsible for determining the limits of his/her own abilities based on legal requirements, training, knowledge, skills, experience, and other relevant considerations.

3. Maintain and respect the confidentiality of sensitive information obtained in the course of all work and pharmacy-related activities, as directed by the supervising pharmacist and consistent with legal requirements, unless: the information is reasonably understood to pertain to unlawful activity; a court or governmental agency lawfully directs the release of the information; the patient or the employer expressly authorizes the release of specific information; or, the failure to release such information would likely result in death or serious physical harm to employees and/or patients.

4. Use pharmacy technician credentials properly, and provide truthful and accurate representations concerning education, experience, competency, and the performance of services.

5. Provide truthful and accurate representations to the public and employers.

6. Follow appropriate health and safety procedures with respect to all pharmacy-related activities and duties.

7. Protect the public, employees, and employers from conditions where injury and damage are reasonably foreseeable.

8. Disclose to patients or employers significant circumstances that could be construed as a conflict of interest or an appearance of impropriety.

9. Avoid conduct that could cause a conflict of interest with the interests of a patient or employer.

10. Assure that a real or perceived conflict of interest does not compromise legitimate interests of a patient or employer, and does not influence or interfere with work-related judgments.

Code of Conduct, Pharmacy Technician Certification Board, 2014, https://www.ptcb.org/resources/code-of-conduct

ONE: PHARMACOLOGY

Pharmacology is one of the most challenging subjects for pharmacy technicians. Studying anatomy, physiology, chemistry, and pathology in combination with pharmacology achieves a better understanding of how drugs work within the body. The *PTCB Exam Study Guide* will connect these sciences to foster a generalized comprehension of the most common current concepts, terminology, and drugs used in pharmacy practice.

The Principles of Pharmacology

Pharmacology is the study of the origin, uses, preparation, and effects of drugs on the body systems. The history of pharmacology is as ancient as the human race. In the beginning, experimentation with natural substances through trial and error developed an understanding that certain plants and plant extracts could cure or help ease the symptoms of diseases.

By the mid-seventeenth century, after the development of alchemy and an improved knowledge of chemical elements and minerals, experimentation with synthetic substances evolved and continued well into the twentieth century. The advent of pharmaceutical laboratories supported experimentation and production of cost-effective synthetic substances that could be supplied in bulk. By identifying, in laboratories, the molecular structure of a natural curative substance, scientists were able to synthesize and build upon that structure, modifying the components until the resulting drug was more efficient, better able to be absorbed, and presented fewer side effects.

Today, through biotechnology, the proteins of plants and animals, taken from cells and tissues, are used to produce highly complex compounds for medicines and treatments. Scientists manipulate these chemical bonds and structures from microbes and the human genome. This process is called **genetic engineering**.

Pharmacokinetics, pharmacodynamics, and clinical trials build on biotechnology research, advancing pharmacology. With a basic knowledge of how drugs perform in the body and the effects they have on each of the body systems, a pharmacy technician can more effectively administer drug treatments to cure and treat diseases.

PRACTICE QUESTION

Pharmacology is the study of a combination of all these aspects of a drug EXCEPT its

A) origin.

B) effects.

C) uses.

D) cost.

Answers:

A)   Incorrect. Pharmacology includes the study of a drug's origin—from what it was derived (e.g., a plant, an animal, chemical synthesis).

B)   Incorrect. Pharmacology is concerned with the effects of a drug on the body.

C)   Incorrect. Pharmacology requires knowledge of a drug's uses.

D)   **Correct.** How much a drug costs is not part of the science of how a drug works in the body.

PHARMACODYNAMICS

Pharmacodynamics is the branch of pharmacology that involves how a drug affects the body. The majority of drugs act on the system in two ways: by mimicking or suppressing normal anatomical processes in the body or by inhibiting the growth of certain microbial or parasitic organisms.

The seven actions of drugs on the system occur at a molecular, or cellular, level. This means these actions work on the smallest structural units of the body.

+ **Stimulating action** refers to the direct effects from a receptor agonist that stimulates the body. (A **receptor** is a protein molecule in a cellular membrane that can bind to a complementary molecule. An **agonist** is a chemical capable of activating a receptor to generate a therapeutic response. A **partial agonist** only partially activates a receptor.)

+ **Depressing action** refers to the direct effects from a receptor agonist that depresses the body.

+ **Antagonizing action** refers to a drug binding to a receptor without activating it.

+ **Stabilizing action** refers to a drug causing a neutral reaction, neither stimulating nor depressing the system.

- **Replacing action** refers to the accumulation of a substance in the system, such as glycogen stored as carbohydrates.
- **Direct constructive chemical reaction** refers to a drug producing beneficial results.
- **Direct harmful chemical reaction** refers to a drug causing cell destruction, which can be beneficial in situations such as cancer treatment.

Through these actions, and by targeting specific enzymes, receptors, or ion channels within a cellular membrane, a drug causes desired activities, such as the following:

- cellular membrane disruption
- chemical reaction
- interaction with **enzymes**, or proteins that are capable of producing chemical changes
- interaction with structural proteins
- interaction with **transport molecules**, or molecules capable of transporting proteins from one cellular structure to another
- interaction with **ion channels**, or membrane proteins
- interaction with **ligand**, a substance that forms a complex with a molecule, binding to a hormone, to a neurotransmitter, or to neuromodulator receptors

Although the aim with pharmacology is to produce the best possible effects, beneficial drugs sometimes cause undesirable effects. Pharmacology relies on **affinity**—the evolutionary relationship between a group of relative organisms—to develop drugs. This normally causes **efficacy**, creating a desired result or effect for most of the population though not all. Since not everyone's biological makeup is the same, a drug can cause side effects, and sometimes the side effects can be adverse. Undesirable effects include a harmful chemical reaction; cell mutation; multiple actions occurring at the same time that could be hazardous or cause injury to a patient's health; a drug interaction caused by multiple drug intake, a genetic condition, or additives in drugs; and an unexpected reaction when treating an abnormal chronic condition, such that a drug may be beneficial to one condition but not to another.

To determine how much of a medication is needed to effectively treat a disease or condition, a **therapeutic window** is calculated, which measures the dose required for the medication to be effective against the amount of it that would cause adverse side effects. For example, warfarin (brand name Coumadin), which is used for blood clotting, has a very narrow therapeutic window; its use must be monitored, and the effective dose must be adjusted based on blood testing and other factors.

Once the therapeutic window is determined, a **duration of action** is compiled, which is how long the drug will be effective. This usually relies on the **peak concentration** of the drug, and this is dependent upon the target **plasma concentration**—how much of the drug is present in a sample of plasma—required for the desired level of response.

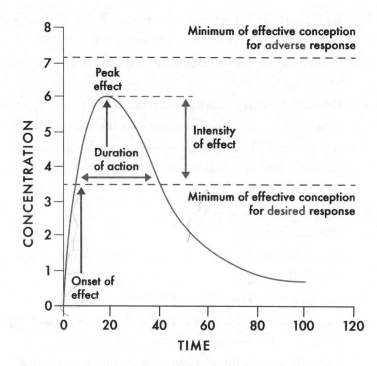

Figure 1.1. Therapeutic Window of Warfarin (Coumadin)

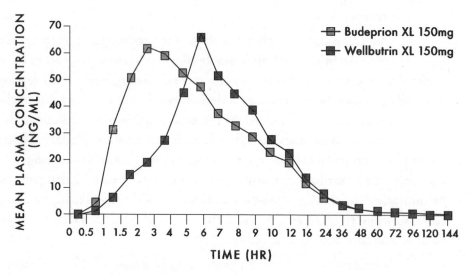

Figure 1.2. Bupropion's Duration of Action

PRACTICE QUESTIONS

1. Which is NOT considered a drug action?

   A) cellular membrane distribution

   B) antagonizing action

   C) substance replacement

   D) direct harmful chemical reaction

Answers:

A) **Correct.** Cellular membrane distribution is a desired effect.

B) Incorrect. Antagonizing action is when a drug binds to a receptor without activating it.

C) Incorrect. Substance replacement, or replacing action, refers to a substance's accumulation or storage in the body.

D) Incorrect. Direct harmful chemical reactions, which entail cell destruction, are used with chemotherapy.

2. Which is considered an undesired effect of a drug?

A) a chemical reaction

B) cell mutation

C) plasma concentration

D) an interaction with enzymes

Answers:

A) Incorrect. A chemical reaction is a desired activity.

B) **Correct.** Cell mutation is indeed an undesired effect.

C) Incorrect. Plasma concentration is not an effect but is the amount of a drug present in a sample of plasma, and it helps when plotting a drug's duration of action.

D) Incorrect. Interaction with enzymes is also a desired activity.

3. A therapeutic window is

A) how long a drug will be effective.

B) multiple actions occurring at the same time.

C) a desired drug action.

D) a quantity of medication that is both an effective dose and an amount that avoids adverse side effects.

Answers:

A) Incorrect. How long a drug is effective is its duration of action.

B) Incorrect. Multiple actions occurring at the same time is considered an undesired effect.

C) Incorrect. A therapeutic window is not a drug action.

D) **Correct.** A therapeutic window is a workable range calculated by comparing the effective dose of a drug with the amount of it that produces adverse side effects.

CONTINUE

PHARMACOKINETICS

Pharmacokinetics is the branch of pharmacology that interprets what happens to a drug after it enters the body, from when it is administered to the point of its elimination. Pharmacokinetics is based upon mathematical equations that help to predict a drug's behavior through the relationship between drug-plasma concentration and the time elapsed since the drug was administered. This process determines the drug's **bioavailability**, or the useable amount of the drug that reaches the body's circulation.

> 🔍 The difference between pharmacokinetics and pharmacodynamics is easily understood. Pharmacokinetics is the way drugs move through the body, while pharmacodynamics is the effect drugs have on the body.

Bioavailability depends on specific factors essential to each individual drug: pharmaceutical form, chemical form, route of administration, stability, and metabolism. When two drugs have the same bioavailability, they are considered **bioequivalent**, which means they are the same chemical form, just formulated differently, but they are absorbed equally by the body. This is how generic drugs are made.

The following are the mechanisms of pharmacokinetics:

+ **Liberation** is the release of a drug from its pharmaceutical formulation.
+ **Absorption** is the process of a drug entering the blood.
+ **Distribution** is the dispersion of a drug throughout the body's fluid and tissue.

ADME
(Absorption, Distribution, Metabolism, Excretion)

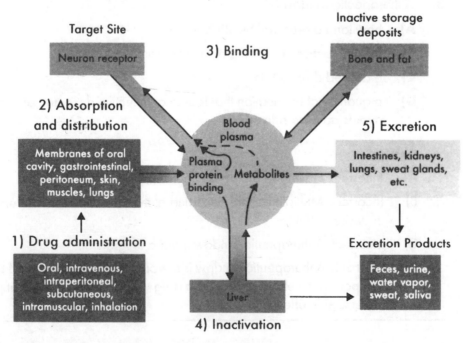

Figure 1.3. Mechanisms of Pharmacokinetics

✦ **Metabolism** is the transformation of a drug's compounds into drug metabolites.

✦ **Excretion** is the elimination of a drug from the body.

One of the specific factors that influences a drug's bioavailability and how it distributes through the system is its **route of administration** (ROA), which could be one of the following:

✦ oral (by mouth)
✦ sublingual (under the tongue)
✦ transdermal (through the skin)
✦ intramuscular (into the muscle)
✦ intravenous (into the vein)

✦ rectal (into the rectum)
✦ vaginal (into the vagina)
✦ intranasal (through the nose)
✦ inhalational (into the lungs)
✦ subcutaneous (under the skin)

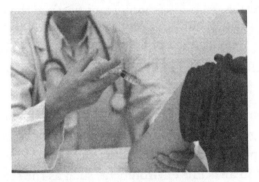

Figure 1.4. Intramuscular Injection

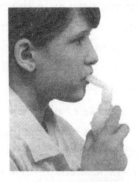

Figure 1.5. Inhalation

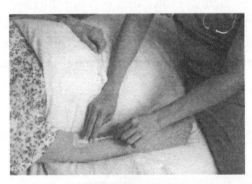

Figure 1.6. Intravenous Delivery

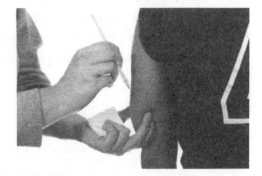

Figure 1.7. Subcutaneous Injection

 Many drugs have more than one route of administration. Injectables usually have the quickest effect, while taking a drug orally usually has the longest duration.

A drug's bioavailability often depends on its ROA, meaning a drug may be taken several ways, but some ROAs are more effective than others. Certain drugs, such as biologics, can only be administered intravenously because they would break down too quickly if they came into contact with the gastric acids of the stomach and would therefore be ineffective. As another example, fentanyl, a strong pain medication, has a wide range of bioavailability. When taken as a lozenge, its bioavailability is 50 percent;

when used intranasally, its bioavailability is 70 to 90 percent; and when swallowed, its bioavailability reduces to 33 percent. This happens because of **first-pass effect**, which is when a drug's metabolism is greatly diminished before it is distributed into the circulatory system. This reduction happens in either the liver or the small intestine.

The pH level of a patient's stomach or intestines can have a significant effect on drug distribution as well. The **pH level** is a measure of acidity or alkalinity. Most drugs are *weak acids* or *weak bases*. When in a solution, they are in between an ionized (charged) and non-ionized (uncharged) state. Within the solution, weak bases release a proton, while weak acids disassociate and release a proton and a negatively charged ion, or anion. Weakly acidic drugs are more ionized in basic solutions and less ionized in acidic solutions. Weakly basic drugs are the opposite. When a drug is transported through the body, it passes through acidic solutions, such as in the stomach, and basic solutions, such as in the small intestine, and this is important because the efficacy of the drug will depend on the pH of the body fluids, as well as the drug's ability to pass over a cellular membrane. A pH of 1 is very acidic, a pH of 7 is neutral, and a pH higher than 7 is considered alkaline. Blood plasma has a pH of 7.35 to 7.45, whereas stomach acid has a pH of 1.

Because of pH levels, diffusion across a cell membrane is higher when a drug is lipid—or fat—soluble and uncharged. As an example, a weakly acidic drug is easily absorbed and the amount of absorption is high. It will ionize in a basic environment, such as the small intestine, and not in an acidic environment, such as the stomach.

Another factor of drug distribution in the body is the process of **passive diffusion**, which is the inactive transport of a biochemical substance without the need for energy input. **Lipid—water partition** is a form of passive diffusion. Drug molecules can cross over cell membranes via either a lipid pathway or a water channel. Since some drugs are water soluble and some are lipid soluble, the concentration of water in the lipid and the

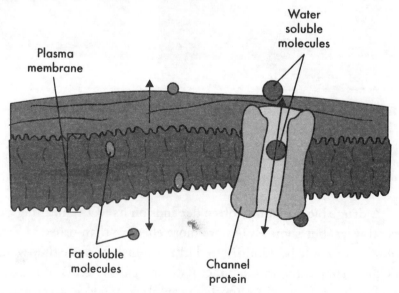

Figure 1.8. Diffusion Across the Membrane

surface of a cell membrane will determine which pathway the drug will take for better absorption.

Volume of distribution is the calculated volume of a drug present both in the body and in blood plasma when drug concentrations in tissues and plasma are at equilibrium. For example, drugs that have high fat solubility, low ionization rates, or low plasma-binding abilities have a higher volume of distribution than the opposite. If a drug has a low volume of distribution, then the drug is mainly confined in the blood and distributes to a lesser degree into tissues.

Individual patient factors can cause a change in the volume of distribution of a drug too. Both renal failure and liver failure increase volume, and these conditions can cause **plasma protein binding**; the way proteins bind within plasma affects drug efficiency as well as how proficiently a drug diffuses through a cell membrane. CD, LA, ER, XR

Another way a drug is distributed is through the **blood–brain barrier**, the highly permeable cell barrier that makes up the walls of brain capillaries. This barrier stops certain substances from flowing freely through the blood and entering the brain. Passage through the blood–brain barrier is determined by fat solubility and/or whether a substance's transport molecule is detectable.

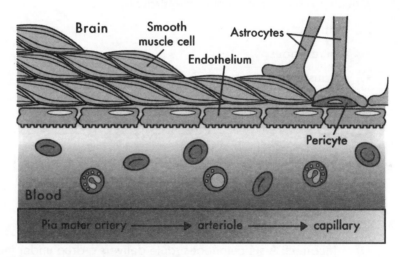

Figure 1.9. The Blood-Brain Barrier

In pregnant women, there is also the **placental barrier**, a semipermeable layer of tissue in the placenta that restricts substances passing from a mother's to a fetus's blood.

An understanding of these and all elements of pharmacokinetics can only be achieved through analysis, mathematical equations, and clinical studies. Processes can change based on each individual patient, but as a whole, pharmacokinetics informs how basic characteristics of drugs—such as solubility, bioavailability, and measures of acidity, absorption, and distribution—affect living organisms.

CONTINUE

PRACTICE QUESTIONS

1. Bioavailability relies on all these factors EXCEPT
   - **A)** chemical form.
   - **B)** stability.
   - **C)** liberation.
   - **D)** metabolism.

   Answers:
   - A) Incorrect. Chemical form, even when presented differently as a generic, is a factor of bioavailability.
   - B) Incorrect. Stability of a drug is also a factor of bioavailability.
   - **C) Correct.** Liberation—the release of a drug from its pharmaceutical formulation—is a phase of pharmacokinetics but not specific to bioavailability.
   - D) Incorrect. Metabolism is another factor of bioavailability.

2. Which is a NOT a route of administration?
   - **A)** absorption
   - **B)** intravenous
   - **C)** transdermal
   - **D)** subcutaneous

   Answers:
   - **A) Correct.** Absorption—the process of a drug entering the blood—is a mechanism of pharmacokinetics but not a ROA.
   - B) Incorrect. An intravenous route is into the vein.
   - C) Incorrect. A transdermal route is through the skin.
   - D) Incorrect. A subcutaneous route delivers a drug under the skin.

3. Which is NOT a mechanism of pharmacokinetics?
   - **A)** bioequivalence
   - **B)** liberation
   - **C)** excretion
   - **D)** absorption

   Answers:
   - **A) Correct.** When two drugs have the same bioavailability they have the same chemical form and are considered bioequivalent.

B)   Incorrect. Liberation is the release of a drug from its pharmaceutical formulation and a mechanism of pharmacokinetics.

C)   Incorrect. Excretion is also a mechanism of pharmacokinetics. It is the elimination of a drug from the body.

D)   Incorrect. Absorption too is a mechanism of pharmacokinetics and refers to the process of a drug entering the bloodstream.

CLINICAL TRIALS

Clinical trials are pharmaceutical, biomedical, or behavioral clinical research studies and include the voluntary participation of human subjects. In regards to pharmacology, clinical trials are normally conducted for investigational drugs. Once these drugs have been approved by the FDA for testing in human participants, patients can apply to be part of the study. The purpose of a clinical trial is to compile data and research on a specific drug as well as on the participants' responses to it to see whether it is safe and effective.

Patients agree to participate in clinical trials for many different reasons. Some may believe the investigational drug will be more effective than their current treatment. Other people volunteer to help expand studies for the future development of medicine.

Clinical trials also involve taking risks. Participants may experience unpleasant or severe side effects, treatment results may be ineffective, or the participants' treatment may require excessive time and attention, extensive trips to the study site, or hospital stays.

Some examples of clinical trials include

+   treatment trials, which focus on new treatments and/or new combinations of drugs;

+   prevention trials, which seek ways to prevent disease;

+   diagnostic trials, which attempt to refine tests used in diagnosing diseases;

+   screening trials, which aim to enhance disease detection; and

+   quality of life trials, which research how to improve patient comfort and quality of life.

With investigational drugs, trials are usually classified into one of five phases. Each phase is a different trial, and the development process for all phases takes many years to conclude. Before a clinical trial begins, preclinical studies must be conducted, and based on the questions asked in these studies, each phase serves a different function. The five phases are listed below:

1.   Pharmacodynamics and pharmacokinetics are explored, which includes liberation, absorption, distribution, metabolism, and excretion as well as drug interactions within the body. In vitro studies—studies performed in test tubes in labs before testing on humans—are done in the developmental stages.

2. Safety screenings are carried out, testing a small group to evaluate drug dosage safety and identify side effects.

3. This phase establishes the efficacy of the drug against a placebo for safety and effectiveness. Sometimes a **placebo**, or a drug that has no pharmacological effect, will be key in pointing out the true efficacy of the investigational drug.

4. Tests take place on a larger group of 1,000 to 3,000 patients to confirm the safety, effectiveness, and side effects of the drug.

5. Safety studies take place during sales. This includes ongoing studies after the drug is on the market, meant to establish the risks, benefits, and best uses of it.

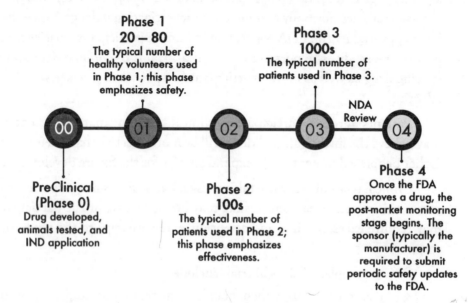

Figure 1.10. Timeline for Drug Evaluation

Researchers, when documenting a clinical trial, formulate a graph representing a **dose–response curve**, which plots responses to the drug against dosage, revealing the drug's effectiveness based on the percentage of people who responded well to it.

Three different doses are used in a dose–response curve: the **effective dose** (ED50), of which 50 percent of participants experience some therapeutic effect; the **toxic dose** (TD50), of which 50 percent of participants experience some toxic effect; and the **lethal dose** (LD50), of which 50 percent of participants will die. Each represents the dosage at 50 percent of comparable responses.

When a drug dosage that causes adverse or toxic effects is divided by a dosage that leads to the drug's desired effect, a **therapeutic index** (TI) is established:

$$\text{Therapeutic Index} = \frac{TD_{50}}{ED_{50}}$$

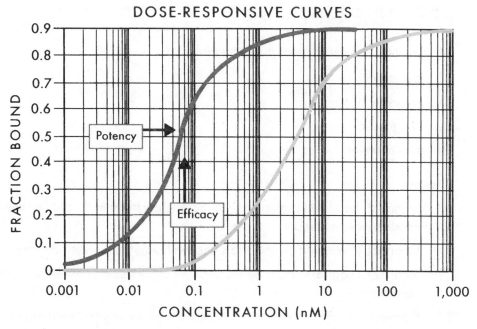

Figure 1.11. Dose-Response Curve

A **graded dose–response curve** calculates concentrated compounds, using **half maximal effective concentration (EC50)** and **half maximal inhibitory concentration (IC50)**. EC50 refers to the concentration of a drug after a specific exposure time that activates a response halfway between the baseline and maximum dose. IC50 measures how much of a dose is needed to activate a biochemical function.

Clinical trials are normally performed in hospitals and require participants and researchers adhere to strict protocols, regulated through the Food and Drug Administration (FDA) and the Joint Commission, an organization that accredits healthcare programs and organizations, such as hospitals. These protocols cover ordering, storing, inventory, and proper disposal of the drug. Investigational drugs are stored separately from other drugs and require a logbook, which must contain the following:

+ drug name
+ drug strength
+ unit size
+ protocol titles and numbers
+ principal investigator
+ drug lot number

+ identification
+ date dispensed
+ doses dispensed
+ stock balance
+ pharmacist's initials

Pharmacy technicians are responsible for preparing, maintaining, and auditing for clinical trials. Study sponsors conduct site visits throughout trials, collecting copies of paperwork they need for their records. A pharmacy is required to keep an investigational drug's logbook for a specified period of time after the study ends, after which the unused portion of the drugs are sent back to the sponsor.

Which is NOT an example of a clinical trial?

A) treatment

B) prevention

C) diagnostic

D) identification

Answers:

A) Incorrect. Treatment clinical trials focus on new treatments and/or new combinations of drugs.

B) Incorrect. Prevention clinical trials deal with ways to prevent diseases.

C) Incorrect. Diagnostic trials aim to improve on or design new ways of diagnosing conditions.

D) **Correct.** Identification is one of the details pharmacy technicians must record in the logbook of an investigational drug.

An Introduction to Medical Terminology

Medical terminology derives from either Greek or Latin and can be described as the language of the practice of medicine. Medical terms typically have three components: the prefix, the word root, and the suffix. Forming these components into a word is called **word building.** Having the ability to recognize and translate these components helps a pharmacy technician understand medical and pharmacy terms and abbreviations, since these define diseases, conditions, procedures, anatomy, and physiology. Specific Latin phrases used to this day describe how or when medications are to be taken. The phrases, in abbreviated form, enable medical professionals to proficiently document treatments in a timely manner. The medical terminology and abbreviations can then be interpreted into easy-to-read instructions for a patient.

A **word root** is the core of a word. Most commonly the root describes the part of the body afflicted, but less commonly it can specify color. All medical terms have at least one word root; some have more than one, which are merged with a **combining vowel**—a vowel that joins various parts of a term.

Table 1.1. The Most Common Word Roots in Pharmacy Practice

Word Root	Definition	Example
acous/o ✓	hearing	acoustic
acusis ✓	hearing	hyperacusis
aden/o ✓	gland	adenoid
adip/o ✓	fat	adipose
alb ✓	white / Albino	albumin
ambul/o ✓	walk	ambulatory
andr/o ✓	male	androgen
angi/o	vessel	angiogram
arthr/o	joint	arthritis
bucc/o	cheek	buccal
canc	crab	cancerous
carcin/o	cancer	carcinogen
cardi	heart	cardiology
cereb	brain	cerebellum
chem/o	chemistry	chemotherapy
chol	bile	cholesterol
cyan	blue	cyanosis (blue lips)
cyst/o	bladder	cystitis
cyt/o	cell	cytology
dactyl	finger	syndactylism
derm/a	skin	dermatitis
duoden/o	duodenum	duodenostomy
enter/o	intestine	enteralgia
erythr/o	red	erythrocyte
esophag/o	esophagus	esophageal
fibr/o	fibrous tissue	fibromyalgia
gastr/o	stomach	gastritis
gluc/o	sugar	glucose
glyc/o	sugar	glycogen
gynec/o	woman	gynecology

A -Dip

Table 1.1. The Most Common Word Roots in Pharmacy Practice (continued)

Word Root	Definition	Example
hemat/o, hem/o	blood	hemoglobin
hepat/o	liver	hepatic
hist/o	body tissue	histamine
hyster/o	uterus	hysterectomy
lact/o	milk	lactating
lapar/o	abdomen	laparotomy
leuk/o	white	leukemia
lipid	fat	sphingolipid
lymph/o	lymphoid tissue	lymphocyte
mamm/o, mast/o	breast tissue	mammogram
melan/o	black	melanoma
myel/o, my/o	muscle	myalgia
nas/o	nose	nasal
necr/o	dead	necrosis
nephr/o	kidney	nephrology
neur/o	nerve	neuralgia
ocul/o	eye	ocular
ophthalm/o	eye	ophthalmologist
orchid/o	testes	orchidectomy
oste/o	bone	osteoarthritis
ot/o	ear	otalgia
ox, oxy	oxygen	oxyhemoglobin
pancreat/o	pancreas	pancreatitis
path	disease	pathogen
pector/o	chest	pectoral
ped/o	foot	bipedal
pelv/o	pelvis	pelvic
phleb/o	vein	phlebotomist
pneum/o	lungs	pneumonia
proct/o	rectum	proctologist

Word Root	Definition	Example
prostat/o	prostate	prostatic
psych/o	mind	psychology
pulm/o	lungs	pulmonary
ren/o	kidney	renal
retin/o	retina	retinal
rhin/o	nose	rhinoplasty
somat/o	body	somatotonia
spir/o	breathing	spirometer
spondyl/o	spine	spondylosis
stenosis	narrowing	spinal stenosis
thromb/o	blood clot	thrombolysis
thym/o	thymus gland	thymogenic
tox/o	poisonous	toxoplasmosis
tympan/o	ear drum	tympanoplasty
urethr/o	urethra	urethroplasty
uria	excess	glycosuria
uro, ur	urine	urology
uter/o	uterus	intrauterine
vas, vascul/o	blood vessel	vasoconstriction
ven/o	vein	ventostasis
vesic, vesicul/o	vesicle, bladder	vesicular
xanth/o	yellow	xanthin

A **prefix**—the beginning part of a word—modifies a suffix or a root by adding placement, color, number, measurement, or position. As an example, in the word *biology*, *bio–* is the prefix. *Bio–* means life, and the suffix *–logy* means study of. The definitions combine as the study of life.

Understanding can be tested by deciphering the meaning of example words provided or other common medical terms using these tables of word roots, prefixes, and suffixes.

CONTINUE

Table 1.2. The Most Common Prefixes in Pharmacy Practice

Prefix	Definition	Example
a–	without, not, no	aphasia
ab–	away from	abnormal
ad–	toward	adduct
ambi–	both	ambidextrous
an–	not, without	anorexia
ante–	before	anteroom
anti–	against	antivenin
auto–	self	autograft
bi–	two	bilateral
bio–	life	biochemical
brady–	slow	bradycardia
chlor–	green	chlorosis
circum–	around	circumcision
cirrh–	yellow	cirrhosis
con–	together	congenital
contra–	against	contradiction
cyan–	blue	cyanide
dia–	completely	diagnosis
dys–	bad, painful, abnormal	dysfunction
ec–	out of	ecbolic
ecto–	out, outside	ectopic
endo–	within, inner	endometriosis
epi–	upon, above	epidermis
eryth–	red	erythrocyte
eu–	good, normal	euphoria
ex–, exo–	out, away from	exoskeleton
extra–	outside	extracellular
hemi–	half	hemisphere
hyper–	over, above	hyperglycemia
hypo–	below, under	hypoallergenic

Prefix	Definition	Example
im–	not, without	imperfect
immun–	having immunity	immunosuppressant
in–	not, without	incorrect
infra–	below, under	infracostal
inter–	between, among	intervertebral
intra–	within, inside	intradermal
iso–	equal	isochromatic
leuk–	white	leukemia
macro–	large	macrocephaly
mal–	poor	malnutrition
medi–	middle	medicine
melan–	black	melanoma
meso–	middle	mesothelioma
meta–	after, beyond	metamorphic
micro–	small	microscopic
mid–	middle	midsection
mono–	one	monochromatic
multi–	many	multicellular
neo–	new	neonatal
pan–	all	pandemic
para–	near, alongside, abnormal	parathyroid
per–	through	percutaneous
peri–	around	pericardial
poly–	many, excessive	polycystic
post–	after	postsurgical
pre–	before	prenatal
pro–	to go forth	procreation
pseudo–	false	pseudonym
purpur–	purple	purpuriferous
quadri–	four	quadriplegic
re–	again	regenerate

Table 1.2. The Most Common Prefixes in Pharmacy Practice (continued)

Prefix	Definition	Example
retro–	behind, backward	retroactive
rube–	red	rubella
semi–	half	semicircle
sub–	below, under	sublingual
super–	above, excess	supernumerary
supra–	above	suprarenal
sym–, syn–	together	synthetic
tachy–	fast	tachycardia
trans–	across	transverse
tri–	three	triangle
ultra–	beyond, excessive	ultrasound
uni–	one	unilateral
xanth–	yellow	xanthine
xer–	dry	xerodermatic

Flash cards of word parts can aid memorization and be used while a student is waiting for an appointment, during television commercial breaks, and at lunchtime at work or school.

A **suffix** is a word part that follows the root. It also modifies the root and is normally added with a combining vowel. For example, in the word *pharmacology*, *–logy* is the suffix—defined as study of. *Pharmac* is the word root (meaning drug). When the combining vowel *o* is added to it, it becomes the compound *pharmaco*, what is called the **combining form** of the word, which is any word element that occurs only in combination with other word elements. Pair that combining form with the suffix, the word is complete: pharmacology.

Table 1.3. The Most Common Suffixes in Pharmacy Practice

Suffix	Definition	Example
–ac	pertaining to	cardiac
–al	pertaining to	buccal
–algia	pain	neuralgia
–ar, –ary	pertaining to	urinary
–asthenia	weakness	myasthenia

Suffix	Definition	Example
–cele	hernia, bulging	hydrocele
–centesis	surgical puncture for removal of fluid	amniocentesis
–cyte	cell	leukocyte
–dipsia	thirst	polydipsia
–dynia	pain	encephalodynia
–eal	pertaining to	esophageal
–ectasis	dilation or distension of an organ	lymphangiectasis
–ectomy	surgical removal	hysterectomy
–emia	blood condition	leukemia
–genic	producing, forming	carcinogenic
–gram	record, picture	electrocardiogram
–graphy, –graph	instrument for recording	electrocardiograph
–ia	disease, abnormal condition	anorexia
–iasis	pathological condition	elephantiasis
–iatry	treatment	psychiatry
–ic	pertaining to	anorexic
–icle	small	ventricle
–ism	state, condition	alcoholism
–itis	inflammation of	arthritis
–ium	metallic element	barium
–lepsy	seizure	epilepsy
–lith	stone	tonsillolith
–logy	study of	biology
–lysis	breaking down	thrombolysis
–lytic	destroy, reduce	hemolytic
–malacia	softening	osteomalacia
–megaly	enlarged	osteomegaly
–meter	measuring instrument	cytometer
–metry	process of measuring	optometry
–oid	resembling, like	carcinoid

Table 1.3. The Most Common Suffixes in Pharmacy Practice (continued)

Suffix	Definition	Example
–oma	tumor	hematoma
–opia, –opsia	vision	presbyopia
–osis	abnormal condition	cyanosis
–osmia	odor, smell	dysosmia
–ous	processing, full of	ferrous
–paresis	incomplete, partial	hemiparesis
–path, –pathy	disease	osteopath
–penia	deficiency, decreased number	leukocytopenia
–pepsia	digestion	dyspepsia
–phagia	eating, swallowing	dysphagia
–philia	attraction to	hemophilia
–phobia	fear of	agoraphobia
–plasia	formation	dysplasia
–plasty	surgical repair	rhinoplasty
–plegia	paralysis, stroke	paraplegia
–rrhage	blood bursting forth	hemorrhage
–rrhea	flow, discharge	amenorrhea
–sclerosis	hardening	arteriosclerosis
–scope	instrument to view	microscope
–scopy	process of viewing	endoscopy
–spasm	twitching, involuntary contraction	neurospasm
–stasis	control, stop	homeostasis
–stenosis	narrowing	tracheostenosis
–stomy	artificial opening	colostomy
–therapy	treatment	hydrotherapy
–tic	pertaining to	paralytic
–tocia	conditions of labor	tomotocia
–tomy	incision, cut	cystotomy
–toxic	poison	cardiotoxic

Suffix	Definition	Example
–tripsy	rubbing, crushing	lithotripsy
–trophy	nourishment, development	atrophy
–tropic, –tropia	turning	exotropia
–ula, –ule	small	globule
–uria	urine, urination	nocturia

PRACTICE QUESTIONS

1. In the word *electrocardiogram,* –*gram* is defined as

   A) relating to the heart.

   B) pertaining to.

   C) to record or picture.

   D) the process of viewing.

   Answers:

   A) Incorrect. The word root *cardi* is related to the heart.

   B) Incorrect. *Pertaining to* relates to the suffixes –*ac,* –*al,* –*ar,* –*ary,* –*eal,* –*ic,* and –*tic.*

   C) **Correct.** The suffix –*gram* means to record or picture.

   D) Incorrect. The suffix –*scopy* translates as a process of viewing.

2. If a person has myasthenia, he or she has

   A) motion sickness.

   B) muscle weakness.

   C) a hardening of the arteries.

   D) a stroke.

   Answers:

   A) Incorrect. None of the common word parts in the tables point to motion sickness in particular, though some refer to abnormality or pain and the word root *gastr* relates to the stomach.

   B) **Correct.** The word root *my* relates to muscles, and the suffix *asthenia* means weakness.

   C) Incorrect. Arteriosclerosis is a hardening of the arteries. The suffix –*sclerosis* means hardening, and though *arterio* is not found in these tables, this word part is so similar to the word *artery,* it is easily deciphered.

   D) Incorrect. The suffix –*plegia* signifies a stroke or paralysis.

3. In the word *xerodermatic*, *xer–* would be the

A) prefix.

B) suffix.

C) word root.

D) combining vowel.

Answers:

A) **Correct.** *Xer–* is the prefix, which means dry.

B) Incorrect. The suffix of the word is *–tic*, which means pertaining to.

C) Incorrect. The word root is *derm* or *derma*, which is the Greek word for skin.

D) Incorrect. The combining vowel could be the *a* between *derm–* and *–tic*, but the word root can take the form of either *derm* or *derma*.

4. What is the definition of leukocytopenia?

A) cancer of the white blood cells

B) bone marrow tumor

C) excessive white blood cells

D) decreased number of white blood cells

Answers:

A) Incorrect. *Leuk–* relates to white, but the rest of the word parts do not point to cancer, which is found in the word roots *canc* and *carcin*.

B) Incorrect. The word root *oste* or *osteo* signifies bone, the suffix *–oma* relates to a tumor, and both word parts are missing from leukocytopenia.

C) Incorrect *Leuk–* signifies white, and the word root *cyto* means cell, but the rest of the word does not point to the blood.

D) **Correct.** The prefix *leuk–* means white, the o is a combining vowel, the word root *cyto* means cell, and the suffix *–penia* means a deficiency or decreased number.

5. When all the word parts are put together to form a word, it is called

A) a suffix.

B) a combining form.

C) word building.

D) a combining vowel.

Answers:

A) Incorrect. A suffix is the word part found after the root in a word.

B) Incorrect. A combining form is any word element that occurs only in combination with other word elements.

C) **Correct.** Word building is combining all the word parts to form a word.

D) Incorrect. A combining vowel is the vowel used to combine two word parts.

6. Amniocentesis is

A) a water treatment.

B) a nerve spasm.

C) head pain.

D) a surgical procedure for collecting amniotic fluid.

Answers:

A) Incorrect. A water treatment is hydrotherapy.

B) Incorrect. A nerve spasm is a neurospasm.

C) Incorrect. Head pain is encephalodynia.

D) **Correct.** The suffix –*centesis* provides the clue, meaning surgical puncture for removal of fluid.

7. In the word *epidermal*, which word part means upon, above?

A) *epi–*, the prefix

B) –*al*, the suffix

C) *derm*, the word root

D) all of the above

Answers:

A) **Correct.** The prefix *epi–* means upon or above.

B) Incorrect. The suffix –*al* means pertaining to.

C) Incorrect. The word root *derm* means skin.

D) Incorrect.

8. In the word *osteomyelitis*, which word part means muscle?

A) *osteo–*, the prefix

B) *myel*, one of the word roots

C) –*itis*, the suffix

D) all of the above

Answers:

A) Incorrect. The prefix *osteo–* means bone.

B) **Correct.** The word root *myel* means muscle.

C) Incorrect. The suffix –*itis* means inflammation of.

D) Incorrect.

Systems Pharmacology

The human body has ten systems: cardiovascular, nervous, musculoskeletal, digestive, endocrine, respiratory, integumentary, reproductive, urinary, and immune. Systems pharmacology entails applying systems biology principles to the field of pharmacology and includes understanding what each system does, the most common diseases and conditions related to each system, and the **brand name** (proprietary name) and **generic name** (scientific name) of the most commonly prescribed drugs used for each system.

The brand name of a drug is the name it is given by the pharmaceutical company that funded its research and development. This company holds the drug's patent for up to twenty years after its initial development, but when the patent expires, other pharmaceutical companies can produce the drug. A generic drug must have the same active ingredient, strength, and dosage form as the brand name drug, but the inactive ingredients do not need to be the same. Many generic drugs cost less to produce because generic manufacturers do not need to recoup the cost of research and development.

A **drug class** is a group of medications that have similar structures, the same targeted mechanism, a similar mode of action, and/or they are used to treat the same disease or condition. Drugs within a single drug class usually have the same suffix, to make them easier to identify, although the suffixes of older drugs may differ because grouping generic drugs by suffix is a relatively new concept.

PRACTICE QUESTIONS

1. A generic drug must have all the same characteristics as a brand name drug EXCEPT its

    A) active ingredient.

    B) color.

    C) dosage.

    D) strength.

    Answers:

    A) Incorrect. The active ingredient of a drug is vital to its efficacy.

    B) Correct. The color of a drug does not affect its ability to treat its targeted disease or condition.

    C) Incorrect. The dosage of a generic drug must be the same as the brand name drug.

    D) Incorrect. The strength of a drug is another factor crucial to that drug's efficacy.

2. Drugs in a <u>drug class</u> must have all these traits in common EXCEPT

    A) the same targeted mechanism.

    B) a similar mode of action.

    C) the same active ingredient.

    D) similar structures.

<u>Answers:</u>

    A) Incorrect. Drugs in the same drug class must have the same targeted mechanism in order to concentrate the drugs' properties in the body as expected.

    B) Incorrect. Having the same mode of action is important for uniformity and dependability of treatment among drugs in the same class.

    C) **Correct.** Drugs do not have to have the same active ingredient to be in the same drug class since each drug is chemically different.

    D) Incorrect. Drugs in the same drug class must have similar molecular structures even if their active ingredients vary.

GENERIC DRUG SUFFIXES

Suffixes used in generic drug names help identify which class each drug is in. As more drugs are developed, the use of predetermined suffixes has made it easier to discern which drugs are used for specific diseases and conditions. Knowledge of these suffixes enables quicker learning of the diseases and conditions associated with various drugs and the related drugs within each drug class.

🔍 Memorizing drug class suffixes assists in deciphering what a drug is used for.

Table 1.4. The Most Common Generic Drug Suffixes

Drug Suffix	Drug Class	Description	Body System	Drug Example
–actone	potassium sparing diuretics	increase the flow of urine and enhance the loss of sodium	cardiovascular	spironolactone
–artan	angiotensin II receptor blockers (A2RBs)	block angiotensin II enzymes from specific receptor sites; help prohibit vasoconstriction	cardiovascular	candesartan
–azosin	alpha-adrenergic blockers	relax the veins and arteries so blood can easily pass through; antihypertensives	immune	terazosin

Table 1.4. The Most Common Generic Drug Suffixes (continued)

Drug Suffix	Drug Class	Description	Body System	Drug Example
–cillin	antibiotics	inhibit the growth of or kill bacterial microorganisms	musculoskeletal, nervous	penicillin
–codone	opioid pain relievers	help to block pain signals in the brain to make a patient "forget" about his or her pain	immune	oxycodone
–cycline	antibiotics	inhibit the growth of or kill bacterial microorganisms	cardiovascular	doxycycline
–emide	loop diuretics	increase the flow of urine and enhance the loss of sodium	immune	furosemide
–floxacin	antibiotics	inhibit the growth of or kill bacterial microorganisms	immune	moxifloxacin
–mycin	antibiotics	inhibit the growth of or kill bacterial microorganisms	cardiovascular	vancomycin
–olol	beta-blockers (B1s) or beta-adrenergic blocking agents	block adrenaline receptors and mediate a flight-or-fight response, which causes actions in the heart	respiratory, immune, musculoskeletal	propranolol
–olone, –sone	corticosteroids	reduce inflammation	nervous	prednisolone
–pam	benzodiazepines	reduce anxiety, relax muscles, sedate, induce sleep	cardiovascular	diazepam
–pine	calcium channel blockers	relax the veins and arteries so blood can easily pass through; antihypertensives	cardiovascular	amlodipine
–pril	angiotensin converting enzyme (ACE) inhibitors	block the conversion of angiotensin I to angiotensin II; may reduce the chance of increased vasoconstriction or blood pressure	digestive	enalpril

Drug Suffix	Drug Class	Description	Body System	Drug Example
–razole	proton pump inhibitors	inhibit the action of the gastric proton pump, reducing gastric acid production	immune	pantoprazole
–statin	HMG-CoA reductase inhibitors	inhibit cholesterol production	cardiovascular	rosuvastatin
–tidine	histamine-2 blockers	reduce the amount of acid in the stomach	digestive	ranitidine
–vir	antivirals	inhibit the growth of or kill viral microorganisms	immune	tamvir

PRACTICE QUESTIONS

1. Drugs in the class with suffixes –olone and –sone address all these body systems EXCEPT the

   A) cardiovascular system.

   B) respiratory system.

   C) immune system.

   D) musculoskeletal system.

   Answers:

   A) **Correct.** The suffixes listed distinguish corticosteroids, which reduce inflammation; they do not work with the cardiovascular system.

   B) Incorrect. Corticosteroids can work with the respiratory system to reduce lung inflammation.

   C) Incorrect. Corticosteroids can work with the immune system too, by reducing inflammation in autoimmune diseases.

   D) Incorrect. Corticosteroids can also work with the musculoskeletal system, reducing joint inflammation.

2. Which drug class suffix does NOT refer to drugs that kill or inhibit the growth of bacterial microorganisms?

   A) –cillin

   B) –vir

   C) –mycin

   D) –cycline

Answers:

A) Incorrect. Drugs with the suffix –*cillin*, like penicillin, are antibiotics, which kill bacteria.

B) **Correct.** Drugs with the suffix –*vir* are antivirals.

C) Incorrect. Drugs with the suffix –*mycin*, like erythromycin, are also antibiotics, which kill bacteria.

D) Incorrect. Drugs with the suffix –*cycline*, like doxycycline, are antibiotics too, which kill bacteria.

THE CARDIOVASCULAR SYSTEM

The **cardiovascular system** includes the heart, blood vessels, and blood. This is where circulation begins, ends, and begins again.

The cardiovascular system plays a vital role in the functioning of humans, since it distributes oxygen, nutrients, and hormones to the entire body. The whole system relies on the **heart**, a cone-shaped muscular organ that is no bigger than a closed fist. The heart must pump the blood low in oxygen to the lungs; once the blood is in the lungs, it is oxygenated and returned to the heart. The heart then pumps the oxygenated blood through the whole body.

The heart is located inside the rib cage. It can be found approximately between the second and the sixth rib from the bottom of the rib cage. It does not sit on the body's midline; rather, two-thirds of it is located on the left side of the body. The narrower part of the heart is called the **apex**, and it points downward and to the left of the body; the broader part of the heart is called the **base**, and it points upward.

The cavity that holds the heart is called the **pericardial cavity**. It is filled with serous fluid produced by the pericardium, which is the lining of the pericardial cavity. The serous fluid acts as a lubricant for the heart. It also keeps the heart in place and empties the space around the heart. The heart wall has three layers:

+ The **epicardium** is the outermost layer of the heart and is one of the two layers of the pericardium.

+ The **myocardium** is the middle layer and the most massive part of the heart. It contains the cardiac muscular tissue and performs the function of pumping what is necessary for the circulation of blood.

+ The **endocardium** is the smooth innermost layer that keeps the blood from sticking to the inside of the heart.

The heart wall is uneven because some parts of the heart—such as the atria—do not need a lot of muscle power to perform their duties. Other parts—such as the ventricles—require a thicker muscle to pump the blood.

The heart consists of four chambers: the right and left **atria**, and the right and left **ventricles.** The atria (plural for atrium), smaller than the ventricles, have thin walls; their function is to receive blood from the lungs and the body and pump it to the ventricles. The ventricles have to pump the blood to the lungs and the rest of the body, so they are larger and have thicker walls. The left half of the heart, which is responsible for pumping the blood through the body, has thicker walls than the right half, which pumps the deoxygenated blood to the lungs.

The heart has one-way valves, allowing the blood to flow in only one direction. The valves that keep the blood from going back into the atria from the ventricles are called the **atrioventricular valves**, and the valves that keep the blood from going back into the ventricles from the arteries are called the **semilunar valves**.

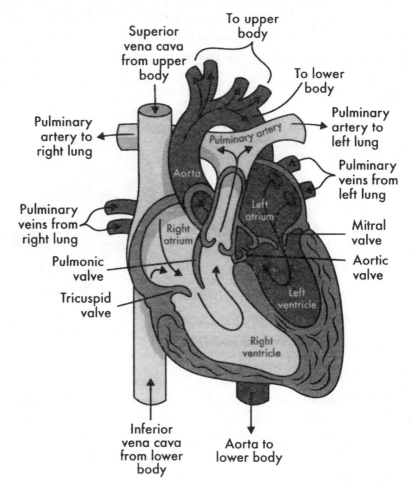

Figure 1.12. The Heart

Two groups of cells make possible the pumping function of the heart: the **sinoatrial node** and the **atrioventricular node**. They keep the heart well coordinated. The sinoatrial node sets the pace and signals the atria to contract; the atrioventricular node picks up this signal and tells the ventricles also to contract.

Blood vessels carry the blood from the heart throughout the body and then back. They vary in size depending on the amount of blood that needs to flow through them. The blood flows through the hollow part in the middle, called the **lumen**. All blood vessels are lined with **endothelium**, which is made out of the same type of cells as the endocardium and serves the same purpose: to keep the blood from sticking to the walls and clotting.

Arteries are blood vessels that transport the blood away from the heart. They work under a lot more pressure than the other types of blood vessels; hence, they have thicker, more muscular walls, which are also highly elastic. The smaller arteries are usually more muscular, while the larger are more elastic.

The largest artery in the body, the **aorta**, ascends from the left ventricle of the heart, arches to the back left, and descends behind the heart. Narrower arteries, called **arterioles**, branch off the main arteries and carry blood to the capillaries. The descending part of the aorta carries blood to the lower parts of the body, except for the lungs. The lungs get blood through the **pulmonary artery**, exiting the right ventricle.

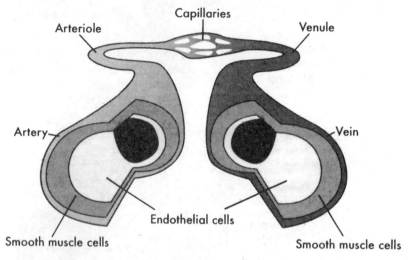

Figure 1.13. Arteries and Veins

The arching part of the aorta—the **aortic arch**—branches into three arteries: the **brachiocephalic artery**, the **left common carotid artery**, and the **left subclavian artery**. The brachiocephalic artery carries blood to the brain and head; it divides into the right subclavian artery, which brings the blood to the right arm. The left common carotid artery also carries blood to the brain, and the left subclavian artery carries blood to the left arm.

Veins—blood vessels that bring blood to the body and then back to the heart—do not work under the same pressure as arteries, so they are much thinner and not as muscular or elastic. They use inertia, muscle work, and gravity to get the blood to the heart, and like the heart, they have a number of one-way valves that stop the blood from going back through them. Of the two main veins—the **superior vena cava** and the **inferior vena cava**—the superior vena cava ascends from the right atrium and delivers blood to the head and neck; it also connects to the arms via both subclavian and brachiocephalic veins. The inferior vena cava descends from the right atrium, carrying the blood from the lumbar, gonadal, hepatic, phrenic, and renal veins.

The lungs have their own set of veins: the **left and right superior** and **inferior pulmonary veins**. These vessels enter the heart through the left atrium.

Thin veins that connect to the capillaries are called **venules. Capillaries**, the smallest blood vessels and the most populous in the body, can be found in almost every tissue. They connect to arterioles on one end and venules on the other end. Also, capillaries carry the blood very close to the cells and thus enable cells to exchange gases, nutrients, and cellular waste. The walls of capillaries have to be very thin for this exchange to happen.

Blood—consisting of red blood cells, hemoglobin, white blood cells, platelets, and plasma—is the medium for the transport of substances throughout the body. The human body contains 4 to 5 liters of this liquid connective tissue.

Red bone marrow produces **red blood cells** (RBCs), also called **erythrocytes**, and RBCs transport oxygen. The red pigment found in red blood cells, **hemoglobin** (HGB), is rich in iron and proteins, both of which allow these cells to transport the oxygen. Hemoglobin also has a biconcave shape—round and thinner in the middle—which gives them a larger surface area, making them more effective.

White blood cells (WBCs), also called **leukocytes**, are essential to the human immune system and consist of two classes of cells: granular and agranular leukocytes. Of the three classes of granular leukocytes, the neutrophils digest bacteria, the eosinophils digest viruses, and the basophils release histamine. Of the two classes of agranular leukocytes, lymphocytes fight off viral infections and produce antibodies for fighting pathogen-induced infection; monocytes play a role in removing pathogens and dead cells from wounds.

Platelets, also called **thrombocytes**, are vital for blood clotting. Like red blood cells, they are formed in the red bone marrow, and they serve many functions in the body. Finally, **plasma**—the liquid part of blood—forms 55 percent of the total blood volume. Plasma consists of up to 90 percent water, as well as proteins, such as antibodies and albumins. Other substances circulating in the blood plasma include glucose, nutrients, cell waste, and various gases.

All these components work together in the cardiovascular system, driven by the actions of the heart, which shifts between two states: systole and diastole. In **systole**, the cardiac muscles contract and move blood from any given chamber. During **diastole**, the muscles relax and the chamber expands to fill with blood. The systole and diastole are responsible for the pressure in the major arteries, resulting in the blood pressure measured in a regular exam. The two values represent the systolic and diastolic pressures respectively, with the former being greater than the latter.

The series of events that occur in the heart during one heartbeat—called a **cardiac cycle**—includes four steps, which together result in blood cell oxygenation:

1. The poorly oxygenated blood enters the right atrium through the superior and inferior vena cava.
2. The blood then passes to the right ventricle, which sends it through the pulmonary artery into the lungs, where oxygenation occurs.

3. The oxygen-rich blood then enters the left atrium through the pulmonary veins and moves from the left atrium into the left ventricle.

4. By way of blood pressure, the blood travels from the left ventricle through the aorta and the aortic arch into the arteries and through the whole body.

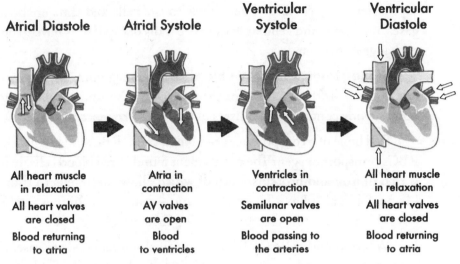

Atrial Diastole	Atrial Systole	Ventricular Systole	Ventricular Diastole
All heart muscle in relaxation	Atria in contraction	Ventricles in contraction	All heart muscle in relaxation
All heart valves are closed	AV valves are open	Semilunar valves are open	All heart valves are closed
Blood returning to atria	Blood to ventricles	Blood passing to the arteries	Blood returning to atria

Figure 1.14. The Cardiac Cycle

After leaving the left ventricle in the fourth step, the blood passes from the arteries to the arterioles and on to the capillaries, where the exchange of gases, nutrients, wastes, and hormones occurs. The blood then passes into the venules and returns to the heart through the veins. A healthy, resting heart can pump around 5 liters per minute through this cycle.

Unlike the body's other veins, the veins of the stomach and intestines do not carry the blood directly to the heart. Rather, they divert it to the liver first, through the hepatic portal vein, so the liver can store sugars, remove toxins, and process the products of digestion. This blood then goes to the heart through the inferior vena cava.

A list of diseases and conditions common to the cardiovascular system follows, along with tables detailing some of the most common drug treatments used currently:

Hypertension—also called **high blood pressure**—is defined as having a blood pressure higher than 140/90 mmHg. This means the systolic reading, or the pressure as the heart pumps blood throughout the body, is over 140 millimeters of mercury and the diastolic reading, or the pressure as the heart relaxes and fills back up with blood, is over 90 millimeters of mercury. Blood pressure rates can rise and fall throughout the day and when physical activity and stress increase.

Causes of hypertension include physical inactivity, high intake of salt and fatty foods, obesity, and alcohol and tobacco use. Other risk factors include age, race, and lifestyle. Some people also have secondary hypertension, which results from another condition, such as kidney disease. Changes in lifestyle and taking an antihypertensive drug can help reduce high blood pressure.

A **myocardial infarction**—a heart attack—affects the **myocardium**, or heart muscle. **Necrosis**, or death, of the myocardial tissue from oxygen deprivation usually causes the event. When one of the two coronary arteries supplying blood to the heart becomes blocked by a clot or plaque, the arteries narrow and blood supply and oxygen is thwarted, causing **atherosclerosis**.

Some factors that cause a myocardial infarction include genetic traits, sex, age, diabetes, and lifestyle factors, such as smoking, hypertension, and high cholesterol. Symptoms of a myocardial infarction vary and are often based on the sex of the individual. Men normally feel crushing pressure in the chest, with pain and numbness radiating down the arms, throat, and back. Women tend to feel a squeezing pressure with pain and discomfort in both arms as well, but they also have pain in the back, neck, jaw, or stomach associated with nausea and vomiting. Both men and women can have shortness of breath and other symptoms of shock, such as a cold sweat. Both sexes can experience any of these symptoms, but as more research develops, the importance of knowing the most common symptoms between the sexes becomes more important to ensure the patient gets timely medical attention.

Arrhythmia occurs when the heart beats with an irregular rhythm, whether too slow, too fast, or otherwise abnormally. Rapid arrhythmia is called **tachycardia**, when the heart beats more than one hundred beats per minute. **Bradycardia** is when the heart beats too slowly, at less than sixty beats per minute. Irregular rhythms, called **fibrillations**, fall into two types: **atrial** and **ventricular**. These can be life threatening because the heart beats erratically, with rapid, electrical impulses. The ventricles of the heart palpitate uselessly instead of pumping blood.

Symptoms of arrhythmia include a fluttering in the chest, a fast heartbeat, a slow heartbeat, chest pain, shortness of breath, lightheadedness, sweating, and fainting. The causes of arrhythmia include heart attacks, scarred heart tissue, clogged arteries, high blood pressure, thyroid problems, smoking, drinking caffeine or alcohol, drug abuse, stress, diabetes, medications, and genetics.

Congestive heart failure occurs with a weakening heart, which causes fluids to build up in the lungs and surrounding tissues. Coronary artery disease, diabetes, obesity, smoking, and high blood pressure can gradually make the heart unable to pump blood through the body correctly.

Although congestive heart failure cannot be fully reversed, some of the symptoms can be treated with medication and lifestyle changes, such as exercise, a reduction in salt intake, changes in diet, stress management, and weight loss. This can help control conditions that caused the heart failure.

Angina is defined as severe pain in the chest that can radiate into the shoulders, arms, and neck. An inadequate blood supply to the heart causes the condition, and the pain can be pressure, squeezing, heaviness, or tightness, usually caused by coronary artery disease. Other symptoms include nausea, fatigue, shortness of breath, sweating, and dizziness.

As a recurring problem, called **stable angina**, the symptoms come with exertion and go away with rest. But angina can be sudden and life threatening. The risk factors include smoking, caffeine intake, diabetes, high blood pressure, high cholesterol, older age, obesity, and stress.

Hypercholesterolemia—high cholesterol—can cause enough narrowing of the blood vessels due to plaque formation to result in heart attacks or strokes. Cholesterol is the waxy substance derived from lipids in the body. Healthy cholesterol builds healthy cells, but an excess of cholesterol can cause fatty deposits and plaque to develop in blood vessels, which decreases oxygen to the heart.

The body contains different types of cholesterol. As cholesterol attaches to proteins in the blood, it forms combinations called **lipoproteins. Low-density lipoproteins** (LDLs)—considered the "bad" cholesterol—build up on arterial walls, causing them to harden and narrow. LDL levels should be below 100 mg/dL. **High-density lipoproteins** (HDLs)—considered the "good" cholesterol—pick up cholesterol in the body and deliver it to the liver. High cholesterol has no symptoms but is confirmed through regular blood tests. HDLs should range between 40 and 50 mg/dL for men and 50 and 60 mg/dL for women. Total cholesterol should be below 200 mg/dL.

Hypertriglyceridemia denotes having a high level of triglycerides, another type of lipid in the blood, which are checked when a doctor checks cholesterol levels. The body converts food calories into triglycerides and stores them in fat cells. They release as energy between meals, but when the body takes in more calories than it burns, through fats and carbohydrates, the triglyceride count in the body can get too high. Triglyceride counts should be less than 150 mg/dL.

Some factors that cause hypertriglyceridemia, as well as **hypercholesterolemia**, are poor diet, obesity, inactivity, smoking, diabetes, and genetics. High triglyceride levels are preventable through lifestyle changes and medications.

The following group of tables, and similar tables in later sections addressing the other body systems, list commonly used drugs—in this case, associated with cardiovascular system diseases and conditions—sorted by drug class. It is important for the pharmacy technician to have an understanding of the generic and brand names of a drug, what it is used for, its most common side effects, and any drug, food, or drink interactions.

Table 1.5. Angiotensin II Receptor Blockers (A2RBs)

Drug Suffix	Generic Name (Brand Names)	Common Side Effects	Common Interactions
—artan	candesartan (Atacand) irbesartan (Avapro) losartan (Cozaar) telmisartan (Micardis) valsartan (Diovan)	changes in urination, weakness, weight gain, lightheadedness, fainting	other blood pressure medications, including ACE inhibitors, aliskiren, lithium, NSAIDS; anything containing potassium; alcohol

These drugs block angiotensin II enzymes from specific receptor sites and help prohibit vasoconstriction.

Table 1.6. Beta-Blockers for High Blood Pressure

Beta Blockers for High BP

Drug Suffix	Generic Name (Brand Names)	Common Side Effects	Common Interactions
—olol	acebutolol (Sectral) atenolol (Tenormin) betaxolol (Kerlone) bisoprolol (Zebeta) carvedilol (Coreg) metoprolol (Lopressor) nadolol (Corgard) penbutolol (Levatol) pindolol (Visken) propranolol (Inderal)	fatigue, cold hands, upset stomach, constipation, diarrhea, dizziness, shortness of breath, trouble sleeping, erectile dysfunction, depression, bradycardia, hypotension/syncope	amiodarone, clonidine, diltiazem, cyclosporine, digoxin, fluconazole, reserpine, rifampin, verapamil, MAO inhibitors, alcohol

Table 1.7. Calcium Channel Blockers

Calcium Blockers

Drug Suffix	Generic Name (Brand Names)	Common Side Effects	Common Interactions
—pine	amlodipine (Norvasc) felodipine (Plendil) isradipine (Dynacirc) nicardipine (Cardene) nifedipine (Procardia) nisoldipine (Sular)	dizziness, swelling of the ankles or feet, blurred vision, cough, fatigue, weight gain, cold sweats	clarithromycin, cyclosporine, diltiazem, itraconazole, ritonavir, sildenafil, simvastatin, tacrolimus, alcohol

Table 1.7. Calcium Channel Blockers (continued)

Drug Suffix	Generic Name (Brand Names)	Common Side Effects	Common Interactions
other suffix	diltiazem (Cardizem)	body aches, congestion, cough, hoarseness, runny nose, tender glands in the neck, trouble swallowing	busiprone, carbamazepine, cimetidine, cyclosporine, clonidine, digoxin, lovastatin, midazolam, quinidine, rifampin, simvastatin, triazolam, beta-blockers

Calcium Blockers [handwritten annotation]

Calcium channel blockers are used as antihypertensive drugs and include dihydropyridines (DHPs). They disrupt the movement of calcium ions by blocking the calcium channels to lower blood pressure, regulate heart rate, and/or reduce chest pain. An older generation calcium channel blocker, diltiazem—a non-dihydropyridine (NDHP)—is also listed, with slightly different side effects and drug interactions.

Table 1.8. ACE Inhibitors

Drug Suffix	Generic Name (Brand Names)	Common Side Effects	Common Interactions
–pril	benazepril (Lotensin) captopril (Capoten) enalapril (Vasotec) fosinopril (Monopril) lisinopril (Zestril, Prinivil) moexipril (Univasc) quinapril (Accupril) ramipril (Altace) trandolapril (Mavik)	dry cough, nausea, vomiting, loss of appetite, stomach discomfort	other blood pressure medications, insulin, diabetes medications, NSAIDs, arthritis medications, aliskerin, alcohol

These drugs block the conversion of angiotensin I to angiotensin II. They may be used to avoid increased vasoconstriction or high blood pressure.

Table 1.9. HMG-CoA Reductase Inhibitors

Drug Suffix	Generic Name (Brand Names)	Common Side Effects	Common Interactions
–statin	atorvastatin (Lipitor) fluvastatin (Lescol) lovastatin (Mevacor) rosuvastatin (Crestor) simvastatin (Zocor)	diarrhea, lower back pain, tiredness, muscle cramps, headache, hoarseness, constipation, gas, heartburn, loss of appetite, trouble sleeping	boceprevir, cimetidine, colchicine, cyclosporine, digoxin, niacin, rifampin, spironolactone, telaprevir, HIV/AIDS drugs; not to be used if the patient has liver disease or uses birth control
other suffixes	fenofibrate (Tricor) gemfibrozil (Lopid)	sour stomach, belching, itching, numbness, diarrhea, heartburn, nausea, vomiting	warfarin, –statin medications, repaglinide, colchicine, colestipol; not to be used if the patient has gallbladder, kidney, or liver diseases

These drugs inhibit the body's cholesterol production. The last two in the table are fibrates—fibric acid derivatives—which are used to treat high cholesterol.

Table 1.10. Alpha Adrenergic Blockers

Drug Suffix	Generic Name (Brand Names)	Common Side Effects	Common Interactions
–zosin	doxazosin (Cardura) prazosin (Minipress) tamsulosin (Flomax) terazosin (Hytrin)	headache, tiredness, dizziness, painful prolonged erection, alcohol	sildenafil, tadalafil, vardenafil, beta-blockers, diuretics

Like calcium channel blockers, these are used as antihypertensive drugs. They inhibit alpha adrenergic receptors to dilate veins and arterioles, and they decrease blood pressure.

CONTINUE

Table 1.11. Blood Thinners

Generic Name (Brand Names)	Common Side Effects	Common Interactions
clopidogrel (Plavix) enoxaparin (Lovenox) rivaroxaban (Xarelto) warfarin (Coumadin)	unusual bleeding, red or brown urine or stools, vomiting blood, heavy menstrual bleeding, blood clotting problems	NSAIDs, antiviral drugs, other blood thinners, steroid medications, antidepressants

All these drugs are meant to prevent and treat blood clots. They do not fall into the suffix-based system of identification.

Table 1.12. Vasodilators

Generic Name (Brand Names)	Description	Common Side Effects	Common Interactions
nitroglycerin (Nitro-Bid)	for chest pain or palpitations	flushing, tachycardia, bradycardia, tinnitus, hypotension, cyanide toxicity, heart palpitations	erectile dysfunction drugs, −caine drugs (local anesthetics), tizanidine
sodium nitroprusside (Nitropress)	for severe high blood pressure, acute decompensated heart failure, and, in rare cases, low blood sugar		
diazoxide (Proglycem) hydralazine (Apresoline) minoxidil (Minoxidil) tolazoline (Priscoline)	for severe high blood pressure, acute decompensated heart failure, and, in rare cases, low blood sugar	nausea, vomiting, diarrhea, dizziness, increased hunger or thirst	phenytoin, blood pressure and blood thinner medications, diuretics

The first two vasodilators in this table share specific actions, side effects, and drug interactions that the last four do not.

Table 1.13. Antiarrythmals

Generic Name (Brand Names)	Description	Common Side Effects	Common Interactions
digoxin (Lanoxin) digitoxin (Digitaline)	cardiac glycosides for heart failure and heart rhythm problems	headache, dizziness, nausea, vomiting, loss of appetite	excessive drug interactions; need to be checked with each individual patient depending on condition and drugs used
isosorbide dinitrate/ isosorbide mononi-trate (Isordil, Imdur, Monoket, Ismo)	for angina		NSAIDs, erectile dysfunction drugs, OTC cough and cold medications; may interfere with certain drug tests
quinidine (no brand name available)	for angina; also an anti-malarial		blood thinners, acetazolamide, pimozide
disopyramide (Norpace) flecainide (Tambocor) mexiletine (Mexitil) procainamide (Pronestyl, Procan, Procanbid)	for angina		if patient has lupus or heart block, or is taking any other antiarrhyth-mic, phenytoin, or pimozide
adenosine (Adenocard) amiodarone (Cordarone) propafenone (Rythmol)	for angina		cimetidine, SSRIs, rifampin, orlistat, MAO inhibitors, prochlorperazine, promethazine, −statin drugs, lithium, phenytoin, loratadine, dipyrid-amole, verapamil, theophylline, caffeine

These treat angina but a few have other uses too.

 Diseases and conditions not covered in this section and not related to the car-diovascular system can also be treated by some of the drugs in this section.

Table 1.14. Diuretics

Generic Name (Brand Names)	Description	Common Side Effects	Common Interactions
furosemide (Lasix)	loop diuretic or water pill	dry mouth, muscle twitching, weakness, loss of appetite, diarrhea, stomach cramps, ringing in ears	hormones, laxatives, high blood pressure drugs, steroid medications, NSAIDs, methotrexate, lithium, cisplatin, cyclosporine, digoxin, indomethacin, licorice, phenytoin
hydrochlorothiazide (Microzide)	diuretic		
spironolactone (Aldactone)	potassium sparing diuretic		ACE inhibitors, amiloride, digoxin, lithium, methenamine, blood thinners, chlorpropamide, diabetes medications, NSAIDs, laxatives, steroid medications
triamterene (Maxzide, Dyazide)	potassium sparing diuretic, antihypertensive		

These treat angina but a few have other uses too.

PRACTICE QUESTIONS

1. The systolic reading in blood pressure measures
   A) the heart when it relaxes and fills back up with blood.
   B) the number of heart beats per minute.
   C) the pressure as the heart pumps blood through the body.
   D) the oxygen level in the coronary arteries.

Answers:

A) Incorrect. Diastolic readings measure when the heart relaxes and fills with blood.

B) Incorrect. The number of beats per minute is the pulse.

C) **Correct.** Systolic readings measure the pressure as the heart pumps blood through the body.

D)   Incorrect. Oxygen levels are not measured by systolic readings. (They can be measured with a blood test or with the use of a device called a pulse oximeter.)

2.   Triglycerides are

   A)   what calories are converted to in the body.

   B)   the "bad" cholesterol in the body.

   C)   the "good" cholesterol in the body.

   D)   the waxy substance derived from lipids.

   Answers:

   A)   **Correct.** Triglycerides are what calories are converted to in the body.

   B)   Incorrect. "Bad" cholesterol is LDL.

   C)   Incorrect. "Good" cholesterol is HDL.

   D)   Incorrect. The waxy substance derived from lipids is cholesterol.

3.   Drugs with the suffix –*pril* are

   A)   calcium channel blockers.

   B)   beta-blockers.

   C)   fibric acid.

   D)   ACE inhibitors.

   Answers:

   A)   Incorrect. Calcium channel blockers have the –*pine* suffix.

   B)   Incorrect. Beta-blockers have the –*olol* suffix.

   C)   Incorrect. Fibric acid derivatives, such as fenofibrate (Tricor) and gemfibrozil (Lopid), reduce cholesterol.

   D)   **Correct.** ACE inhibitors, such as benazepril, fosinopril, and quinapril, indeed have the –*pril* suffix.

4.   Vasodilators

   A)   reduce cholesterol in the body.

   B)   thin the blood.

   C)   treat severe high blood pressure.

   D)   are diuretics.

   Answers:

   A)   Incorrect. HMG-CoA reductase inhibitors are used to reduce cholesterol in the body by inhibiting its production.

B) Incorrect. Blood thinners, such as warfarin and enoxaparin, thin the blood.

C) **Correct.** Vasodilators treat severely high blood pressure.

D) Incorrect. Diuretics, such as furosemide and spironolactone, make you urinate more frequently.

THE NERVOUS SYSTEM

The **nervous system** consists of the brain, the spinal cord, the nerves, and the sensory organs. This system is responsible for gathering, processing, and reacting to information from both inside and outside the body. Of the two parts of the nervous system—the central nervous system and the peripheral nervous system—the **central nervous system** (CNS) consists of the brain and spinal cord, and is responsible for processing and storing information as well as deciding on appropriate actions and issuing commands. The **peripheral nervous system** (PNS) is responsible for gathering information, transporting it to the CNS, and then delivering commands from the CNS to the appropriate organs. Sensory organs and nerves do the gathering and transporting of information while the efferent nerves deliver the commands.

The nervous system consists mostly of nervous tissue, which in turn consists of two classes of cells: neurons and neuralgia. **Neurons** are the nerve cells. They comprise several distinct parts. The **soma**—the body of the neuron—contains most of the cellular organelles. **Dendrites**—small, treelike structures—extend from the soma; their main responsibility is to carry information to the soma, and sometimes away from it. The long, thin **axon** also extends from the soma. Usually each soma has one axon, but the axon can branch out farther. The axon sends information from the soma, rarely to it. Lastly, the places where two neurons meet, or where they meet other types of cells, are called **synapses**.

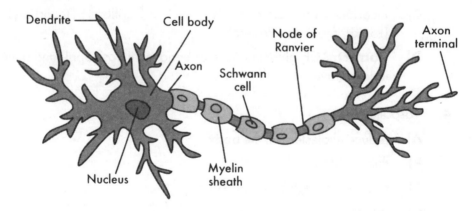

Figure 1.15. Neuron

Neurons fall into three classes. **Efferent neurons** transmit signals from the CNS to the effectors in the body, while **afferent neurons** transmit signals from receptors in the body to the CNS. **Interneurons**—the third class of neurons—form complex networks in the CNS. They integrate the signals received from the afferent neurons and control the body by sending signals through the efferent neurons.

Together, these three types of neurons perform the main tasks of the nervous system:

+ Efferent neurons (also called motor neurons) signal effector cells in muscles and glands to react to stimuli.

+ Afferent neurons (also called sensory neurons) take in information from inside and outside the body through the sensory organs and receptors.

+ Interneurons transmit information to the CNS, where it is evaluated, compared to previously stored information, stored or discarded, and used to make a decision—a process called **integration**.

Neurons are so specialized that they almost never reproduce. Therefore, they need **neuroglia cells** (also called glial cells), the maintenance cells for neurons. A number of neuroglia surround every neuron, protecting and feeding it.

The brain and spinal cord of the CNS have their own protection within the cavities of skeletal structures: the brain, housed in the cranial cavity of the skull, and the spinal cord, enclosed in the vertebral cavity in the spine.

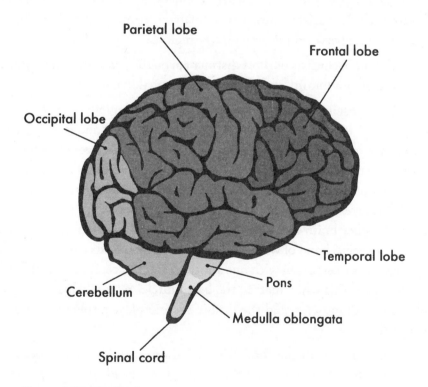

Figure 1.16. The Brain

Since the organs that form the CNS are vital to the body's survival, two other important structures also protect them: the meninges and the cerebrospinal fluid. The **meninges**, which covers the CNS, consists of three distinct layers. The dura mater, as its name suggests, is the most durable, outer part of the meninges. Made out of collagen fibers—rich and thick connective tissue—it forms a space for the cerebrospinal fluid around the CNS. Next is the arachnoid mater, the thin lining on the inner side of the dura mater. It forms many tiny fibers that connect the dura mater with the next layer, the pia mater, which is separated from the arachnoid mater by the subarachnoid space. The pia mater directly covers the surface of the brain and the spinal cord, and it provides sustenance to the nervous tissue through its many blood vessels.

Cerebrospinal fluid (CSF), a clear fluid formed from blood plasma, fills the subarachnoid space. The ventricles (the hollow spaces in the brain) and the central canal (a cavity found in the middle of the spinal cord) also contain CSF.

As the components of the central nervous system float in the CSF, they seem lighter than they really are. This is especially important for the brain, because the fluid keeps it from being crushed by its own weight. The floating also protects the brain and the spinal cord from shock, such as sudden movements and trauma. Additionally, the CSF possesses the necessary chemical substances for the normal functioning of the nervous tissue, and it serves to remove cellular waste from the neurons.

Two classes divide the nervous tissue that makes up the **brain**. **Gray matter**, which consists mostly of unmyelinated interneurons, is the tissue where the actual processing of signals happens as well as where connections between neurons are made. **White matter**, which consists mostly of myelinated neurons, is the tissue that conducts signals to, from, and between the gray matter regions.

The brain consists of three distinct parts: the prosencephalon (forebrain), the mesencephalon (midbrain), and the rhombencephalon (hindbrain).

The **prosencephalon**, or forebrain, has two regions: the cerebrum and the diencephalon. A longitudinal fissure divides the outermost and largest part of the brain, the **cerebrum**, into left and right hemispheres, each of which contains four lobes: the frontal, parietal, temporal, and occipital. The surface of the cerebrum, called the **cerebral cortex**, is made out of gray matter with characteristic grooves (**sulci**) and bulges (**gyri**). The cerebral cortex is where the actual processing happens in the cerebrum: it's responsible for the higher brain functions like thinking and using language. Under the cerebral cortex, a special band of white matter, called the **corpus callosum**, connects the hemispheres of the cerebrum with one another, and the cerebrum itself with the rest of the body. Under this white matter, the **basal nuclei** region helps control and regulate the movement of muscles, and the **limbic system** plays a role in memory, emotions, and survival.

Also present in the forebrain, the **diencephalon** is a structure formed by the thalamus, hypothalamus, and the pineal gland. Made out of two gray matter masses, the **thalamus** is located around the third ventricle of the brain. It routes the sensory signals to the correct parts of the cerebral cortex. Under the thalamus, the **hypothalamus** plays a role in regulating hunger, thirst, blood pressure, and body temperature as well as heart rate and the production of hormones. The **pineal gland**, beneath the hypothalamus—and directly controlled by it—produces the hormone melatonin, which plays a vital role in sleep.

The topmost part of the brain stem—the **mesencephalon**, or midbrain—contains two regions as well. The first, the **tectum**, plays a role in reflex reactions to visual and auditory information. The second, the **cerebral peduncles**, connect the cerebrum and thalamus with the lower parts of the brain stem and the spinal cord. The cerebral peduncles contain the **substantia nigra** too, which is involved in muscle movement, reward seeking, and learning.

The **rhombencephalon**, or hindbrain, encompasses the brain stem and the cerebellum. The **brain stem** further divides into the medulla oblongata and the pons. The **medulla oblongata**, which connects the spinal cord with the pons, is mostly made out of white matter, but it also contains gray matter that processes involuntary body functions, such as blood pressure, the level of oxygen in the blood, and reflexes like sneezing, coughing, vomiting, and swallowing. The **pons**—located between the medulla oblongata and the midbrain, and in front of the cerebellum—transports signals to and from the cerebellum, and between the upper regions of the brain, the medulla oblongata, and the spinal cord.

The **cerebellum** in the hindbrain looks like a smaller version of the cerebrum: with two spheres and wrinkled. Its outer layer, called the **cerebellar cortex**, consists of gray matter, while the inner part, called the **arbor vitae**, consists of white matter, which transports signals between the cerebellum and the rest of the body. The cerebellum controls and coordinates complex muscle activities plus helps the body to maintain its posture and keep its balance.

The **spinal cord**, located inside the vertebral cavity, is made out of both white and gray matter. It carries signals and processes some reflexes to stimuli. The spinal nerves stretch out from it.

Moving away from the central nervous system, the **nerves** that form the peripheral nerve system (PNS) consist of bundled axons that carry signals to and from the spinal cord and the brain. A single axon, covered with a layer of connective tissue called the **endoneurium**, bundles with other axons to form **fascicles**. Another sheath of connective tissue covers these, called the **perineurium**. Groups of fascicles wrapped together in yet another layer of connective tissue, the **epineurium**, form a whole nerve.

Of the five types of peripheral nerves, the **afferent**, **efferent**, and **mixed** nerves are formed out of the neurons that share the same name and perform the same roles. The **spinal nerves**—thirty-one pairs in total—extend from the side of the spinal cord. They exit the spinal cord between the vertebrae and carry information to and from the spinal cord and the neck, arms, legs, and trunk. They are grouped and named according to the region where they originate: eight pairs of cervical, twelve pairs of thoracic, five pairs of lumbar, five pairs of sacral, and one pair of coccygeal nerves. Last of the peripheral nerves, the **cranial nerves**—twelve pairs in total—extend from the lower side of the brain. Numbers identify them, and they connect the brain with the sensory organs, head muscles, neck and shoulder muscles, heart, and gastrointestinal tract.

The final component of the nervous system, the **sensory organs**, includes the specialized sense organs, which are responsible for the specialized senses: hearing, sight, balance (in addition to the cerebellum), smell, and taste. Sense organs also have sensory receptors for the general senses, which include touch, pain, and temperature. These senses are part of the PNS, and they detect stimuli and send signals to the CNS when detection occurs.

The ability of the body to exert conscious control divides the peripheral nervous system. The **somatic nervous system** (SNS)—the part of the PNS that can be consciously controlled—stimulates the skeletal muscles. The **autonomic nervous system** (ANS) portion of the PNS cannot be consciously controlled; it stimulates the visceral and cardiac muscle as well as the glandular tissue.

The ANS further divides into the sympathetic, parasympathetic, and enteric nervous systems. The **sympathetic nervous system** forms the fight-or-flight reaction to stimuli like emotion, danger, and exercise. It increases respiration and heart rate, decreases digestion, and releases stress hormones. The **parasympathetic nervous system** stimulates activities that occur when the body is at rest, including digestion and sexual arousal. Lastly, the **enteric nervous system** is responsible for the digestive system and its processes. This system works mostly independently from the CNS, although it can be regulated through the sympathetic and parasympathetic division.

A list of diseases and conditions common to the nervous system follows, along with tables detailing some of the most common drug treatments used currently:

Anxiety disorders are one of the most common conditions of the nervous system. Some anxiety disorders can be so severe they disrupt a patient's life and relationships. Each patient is different and presents with different symptoms, and some disorders have their own unique set of symptoms. Anxiety disorders include social anxiety, panic disorder, post-traumatic stress disorder (PTSD), obsessive-compulsive disorder (OCD), and generalized anxiety disorder (GAD).

Symptoms of anxiety disorders include fatigue, headaches, tremors, shakiness, sweating, twitching, irritability, hot flashes, and muscle tension and aches. These disorders can develop at any time in life and can be brought on by lifestyle changes, such as stress. Many people who suffer from anxiety also suffer from depression.

Depression, another common nervous system disorder, is considered a mood disorder. Symptoms of a depressive disorder can affect a patient to the point that he or she can no longer do normal activities, such as sleeping, eating, and working. As with anxiety disorders, patients may present with different symptoms, but some disorders have a unique set of symptoms. Depressive disorders include clinical depression, postpartum depression, bipolar depression, seasonal affective disorder, and psychotic depression.

Symptoms of depression include anxiety, manic episodes, sadness, hopelessness, irritability, feelings of guilt, fatigue, feeling restless, difficulty with concentration, aches and pains, appetite and weight changes, insomnia, and thoughts of death or suicide. Risk factors of depression include genetic history, lifestyle changes, stress, trauma, and illness.

Parkinson's disease is caused by nerve cell damage in the brain, which in turn causes a drop in dopamine. It often starts out with slight tremors and slowly develops to extensive tremors, slow movement, and lack of coordination. Unfortunately, no cure exists for Parkinson's disease; it is a chronic condition, but available medications help ease the symptoms. Parkinson's disease usually afflicts the elderly population.

Alzheimer's disease affects the elderly population as well. With Alzheimer's, brain cells and their connections degenerate and die. Eventually, the patient loses memory cells and mental functions, causing confusion and forgetfulness. No cure exists for Alzheimer's disease, but available medications help slow the progress.

Multiple sclerosis (MS) is an autoimmune disorder that disrupts communication between the brain and body through nerve degeneration and lesions in the brain. Multiple sclerosis is very hard to diagnose due to the fact that its symptoms mimic a number of other conditions and in many people it falls into a relapsing remission. Also, different levels of MS present, ranging from mild to severe.

MS is a chronic condition and has a slow progression. The main symptoms of MS include pain, fatigue, vision loss, impaired coordination, memory problems, and vision loss. Medications and physical therapy help ease these symptoms.

Epilepsy, another chronic disorder, cannot be cured. It can be caused by genetics, a stroke, a brain injury, or a trauma. During a seizure, a patient may experience symptoms that frighten an onlooker. The patient may cry out, stiffen, have repetitive or jerky movements, seem confused, roll his or her eyes back in the head, repetitively blink, or stare blankly.

Although some patients can "grow out" of having seizures as they get older, the chance of experiencing another seizure is higher if a patient has experienced one in the past. The several types of seizure disorders include generalized seizures, partial seizures, absent seizures, and grand-mal seizures. Through patient-specific drug therapies, the majority of epileptic seizures can be controlled by medications.

Migraines—intense headaches that cause throbbing in a particular area of a patient's head—can vary in intensity depending on the patient and/or risk factors. Most people who have migraines are chronic sufferers. Normally, triggers bring on migraines. Common triggers include hormonal changes, food and drink, stress and exercise, and a change of the seasons.

Symptoms of a migraine include pounding headache, light sensitivity, nausea, vomiting, pain, and vision changes. Preventative medications, physical therapy, pain relievers, and antinausea medications can help treat migraines.

Sleep disorders present as many different types. Some abnormal sleep behavior disorders, such as insomnia, nightmares, REM behavior disorders, and light sleeping patterns, can cause fatigue, lack of concentration during the day, and other disruptions. Rhythmic sleep disorders, such as non-24-hour sleep–wake disorder, nightshift work disorders, and delayed sleep phase disorders, can cause fatigue, depression, and anxiety due to the lack of a normal sleep pattern. Other disorders can be more severe. With sleep apnea, the patient stops breathing and requires use of a mask to sleep. With narcolepsy, a patient is unable to regulate the sleep–wake cycle normally, which can cause the patient to fall asleep in dangerous situations, such as driving.

Sleep disorders are treatable dependent upon what is causing the disruption in sleep. Drug therapies, such as hypnotics and benzodiazepines, can help regulate sleep. Some patients also participate in sleep studies and treatments to help find a solution to their sleep disorders.

Attention-deficit/hyperactivity disorder (ADHD) normally starts in childhood and, for many, continues into adulthood as a chronic condition. Because ADHD causes hyperactivity, limited attention, and sometimes uncontrollable impulses, patients often have issues with low self-esteem, relationships, and difficulty at school. No cure exists for ADHD, but some patients grow out of it and others can control it with drugs and behavioral therapies.

Of the most common drugs used for the nervous system, two categories of drugs work with the sympathetic nervous system (some of which can be found in table 1.25):

+ **Sympathomimetic** drugs, or **adrenergic agonists**, stimulate the sympathetic nervous system. They mimic the organic compounds dopamine, norepinephrine, and adrenaline in the body. These drugs are used for cardiac arrest, ADHD, and low blood pressure. Examples of drugs in this group are dobutamine and amphetamines like Adderall.

+ **Parasympathomimetic**, or **cholinergic**, drugs stimulate the parasympathetic nervous system. Acetylcholine is the neurotransmitter of this system. The chemicals used in this group are stimulated by nicotinic or muscarinic receptors. Examples of drugs in this category are varenicline (Chantix) and atropine.

Other nervous system drugs work in the central nervous system, such as benzodiazepines like diazepam (Valium) and antidepressants like paroxetine (Paxil) (found in tables 1.15 and 1.18 respectively).

 Diseases and conditions not covered in this section and not related to the nervous system can also be treated by some of the drugs in this section.

Table 1.15. Benzodiazepines

Drug Suffix	Generic Name (Brand Names)	Description	Common Side Effects	Common Interactions
–pam, –lam	alprazolam (Xanax) clonazepam (Klonopin) lorazepam (Ativan) diazepam (Valium) estazolam (Prosom) flurazepam (Dalmane) quazepam (Doral) temazepam (Restoril) triazolam (Halcion)	for seizure disorders, sleep disorders, anxiety disorders; also used as a muscle relaxant and as a hypnotic	depression, confusion, dizziness, clumsiness, fatigue; may be habit forming and cause with-drawals	alcohol, theophylline, aminophylline, clozapine, probenecid, valproate, other seizure drugs, narcotic drugs, allergy medications

These drugs predominantly act as sedatives to treat seizure, sleep, and anxiety disorders.

Table 1.16. Barbituates

Generic Name (Brand Names)	Common Side Effects	Common Interactions
amobarbital (Amytal Sodium) butabarbital (Butisol Sodium) mephobarbital (Mebaral) phenobarbital (Nembutal) secobarbital (Seconal)	headache, nervousness, nausea, talkativeness, irritability, confusion, euphoria, weakness, tremor, lack of concentration, lack of coordination, depression, heart palpitations; may be habit forming	alcohol, narcotic pain medications, OTC cough and cold medications, oral contraceptives, cimetidine, isoniazid, benzodiazepines, SSRIs, disulfiram, diazepam, digoxin

These drugs treat anxiety, insomnia, and seizure disorders.

Table 1.17. Hypnotics

Generic Name (Brand Names)	Common Side Effects	Common Interactions
chloral hydrate (Noctec) eszopiclone (Lunesta) ramelteon (Rozerem) zalepion (Sonata) zolpidem (Ambien)	daytime drowsiness, dizziness, headache, nausea, dry mouth; may be habit forming	imipramine, chlorpromazine, haloperidol, alcohol, SSRIs, rifampin, ketoconazole, CNS-active medications

These drugs treat anxiety, insomnia, and seizure disorders.

Table 1.18. Antidepressants

Generic Name (Brand Names)	Description	Common Side Effects	Common Interactions
citalopram (Celexa) fluoxetine (Prozac) paroxetine (Paxil) sertraline (Zoloft)	selective serotonin reuptake inhibitors (SSRIs) that treat depression, anxiety, and peripheral neuropathy by increasing the neurotransmitter serotonin level in the brain	headache, drowsiness, dizziness, insomnia, restlessness, decreased sex drive, dry mouth, yawning, ringing in the ears	alcohol, MAO inhibitors, pimozide, tryptophan, thioridazine, warfarin, triptans, cimetidine, phenobarbital, phenytoin, NSAIDs, lithium, digoxin, diazepam, beta-blockers, electroconvulsive therapy
desvenlafaxine (Pristiq) duloxetine (Cymbalta) mirtazapine (Remeron) venlafaxine (Effexor)	serotonin and norepinephrine reuptake inhibitors (SNRIs) that treat depression, anxiety, and chronic pain by increasing the levels of neurotransmitters serotonin and norepinephrine in the brain		
bupropion (Wellbutrin, Zyban)	for depression, help to stop smoking, and seasonal affective disorder	dry mouth, eye pain, headache, dizziness, nausea, vomiting, upset stomach, weight gain or loss	alcohol, MAO inhibitors, linezolid, methylene blue, beta-blockers, diabetic medications, seizure medications, cimetidine, steroid medications, HIV/AIDS medications, arrhythmia medications
nortriptyline (Pamelor)	tricyclic antidepressant also for nerve pain	anxiety, seizures, eye pain, stomach upset	
trazodone (Desyrel)	antidepressant and sedative used as a serotonin antagonist and reuptake inhibitor	constipation, nausea, dry mouth, vision changes, headache, unusual sleepiness	
amitriptyline (Elavil)	tricyclic antidepressant also for nerve pain		

Each antidepressant in the list acts somewhat differently but most address serotonin levels.

Table 1.19. Antipsychotics

Generic Name (Brand Names)	Description	Common Side Effects	Common Interactions
aripiprazole (Abilify) olanzapine (Zyprexa) quetiapine (Seroquel) risperidone (Risperdal)	atypical antipsychotics for bipolar disorder, schizophrenia, and Tourette's syndrome	headache, nausea, vomiting, constipation, upset stomach, restlessness, weight gain or loss	alcohol, carbamazepine, clarithromycin, fluoxetine, paroxetine, ketoconazole, rifampin, benzodiazepines, blood pressure medications
lithium carbonate (Lithium)	for manic episodes of bipolar disorder	hand tremors, weakness, lack of coordination, nausea, vomiting, loss of appetite, upset stomach, thinning of the hair, itchy skin	
haloperidol (Haldol)	typical antipsychotic	breast pain, change in menstruation, dry mouth, loss of appetite, nausea, vomiting, diarrhea, constipation, restlessness	medications that may cause low blood pressure, overheating; lithium; Parkinson's medications; alcohol; avoid if patient has liver disease, seizures

Table 1.20. Antihistamines and Anticholinergics

Generic Name (Brand Names)	Description	Common Side Effects	Common Interactions
diphenhydramine (Benadryl) hydroxyzine (Atarax) meclizine (Antivert) promethazine (Promethegan)	antihistamine for motion sickness, nausea, vomiting, rash, hives, and itching	blurred vision, drowsiness, dry mouth, headache, constipation	alcohol, narcotic pain medications, allergy medications, tricyclic antidepressants
scopolamine (TransdermScop)	anticholinergic for nausea and vomiting caused by motion sickness		

Table 1.20. Antihistamines and Anticholinergics (contined)

Generic Name (Brand Names)	Description	Common Side Effects	Common Interactions
atropine (no brand name available)	anticholinergic involuntary nervous system blocker	blurred vision, constipation, dry mouth, muscle weakness, upset stomach, decreased sweating	allergy medications, narcotic pain medications, alcohol

Table 1.21. Cognition-Enhancing Drugs

Generic Name (Brand Names)	Common Side Effects	Common Interactions
donepezil (Aricept)	nausea, vomiting, fainting, weight loss	bethanechol, carbamazepine, dexamethasone, ketoconazole, phenobarbital, phenytoin, quinidine, rifampin, NSAIDs
memantine (Namenda)	back pain, headache, weight gain, nausea, vomiting	amantadine, cimetidine, ketamine, metformin, quinidine, ranitidine, diuretics, sodium bicarbonate
galantamine (Razadyne)	dizziness, nausea, vomiting	bethanechol, cimetidine, ketoconazole, paroxetine, arrhythmia medications, NSAIDs

All these drugs help treat Alzheimer's disease.

Table 1.22. Dopamine Promoters and Precursors

Generic Name (Brand Names)	Description	Common Side Effects	Common Interactions
carbidopa/ levodopa (Sinemet)	dopamine precursor	drowsiness, headache, dizziness, fainting, nausea	MAO inhibitors, isoniazid, metoclopramide, papaverine, promethazine, prochlorperazine, thioridazine, blood pressure medications, antidepressants

Generic Name (Brand Names)	Description	Common Side Effects	Common Interactions
ropinirole (Requip)	dopamine promoter	drowsiness, headache, dizziness, fainting, nausea	MAO inhibitors, isoniazid, metoclopramide, papaverine, promethazine, prochlorperazine, thioridazine, blood pressure medications, antidepressants
benztropine (Cogentin)	for reducing tremors		haloperidol, MAO inhibitors, phenothiazine medications
entacapone (Comtan) rotigotine (Neupro)	dopamine promoters	dizziness, fainting, nausea	blood pressure medications, phenothiazine medications, anti-depressants, metoclopramide, papaverine

All these drugs address Parkinson's symptoms.

Table 1.23. Anticonvulsants

Generic Name (Brand Names)	Common Side Effects	Common Interactions
carbamazepine (Tegretol)		excessive drug interactions; should be decided on patient-specific basis; do not drink grapefruit juice or eat grapefruits while taking this medication
lamotrigine (Lamictal) topiramate (Topamax)	anxiety, restlessness, trouble sleeping, blurred vision, nausea, vomiting, dry mouth, drowsiness, runny nose	diuretics, digoxin, lithium, metformin, other seizure medications, antivirals
valproic acid (Valproic)		aspirin, rifampin, tolbutamide, zidovudine, other seizure medications, sedatives, blood thinners
phenytoin (Dilantin)		albendazole, amiodarone, aspirin, diazoxide, digoxin, disulfiram, folic acid, furosemide, isoniazid, methylphenidate, nisoldipine, quinidine, reserpine, rifampin, sucralfate, theophylline, tolbutamide, cholesterol medications, antidepressants, blood thinners

These drugs treat seizures, nerve pain, and bipolar disorder.

Table 1.24. Antimigraine Drugs

Generic Name (Brand Names)	Common Side Effects	Common Interactions
almotriptan (Axert) ergotamine (Ergomar) sumatriptan (Imitrex) zolmitriptan (Zomig)	muscle pain, nausea, vomiting, diarrhea, upset stomach, nervousness, irritability, dizziness, leg weakness	dopamine, some antibiotics, blood pressure medications, HIV/AIDS medications, other triptan migraine medications

These drugs treat migraines and cluster headaches.

Table 1.25. Miscellaneous Stimulants and Other Sympathomimetic and Parasympathomimetic Drugs

Generic Name (Brand Names)	Description	Common Side Effects	Common Interactions
amphetamine/dextroamphetamine (Adderall)	stimulants for ADD/ADHD	dry mouth, diarrhea, nausea, headache, loss of appetite, insomnia, weight loss	MAO inhibitors, acetazolamide, antacids, haloperidol, diuretics, lithium, meperidine, omeprazole, phenytoin, reserpine, sodium bicarbonate
methylphenidate (Ritalin)			MAO inhibitors, antacids, blood thinners, antidepressants, seizure medications
atomoxetine (Strattera)			MAO inhibitors, asthma medications, antidepressants, dobutamine, dopamine, arrhythmia medications
gabapentin (Neurontin) pregabalin (Lyrica)	GABA analogs used as nerve pain medications and anticonvulsants	drowsiness, dizziness, blurred vision	narcotic pain medications, allergy medications, alcohol, ACE inhibitors

Generic Name (Brand Names)	Description	Common Side Effects	Common Interactions
varenicline (Chantix)	for help to stop smoking	headache, nausea, constipation, gas, trouble sleeping	alcohol, bupropion, nicotine, quinolone antibiotics, H-2 antagonists, trimethoprim
buspirone (Buspar)	non-narcotic for anxiety	dry mouth, drowsiness, restlessness, headache, nausea, constipation	MAO inhibitors, cimetidine, dexamethasone, diltiazem, erythromycin, itraconazole, nefazodone, rifampin, verapamil, seizure medications
phentermine (Ionamin)	stimulant for weight loss	hypertension, dizziness, changes in sex drive, tremors, insomnia	
dopamine (no brand name available)	for blood pressure and symptoms of shock; used as a supplement to the neurotransmitter in the brain	headache, anxiety, nausea, vomiting, tingly sensation	not applicable
neostigmine (Prostigmin) sulfaguanidine (Guanidine)	for strengthening muscles	dry mouth, nausea, vomiting, diarrhea, loss of appetite, numbness, tingling, muscle cramps	amphetamines, insulin or diabetic medications, MAO inhibitors, glaucoma medications, migraine medications, haloperidol, diuretics, blood pressure medications, antidepressants; overactive thyroid, heart disease

This mix of drug types include GABA/peripheral acetylcholinesterase inhibitors and treatments for ADHD.

PRACTICE QUESTIONS

1. Which is NOT a class of neurons?

    A) central neurons

    B) efferent neurons

    C) interneurons

    D) afferent neurons

Answers:

A) **Correct.** *Central* is not an actual class of neurons, though it can be confused with the central nervous system.

B) Incorrect. Efferent neurons are motor neurons.

C) Incorrect. Interneurons form complex networks in the CNS.

D) Incorrect. Afferent neurons transport signals from receptors to the CNS.

2. Which is NOT a trigger for migraines?

A) food or drink

B) hormones

C) stress

D) obesity

Answers:

A) Incorrect. Various types of food or drink can indeed trigger a migraine.

B) Incorrect. Hormonal changes can also trigger a migraine.

C) Incorrect. Stress too can trigger a migraine.

D) **Correct.** Obesity is not a known trigger for a migraine.

3. Which is NOT a cognition-enhancing medication?

A) donepezil

B) memantine

C) diazepam

D) galantamine

Answers:

A) Incorrect. Donepezil is a cognition-enhancing medication.

B) Incorrect. Memantine is also a cognition-enhancing medication.

C) **Correct.** Diazepam is a benzodiazepine.

D) Incorrect. Galantamine is another cognition-enhancing medication.

4. Which drug class suffix refers to benzodiazepines?

A) –artan

B) –pam

C) –ine

D) –olol

Answers:

A) Incorrect. –*artan* is the drug class suffix for angiotensin II receptor blockers (A2RBs).

B) **Correct.** *–pam* is the drug class suffix for benzodiazepines.

C) Incorrect. *–ine* is not a drug class suffix but is used in chemistry to denote specific substances.

D) Incorrect. *–olol* is the drug class suffix for beta-blockers or beta-adrenergic blocking agents.

The Musculoskeletal System

In the **muscular system** portion of the musculoskeletal system, movement is the main function. Muscles, attached to the bones in the body, allow movement of the limbs. They also work in the heart, blood vessels, and digestive organs, where they facilitate movement of substances through the body. In addition to movement, muscles help support the body's posture and create heat.

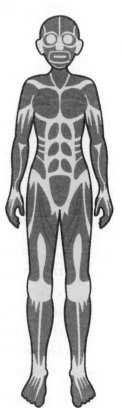

Of the three types of muscle—visceral, cardiac, and skeletal—**visceral muscle** is the weakest. Found in the stomach, intestines, and blood vessels, it helps contract and move substances through those areas. Only the unconscious part of the brain controls visceral muscle, which is why it is sometimes referred to as **involuntary muscle**. It is also called **smooth muscle** because of its appearance under a microscope. The cells of visceral muscle form a smooth surface, unlike the other two types of muscle.

Cardiac muscle—found only in the heart—enables the heart to contract and pump blood through the body. Like visceral muscle, cardiac muscle cannot be voluntarily controlled. Unlike visceral muscle, however, the cardiac muscle is quite strong. Individual muscle cells called **cardiomyocytes**, within the cardiac muscle, are joined together by **intercalated discs**. These discs allow the cells of the muscle to contract in sync. The muscle, when observed under a microscope, reveals a pattern of light and dark stripes, caused by the arrangement of proteins.

Skeletal muscle is the only muscle type that contracts and relaxes by voluntary action. Tendons, formed out of connective tissue rich in collagen fibers, attach this muscle to bone. Skeletal muscle consists of cells lumped together to form fiber structures. These fibers are covered by a cell membrane called the **sarcolemma**, which serves as a conductor for electrochemical signals that tell the muscle to contract or expand. The **transverse tubes**, connected to the sarcolemma, transfer the signals deeper into the middle of the muscle fiber, and a system of tubules called the **sarcoplasmic reticulum** stores **calcium ions**, necessary for muscle contraction. Skeletal muscle fibers are also rich in **mitochondria**, which act as power stations, fueled by sugars and providing the energy necessary for the muscle

Figure 1.17. The Muscular System

to work. Muscle fibers mostly consist of **myofibrils**, which do the actual contracting. The myofibrils consist of protein fibers arranged into small subunits called **sarcomeres**.

The way a skeletal muscle produces and uses energy defines its type. **Type I** muscle fibers contract slowly and are used for stamina and posture. They produce energy from sugar using aerobic respiration, making them resistant to fatigue. **Type II** muscle fibers contract more quickly. **Type IIA** muscle fibers, found in the legs, are weaker and show more endurance than **Type IIB** muscle fibers, found mostly in the arms.

Skeletal muscles work by contracting. This shortens the length in their middle part, called the **muscle belly**, which in turn pulls one bone closer to another. The bone that remains stationary is called the **origin**. The other bone—the one actually moving toward the other—is called the **insertion**.

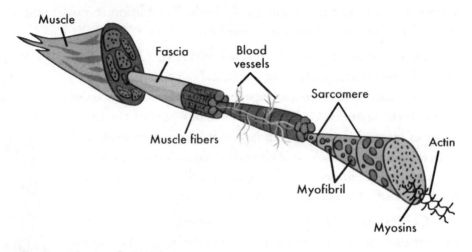

Figure 1.18. Muscle Structure

Skeletal muscles also usually work in groups. The muscle mainly responsible for the action, called the **agonist**, always pairs with another muscle that does the opposite action, called the **antagonist**. If the two contracted together at the same time, they would cancel each other out and produce no movement. Other muscles that support the agonist include **synergists**, which are found near the agonist, attach to the same bones, stabilize the movement, and reduce unnecessary movement. **Fixators** are support muscles that keep the origin stable.

Naming the more than six hundred skeletal muscles found in the human body employs several methods. Muscles can be named according to

+ the region of the body in which they are located (e.g., transverse abdominis);
+ the number of origins (e.g., biceps);
+ the bones to which they are attached (e.g., occipitofrontalis);
+ their function (e.g., flexor); and/or
+ their relative size (e.g., gluteus maximus).

The neurons that control muscles—**motor neurons**—control a number of muscle cells that together are called a **motor unit**. Big muscles that need more strength, like those in the arms and legs, require a larger number of cells in their motor units. Small muscles, in which precision is more important than strength, such as the muscles in the fingers and around the eyes, contain a smaller number of cells in their motor units.

When signaled by motor neurons, muscles can contract in several different ways:

+ isotonic muscle contraction, which produces movement
+ isometric muscle contraction, which maintains posture and stillness
+ muscle tone, a naturally occurring, constant semi-contraction of the muscle
+ twitch contraction, a short contraction caused by a single short nerve impulse
+ temporal summation, a phenomenon in which a few short impulses delivered over time build up the muscle contraction in strength and duration
+ tetanus, a state of constant contraction caused by many rapid, short impulses

Muscles get energy—metabolize—through both **aerobic respiration**, which is most effective, and **lactic acid fermentation**, which is a type of anaerobic respiration and is less effective; lactic acid fermentation happens only when blood cannot get into the muscle due to very strong or prolonged contraction. In both these methods, the goal is to produce from glucose **adenosine tri-phosphate** (ATP), the body's most important energy molecule. During ATP's conversion to **adenosine di-phosphate** (ADP), energy is released.

Muscles also use other molecules to help in the production of energy. **Myoglobin** stores oxygen, allowing muscles to use aerobic respiration even when no blood is coming into the muscles. **Creatine phosphate** creates ATP by giving its phosphate group to the energy-depleted ADP. Lastly, muscles use **glycogen**, a large molecule made out of several glucose molecules, which helps muscles make ATP.

When it runs out of energy, a muscle goes into a state called **muscle fatigue**. This means it contains little or no oxygen, ATP, or glucose and has high levels of lactic acid and ADP. A fatigued muscle needs more oxygen to replace the oxygen used up from myoglobin sources and to rebuild its other energy supplies.

In the **skeletal system**, the other portion of the musculoskeletal system, bones and joints:

+ provide support and protection;
+ allow movement;
+ create blood cells;
+ store fat, iron, and calcium; and
+ guide the growth of the entire body.

Generally, the skeleton can be divided as the axial skeleton and the appendicular skeleton. The **axial skeleton** consists of 80 bones placed along the body's midline axis and grouped into the skull, ribs, sternum, and vertebral column. The **appendicular skeleton** consists of 126 bones grouped into the upper and lower limbs and the pelvic and pectoral girdles. These bones anchor muscles and allow for movement.

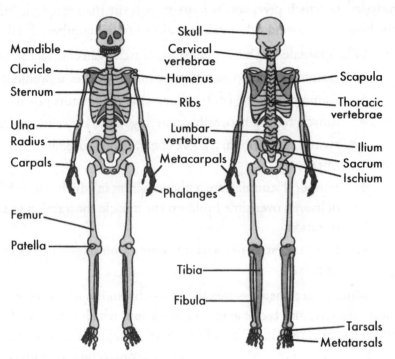

Figure 1.19. The Skeletal System

On the cellular level, bone consists of distinctively different components: the **bone matrix**, the non-living part of the bone, made out of water, collagen, protein, calcium phosphate, and calcium carbonate crystals, and **living bone cells—osteocytes**—found at the edges of bones and throughout the bone matrix in small cavities. Bone cells play a vital part in the growth, development, and repair of bones, and can be used for the minerals they store.

A cross section of a bone reveals its layers. These include the **periosteum**, the topmost layer of the bone, which acts as a layer of connective tissue. The periosteum contains collagen fibers that anchor the tendons and the muscles; it also holds the stem and the osteoblast cells necessary for growth and repair of the bones. Nervous tissue, nerve endings, and blood vessels are also present in the periosteum.

Under the periosteum, a layer of **compact bone** gives the bone its strength. Made out of mineral salts and collagen fibers, it contains many cavities where osteocytes can be found.

Under the compact bone is a layer where the bone tissue grows in columns called **trabeculae**. The bone tissue forms space that contains the red bone marrow. The trabeculae provide structural strength, even while keeping the bones light.

Inside the red bone marrow, located in the medullar cavity of the bones, a process called **hematopoiesis** occurs. In the process, stem cells produce white and red blood cells. The amount of the red bone marrow declines at the end of puberty, since yellow bone marrow replaces a significant part of it.

At birth, the body contains 300 bones. As the body grows, the structure of the bones changes. In **calcification**, bones transform from mostly hyaline cartilage and connective tissue to osseous tissue. They also fuse together, which is why adults have 206 instead of 300 bones.

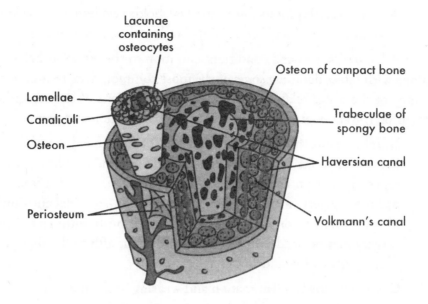

Figure 1.20. Bone Structure

Human bones are grouped into five types:

+ **Long bones** make up the major bones of the limbs. They are longer than they are wide, and they determine most of the body's height. The **epiphyses** region of long bones is located at the ends of the bone, and the **diaphysis** region is located in the middle. The middle of the diaphysis contains a hollow medullary cavity, which serves as a storage for bone marrow.

+ **Short bones** are roughly as long as they are wide, and they are generally cube shaped or round. Short bones in the body include the carpal bones of the wrist and the tarsal bones of the foot.

+ **Flat bones** do not have the medullary cavity because they are thin, and usually thinner on one end region. Flat bones in the body include the ribs, the hip bones, and the frontal, parietal, and occipital bones of the skull.

+ **Irregular bones** do not fit the criteria of long, short, or flat bones. The vertebrae and the sacrum, among others, are irregular bones.

+ Only two **sesamoid bones** actually count as proper bones: the patella and the pisiform bones. Sesamoid bones form inside the tendons located across the joints, and apart from the two mentioned, are not present in all people.

The **joints**, also known as articulations, are where bones come into contact with one another, with cartilage, or with teeth.

+ **Synovial joints** are the most common in the body, and they allow the most movement. They feature a small gap between the bones, filled with synovial fluid, which lubricates the joint.

+ **Fibrous joints**, found where bones fit tightly together, permit little or no movement. These joints also hold teeth in their sockets.

+ In a **cartilaginous joint**, cartilage holds two bones; these joints allow more movement than fibrous joints but less than synovial ones.

A list of diseases and conditions common to the musculoskeletal system follows, along with tables detailing some of the most common drug treatments used currently. Many of the drugs related to diseases and conditions of the musculoskeletal system focus on the elimination or prevention of inflammation and pain:

Bursitis is inflammation of the **bursae**, the fluid-filled sacs that act like a cushion in between joints. Bursitis normally occurs around middle age and is caused by repetitive motion. Symptoms include swelling, pain, and stiffness. Treatment includes ice, rest, and pain relievers such as non-steroidal anti-inflammatory drugs (NSAIDs) or opioids. Usually bursitis heals within a few months, but surgery may be needed in severe cases. Bursitis afflicts the shoulders, elbows, wrists, knees, hips, and ankles.

Osteoarthritis is inflammation and wearing of the tissue at the ends of bones and/or cartilage. Considered a degenerative disease, it worsens gradually over a long period of time. Osteoarthritis is a chronic condition that cannot be cured but can be helped through drug treatments, with NSAIDs and steroids to reduce inflammation and pain, as well as physical therapy. Surgery may be needed in severe cases. The joint pain normally occurs in the neck, back, knees, hips, and hands. Although osteoarthritis can occur at any age, it is normally seen in patients over forty years old.

Osteoporosis is the weakening and fracturing of bone. Normally, the body continually replaces and absorbs bone tissue, but as a person gets older and is unable to supplement the calcium, phosphorus, and vitamin D needed to replace degenerated bone tissue, bone mass reduces and weakening of the bones occurs, causing fractures. Osteoporosis is a degenerative disease that cannot be cured, although calcium and vitamin D therapies help to strengthen and regrow bone tissue. Also, eating a healthy diet and doing weight-bearing exercises can strengthen weak bones.

With **rheumatoid arthritis**, the body's immune system attacks its own tissue, cartilage, ligaments, and joints. In advanced cases, it can attack internal organs as well. Over a period of time, rheumatoid arthritis causes inflammation so severe it can cause painful swelling, erosion of the bone, and joint deformities. Although rheumatoid arthritis cannot be cured, medications such as steroids, biologic drugs, and NSAIDs can slow the progression. Keeping the body active and utilizing physical therapy helps as well. Rheumatoid arthritis may happen at any time of life, can be a lifelong disease, and has different levels of severity.

 Diseases and conditions not covered in this section and not related to the musculoskeletal system can also be treated by some of the drugs in this section.

Table 1.26. Antispasmodics

Generic Name (Brand Names)	Common Side Effects	Common Interactions
carisoprodol (Soma)	headache, nausea, constipation, ankle swelling, trouble sleeping, weakness	same as the first four antispasmodics as well as omeprazole and rifampin
baclofen (Lioresal) metaxalone (Skelaxin) methocarbamol (Robaxin) tizanidine (Zanaflex)		sleeping pills, cold and allergy medications, narcotic pain relievers, sedatives, alcohol
cyclobenzaprine (Flexeril)		same as the first four antispasmodics as well as MAO inhibitors, buproprion, meperidine, tramadol, and verapamil

These drugs treat muscle spasms and are used as skeletal muscle relaxants.

Table 1.27. Corticosteroids and Anti-Gout Medications

Generic Name (Brand Names)	Description	Common Side Effects	Common Interactions
methylprednisolone (Medrol) prednisone (Sterapred)	glucosteroids for inflammation, allergies, and flares of chronic illnesses	round, puffy, or "moon" face; increased appetite; weight gain; upset stomach	cyclosporine, phenobarbital, phenytoin, rifampin, ketoconazole, aspirin, blood thinners, diabetes medications, diuretics, hormonal replacement therapies, NSAIDs
dexamethasone (Decadron) hydrocortisone (Solu-Cortef)		same as the first two glucosteroids as well as irregular menstruation and thinning skin	
allopurinol (Zyloprim)	uric acid reducers for gout	nausea, vomiting, diarrhea	alcohol, blood thinners, diuretics, –cillin medications, azathioprine

Table 1.27. Corticosteroids and Anti-Gout Medications (continued)

Generic Name (Brand Names)	Description	Common Side Effects	Common Interactions
colchicine (no brand name available)	uric acid reducers for gout	nausea, vomiting, diarrhea	HIV/AIDS medications, certain antibiotics, cholesterol medications
febuxostat (Uloric)		anxiety, depression, upset stomach, blurred vision, constipation, loss of appetite, hair loss, rash, dizziness, drowsiness	theophylline, azathioprine

> Some diseases and conditions can affect multiple body systems, and the drugs used to treat them can be used for multiple systems. Gout, an example in this section, is a form of arthritis, which affects the musculoskeletal system, but high uric acid causes gout, and uric acid is related to the urinary system.

Table 1.28. Non-Steroidal Anti-Inflammatory Drugs (NSAIDs)

Generic Name (Brand Names)	Description	Common Side Effects	Common Interactions
celecoxib (Celebrex) diclofenac (Voltaren) etodolac (Lodine) ibuprofen (Motrin, Advil) meloxicam (Mobic) nabumetone (Relafen) naproxen (Aleve, Naprosyn) sulindac (Clinoril)	for mild to severe pain, fever, or inflammation	headache, ringing in the ears, upset stomach, diarrhea, constipation, unusual bleeding	corticosteroids, lithium, methotrexate, blood thinners, diuretics, ACE inhibitors, alcohol
aspirin (Ecotrin, Bayer)	for pain and inflammation; can also thin the blood		

Table 1.29. Analgesics

Generic Name (Brand Names)	Description	Common Side Effects	Common Interactions
acetaminophen (Tylenol)	for pain and fever	lightheadedness, fainting, bleeding problems, loss of appetite, nausea, vomiting; can cause liver toxicity in high doses	blood thinners, alcohol
tramadol (Ultram)	opioid-derived narcotic pain reliever		
methadone (Methadose)	same treatment as the others in this category but also used as a substitute to opioid and heroin dependencies		
butorphanol (Stadol) codeine (Tylenol #3) fentanyl (Duragesic, Actiq) hydrocodone (Norco, Vicodin, Lortab—all examples have been formulated with acetaminophen as a combination product) hydromorphone (Dilaudid) morphine (Astramorph, Duramorph) oxycodone (Percocet and Endocet are combined with acetaminophen; Percodan is combined with aspirin; Oxycontin and Roxicodone have oxycodone only)	opioid narcotic pain reliever; can be formulated with other analgesics and NSAIDs, such as acetaminophen, aspirin, and ibuprofen	headache, itching, nausea, vomiting, constipations, loss of appetite, weakness, respiratory distress; may be habit forming	MAO inhibitors, SSRIs, blood thinners, alcohol, lithium, rifampin, promethazine, digoxin

Table 1.30. Immunosupressants and Biologics

Generic Name (Brand Names)	Description	Common Side Effects	Common Interactions
hydroxychloroquine (Plaquenil)	immunosuppressant for autoimmune diseases, such as lupus and rheumatoid arthritis; also used to treat malaria	headache, nausea, vomiting, diarrhea, appetite loss, hair loss	a doctor or pharmacist should be consulted with
azathioprine (Imuran) methotrexate (Trexall)	immunosuppressants		NSAIDs, antibiotics, folic acid, radiation therapies, gout medications
adalimumab (Humira)	immunosuppressant and for chemotherapy	itching, hives, bruising, bleeding, pain or swelling where shot was given	blood thinners; medications that weaken the immune system, such as steroids or cancer medications
anakinra (Kineret) infliximab (Remicade) leflunomide (Arava)	immunosuppressants	rash, muscle pain, nausea, vomiting, pain redness or bruising where shot was given	
etanercept (Enbrel)	immunosuppressant and biopharmaceutical for autoimmune disorders		

All these drugs are immunosuppressants, but some have other uses.

Table 1.31. Bone Reabsorption Inhibitors

Generic Name (Brand Names)	Description	Common Side Effects	Common Interactions
risedronic acid (Actonel)	for osteoporosis	mild bone pain, stomach pain or upset	cancer medications, NSAIDs, steroids

Generic Name (Brand Names)	Description	Common Side Effects	Common Interactions
zoledronic acid (Reclast)	for high blood calcium levels; can be used to reduce the risk of fractures when bones are damaged	fever, chills, cough, sore throat, headache, nausea, constipation, diarrhea, stomach pain	NSAIDs, digoxin, antibiotics, diuretics, steroids, cancer medications
ibandronate (Boniva)	bisphosphonate derivative for osteoporosis	cough, stuffy nose, sore throat	
raloxifene (Evista)	estrogen modulator for women at high risk of breast cancer and for treating osteoporosis	depression, hot flashes, leg cramps, muscle and joint pain, upset stomach, nausea and vomiting, skin rash, weight gain	
calcitonin (Miacalcin)	for osteoporosis	stomach upset; redness of the face, neck, arms, hands, or chest	lithium

Table 1.32. Neuromuscular Blockers and Local Anesthetics

Generic Name (Brand Names)	Description	Common Side Effects	Common Interactions
pancuronium (Pavulon) rocuronium (Zemuron) succinylcholine (Quelicin) tubocurarine (no brand name available)	paralytic agents for anesthesia	muscle weakness, stiffness	lithium, procainamide, quinidine, antibiotics, magnesium salts, seizure medications, steroids

CONTINUE

Table 1.32. Neuromuscular Blockers and Local Anesthetics (continued)

Generic Name (Brand Names)	Description	Common Side Effects	Common Interactions
benzocaine (no brand name available)	local anesthetics	possible allergic reaction at application site	arrhythmia drugs, other topicals
bupivacaine (Marcaine)			
cocaine (no brand name available)			
lidocaine (Xylocaine, Lidoderm)			
procaine (Novocaine)			

The local anesthetics are designated by the *–caine* suffix.

PRACTICE QUESTIONS

1. The bones and joints of the skeletal system are responsible for doing all of the following EXCEPT

   A) allowing movement.

   B) storing fat.

   C) metabolizing sugar.

   D) creating blood cells.

   Answers:

   A) Incorrect. Though movement is the main function of the muscular system, the skeletal system also allows movement.

   B) Incorrect. The skeletal system does store fat.

   C) **Correct.** The skeletal system does not metabolize sugar though the muscular system produces adenosine tri-phosphate, the body's most important energy molecule, from glucose.

   D) Incorrect. The skeletal system does create blood cells through the process called hematopoiesis.

2. Muscles can contract through motor neurons in all these ways EXCEPT

   A) calcification.

   B) isotonic movements.

   C) isometric movements.

   D) muscle tone.

Answers:

A) **Correct.** Calcification does not occur in the muscle's motor neurons.

B) Incorrect. Isotonic movements produce movement.

C) Incorrect. Isometric movements maintain posture and stillness.

D) Incorrect. Muscle tone movements occur naturally and are a constant semi-contraction of the muscle.

3. All these drugs are considered NSAIDs EXCEPT

A) aspirin.

B) acetaminophen.

C) naproxen.

D) ibuprofen.

Answers:

A) Incorrect. Aspirin is an NSAID.

B) **Correct.** Acetaminophen is an analgesic.

C) Incorrect. Naproxen is an NSAID.

D) Incorrect. Ibuprofen is an NSAID.

4. All these drugs are opioid analgesics EXCEPT

A) oxycodone.

B) tramadol.

C) fentanyl.

D) cocaine.

Answers:

A) Incorrect. Oxycodone is an opioid analgesic.

B) Incorrect. Tramadol is an opioid derivative analgesic.

C) Incorrect. Fentanyl is an opioid analgesic.

D) **Correct.** Cocaine is a local anesthetic.

THE DIGESTIVE SYSTEM

The **digestive system** comprises a system of organs in the body responsible for the intake and processing of food and the removal of food waste products. The digestive system ensures that the body has the necessary nutrients and energy it needs to function.

The digestive system includes the **gastrointestinal (GI) tract**, which consists of the organs through which food passes into and through the body: the mouth, the pharynx, the esophagus, the stomach, the small intestine, the large intestine, the rectum, and the anus.

Other organs also have a role in processing food even though food does not pass through them directly. These include the teeth, the tongue, the salivary glands, the liver, the gallbladder, and the pancreas.

The digestive system begins with the **mouth**, also known as the oral cavity, which contains other organs that play a role in digestion. The **teeth**—the small, very hard organs that cut and grind food—are located on the edges of the mouth. Made out of **dentin**, a substance that resembles bone, they are covered by enamel. Each tooth has its own blood vessels and nerves, located in the matter that fills it, called the **pulp**.

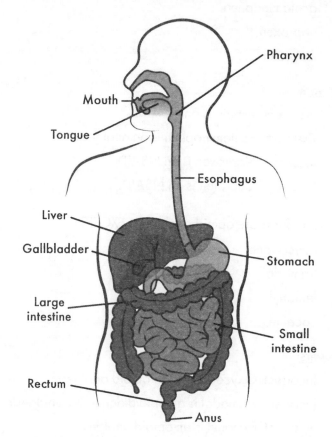

Figure 1.21. The Digestive System

Also in the mouth is the **tongue**, a muscle located behind the teeth. The tongue contains the taste buds and moves food around the mouth as the teeth process it. The tongue then moves food toward the pharynx when it is time to swallow. The three pairs of **salivary glands**, located around the mouth, produce saliva to lubricate and digest carbohydrates.

The **pharynx**—the tube that enables the passage of food and air further into the body—performs with the help of the **epiglottis**, which allows food to pass to the esophagus by covering the opening of the **larynx**, a structure that carries air into the lungs. When the body needs to breathe in, the esophagus closes, so the air passes only into the larynx.

The **esophagus** begins at the pharynx and continues to carry food all the way to the stomach. The esophagus is a muscular tube, and the muscles in its wall push food down. During vomiting, it pushes food up.

The esophagus has two rings of muscle, called **sphincters**. These sphincters close at the top and the bottom ends of the esophagus when food is not passing through it. Heartburn occurs when the bottom sphincter cannot close entirely and allows the contents of the stomach to enter the esophagus.

The **stomach**—the round organ located on the left side of the body just beneath the diaphragm—consists of four regions. The **cardia** connects the stomach to the esophagus, transitioning from the tube-like shape of the esophagus into the sack-like shape of the rest of the stomach. The cardia also houses the lower sphincter of the esophagus.

The **body** of the stomach is its largest part, and the **fundus** is located above the body. The **pylorus**—a funnel shaped region located beneath the body of the stomach—controls the passage of partially digested food further down the GI tract through the **pyloric sphincter.**

These four regions of the stomach are made out of four layers of tissue. The innermost layer, the **mucosa**, contains a smooth muscle and the mucus membrane that secretes digestive enzymes and hydrochloric acid. The cells that secrete these products are located within small pores called **gastric pits.** The mucus membrane also secretes mucus to protect the stomach from its own digestive enzymes.

The **submucosa**, the layer located around the mucosa, is made of connective tissue and consists of nerves and blood vessels. The **muscularis** layer, containing three layers of smooth muscle, enables the movement of the stomach. The outermost layer of the stomach is the **serosa**, which secretes **serous fluid** that keeps the stomach wet and reduces friction between the stomach and the surrounding organs.

The **small intestine** extends from the stomach and takes up most of the space in the abdomen. It is attached to the wall of the abdomen and measures approximately twenty-two feet in length.

In the small intestine, the part called the **duodenum** receives the food and chemicals from the stomach. The **jejunum**, which continues from the duodenum, enables absorption of most of the nutrients into the blood. Lastly, the **ileum**, which continues from the jejunum, absorbs the rest of the nutrients.

Absorption in the small intestine is helped by **villi**, which are small protrusions that increase the surface area available for absorption. The villi are made out of smaller microvilli.

Though the **liver** is not a part of the GI tract, it performs roles vital for digestion and life itself. Located just beneath the diaphragm, it is the largest organ in the body after the skin. Its triangular shape extends across the whole width of the abdomen.

Four lobes divide the liver: the **left lobe**, the **right lobe**, the **caudate lobe** (which wraps around the inferior vena cava), and the **quadrate lobe** (which wraps around the gallbladder). The liver is connected to the peritoneum by the **coronary, left, right,** and **falciform ligaments.**

A number of functions fall to the liver, including detoxification of the blood, storage of nutrients, and production of components of blood plasma. Its role in digestion is to produce **bile,** a fluid that aids in the digestion of fats. After its production, bile passes through the bile ducts to the **gallbladder,** a small, muscular, pear-shaped organ that stores and releases bile.

The **pancreas,** another organ that is not part of the GI tract, also plays a role in digestion. Located below and to the left of the stomach, it secretes both the enzymes that digest food and the hormones insulin and glucagon, which control blood sugar levels.

The pancreas is a **heterocrine gland,** which means it contains both endocrine tissue, which produces insulin and glucagon that move directly into the bloodstream, and exocrine tissue, which produces digestive enzymes that pass into the small intestine. These enzymes include

+ pancreatic amylase, which breaks large polysaccharides into smaller sugars;

+ trypsin, chymotrypsin, and carboxypeptidase, which break down proteins into amino acid subunits;

+ pancreatic lipase, which breaks down large fat molecules into fatty acids and monoglycerides; and

+ ribonuclease and deoxyribonuclease, which digest nucleic acids.

The **large intestine** continues from the small intestine and loops around it. No digestion actually takes place in the large intestine. Rather, it absorbs water and some leftover vitamins. The large intestine carries waste (feces) to the **rectum,** where it is stored until it is expelled through the **anus.**

A list of diseases and conditions common to the digestive system follows, along with a table detailing some of the most common drug treatments used currently:

Acid reflux is a chronic but treatable condition that happens when acid in the stomach and/or bile flows up into the esophagus, which causes burning and irritation to the esophageal lining. When acid reflux lasts more than a couple of weeks, it is called **gastroesophageal reflux disease** (GERD).

Common systems of acid reflux include an upset stomach as well as a burning pain in the chest and esophageal tract that occurs after eating and gets worse while lying down. Lifestyle changes and medications can help alleviate the systems of acid reflux.

Celiac disease is an immune reaction to eating foods with gluten in them. It causes inflammation and discomfort in the small intestines and can lead to damage of the intestinal lining. It can also cause malabsorption of important nutrients due to the symptoms, which include diarrhea, bloating, gas, fatigue, anemia, and osteoporosis. Celiac disease cannot be cured but can be managed with lifestyle changes and medications.

Crohn's disease also cannot be cured and can be life threatening. This inflammatory bowel disease affects the lining of the digestive tract. Some of the symptoms of Crohns disease include abdominal pain, colitis (inflammation of the colon), malnutrition, weight loss, anemia, and fatigue.

Medications, such as immunosuppressants and steroids, can relieve inflammation and slow the progression of the disease. Surgery may be required if all other treatment options fail.

Gastritis is a group of conditions that affect the stomach lining. Some conditions that can cause gastritis are infections, injuries, use of NSAIDs, and too much alcohol. Chronic gastritis can lead to **peptic ulcers**—sores that develop on the lining of the stomach.

Treatment for gastritis depends on the condition being treated. Most conditions are short-term and can be treated with antacids, antibiotics, and a change in diet.

Hepatitis loosely defines as inflammation of the liver. It is commonly caused by a viral infection, but other conditions cause hepatitis as well. Some include autoimmune disorders and secondary conditions caused by drug and alcohol abuse, medications, toxins, and other diseases.

+ **Hepatitis A** is a highly contagious viral liver infection and is preventable with use of a vaccine. Contaminated food and water cause it, and it normally clears up on its own within a few months.

+ **Hepatitis B** is a severe viral liver infection that can also be prevented by use of a vaccine. It is spread through shared body fluids. Some symptoms of hepatitis B are jaundice, abdominal pain, and dark urine. It is treatable by a medical professional and clears up on its own.

+ **Hepatitis C** is a virus of the liver that causes inflammation. It can spread easily and is normally transmitted through shared body fluids. Some people have no symptoms, while others develop jaundice, nausea, and a loss of appetite. It can be treated with antivirals and medications developed recently that have the ability to eradicate the disease.

+ **Autoimmune hepatitis** develops when the body's immune system attacks the liver, causing inflammation, fatigue, abdominal discomfort, and joint pain. The cause of this disease is unknown, but when treated early, it can often be controlled with immunosuppressant drugs, although in severe cases a liver transplant may be necessary.

 Diseases and conditions not covered in this section and not related to the digestive system can also be treated by some of the drugs in this section.

Many of the drugs used for the digestive system are available **over the counter** (OTC) and may alleviate digestive symptoms developed from heartburn, diet, flu, gas, and nausea. **Antacids** are used primarily for heartburn but also as a calcium supplement. Some common brands of antacids are Tums and Rolaids. **Antidiarrheal drugs** help reduce or stop diarrhea. A common OTC antidiarrheal drug is loperamide (Imodium A-D). **Laxatives** treat constipation. OTC laxatives include bisacodyl (Dulcolax), polyethylene glycol (MiraLAX), and sennoside (Milk of Magnesia, Ex-Lax). **Stool softeners**, like docusate sodium (Colace), soften the stool and do not cause as much urgency and cramping as laxatives do. **Fiber supplements**, such as methylcellulose (Metamucil), help to keep the body regular and prevent constipation.

Table 1.33. Other Common Drugs for the Digestive System

Generic Name (Brand Names)	Description	Common Side Effects	Common Interactions
ondansetron (Zofran)	for preventing nausea and vomiting	constipation, diarrhea, headache	tramadol, diuretics
metoclopramide (Reglan)	for preventing nausea; a gut motility stimulator		acetaminophen, cyclosporine, digoxin, levodopa, tetracycline, MAO inhibitors
dicyclomine (Bentyl)	antispasmodic for irritable bowel syndrome	decrease in urination, dry mouth, drowsiness, weakness, nausea, vomiting, constipation, stomach pain, vision changes	belladonna medications, digoxin, MAO inhibitors, scopolamine, atropine, hyoscyamine, arrhythmia medications, diphenhydramine
hyoscyamine (Levsin)	for gut spasms	dry mouth	
prochlorperazine (Compazine) trimethobenzamide (Tigan)	for nausea	blurred vision, sleepiness, restlessness, headache	lithium, blood thinners, diuretics, blood pressure medications, seizure medications
dimenhydrinate (Dramamine)	for nausea and motion sickness		
diphenoxylate/atropine (Lomotil)	for diarrhea	dry mouth, blurred vision, headache, trouble urinating	antidepressants, narcotics, cold and allergy medications, tranquilizers, MAO inhibitors

Generic Name (Brand Names)	Description	Common Side Effects	Common Interactions
polyethylene glycol (GoLYTELY, NuLYTELY)	laxative for use before a colonoscopy	nausea, bloating stomach cramps, vomiting	no common interactions
orlistat (Xenical)	weight loss medication used to block some fat ingested and send it to the digestive tract	increase in bowel movement, gas with oily discharge	diabetes medications, blood thinners, seizure medications, levothyroxine
pancrelipase (Creon)	for improving digestion	bowel blockage, headache, diarrhea, nausea, stomach cramps	no common interactions
sucralfate (Carafate)	for ulcers	constipation, dry mouth, stomach cramps, diarrhea, gas, dizziness	no common interactions
misoprostol (Cytotec)	for preventing stomach ulcers	headache, diarrhea, constipation, nausea, gas, stomach pain	do not take if pregnant
cimetidine (Tagamet) famotidine (Pepcid) nizatidine (Axid) ranitidine (Zantac)	for ulcers and use as an antacid; histamine-2 blockers	diarrhea, dizziness, headache, swollen breast	alcohol, meperidine, morphine, theophylline, tizanidine, blood thinners, aspirin
esomeprazole (Nexium) lansoprazole (Prevacid) omeprazole (Prilosec) pantoprazole (Protonix)	proton pump inhibitors	diarrhea, headache	blood thinners, diuretics, iron supplements, methotrexate, alcohol

CONTINUE

PRACTICE QUESTIONS

1. The GI tract is composed of everything EXCEPT the

   A) stomach.

   B) kidneys.

   C) intestines.

   D) esophagus.

   Answers:

   A) Incorrect. The stomach is part of the digestive system.

   B) **Correct.** The kidneys are part of the urinary system.

   C) Incorrect. Both the small and large intestines are part of the digestive system.

   D) Incorrect. The esophagus is part of the digestive system.

2. What do antiemetics do?

   A) treat vomiting

   B) treat diarrhea

   C) treat constipation

   D) treat gas

   Answers:

   A) **Correct.** Antiemetics treat vomiting.

   B) Incorrect. Antidiarrheals treat diarrhea.

   C) Incorrect. Laxatives treat constipation.

   D) Incorrect. Antacids treat gas.

3. Which is NOT a symptom of Crohn's disease?

   A) malnutrition

   B) weight gain

   C) anemia

   D) fatigue

   Answers:

   A) Incorrect. Malnutrition is indeed a symptom of Crohn's.

   B) **Correct.** Weight loss, not gain, is a symptom of Crohn's.

   C) Incorrect. Anemia is also a symptom of Crohn's.

   D) Incorrect. Fatigue is another symptom of Crohn's.

4. Which of these medications is a proton pump inhibitor?

A) misoprostol

B) famotidine

C) sucralfate

D) pantoprazole

Answers:

A)   Incorrect. Misoprostol prevents stomach ulcers.

B)   Incorrect. Famotidine is a histamine-2 blocker.

C)   Incorrect. Sucralfate treats ulcers.

D)   Correct. Pantoprazole is a proton pump inhibitor.

THE ENDOCRINE SYSTEM

The **endocrine system** consists of many glands that produce and secrete hormones, which send signals to molecules traveling through the bloodstream. **Hormones** allow cells, tissues, and organs to communicate with one another, and they play a role in almost all bodily functions, including growth, sleep, digestion, stress response, and sexual functioning. The glands of the endocrine system are scattered throughout the body, and each has a specific task.

The **pituitary gland** hangs from the base of the brain and produces the hormone that controls growth and some aspects of sexual functioning. The pituitary gland produces the growth hormone, thyroid-stimulating hormone, oxytocin, follicle-stimulating hormone, antidiuretic hormone, and adrenocorticotropic hormone.

Also located in the brain, the **hypothalamus** mainly controls the pituitary gland, and many of the hormones it releases stimulate the pituitary gland to in turn release hormones itself. The hypothalamus produces dopamine, thyrotropin-releasing hormone, and growth-hormone releasing hormone.

The **pineal body**, also in the brain, releases melatonin, a hormone that induces drowsiness and lowers body temperature.

The **thyroid gland**, found in the neck just below the Adam's apple, controls protein production and the body's use of energy. It is regulated by thyroid-stimulating hormone, released by the pituitary gland. The thyroid gland produces the hormones T_3 and thyroxine.

The **parathyroid glands**, located behind the thyroid, produce parathyroid hormone, which regulates calcium and phosphate levels in the body.

The **pancreas**, discussed in the digestive system section, is located behind the stomach and releases hormones that regulate digestion and blood-sugar levels. The alpha-cells, which are endocrine cells, secrete the peptide hormone glucagon and the beta-cells produce the hormone insulin. The pancreas also produces somatostatin.

The **adrenal glands** sit atop the kidneys and have two regions that produce two sets of hormone: the adrenal cortex releases corticosteroids and androgens, while the adrenal medulla regulates the fight-or-flight response. The adrenal hormones consist of cortisol, testosterone, adrenaline (epinephrine), noradrenaline, and dopamine.

The **testes**—the glands found in males—regulate maturation of sex organs and secondary sex characteristics, such as muscle mass and growth of axillary hair. The testes produce testosterone and estradiol.

The **ovaries**—the glands found in females—regulate the menstrual cycle, pregnancy, and secondary sex characteristics, such as the enlargement of breasts and the widening of the hips. The ovaries produce progesterone and estrogen.

A list of diseases and conditions common to the endocrine system follows, along with tables detailing some of the most common drug treatments used currently. Hormone replacement therapy is among the treatments that address some endocrine-related conditions, including osteoporosis and menopause:

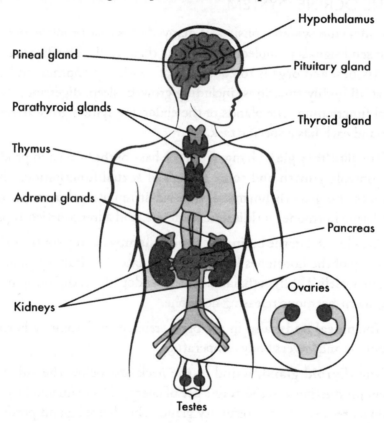

Figure 1.22. The Endocrine System

Type 1 diabetes, or **juvenile diabetes**, typically appears in adolescence and is a chronic condition in which the pancreas produces little or no insulin. Symptoms include fatigue, blurred vision, excessive thirst, frequent urination, and hunger.

Treatment of juvenile diabetes consists of insulin therapy, diet, exercise, regular monitoring, and maintaining normal blood sugar levels. Insulin therapy prevents the autoimmune destruction of the insulin-producing beta-cells in the pancreas.

Type 2 diabetes is also a chronic condition and affects the way a body produces blood sugar. With this condition, the body either does not produce enough insulin or resists insulin. Type 2 diabetes has the same symptoms as type 1 diabetes, but it typically appears in middle age or obese patients. Treatments include lifestyle and diet changes, insulin and drug therapies, and exercise. Patients regularly monitor blood sugar and A1C levels. (A1C is a blood plasma test that provides information about a patient's average levels of blood sugar over a three-month period.)

Hypothyroidism is a chronic condition in which the thyroid gland does not produce enough thyroid hormone. This can affect a patient's heart rate, body temperature, and metabolism. Symptoms include weight gain, dry skin, fatigue, and sensitivity to cold. Treatments for hypothyroidism include diet and thyroid hormone replacement medication.

Hyperthyroidism is a chronic condition in which the thyroid gland produces too much thyroid hormone. Symptoms include weight loss, sweating, irritability, and a rapid heartbeat. Treatments include medications and sometimes thyroid surgery.

Hypercalcemia is a treatable condition in which the parathyroid glands become overactive, causing the blood to have a high calcium level. Symptoms can range from mild to severe and include increased thirst and urination, nausea, bone pain, muscle weakness, confusion, and fatigue. Treatments include medications and surgery to remove the parathyroid glands.

Grave's disease is an immune system disorder that affects the thyroid gland and usually occurs in women over forty. It is a cause of hyperthyroidism. Symptoms include weight loss, enlarged thyroid, puffy eyes, heat sensitivity, anxiety, and hand tremors. Treatments include a thyroidectomy and medications.

Cushing syndrome is caused by exposure to high cortisol levels over an extended period of time, including an overuse of steroid medication and an overproduction of cortisol from the adrenal glands. Symptoms include fat loss in the arms and legs, weight gain in the midsection, and fatty deposits around the face and upper back. Treatment options include a reduction in steroid use, surgery, medication, and sometimes radiation.

 Diseases and conditions not covered in this section and not related to the endocrine system can also be treated by some of the drugs in this section.

Table 1.34. Manufactured Insulin Hormones

Generic Name (Brand Names)	Common Side Effects	Common Interactions
insulin detemir (Levemir) insulin glargine (Lantus) insulin glulisine (Apidra) insulin isophane (Humulin/ Novolin N) insulin lispro (Humalog) insulin aspart (NovoLog) insulin regular (Humulin/ Novolin R) insulin zinc (Humulin/ Novolin Lente)	headache, hunger, sweating, pale skin, irritability, dizziness, shakiness, trouble concentrating	alcohol

Table 1.35. Antidiabetics

Generic Name (Brand Names)	Description	Common Side Effects	Common Interactions
glimepiride (Amaryl) glipizide (Glucotrol) glyburide (Diabeta)	antidiabetics, sulfo-nylurea	weight gain, heartburn, gas	SSRIs, blood thinners, pheno-barbital, ACE inhibitors, thyroid medications
nateglinide (Starlix) repaglinide (Prandin)	antidiabetics, meg-lintinides	back pain, joint pain, diarrhea, nausea, dizziness, runny or stuffy nose, cough, sneezing	blood pressure medications, other diabetic medi-cations, MAO inhibitors, NSAIDs, thyroid medica-tions, steroid medi-cations, alcohol
dulaglutide (Trulicity) liraglutide (Victoza)	antidiabetic glp-1 receptor agonists		

Table 1.35. Antidiabetics (continued)

Generic Name (Brand Names)	Description	Common Side Effects	Common Interactions
acarbose (Precose) canagliflozin (Invokana) dapagliflozin (Farxiga) metformin (Glucophage) pioglitazone (Actos) rosiglitazone (Avandia) saxagliptin (Onglyza) sitagliptin (Januvia)	antidiabetics	diarrhea, gas, nausea	estrogen, diuretics, steroids, thyroid medications, heart and blood pressure medications, nicotinic acid

Not all antidiabetic medications possess the suffix –ide, though many in this table do. Another suffix related to antidiabetics is –gliptin.

Table 1.36. Hormone Replacements and Mineral Supplements

Generic Name (Brand Names)	Description	Common Side Effects	Common Interactions
estrogen (Premarin, Prempro, Climara, Depo-Estradiol)	hormone replacement, estrogen derivative	breast pain, tenderness, change in weight or hair growth, nausea and vomiting, cramps, stomach pain	blood thinners, heart medications, thyroid medications, dementia
progesterone (Prometrium)	hormone replacement	breast pain, tenderness, light bleeding, cramps, warmth/redness in upper body	some blood thinners and cancer treatments
testosterone (Depo-Testosterone)	hormone replacement, androgen	nausea, vomiting, anxiety, depression, increase/decrease in sexual desire, oily skin, hair loss, numbness, acne	zolpidem, blood thinners, heart medications

Generic Name (Brand Names)	Description	Common Side Effects	Common Interactions
propylthiouracil (PTU)	antithyroid agent	headache	beta-blockers, potassium, blood thinners, theophylline, digoxin
levothyroxine (Synthroid)	hormone replacement for hypothyroidism	hair loss, appetite or weight change, menstruation change	diabetic medications, blood thinners, MAO inhibitors, digoxin
oxytocin (Pitocin)	hormone replacement for labor induction	nausea, vomiting	
levonorgestrel (Norplant)	progestin implant for birth control	breast tenderness, dizziness, cramping, fatigue	heart medications
megestrol acetate (Megace)	progestin hormone replacement	depression, headache, dizziness, stomach cramps, light bleeding	blood clotting medications, heart medications
cortisone (Solu-Cortef)	cortisol hormone/ steroid	some steroids (see musculoskeletal system)	see interactions under steroids in the musculoskeletal system
dinoprostone (Cervidil)	prostaglandin for hormone replacement	back or stomach pain, diarrhea, vomiting, nausea, headache	blood thinners, heart medications
magnesium sulfate (Mag-Ox)	mineral supplement	dizziness, low blood pressure, weakness	some antibiotics
potassium iodide (SSKI)	for certain hyperthyroid conditions	diarrhea, metallic taste in the mouth, headache, acne	ACE inhibitors, diuretics, A2RBs

Mineralocorticoids and glucocorticoids are steroid hormones. Mineralocorticoids are corticosteroids that influence salt and water balances. The primary mineralocorticoid is aldosterone. Glucocorictoids regulate glucose. Both of these steroid hormones can be supplemented for treatment of autoimmune disorders, sepsis, allergies, and asthma as well as lymphomas and leukemia.

PRACTICE QUESTIONS

1. The pancreas releases which hormone?

    A) melatonin

    B) thyroxine

    C) glucagon

    D) epinephrine

    Answers:

    A) Incorrect. Melatonin is released through the pineal body.

    B) Incorrect. Thyroxine is released from the thyroid gland.

    C) **Correct.** The alpha-cells in the pancreas release glucagon.

    D) Incorrect. Epinephrine is released through the adrenal glands.

2. What do mineralocorticoids do?

    A) regulate glucose

    B) influence salt and water balances

    C) release adrenalin

    D) replace hormones

    Answers:

    A) Incorrect. Glucocorictoids regulate glucose.

    B) **Correct.** Mineralocorictoids influence salt and water balances.

    C) Incorrect. The adrenal glands release adrenalin.

    D) Incorrect. Hormone replacement therapy replaces hormones.

3. Which is NOT a type of manufactured insulin?

    A) lispro

    B) detemir

    C) glargine

    D) dulaglutide

    Answers:

    A) Incorrect. The brand name for lispro is Humalog/NovoLog.

    B) Incorrect. The brand name for detemir is Levemir.

C) Incorrect. The brand name for glargine is Lantus.

D) Correct. Dulaglutide's brand name is Trulicity, an antidiabetic, not an insulin.

4. Which is NOT a hormone replacement drug?

A) levothyroxine

B) propylthiouracil

C) sitagliptin

D) estrogen

Answers:

A) Incorrect. Levothyroxine (Synthroid) is indeed a hormone replacement drug.

B) Incorrect. Propylthiouracil (PTU) is also hormone replacement drug.

C) Correct. Sitagliptin (Januvia) is used to treat type 2 diabetes.

D) Incorrect. Estrogen is another hormone replacement drug. Some of its brand names are Premarin, Prempro, Climara, and Depo-Estradiol.

THE RESPIRATORY SYSTEM

The human body needs oxygen in order to function. The **respiratory system**, with its upper and lower tracts, is responsible for the intake of oxygen plus the removal carbon dioxide from the body, an equally important task.

The **upper respiratory tract** consists of the nose, the nasal cavity, the olfactory membranes, the mouth, the pharynx, the epiglottis, and the larynx.

The **nose**—the primary body part for air intake and carbon dioxide removal—is made out of bone, cartilage, muscle, and skin. It serves as a protector of the hollow space behind it called the **nasal cavity**. The hair and mucus covering the nasal cavity together serve an important function: they prevent contaminants, such as dust, mold, and other particles, from entering the respiratory system. The nasal cavity warms and moisturizes air too.

The nose and the nasal cavity contain **olfactory membranes**, located on the top of the nasal cavity, just under the bridge of the nose. These small organs are responsible for the sense of smell.

Breath also enters through the **mouth**, although the mouth does not perform as well when it comes to the three functions of the primary opening: filtering, moisturizing, and warming of air. However, it has its advantages over the nose for breathing, including its larger size and its proximity to the lungs.

The next part of the respiratory system, the throat—also called the **pharynx**—is a smooth, muscular structure lined with mucus and divided into three regions: the nasopharynx, the oropharynx, and the laryngopharynx.

Air enters through the nose and then passes through the **nasopharynx**, which is also where the **Eustachian tubes** from the middle ears connect with the pharynx. The air then enters the **oropharynx**, where air from the mouth enters the pharynx; this is the same passageway used for transporting food when eating. Both air and food also pass through the **laryngopharynx**, where these substances travel on to different systems.

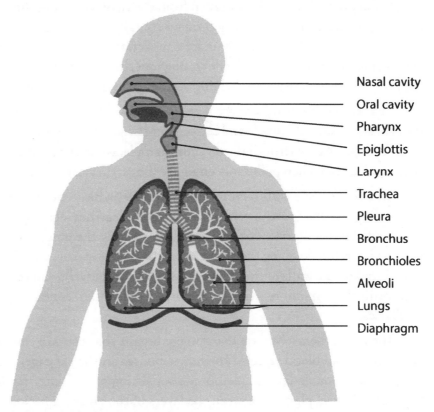

Nasal cavity
Oral cavity
Pharynx
Epiglottis
Larynx
Trachea
Pleura
Bronchus
Bronchioles
Alveoli
Lungs
Diaphragm

Figure 1.23. The Respiratory System

The **epiglottis** ensures that air enters the trachea and food enters the esophagus. This flap, made of elastic cartilage, covers the opening of one passageway to allow the air or food to enter the other passageway. During respiration, the epiglottis covers the opening of the esophagus; during food ingestion, it protects the opening of the trachea.

The part of the airway called the **larynx** sits between the pharynx and the trachea. It is also called the **voice box**, because it contains mucus membrane folds—**vocal folds**—that vibrate when air passes through them to produce sound. The larynx is made out of three cartilage structures: the epiglottis, the thyroid cartilage (also called the Adam's apple), and the cricoid cartilage, a ring-shaped structure that keeps the larynx open.

The second portion of the respiratory system, the **lower respiratory tract**, consists of the trachea, the bronchi, the lungs, and the muscles that help with breathing.

The lower respiratory tract begins with the **trachea**, also known as the windpipe. The trachea—made out of fibrous and elastic tissues, smooth muscle, and about twenty cartilage rings—sits between the larynx and the bronchi. As its alternate name suggests, it resembles a pipe, and it is very flexible so it can follow various head and neck movements. Its interior is lined with mucus-producing cells, called **goblet cells**, as well as cells with small fringes that resemble hair. These hair-like structures, called **cilia**, allow air to pass through the trachea, where mucus further filters it. The fringes also help to move mucus up the airways and out, keeping the air passage free.

Connecting to the trachea are **bronchi**. The **primary bronchi**, consisting of many C-shaped cartilage rings, branch into the **secondary bronchi**. Two extend from the left primary bronchi, and three branch from the right, corresponding to the number of lobes in the lungs. The secondary bronchi contain less cartilage and have more space between the rings. The same is true for the **tertiary bronchi**, which are extensions of the secondary bronchi as they divide throughout the lobes of the lungs. Like the trachea, the bronchi are lined with epithelium that contains goblet cells and cilia.

Bronchioles branch from the tertiary bronchi. They contain no cartilage; rather, they consist of smooth muscle and elastic fiber tissue, which allows them to remain quite small yet still change their diameter. For example, when the body needs more oxygen, they expand, and when pollutants enter the lungs, they constrict.

Bronchioles end with **terminal bronchioles**, which connect them with **alveoli**, where the gas exchange happens. Alveoli are small cavities located in **alveolar sacs** and surrounded by capillaries. The **alveolar fluid**, coating the inner surfaces of the alveoli, plays a vital role in keeping the alveoli moist, the lungs elastic, and the thin walls of the alveoli stable. The walls of the alveoli consist of alveolar cells and the connective tissue that forms the respiratory membrane where it comes into contact with the wall of the capillaries.

The **lungs** themselves are two spongy organs that contain the bronchi, bronchioles, alveoli, and blood vessels. The lungs, housed in the rib cage, are surrounded by the **pleura**, a double-layered membrane consisting of the outer **parietal pleura** and the inner **visceral pleura**. Between the layers of the pleura, a hollow space, called the **pleural cavity**, allows the lungs to expand.

The lungs are wider at the top, referred to as the **base**, and narrower at the bottom, called the **apex**. **Lobes** divide the lungs, with the larger lung (the right one) containing three lobes and the smaller lung (the left lung) containing two lobes.

The muscles that play a major role in **respiration** are the diaphragm and the intercostal muscles. The **diaphragm** is made of skeletal muscle and is located under the lungs, forming the floor of the thorax. The **intercostal muscles** are located between the ribs. The **internal intercostal muscles** help with breathing out (expiration) by depressing the ribs and compressing the thoracic cavity; the **external intercostal muscles** help with breathing in (inspiration).

Breathing in and out is also called **pulmonary ventilation**. During **inhalation**, or **inspiration**, the diaphragm contracts and moves a few inches toward the stomach, making more space for the lungs to expand, and this movement pulls air into the lungs. The external intercostal muscles also contract to expand the rib cage and pull more air into the lungs. The lungs, now at a lower pressure than the atmosphere—called **negative pressure**—fill with air until the pressure inside the lungs and the atmospheric pressure outside are the same. During **exhalation**, or **expiration**, the diaphragm and the external intercostal muscles relax, and the internal intercostal muscles contract. This causes the thoracic cavity to become smaller and the pressure in the lungs to climb higher than the atmospheric pressure, which moves air out of the lungs.

Among the various types of breathing, **shallow breathing** entails a circulation of about 0.5 liters of air, a capacity called **tidal volume.** During **deep breathing,** a larger amount of air—usually 3 to 5 liters—circulates, a volume known as **vital capacity.** The abdominal and other muscles are also involved in breathing in and out during deep breathing. **Eupnea**—the breathing the body does when resting—consists of mostly shallow breaths with an occasional deep breath. The lungs are never completely without air; about a liter of air is always present in the lungs.

A list of diseases and conditions common to the respiratory system follows, along with a table detailing some of the most common drug treatments used currently:

Asthma is a condition in which the airways in the lungs narrow, swell, and produce excess mucus. This makes it difficult for the patient to breathe. Asthma is a chronic but treatable condition that ranges from mild to severe. Symptoms include breathing difficulty, chest pain, coughing, and wheezing. Treatments include rescue inhalers that help with flare-ups and controller inhalers that prevent symptoms. In extreme cases, long-acting inhalers used through a nebulizer may be required as well as oral steroids.

Chronic obstructive pulmonary disease (COPD) is in fact a group of lung diseases that block airflow and make breathing difficult. These diseases cannot be cured, but the symptoms can be treated. With the most common of the diseases, **emphysema** and **chronic bronchitis,** the damage cannot be reversed. Many people who suffer from COPD smoke. Symptoms include wheezing, a chronic cough, frequent infections, and shortness of breath. Treatments include rescue and controller inhalers, nebulizer treatment, and the use of steroids and antibiotics.

Allergic rhinitis is an allergic response causing histamine responses in the body, such as itchy, watery eyes; sneezing; stuffy nose; and coughing. **Histamine** is a compound released by the body cells in response to allergies and inflammation. Allergic rhinitis can occur seasonally or at any time. Sometimes doctors will test for what a patient is allergic to so the patient can get treated and/or avoid that allergen. Antihistamines are the most common drugs used for allergic rhinitis.

 Diseases and conditions not covered in this section and not related to the respiratory system can also be treated by some of the drugs in this section.

Many of the drugs used to treat respiratory problems can be purchased over the counter. **Expectorants,** such as guaifenesin (Mucinex), help to loosen up and thin mucus to make coughs more productive. **Antitussives** relieve coughing. Dextromethoraphan is a common OTC medication used to prevent coughing. Decongestants help to relieve stuffy noses. Phenylephrine is the most common drug used in OTC decongestant medicines, although pseudoephedrine (Sudafed, Claritin-D, Allegra-D) is more effective. **Pseudoephedrines** can be purchased over-the-counter, but due to the meth-amphetamine epidemic in the Unites States, it can only be purchased at a drug counter and requires a photo ID and signature, plus the purchaser is limited to five boxes each month. (More information about the Combat Methamphetamine Epidemic Act is covered in pharmacy law.)

Table 1.37. Common Drugs for the Respiratory System

Generic Name (Brand Names)	Description	Common Side Effects	Common Interactions
albuterol (Ventolin, Proventil, Combivent, DuoNeb)	inhaled beta-2 agonist that prevents and treats bronchospasms	dry mouth and throat, shakiness, restlessness, nervousness, excitement, insomnia	diuretics, MAO inhibitors, blood pressure medications, digoxin
tiotropium (Spiriva)	muscarinic antagonist that prevents bronchospasms and reduces flare-ups		other inhaled medications
fexofenadine (Allegra) loratadine (Claritin)	histamine H1 antagonists for allergy symptoms	dry mouth; headache; nervousness; red, irritated eyes; hoarseness	alcohol
aformoterol (Brovana) formoterol (Foradil, Performist) salmeterol (Serevent)	long-acting beta-2 agonists that prevent asthma and bronchospasms and treat COPD	headache, muscle or bone pain, nausea, vomiting, numbness, or tingling in the hands and feet, skin rash	other inhaled medications, MAO inhibitors, some antibiotics, diuretics, steroid medications
aclidinium (Tudorza)	muscarinic antagonist for COPD	cough, diarrhea, inflammation of the nose, vomiting, paradoxical bronchospasm	other inhaled medications
budesonide (Pulmicort) fluticasone (Flonase, Flovent) mometasone (Asmanex, Nasonex)	steroid and decongestants; glucocorticoids	headache	antiviral medications

Table 1.37. Common Drugs for the Respiratory System

Generic Name (Brand Names)	Description	Common Side Effects	Common Interactions
theophylline (Theo-dur)	nonselective phosphodiesterase enzyme inhibitor for symptoms of COPD	diarrhea, headache, insomnia, shakiness, nervousness, increased urination	alcohol, nicotine
montelukast (Singulair)	leukotriene receptor antagonist that prevents allergies and asthma attacks	cough, sore throat, flu symptoms, headache	alcohol
roflumilast (Daliresp)	PDE-4 inhibitor that prevents allergies and asthma attacks	diarrhea	estradiol, phenobarbital, phenytoin, carbamazepine
oseltamivir (Tamiflu)	neuraminidase inhibitor for the flu	stomach problems	influenza vaccines
oxymetazoline (Afrin)	topical decongestant	blurred vision, blood pressure problems, tachycardia, nervousness, trembling, insomnia, weakness	alcohol, blood pressure and arrhythmia medications

THE INTEGUMENTARY SYSTEM

The **integumentary system**, consisting of the skin, hair, and nails, protects the body from damage. The **skin**—the largest organ in the body and accounting for 12 to 15 percent of total body weight—shields the inner organs, regulates temperature, excretes wastes, protects deep tissue, waterproofs, and cushions.

The **epidermis** layer of human skin is the outermost layer, and its main functions are protection, absorption, and homeostasis. Its **epithelial cells** line the surface of the organs of the body to create the **squamous epithelium**, which is made up of four types of cells: keratinocytes, melanocytes, Merkel cells, and Langehans cells. **Keratinocytes** consist of protein, and they waterproof the epidermis. When keratinocytes stiffen the epidermal tissue, it creates nails. **Melanocytes** produce **melanin**, which causes skin color. **Merkel cells** are receptor cells associated with the sense of touch. **Langehans cells** are antigen-presenting immune cells that help the body fight against infection.

The **dermis** layer of skin, between the epidermis and the subcutaneous tissues, has two layers of its own: the **papillary** and the **reticular**. Both layers contain vessels, glands, hair roots, follicles, nerve endings, and muscle tissue as well as connective tissue. The papillary is superficial and has **areolar**—loose—connective tissue, whereas the reticular layer consists of dense connective tissue. In both, connective tissue, such as **collagen** and **elastin**, bundle together in a woven pattern, helping to give elasticity and flexibility to the skin to prevent wrinkling and sagging.

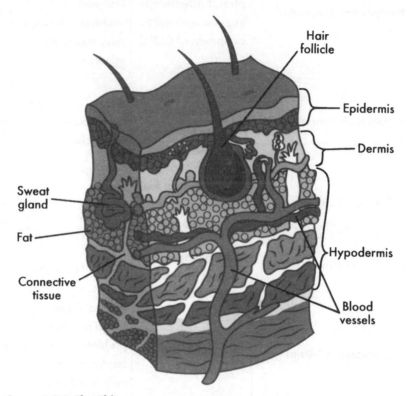

Figure 1.24. The Skin

The **hypodermis**, also known as the **subcutaneous**, is the deepest layer of skin, positioned immediately beneath the dermis and connected to it through collagen and elastin fibers. It is made up of **adipose tissue**, containing **adipocytes**, which accumulate and store fats. The hypodermis stores energy, and when the body requires calories to be transformed into energy, adipocytes enter the blood through the venous route. Because fat is a heat insulator, the hypodermis passively participates in thermoregulation.

A list of diseases and conditions common to the integumentary system follows, which includes some of the most common drug treatments used currently:

Staphylococcus infection is caused by an accumulation of the bacteria staphylococcus, normally found on the skin or nose. It is very contagious and can pass from person to person. Symptoms of staph infections include boils and abscesses—oozing blisters—pain at the site, and redness and swelling. Sometimes, if the infection enters the bloodstream, it can cause fever, nausea, vomiting, joint pain, and flu symptoms. Treatments of staph infection include antibiotics, which can be topically applied, such as with triple antibiotic cream (Neosporin) or taken by mouth.

Methicillin resilient staphylococcus aureus (MRSA) can be very serious and difficult to treat. Only certain antibiotics help to fight the infection and sometimes require months of treatment. There are two different kinds of MRSA. **HA-MRSA** occurs in people who have been hospitalized or in other healthcare settings. **CA-MRSA—community-associated MRSA—**occurs in healthy people and spreads by skin-to-skin contact or contact with an infected wound or object. Antibiotics such as penicillin or other –cillin drugs will not kill the infection. Topically, mupirocin (Bactroban) is used, and depending on the patient, antibiotics such as sulfa drugs (Bactrim-DS, Septra-DS), doxycycline (Vibramycin), or vancomycin (Vancocin) can be taken orally or by IV.

Scabies is caused by a tiny mite that burrows into the skin. Treatment includes **antiparasitic** medicines, such as lindane (Kwell) lotion, applied from the neck down, left on for eight hours, then rinsed off to kill the mites. Scabies is contagious and spreads quickly through school and healthcare settings, such as nursing homes. The most common symptom is intense itching where the mite burrows.

Rosacea is a chronic condition that causes redness and small, pus-filled bumps on the face. It normally affects fair-skinned women. Antibiotics and anti-acne treatments help with the symptoms.

Impetigo is a highly contagious skin infection that causes sores and is mainly seen in children. The sores typically develop around the nose and mouth. After a few days, they erupt and form a yellow crust. Antibiotic creams help to kill the infection, but oral antibiotics may be required.

Acne is the most common skin infection. Although it is most prevalent in adolescents, acne can happen at any age. It is a condition in which the follicles on the face and body, called **comedones**, become blocked with oil and dead skin cells, which causes redness and inflammation. Symptoms can range from blackheads to pus-filled boils. Over-the-counter antiseptic, anti-inflammatory, or vitamin A treatments, such as salicylic acid, benzoyl peroxide, and retinoid creams, can alleviate the symptoms. For chronic conditions, prescription medications may be used. The antibiotic tetracycline helps with chronic acne, as well as isotretinoin (Accutane). The most preventive acne treatment is to regularly wash the face with an antiseptic soap to prevent clogged pores and bacteria from colonizing on the face.

Skin cancer is caused by an abnormal growth of cells on the skin and presents in many forms.

+ **Basal cell carcinoma** is caused mainly by too much sun exposure but is treatable. It usually appears as a white, waxy lump or a brown, scaly patch on the skin. Treatments include prescription creams, such as collagenase

(Santyl), which debrides the skin area affected, or a topical injection called fluorouracil (Efudex). Surgery removes the cancerous area.

+ **Squamous cell carcinoma** is also treatable and caused by too much UV exposure. Symptoms include a lump, ulcer, or scaly patch on the skin. It can also be treated with topical medication and surgery, and it resolves within a couple months.

+ **Melanoma** is the most severe type of skin cancer. Symptoms of melanoma include unusual growth in an existing mole or a new, unusual looking growth. Treatments include surgery, radiation and chemotherapy, and medications.

Human papillomavirus (HPV)—genital warts—spreads by sexual contact. The most common symptom is warts appearing around the genitals and surrounding areas, although many people do not develop any symptoms. No cure exists for the virus, so the treatment focuses on removing the warts. Antiviral medications can help with flare-ups, and imiquimod (Aldara) can treat the genital warts.

Common warts, called **verrucae** can also be infectious but are not spread by sexual contact, nor are they typically painful. Treatments include topical medications and removal through medical procedures.

Fungal infections are caused by an overgrowth of fungus. **Candida** is the most common. Symptoms include a skin rash and itching. Antifungals are used to treat the infections, including clotrimazole (Lotrimin), nystatin, and terbinafine (Lamisil).

Rashes are itchy, inflamed skin usually caused by allergic reactions. The use of antipruritics—anti-itch creams—such as corticosteroid creams (hydrocortisone) help to reduce inflammation and stop itching.

Abrasions, cuts, blisters, and **lesions** can be treated with topical antibiotic creams or with antibiotic drugs, such as co-trimoxazole, erythromycin, cephalexin (Keflex), amoxicillin (Amoxil), floxacillin, and metronidazole (Flagyl), if needed.

Sunburns can be very painful, cause chills or fevers, and lead to sun poisoning. The use of a topical anesthetic, such as benzocaine or dermoplast spray, helps to numb the pain of sunburns.

Seborrhea is a skin condition that causes scaly patches and red skin on the scalp, but it can also be seen in oily areas of the face, chest, and back. Medicated shampoos, such as Selsun Blue, can help treat symptoms. For severe cases, anthralin (Dithranol)—a topical cream that is also used for psoriasis—can help.

PRACTICE QUESTIONS

1. The epidermis functions do NOT include

   A) protection.

   B) absorption.

   C) homeostasis.

   D) housing nerve endings.

   Answers:

   A) Incorrect. The functions of the epidermis include protection.

   B) Incorrect. The functions of the epidermis also include absorption.

   C) Incorrect. The functions of the epidermis include homeostasis too.

   D) Correct. The dermis, not the epidermis, houses nerve endings.

2. Which is NOT considered an antibiotic?

   A) benzoyl peroxide

   B) erythromycin

   C) amoxicillin

   D) cephalexin

   Answers:

   A) Correct. Benzcyl peroxide is an antiseptic.

   B) Incorrect. Erythromycin is indeed an antibiotic.

   C) Incorrect. Amoxicillin is another antibiotic.

   D) Incorrect. Cephalexin is also an antibiotic.

3. Which is used in the treatment of MRSA?

   A) amoxicillin

   B) doxycycline

   C) cephalexin

   D) metronidazole

   Answers:

   A) Incorrect. Amoxicillin does not treat MRSA but treats skin abrasions, lesions, blisters, and cuts.

   B) Correct. Doxycycline does treat MRSA.

   C) Incorrect. Cephalexin does not treat MRSA, but it too treats skin abrasions, lesions, blisters, and cuts.

   D) Incorrect. Metronidazole does not treat MRSA, but it also treats skin abrasions, lesions, blisters, and cuts.

4. Which is considered an antifungal?

A) benzocaine

B) anthralin

C) imiquimod

D) nystatin

Answers:

A) Incorrect. Benzocaine is an anesthetic.

B) Incorrect. Anthralin treats seborrhea and psoriasis.

C) Incorrect. Imiquimod is an antiviral.

D) **Correct.** Nystatin is indeed an antifungal.

THE REPRODUCTIVE SYSTEM

Reproductive systems contain the organs that enable the successful reproduction of a species. In humans, fertilization is internal, with sperm being transferred from the male to the female during copulation.

The organs of the **male reproductive system** produce and ejaculate **sperm**, the male gamete, which are formed in the **testes**. The **scrotum**, located under the **penis**, houses the testes. During sexual arousal, the **vas deferens** carry sperm to the **urethra**, the tube that runs through the penis and carries semen (and urine) out of the body. The **prostate gland** also empties into the urethra and produces a nutrient-filled fluid that

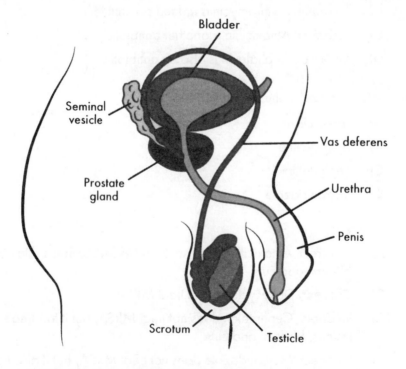

Figure 1.25. The Male Reproductive System

protects sperm as well as makes up the majority of **semen**. Before ejaculation, the **Cowper's gland** produces a thin, alkaline fluid that flushes any remaining urine from the urethra and constitutes a small portion of the semen.

Sexual reproduction in all animals occurs in cycles that depend on the production, in the **female reproductive system**, of an **ovule**, or egg. In humans, the reproductive cycle occurs approximately once a month, when the female's ovaries release an egg.

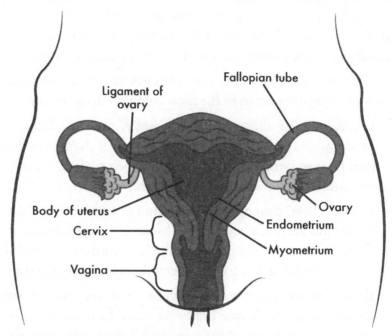

Figure 1.26. The Female Reproductive System

The **ovaries** are the female reproductive organs, or gonads. Each ovary has a follicle that contains **oocytes**, or undeveloped eggs. The surrounding cells in the ovary help to protect and nourish the oocyte until it is needed. During the menstrual cycle, one or more oocytes will mature into an egg with help from the **corpus luteum**, a mass of follicular tissue that provides nutrients to the egg and secretes estradiol and progesterone.

Once it has matured, the egg releases into the **fallopian tube**, where fertilization will take place if sperm are present. The egg then travels into the **uterus**. An unfertilized egg is shed along with the uterine lining during **menstruation**. A fertilized egg, known as a **zygote**, implants in the lining of the uterus, where it continues to develop.

After fertilization, the zygote will start to divide and, after four to five days, becomes a ball of cells known as a **blastocyst**. The blastocyst implants in the **endometrium** of the uterus, after which the placenta develops. The **placenta**, a temporary organ that attaches the embryo to the mother, provides nutrients to the fetus, carries waste away from the fetus, protects the fetus from infection, and produces hormones that support pregnancy. The placenta develops from cells called the **trophoblast**, which come from the outer layer of the blastocyst.

The gestation period of the human **embryo**, or **fetus**, is 266 days—roughly 8.8 months. The development cycle in the womb consists of three trimesters. In the first trimester, the organs responsible for the embryo's growth develop. This includes the placenta and umbilical cord. During this time, **organogenesis** occurs, and the various stem cells from the blastocyst differentiate into the organs of the body. The organs are not fully developed at this point, but they do exist. In the second trimester, the fetus experiences rapid growth, up to 25 to 30 centimeters in length. At this point, it is usually apparent the woman is pregnant, since the uterus grows and extends, and the woman's belly becomes slightly distended. In the third trimester, the fetus finishes developing. The baby exits the uterus through the **cervix** and leaves the body through the **vagina**.

A list of diseases and conditions common to the reproductive system follows, along with a table detailing some of the most common drug treatments used currently:

Prostate cancer afflicts the male prostate, a small walnut-shaped gland that produces seminal fluid. The main symptom is changes in urination. Some men have no symptoms at all. Treatments include monitoring, radiation, chemotherapy, hormone treatments, and medications.

Breast cancer, although most common in women, can afflict men as well. Symptoms include a lump on the breast, nipple discharge, and changes in the shape or texture of the breast or nipple. Treatment depends on the stage of the cancer and includes radiation, chemotherapy, surgery, and medications.

Endometriosis is a disorder in which the tissue that lines the uterus grows outside the uterus. Tissue can be found in the ovaries, fallopian tubes, and intestines. Symptoms of endometriosis include pain and irregular menstrual periods. Treatments include hormone therapy, medications, and surgery.

Menopause is the natural decline in the reproduction of hormones in women, typically when they reach their forties or fifties. It is marked by twelve months of not having a menstrual period. Symptoms include vaginal dryness, hot flashes, sleep disturbances, anxiety, and depression. Treatments include lubrication for vaginal dryness, hormone therapy, and medications for hot flashes, anxiety, and depression.

Sexually transmitted diseases (STDs) are infections transmitted through sexual contact that can be caused by bacteria, viruses, or parasites. HPV, genital herpes, and HIV/AIDS are caused by viruses and are chronic conditions. Chlamydia, gonorrhea, and syphilis are all bacterial infections than can be treated with antibiotics. Genital lice are parasites and are treated with antiparasitics.

Pelvic inflammatory disease (PID) is an infection of the female reproductive organs caused by sexual contact. It occurs when bacteria spread from the vagina to the uterus, fallopian tubes, and ovaries. Symptoms include pelvic pain and fevers. Treatments include mainly antibiotics.

Benign prostatic hypertrophy (BPH) is an age-associated condition in which the prostate gland enlarges, causing urinary difficulty. Symptoms include a weak urinary stream, which can lead to infection, stones, and reduced kidney function. Treatment includes medications that relax the bladder and shrink the prostate, and possibly surgery. Some of the medications used to help treat BPH are also antihypertensive alpha-blockers. These drugs, from the drug class with the suffix –osin, include terazosin, doxazosin, and tamsulosin.

Erectile dysfunction (ED) is when a man cannot achieve or keep an erection strong enough for sexual intercourse. It can be both a physical and a psychological condition and can cause relationship strain, stress, and low self-esteem. Treatment should require an examination for any underlying diseases and conditions. Medication and assistive devices, such as erectile pumps, are then prescribed.

Pregnancy, when not desired, is commonly controlled with birth control methods. The most common are oral contraceptives, which are made from synthetic female hormones, and their use depends on the female patient's hormonal makeup. Some are combined oral contraceptives with variable strengths of the hormones estrogen and progestin. Brands include desogestrel and ethinyl estradiol (Ortho-Cept) and norethindrone and ethinyl estradiol (Ortho-Novum, Ulipristal). Some contraceptives contain only progestin. Brands of these include levonorgestrel (Levonelle, Isteranda, Upostelle, EllaOne), etonogestrel (Nexplanon), and norethisterone (Primolut N, Utovlan, Noristerat).

 Diseases and conditions not covered in this section and not related to the reproductive system can also be treated by some of the drugs in this section.

Table 1.38. Common Drugs for the Reproductive System

Generic Name (Brand Names)	Description	Common Side Effects	Common Interactions
alprostadil (Muse)	prostaglandin; treats impotence (erectile dysfunction, or ED)	prolonged erection, redness around penis	alcohol, blood pressure medications, blood thinners
sildenafil (Viagra) tadalafil (Cialis) vardenafil (Levitra)	PDE-5 inhibitor; treats ED and BPH	headache, runny or stuffy nose, nausea, prolonged erection	nitrates
dutasteride (Avodart) finasteride (Proscar)	5-alpha reductase inhibitor; treats BPH	decrease in sexual desire, trouble keeping an erection	cimetidine, ciprofloxacin, diltiazem, ketoconazole, ritonavir, verapamil

Generic Name (Brand Names)	Description	Common Side Effects	Common Interactions
alfuzosin (Uroxatral) silodosin (Rapaflo)	alpha-blocker; treats BPH	headache, trouble having sex	blood pressure medications, anti-retroviral and antifungal medications
buserelin (Suprecur) nafarelin (Synarel)	synthetic hormone for in-vitro fertilization	headache, dizziness, hot flashes	not available
alverine (Audmonal, Spasmonal)	for uterine spasm		
clomiphene (Clomid)	selective estrogen modulator for infertility	hot flashes, breast tenderness, dizziness, nervousness, headache, stomach pain, mood changes	alcohol
danazol (Danol)	androgen for endometriosis and fibrocystic breast disease	acne, oily skin, weight gain, husky voice, unusual hair growth	insulin, diabetic medications, cholesterol medications, blood thinners
goserelin (Zoladex)	hormone-based chemotherapy	change in breast size, abdominal pain, headache, depression, hot flashes, pain, itching, loss of sexual desire	blood thinners, hormone treatments, alcohol
medroxyprogesterone (Provera) progesterone (Prometrium)	progestin	depression, headache, dizziness, stomach cramps, vaginal bleeding	other hormone medications
estrogen (Premarin)	hormone replacement		

PRACTICE QUESTIONS

1. Which is NOT a part of the female reproductive system?

   A) the prostate

   B) the uterus

   C) the fallopian tubes

   D) the ovaries

   Answers:

   A) **Correct.** Only men have a prostate.

   B) Incorrect. A uterus is indeed part of the reproductive system. A fertilized egg implants in its lining, where it continues to develops.

   C) Incorrect. Fallopian tubes are also a part of the reproductive system and are where fertilization takes place if sperm is present.

   D) Incorrect. Ovaries, or gonads, are part of the reproductive system too and contain undeveloped eggs, or oocytes.

2. Which is a BPH medication?

   A) buserelin

   B) terazosin

   C) progesterone

   D) clomiphene

   Answers:

   A) Incorrect. Buserelin is a synthetic hormone used for in-vitro fertilization.

   B) **Correct.** Terazosin is indeed a benign prostatic hypertrophic drug.

   C) Incorrect. Progesterone is a progestin drug.

   D) Incorrect. Clomiphene is a selective estrogen modulator used for infertility.

3. Which drug is NOT a treatment for erectile dysfunction (ED)?

   A) sildenafil

   B) vardenafil

   C) alprostadil

   D) danazol

   Answers:

   A) Incorrect. Sildenafil is indeed used for ED.

   B) Incorrect. Vardenafil is also used for ED.

   C) Incorrect. Alprostadil is used for ED too.

D) Correct. Danazol is an androgen used for endometriosis and fibrocystic breast disease.

4. Which is NOT a female hormone replacement drug?

   A) progesterone

   B) finasteride

   C) estradiol

   D) desogestrel

   Answers:

   A) Incorrect. Progesterone is a female hormone replacement drug.

   B) Correct. Finasteride is used for male BPH.

   C) Incorrect. Estradiol is also a female hormone replacement drug.

   D) Incorrect. Desogestrel is another female hormone replacement drug.

THE URINARY SYSTEM

The **urinary system**—made up of the kidneys, the bladder, the ureters, and the urethra—eliminates wastes from the body, controls electrolytes, regulates the pH of blood, and regulates blood pressure and volume.

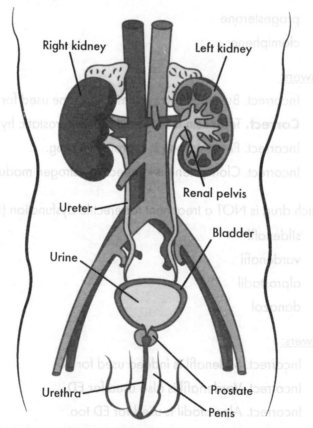

Figure 1.27. The Urinary System

The **kidneys** consist of units called **nephrons**. The main function of nephrons is to filter the blood, regulating what needs to be reabsorbed by the body and what can be excreted. The kidneys have an extensive blood supply, supplied by the renal arteries. In the **Bowman's capsule**, the top part of the nephron, blood from the cardiovascular system filters via the renal arteries, and that filtration is facilitated over the semipermeable membranes of nephrons through osmotic and hydrostatic pressure. Larger membranes, such as protein, are prevented from passing through the membranes and are distributed back into the body. The amount of filtration per minute is called the **glomerular filtration rate**. The body reabsorbs about 99 percent of the blood with about 1 percent extracted as **urine**, the body's waste. The blood that the body reabsorbs leaves the kidneys via the renal vein, while the urine exits the kidney via the ureters.

After exiting the kidneys, urine travels down the **ureters**—tubes made up of smooth muscle fibers—to the bladder. The **bladder** is a sac that expands as it fills with urine. This is where urine is stored until the body is ready to void it. At that time, the urine passes out of the body through another tube, called the **urethra**. In men and women, the urethra is different sizes, with the men's being longer, but the urinary system in men and women is identical. Humans normally produce 800 to 2,000 mL of urine a day.

A list of diseases and conditions common to the urinary system follows, along with a table detailing some of the most common drug treatments used currently:

Cystitis is a urinary tract infection (UTI) and can take place in any part of the urinary system. These infections are more common in women and normally occur in the bladder or urethra. Symptoms of a UTI include pain and discomfort when urinating, pelvic and back pain, fever, and blood in the urine. The most common treatment for a UTI is antibiotics.

Urinary incontinence—loss of bladder control—is a common problem, especially in middle age and older women, and can range from slight to severe incontinence. Normally, it happens when laughing, coughing, or sneezing as well as with urgency and not being able to get to the bathroom on time. Incontinence is a symptom, not a disease, and can be caused by underlying medical issues, everyday habits, or physical problems. People may develop urinary incontinence from a UTI, constipation, bearing children, pregnancy, menopause, cystectomy, BPH, prostate cancer, or neurological disorders. Lifestyle changes, such as limiting alcohol, caffeine, and soda, can help with incontinence. Other treatments include medications and surgery.

Gout is a form of arthritis characterized by severe pain, redness, and tenderness in the joints, especially the big toe. Although the medications associated with gout are covered in the musculoskeletal system, because this disease is caused by the presence of large amounts of uric acid, and because uric acid is normally excreted through the urine, gout is considered a disease of the urinary system. With gout, the body produces more uric acid than it can excrete. The uric acid crystals then deposit in the joints, causing pain and inflammation. Gout usually comes in painful attacks and often happens at night. Treatments include NSAIDs, taken during acute attacks; lifestyle changes, including alcohol limitation, diet, and exercise; and a **uricosuric** drug, such as colchicine, probenecid, or allopurinol, for chronic gout.

 Diseases and conditions not covered in this section and not related to the urinary system can also be treated by some of the drugs in this section.

Table 1.39. Common Drugs for the Urinary System

Generic Name (Brand Names)	Description	Common Side Effects	Common Interactions
phenazopyridine (AZO Standard, Pyridium)	urinary analgesic	stomach upset, dizziness, headache	alcohol; may cause urine to change color to orange or reddish brown
bethanechol (Urecholine)	nonselective muscarinic agonist, urinary retention medication	nausea, vomiting, vision changes, dizziness, gas, the urge to urinate	alcohol
propantheline (Pro-Banthine)	urinary antispas-modics	nausea, vomiting, vision changes, dizziness, gas, the urge to urinate	alcohol, potassium
tolterodine (Detrol LA)			arrhythmia drugs, HIV/AIDS drugs
oxybutynin (Ditropan)			bisphosphonates, alcohol, antibiotics
hyoscyamine (Cystospaz)			antihistamines, narcotic pain medications, phenothiazine medications, MAO inhibitors
flavoxate (Urispas) trospium (Sanctura)			alcohol
solifenacin (VESIcare)			HIV/AIDS drugs, MAO inhibitors, SSRIs, antipsychotics
fesoterodine (Toviaz)			atropine, scopolamine, some antibiotics

PRACTICE QUESTIONS

1. Which is the name for the top part of the nephron?

   A) the ureter

   B) the renal artery

   C) the Bowman's capsule

   D) the urethra

   Answers:

   A) Incorrect. The ureter is the tube that attaches the kidney to the bladder.

   B) Incorrect. The renal artery brings blood to the kidney.

   C) **Correct.** The Bowman's capsule is indeed the top part of the nephron, where blood from the cardiovascular system filters via the renal arteries.

   D) Incorrect. The urethra moves the urine from the bladder to outside the body.

2. How much of the blood in the kidneys is reabsorbed into the body?

   A) 99 percent

   B) 75 percent

   C) 25 percent

   D) 1 percent

   Answers:

   A) **Correct.** The body reabsorbs about 99 percent with about 1 percent extracted as urine.

   B) Incorrect. The body reabsorbs more than 75 percent.

   C) Incorrect. The body reabsorbs much more than 25 percent.

   D) Incorrect. The body reabsorbs 99 percent and excretes about 1 percent as urine.

3. Which drug is NOT an antispasmodic?

   A) solifenacin

   B) propantheline

   C) bethanechol

   D) trospium

   Answers:

   A) Incorrect. Solifenacin is an antispasmodic.

   B) Incorrect. Propantheline is an antispasmodic.

   C) **Correct.** Bethanechol is a nonselective muscarinic agonist and urinary retention medication.

D) Incorrect. Trospium is an antispasmodic.

4. Which is NOT a cause of urinary incontinence?

A) childbirth

B) a UTI

C) BPH

D) gastritis

Answers:

A) Incorrect. Childbirth can cause incontinence.

B) Incorrect. A urinary tract infection can also cause incontinence.

C) Incorrect. Benign prostatic hypertrophy, detailed in the reproductive system section, is another cause of incontinence.

D) **Correct.** Gastritis does not cause incontinence.

The Immune System

The **immune system**, in general, protects the body from disease. It must be able to detect large amounts of pathogens—disease-carrying microorganisms, bacteria, viruses, fungi, and parasites—and defend the body's tissue. Several systems work together within the greater immune system. The **innate immune system** defends the body from infection by pathogens. The **acquired immune system** consists of systemic cells that are highly specified to eliminate or prevent the growth of pathogens. The system of **humoral immunity** involves the body fluids and its secreted **antibodies**, also called **immunoglobulins**, which are proteins produced by plasma cells of the immune system that identify and neutralize pathogens. The system of **cell-mediated immunity** does not involve antibodies but activates **phagocytes**—cells that are able to engulf and absorb pathogens—and antigen-specific cytotoxic **lymphocytes**, small white blood cells. In humans, through barriers such as the blood–brain barrier, the blood–cerebrospinal fluid barrier, and other blood barriers, a separation between the peripheral immune system and the neuro-immune system protects the brain. Finally, the **lymphatic system** eliminates cell debris and pathogenic waste.

Because pathogens can easily evolve and adapt, the body's immune system must be able to detect and neutralize them by using multiple defense mechanisms. Each defense system has a different job to do, and in combination, they block most pathogens from causing serious illness.

When a pathogen successfully enters an organism, the first defense of the immune system is the **innate immune system**, which responds to the pathogen through **pathogen recognition receptors**—primitive proteins that release when a cell is damaged. These receptors recognize components of the pathogen and send out alarm signals. The innate immune system cannot provide long-lasting immunity against the pathogen, but it is the first line of defense in the human body.

Surface barriers protect the body against infection through mechanical, chemical, and biological barriers. By coughing and sneezing, pathogens are expelled from the lungs. By excretion of waste through the digestive and urinary tracts, pathogens are eliminated. Tears and sweat also rid the body of pathogens.

Chemical barriers protect from infection through **antimicrobial peptides**, antibiotics made by the body to deter bacteria. Enzymes in tears, saliva, and breast milk also contain antibacterials. The stomach's gastric acid is so acidic, it proves to be a powerful defense against pathogens too. Within the gastrointestinal and genitourinary tracts, **flora**—good bacteria—compete with pathogenic bacteria for food and space, and can change the environmental conditions, such as the pH balance, which makes the environment unsuitable for the invading pathogen.

Inflammation, another response to infection, causes redness, heat, swelling, and pain, bringing increased blood flow to the affected tissue. Inflammation is produced by eicosanoids and cytokine, released by damaged cells. **Eicosanoids** are molecules created by fatty acids, and they act as messengers. **Leukotrienes**, produced in the white blood cells, induce fever and dilate the blood vessels in inflammation. **Cytokines** are small proteins that also signal in times of distress. Common cytokines, **interleukins**, communicate between white blood cells. **Chemokines**, which promote chemotaxis, and **interferons**, which have antiviral effects, shut down pathogen growth in the host cell. The cytokines then recruit immune cells to promote healing of damaged tissue after the removal of the pathogens.

Cellular barriers, particularly **leukocytes**, work in the innate immune system and include mast cells, eosinophils, basophils, natural killer cells, and phagocytes. **Mast cells** reside in connective tissue and mucus membranes and regulate the inflammatory response. **Eosinophils** fight multicellular parasites. **Basophils** are responsible for the inflammatory reaction during an immune response. **Natural killer cells** respond to viral infected cells. **Phagocytes** engulf the pathogens in a process called **phagocytosis**. The pathogen is then caught in an intracellular **vesicle**—a small structure within the cell—which fuses with another vesicle called a **lysosome**, forming a **phagolysosome**. Digestive enzymes then kill the pathogen.

Neutrophils and **macrophages** are phagocytes that pursue invading pathogens by traveling through the body. Neutrophils—the most common phagocytes—move through the bloodstream and arrive first at the site of an infection. Macrophages live in the tissues and act as scavengers by ridding the body of debris and other dying cells.

Dendritic cells live in the tissues that contact the outside environment, such as the nose, skin, intestines, lungs, and stomach. They serve as a link between body tissue and the innate and adaptive immune systems.

In the **acquired immune system**, pathogens are recognized by the respective antigen through antigen presentation. **Antigen presentation** is an immune process in which macrophages and dendritic cells digest pathogens into smaller fragments so that immune cells can kill the pathogens. **Memory cells** maintain this ability to respond.

They remember pathogens that have already infected the body once and can quickly eliminate them.

Helper T cells work in both the innate and acquired immune systems by determining which immune responses have been made to a particular pathogen. They cannot kill pathogens directly but instead direct the immune responses of other cells. **Gamma delta T cells** seem to share characteristics of helper T cells and are also a regulatory defense, although how they respond is relatively unknown.

B lymphocytes identify pathogens through antibodies on their surface, which bind to foreign antigens. This response is processed through **proteolysis**, or the breaking down of proteins into amino acids or peptides. Proteolysis then attracts a matching helper T cell, which activates **lymphokines** and begins to divide as an active B lymphocyte cell. The B lymphocyte cell then secretes millions of copied antibodies that recognize the pathogen. These antibodies circulate through blood plasma and the lymphatic system.

The **lymphatic system**—part of both the cardiovascular and immune systems—consists of lymphatic vessels, lymph nodes, the spleen, and the thymus. The **lymphatic vessels** carry clear lymphocytic liquid, called **lymph**, to the heart. The main functions of the lymphatic system entail the defense and elimination of cell debris and waste products that contain pathogens.

Lymphocytes are concentrated in the **lymph nodes**, which are linked by lymphatic vessels and are located in the armpits, stomach, tonsils, and other parts of the body. **Peyer patches** are small nodules made up of lymphatic tissue located in the small intestine. They function by analyzing and responding to pathogens in the ileum portion of the small intestine. The pathogen is then absorbed by microfold cells in the lining of the patches.

The **spleen** is structured like a large lymph node and removes old red blood cells, reserves blood, and recycles iron. In the **thymus**—the main organ of the lymphatic system—**T lymphocytes** mature into **thymocytes**. Blood cells are also produced in the bone marrow—the soft, fatty substance in the bone cavity.

A list of diseases and conditions common to the immune system follows, along with tables detailing some of the most common drug treatments used currently:

Hodgkin's lymphoma is cancer of the lymphatic system. As the disease progresses, the immune system has a difficult time fighting infection. Symptoms of Hodgkin's disease include swollen lymph nodes, fever, fatigue, and chills. Treatments include radiation, chemotherapy, and stem cell transplants.

Leukemia—a cancer of blood-forming tissues, such as bone marrow—encompasses different types, such as lymphoblastic leukemia, acute myeloid leukemia, and chronic lymphocytic leukemia. Symptoms of leukemia include fatigue, weight loss, infections, and easy bruising. Treatments include monitoring, chemotherapy, radiation, and stem cell transplants.

Lymphocytosis is an increase of lymphocytes in the blood. If the count is too high, it causes concern of underlying disease or infection in the body. Normally lymphocytosis occurs if the count is over 4,000 per microliter.

Lymphedema is a swelling in the arms or legs caused by blockage in the lymphatic system. It is commonly due to the removal of lymph nodes during cancer treatment. The main symptom is the swelling of arms or legs, which causes pain and discomfort.

HIV/AIDS is a viral infection that interferes with the body's immune system. Spread through sexual contact, bodily fluids, and infected blood, it initially presents with flu-like symptoms, fever, sore throat, and fatigue within a few weeks of contact. Then the HIV disease can become asymptomatic until it develops into AIDS. AIDS symptoms include weight loss, recurrent infection, fever, and night sweats. Although no cure exists for AIDS, antiretroviral treatments can drastically slow the disease's progress and prevent infections and complications.

Autoimmune disorders are diseases in which the immune system attacks healthy cells. Some common types are **rheumatoid arthritis**, a chronic inflammatory disorder that affects the joints; **lupus**, an inflammatory disease in which the body attacks its own tissues; **multiple sclerosis**, an autoimmune disease that attacks the protective covering of nerves; and **vasculitis**, an inflammation of the blood vessels that changes the blood vessels' walls.

Treatments for autoimmune disorders vary by disease, but many disorders can be treated with medications that suppress the immune system, such as biologics and steroids (drugs listed in the musculoskeletal system section).

Table 1.40. Common Drugs for HIV/AIDS Treatment

Generic Name (Brand Names)	Description	Common Side Effects	Common Interactions
amprenavir (Agenerase) indinavir (Crixivan) raltegravir (Ientress) ritonavir (Norvir) saquinavir (Invirase) tipranavir (Aptivus)	antiviral medications for HIV called protease inhibitors	burning sensation in the arms or legs, dry and itchy skin, fatigue, increased cholesterol, increased hunger and thirst, increased urination, skin rash	steroids, −statin medications, hormone medications, narcotic pain medications, belladonna medications, −caine medications, gout medications, some antibiotics, ergot medications, alcohol
atazanavir/cobicistat (Evotaz)	protease inhibitor and CYP3A inhibitor for HIV	headache, tiredness, stuffy or runny nose, weight gain, upset stomach	other HIV medications, steroids, cancer treatments, interferon

Generic Name (Brand Names)	Description	Common Side Effects	Common Interactions
lamivudine/zidovu-dine (Combivir) rilpivirine (Edurant)	HIV nucleoside analog reverse transcriptase inhibitor; HIV antiviral	headache, tiredness, stuffy or runny nose, weight gain, upset stomach	other HIV medications, steroids, cancer treatments, interferon
lamivudine (Epivir)	HIV nucleoside analog reverse transcriptase inhibitor and anti-HBV reverse transcriptase inhibitor; HIV non-nucleoside transcriptase inhibitor	not available	blood thinners, arrhythmia medications, −statin medications, medications used for fungal infections, erectile dysfunction medications, seizure medications, steroids, pain medications
etravirine (Intelence)			

Many of these drugs have the suffixes −vir and −ine.

 Diseases and conditions not covered in this section and not related to the immune system can also be treated by some of the drugs in this section.

Table 1.41. Common Vaccinations

Brand Names	Vaccination Type	Common Side Effects	Common Interactions
Fluzone, FluMist, Flucelvax, Afluria, Flublok, Fluarix	common influenza strains	soreness, redness, and swelling at the injection site, fainting, aches, low-grade fever, nausea	phenytoin, warfarin, aminopyrine, theophylline
Pneumovax 23, Prevnar13	pneumococcal for pneumonia		alcohol, certain antibiotics, certain vitamins, −statin medications
Menomune, Menactra	meningococcal for meningitis	pain at the injection site, fever, nausea, dizziness, fatigue, nausea, vomiting, diarrhea, tooth pain, joint and muscle pain	
Gardasil, Cervarix	human papilloma virus (HPV)		chemotherapy and radiation, biologic medications, organ transplant medications, steroids
Zostavax	herpes zoster, against shingles		thyroid medications, −statin medications, NSAIDs

Table 1.41. Common Vaccinations (continued)

Brand Names	Vaccination Type	Common Side Effects	Common Interactions
numerous brand names available	hepatitis	pain at the injection site, fever, nausea, dizziness, fatigue, nausea, vomiting, diarrhea, tooth pain, joint and muscle pain	NSAIDs, pain medications
numerous brand names available	measles, mumps, and rubella (MMR)		not available
Varicella	chicken pox		steroids, biologics, HIV/AIDS medications

Vaccinations are biological preparations that provide active acquired immunity to particular diseases. They typically contain agents that resemble the diseases being treated and cause the pathogens responsible for the diseases to weaken or become destroyed in the body.

Table 1.42. Other Treatments for the Immune System

Generic Name (Brand Names)	Description	Common Side Effects	Common Interactions
acyclovir (Zovirax)	antiviral for herpes, shingles, and other viral infections	headache, muscle pain, nausea, vomiting, diarrhea, nervousness, vision problems	steroids, chemotherapy, radiation, biologic medications, –statin medications
entecavir (Baraclude)	antiviral for hepatitis B		
famciclovir (Famvir)	antiviral for herpes simplex		
valacyclovir (Valtrex)	antiviral for shingles, herpes, and chicken pox		
boceprevir (Victrelis)	antiviral for hepatitis C		
docosanol (Abreva)	topical antiviral for cold sores	no serious side effects	no drug interactions

CONTINUE

Generic Name (Brand Names)	Description	Common Side Effects	Common Interactions
azithromycin (Zithromax) clarithromycin (Biaxin)	macrolide antibiotics	metallic taste in the mouth, nausea and vomiting, upset stomach	–statin medications, steroids, arrhythmia medications, seizure medications, HIV/AIDS medications, diabetic medications
vancomycin (Vancocin)	glycopeptide antibiotic	back pain, nausea, vomiting, diarrhea, stomach pain	amikacin, gentamicin, streptomycin
levofloxacin (Levaquin) moxifloxacin (Avelox)	floroquinolone antibiotics		diuretics, amikacin, tobramycin, neomycin
gentamicin (Garamycin)	antibiotic	redness, pain, and swelling at the injection site	
belimumab (Benlysta)	immunosuppressant for lupus	diarrhea, nausea, trouble sleeping	cyclophosphamide, vaccinations
interferon alfa-2b (Intron-a)	antiviral	diarrhea, appetite loss, hair loss, headache, joint and muscle pain	theophylline, HIV/AIDS medications
ecallantide (Kalbitor)	anti-inflammatory for hereditary angioedema	redness, pain, and swelling at the injection site	not available
sargramostim (Leukine)	bone marrow stimulant	bone, joint, and muscle pain; fever; stomach issues; redness, pain, and swelling at the injection site	lithium, steroids, chemotherapy agents

Table 1.42. Other Treatments for the Immune System (continued)

Generic Name (Brand Names)	Description	Common Side Effects	Common Interactions
ribavirin (Rebetol)	antiviral for lung infections, such as RSV	dry mouth, headache, hair loss, stomach issues, muscle and joint pain, weight loss	HIV/AIDS medications, alcohol
cyclosporine (Sandimmune, Neoral)	immunosuppressants	diarrhea, stomach issues, swollen gums, increased hair growth	potassium, vaccinations, alcohol, grapefruit juice
sirolimus (Rapamycin)		diarrhea, constipation, stomach issues, mouth sores	antivirals, antifungals, phenobarbital, phenytoin, cyclosporine
lymphocyte immune-globulin (Atgam)		fever, chills, joint pain, diarrhea, headache, nausea, vomiting, night sweats, shortness of breath	alcohol, live vaccinations, steroids, blood thinners
basiliximab (Simulect)	immunosuppressants for use after an organ transplant	vision problems, erectile dysfunction, dizziness, headache, tremors, weakness, pain	steroids, alcohol, HIV/AIDS medications, vaccinations, viral medications, birth control pills
mycophenolate (Cellcept)			

PRACTICE QUESTIONS

1. Which leukocytes do not work in the innate immune system?

   A) phagocytes

   B) eosinophils

   C) mast cells

   D) B lymphocyte cells

Answers:

A) Incorrect. Phagocytes, which are able to engulf and absorb pathogens, indeed work in the innate immune system.

B) Incorrect. Eosinophils also work in the innate immune system, fighting multicellular parasites.

C) Incorrect. Mast cells work in the innate immune system too, regulating the inflammatory response.

D) **Correct.** B lymphocyte cells work in the acquired immune system, identifying pathogens through antibodies on their surface.

2. Which drug is NOT an immunosuppressant?

   A) clarithromycin
   B) belimumab
   C) cyclosporine
   D) mycophenolate

Answers:

A) **Correct.** Clarithromycin is an antibiotic.

B) Incorrect. Belimumab is an immunosuppressant, used for lupus.

C) Incorrect. Cyclosporine is also an immunosuppressant.

D) Incorrect. Mycophenolate is an immunosuppressant, typically used after an organ transplant.

3. Which of these organs is NOT part of the lymphatic system?

   A) the thymus
   B) the lymph nodes
   C) the pancreas
   D) the spleen

Answers:

A) Incorrect. The thymus is the main organ of the lymphatic system.

B) Incorrect. The lymph nodes, located in the armpits, stomach, tonsils, and other parts of the body, are part of the lymphatic system.

C) **Correct.** The pancreas is part of the endocrine system.

D) Incorrect. The spleen is a part of the lymphatic system, removing old red blood cells, reserving blood, and recycling iron.

4. Which drug is NOT an HIV/AIDS medication?

    A) basiliximab

    B) etravirine

    C) ritonavir

    D) indinavir

Answers:

    A) **Correct.** Basiliximab is for use after an organ transplant.

    B) Incorrect. Etravirine is indeed an HIV/AIDS drug.

    C) Incorrect. Ritonavir is also an HIV/AIDS drug.

    D) Incorrect. Indinavir is another HIV/AIDS drug.

RADIOPHARMACEUTICALS

Radiopharmaceutical drugs have a radioactive compound and are used for diagnostic and therapeutic purposes. As with all pharmaceuticals, a standard is required for implementing and developing these drugs.

Most radiopharmaceuticals are used for diagnostic imaging, but they can also be used for chemotherapy and radiation in cancer patients. Chemotherapy radiopharmaceuticals include strontium 89 (Metastron), samarium 153 (Quadramet), and radium-223 (Xofigo) for bone cancers; radioactive iodine for thyroid cancer; and phosphorus 32 for brain tumors.

Monoclonal antibodies, or **radio-labeled antibodies,** are manufactured versions of immune system proteins with radioactive atoms that only attach to their target. This treatment is used for non-Hodgkin's lymphoma.

PRACTICE QUESTION

Which of these is NOT a radiopharmaceutical?

A) monoclonal antibodies

B) radium 450

C) phosphorus 32

D) radium 223

Answers:

A) Incorrect. Monoclonal antibodies are indeed radiopharmaceuticals.

B) **Correct.** Radium 450 is not a radiopharmaceutical.

C) Incorrect. Phosphorus 32 is also a radiopharmaceutical.

D) Incorrect. Radium 223 is a radiopharmaceutical too.

Pharmacy Abbreviations

Pharmacy abbreviations—also called **sig codes**—are used when preparing medical prescriptions and hospital medication orders. These codes are extremely important to the pharmacy technician and must be known in order for the technician to decipher important instructions, measurements, and times needed for a patient's medications.

Table 1.43. Common Sig Codes

Abbreviation	Meaning	Category
ī	one	measurement
s̄	without	other
s̈s; ss	one-half	measurement
a.a., aa	of each	measurement
a.c.	before meals	time
ad	to, up to	measurement
a.d.	right ear	route of administration
ad lib	at one's pleasure	time
agit.	shake, stir	other
alt. h.	every other hour	time
a.m.	morning	time
amp.	ampule	other
app.	apply	route of administration
aq, aqua	water	drug form
aq. ad	add water up to	measurement
a.s., a.l.	left ear	route of administration
A.T.C.	around the clock	time
a.u.	both ears	route of administration
b.i.d., b.d.	twice daily	time
b.m.	bowel movement	other
bol.	bolus	other
B.S.	blood sugar	other
B.S.A.	body surface area	measurement
c	with	other
cap or caps	capsules	drug form

Table 1.43. Common Sig Codes (continued)

Abbreviation	Meaning	Category
cc	cubic centimeter	measurement
comp.	compound	drug form
cr., crm.	cream	drug form
D5NS	dextrose 5% in sodium chloride solution	drug
D5W	dextrose 5% in water	drug
D.A.W.	dispense as written	other
dc, D/C, disc.	discontinue	other
dil.	dilute	measurement
disp.	dispense	other
div.	divide	measurement
d.t.d.	dispense such doses	other
D.W.	distilled water	drug form
elix.	elixir	drug form
emuls.	emulsion	drug form
e.t.	expired time	time
ex aq.	in water	other
fl., fld.	fluid	drug form
fl. oz.	fluid ounce	measurement
g, G, gm	gram	measurement
gtt(s)	drop(s)	measurement
h, hr.	hour	time
h.s.	at bedtime	time
i.d.	intradermal	other
i.m., IM	intramuscularly	route of administration
inj.	inject	route of administration
i.v., IV	intravenously	route of administration
IVP	IV push	route of administration
IVPB	IV piggyback	route of administration
l., L.	liter	measurement

Abbreviation	Meaning	Category
LCD	coal tar solution	drug form
lin.	liniment	drug form
liq.	liquid	drug form
lot.	lotion	drug form
mist.	mixture	drug form
mcg	microgram	measurement
mEq	milliequivalent	measurement
mg	milligram	measurement
min.	minute	time
mL	milliliter	measurement
neb., nebul.	nebulizer	other
NMT	not more than	other
noct.	at night	time
non rep.	do not repeat	time
NR	no refill	other
NS	normal saline, sodium chloride	drug form
½NS	half strength normal saline	drug form
NTE	not to exceed	other
o.d.	right eye	route of administration
o.s., o.l.	left eye	route of administration
o.u.	both eyes	route of administration
oz	ounce	measurement
p.c.	after food, after meals	time
per	by	other
p.m.	afternoon, evening	time
p.o.	by mouth	route of administration
p.r.	rectally	route of administration
prn	as needed	route of administration
pulv.	pulverized	other
q	each, every	time

Table 1.43. Common Sig Codes (continued)

Abbreviation	Meaning	Category
q.a.m.	every morning	time
q.d.	every day	time
q.h.	every hour	time
q.h.s.	every night at bedtime	time
q.i.d.	four times daily	time
q.o.d.	every other day	time
q.s.	a sufficient quantity	measurement
R	rub	other
rep., rept.	repeat	other
RL, R/L	Ringer's lactated	drug form
SC, subc, subQ, subcut	subcutaneous	route of administration
sig	write on label	other
SL	sublingual	route of administration
sol.	solution	drug form
SR, XL, XR	slow release/extended release	drug form
ss	one-half	other
stat.	immediately	time
sup.	suppository	drug form
susp.	suspension	drug form
syr.	syrup	drug form
tab.	tablet	drug form
talc.	talcum	drug form
tbsp	tablespoonful	measurement
t.i.d., tid	three times daily	time
t.i.w.	three times a week	time
top.	topically	route of administration
TPN	total parenteral nutrition	other
tsp	teaspoonful	measurement
troche	lozenge	drug form

Abbreviation	Meaning	Category
tsp	teaspoonful	measurement
u.d., utd., ut. dict.	as directed	other
ung., oint.	ointment	drug form
USP	United States Pharmacopeia	other
vag.	vaginally	route of administration
w	with	other
w/o, wo	without	other
X	times	other
y.o., Y.O.	years old	other

 It is very important to memorize the sig codes. Making flashcards to study them on the go will help to memorize them.

PRACTICE QUESTIONS

1. What does "Take 1 tab. q.i.d. prn pain" mean?

A) Take 1 teaspoonful every 4 hours as needed for pain.

B) Take 1 tablet every day as needed for pain.

C) Take 1 tablet four times daily as needed for pain.

D) Take 1 tablespoonful every day as needed for pain.

Answers:

A) Incorrect. The sig code tab. means tablet, not teaspoonful, which would be tsp.

B) Incorrect. The sig code q.i.d. means four times daily, not every day, which would be q.d.

C) Correct.

D) Incorrect. The sig code tab. means tablet, not tablespoonful, which would be tbsp.

2. What is the translation of "Instill 1 gtt in o.u. b.d."?

A) Instill 1 drop in the left ear twice daily.

B) Instill 1 drop in both eyes twice daily.

C) Instill 1 drop in the left eye twice daily.

D) Instill 1 drop in both ears twice daily.

Answers:

A)   Incorrect. The sig codes for left ear are a.s. and a.l.

B)   **Correct.** The sig code gtt (gutta) means drop; o.u. (oculus uterque) means both eyes; and b.d., or b.i.d. (bis in die), means twice daily.

C)   Incorrect. The sig codes for left eye are o.s. and o.l.

D)   Incorrect. The sig code for both ears is a.u.

3.   What is the sig code for a sufficient quantity?

   A)   q.d.

   B)   q.h.

   C)   q.o.d.

   D)   q.s.

Answers:

A)   Incorrect. The sig code q.d. (quaque die) means every day.

B)   Incorrect. The sig code q.h. (quaque hora) means every hour.

C)   Incorrect. The sig code q.o.d. (quaque alterna die) means every other day.

D)   **Correct.** This sig code q.s. in Latin is quantum sufficiat, which translates as a sufficient quantity.

4.   What does the sig code u.d. translate to?

   A)   label, write

   B)   as directed

   C)   immediately

   D)   dilute

Answers:

A)   Incorrect. The sig code sig (signa) means write (on a label).

B)   **Correct.** The sig code u.d. in Latin is ut dictum—as directed.

C)   Incorrect. The sig code stat. (statim) means immediately.

D)   Incorrect. The sig code dil. is an abbreviation of dilute.

TWO: ASSISTING THE PHARMACIST

A pharmacy technician's most important job is to assist the pharmacist. The pharmacist relies on the pharmacy technician to provide the best possible customer service to the patient. The technician must also identify and perform those tasks necessary to support the pharmacist, enabling him or her to focus on patient care and safely verifying orders.

Tasks for which the pharmacy technician is responsible vary depending on the working environment. In the ambulatory pharmacy setting, technicians are responsible for processing prescriptions and data entry, checking for accuracy, refilling prescriptions, working with third-party payers and insurance companies, filling and preparing orders, customer service, and upkeep of the pharmacy through administrative duties and keeping the pharmacy clean and organized.

In a hospital setting, pharmacy technicians are responsible for preparing IV admixtures, processing and preparing medication orders, and delivering medications to the nursing floors. Technicians are also responsible for filling automated dispensing systems on the floors, communicating with doctors and nurses, administrative duties, and unit-dosing medications.

Ambulatory (Community) Pharmacy

The ambulatory, or community, pharmacy is responsible for providing pharmacy services to ambulatory patients; these include prescriptions, health insurance services, vaccinations, counseling, and other services established by the pharmacy setting. The **ambulatory** pharmacy setting is where pharmacists and pharmacy technicians assist patients who are able to walk to the pharmacy to receive services. Ambulatory pharmacies dispense more drugs than any other pharmacy setting.

Ambulatory pharmacies are not just the "corner drugstore" or independent and chain pharmacies anymore. Many hospitals have outpatient pharmacies where patients released from inpatient hospital services can fill prescriptions. Physicians' clinics and community care clinics provide pharmacy services as well.

The process from entering the prescription in the pharmacy software system to dispensing the prescription to the patient is called the pharmacy workflow. **Pharmacy workflow** in ambulatory pharmacy is broken into five different steps: greeting the patient, data entry, product dispensing and the fill process, verification, and releasing the prescription to the patient. Some ambulatory pharmacies do compounding as well. Because compounding is a responsibility that requires more training and skills, the subject will be discussed in depth in chapter five.

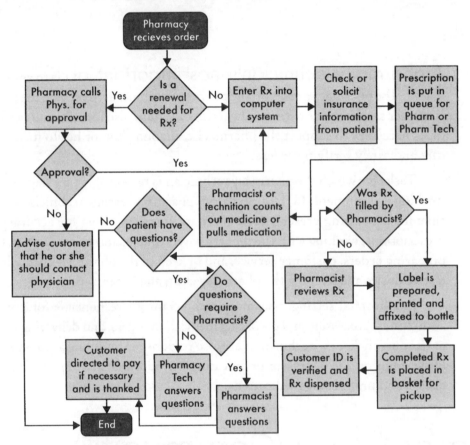

Figure 2.1. Pharmacy Workflow

Although there are different types of ambulatory pharmacies, the skills and tasks required by the pharmacy technician in this setting are driven by the same goal: customer service. This section discusses the many important responsibilities the pharmacy technician performs in an ambulatory setting to assist the pharmacist.

 In all states, pharmacists are held accountable and must supervise all activities performed by a pharmacy technician in a pharmacy setting.

Processing Orders

When a patient comes to drop-off a prescription at the pharmacy, the first person he or she normally encounters is the pharmacy technician. At this time, the pharmacy technician will greet the patient and receive a prescription order, or **hard copy**, written by the patient's physician. It can be either written out by the physician's office or printed out from a computer software program.

A typical hard copy prescription from a prescription pad looks like this:

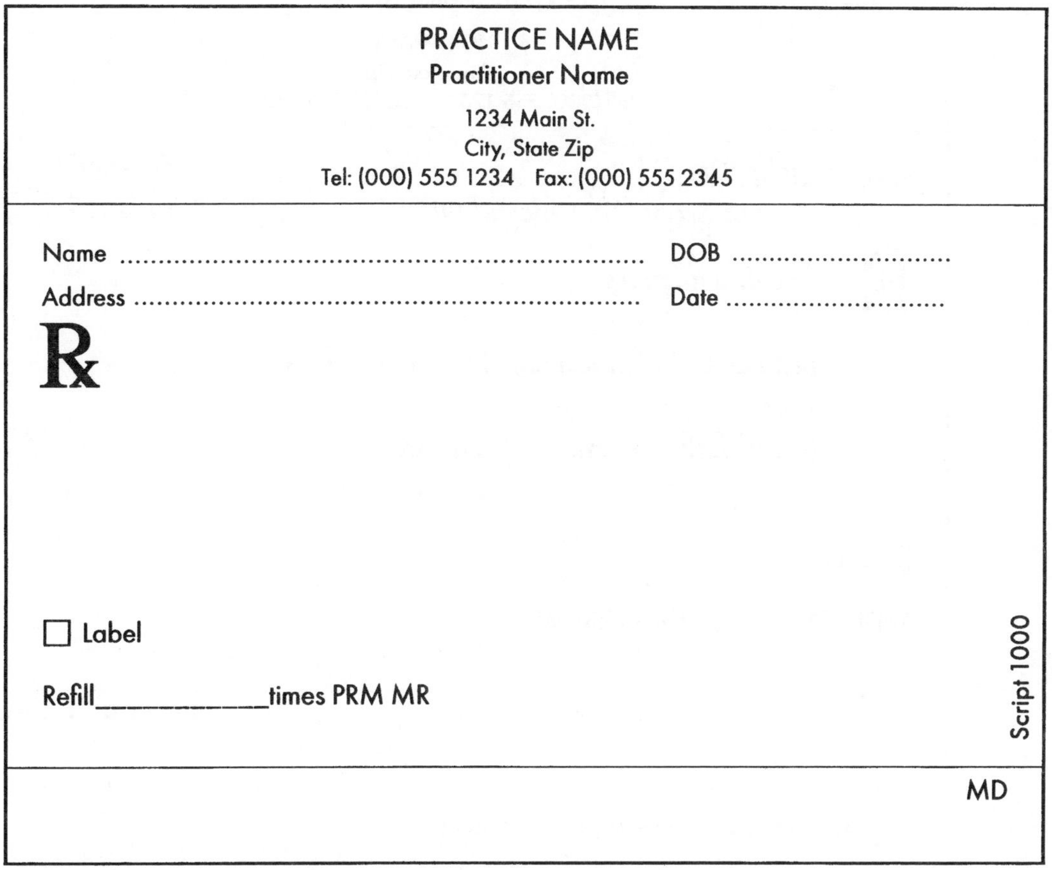

PRACTICE NAME
Practitioner Name

1234 Main St.
City, State Zip
Tel: (000) 555 1234   Fax: (000) 555 2345

Name .... DOB ....

Address .... Date ....

℞

☐ Label

Refill_____times PRM MR

Script 1000

MD

Figure 2.2. Hard Copy Prescription (blank)

As technology continually progresses, so have advancements in pharmacy. These advancements are aimed at making the patient's experience at the pharmacy more convenient. Many pharmacies and physicians' offices use special software programs to communicate with each other. When it comes to processing prescription orders, many physicians' offices now send new prescriptions to pharmacies via the Internet over secured servers to comply with patient privacy laws (the Health Insurance Portability and Accountability Act, or HIPAA). This makes it more convenient for patients because the pharmacy can prepare their orders in advance.

Although these developments are more convenient for the patient, the hard copy is still sent to the pharmacy via the physician's office with the same information; the pharmacy is still required to keep the hard copies on file for at least two years. Prescriptions for some controlled drugs cannot be sent electronically if the provider and pharmacy comply with the DEA rules for electronic prescriptions for controlled substances (see chapter three for more information on electronic prescriptions for controlled substances). If either system does not comply, the prescription must be written on a hard copy and signed by the physician. The patient must still bring the new prescription to the pharmacy to be filled.

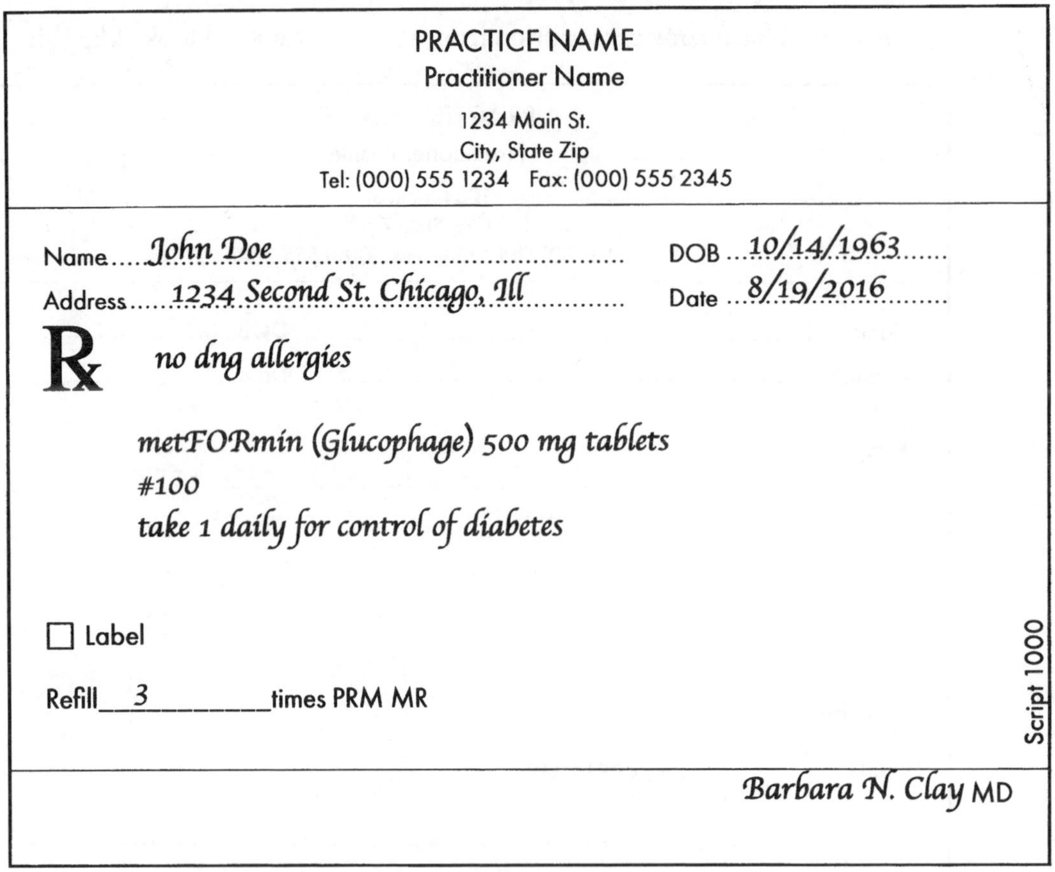

PRACTICE NAME
Practitioner Name

1234 Main St.
City, State Zip
Tel: (000) 555 1234   Fax: (000) 555 2345

Name..... *John Doe*   DOB .. *10/14/1963*
Address..... *1234 Second St. Chicago, Ill*   Date .. *8/19/2016*

Rx   *no drug allergies*

       metFORmin (Glucophage) 500 mg tablets
       #100
       take 1 daily for control of diabetes

☐ Label

Refill___*3*_____times PRM MR

Script 1000

                                    Barbara N. Clay MD

Figure 2.3. Hard Copy Prescription (filled in)

All hard copies of prescriptions are required to have specific information written on them by federal law. The information required is:

+ **patient name:** The patient's name is required for verification.
+ **patient phone number:** Phone numbers must be updated in case the patient needs to be notified of any problems in the filling process. They are also used for verification purposes in case there is more than one patient in the system with the same name. Finally, pharmacies notify patients by phone when their prescriptions are ready to be picked up.
+ **patient date of birth:** Many pharmacies use the patient's date of birth as a verification tool to differentiate patients who may share names.
+ **physician's office name, address, and phone number:** Some physicians have multiple office locations. Pharmacies need accurate information to

limit delays when contacting physicians' offices with questions or requests for refills.

+ **physician's signature:** If the medication is a non-control, the physician can use a copied signature or a physician's assistant or nurse practitioner can sign per rules and regulations allowed by federal or state laws. With controlled substances, the prescription must be physically signed by the physician.

+ **date the prescription was written:** Most prescriptions expire a year after the prescription was written. CII controlled substances may only be filled once. CIII–CV controlled classes may have refills for up to six months depending on how many refills the physician authorizes.

+ **medication, strength, quantity, dose, and dosage form of the medication:** For example, if a physician writes "Metoprolol 25mg, Take 1 tablet by mouth twice daily #60 for a 30-day supply," the medication would be *metoprolol*, the **strength** would be *25mg*, the **quantity** would be *#60*, the **dose** would be *twice daily*, and the **dosage form** would be *tablet*.

+ **administration route:** The administration route in the previous example would be *by mouth*.

+ **signa,** or **labeled directions for use.** The signa is written with sig codes, which are listed in chapter one. In the example above, the **signa** for the directions would be "Take 1 t po bid."

+ **refill information:** This number indicates how many refills the physician authorized on the prescription.

For controlled substances, there are more requirements:

+ **the physician's DEA,** or drug enforcement number
+ **the prescriber's address**
+ **the patient's address**

All prescriptions are required to have the statement, *Caution: Federal Law prohibits dispensing without a prescription* written on the hard copy.

> **?** Translate the sample hard-copy prescriptions in Figure 2.3. using the sig codes learned in chapter one.

The requirements for prescription hard copies help the technician verify information that is legally required to be placed on the prescription label. It is also used for the patient's insurance company for third-party adjudication and reimbursement. At the time of drop-off, it is important to ask if the patient's insurance has changed and to see the patient's insurance card if it has not been used before.

Sometimes, a patient will drop off a prescription bottle and ask for a **refill**. If there are refills left, the technician can enter the order number on the prescription bottle to refill. If it is from the same pharmacy but a different location, the technician can **transfer** the refill to the desired store; however if the prescription is from a different pharmacy, the pharmacist is responsible for getting the refill.

 Always be kind and understanding to the patient. Customer service is one of the most important aspects of ambulatory pharmacy.

PRACTICE QUESTIONS

1. On a hard copy prescription, a prescriber has written "*lorazepam 1 mg, take 1 tablet by mouth at bedtime, #30*" for the patient. Which would be the dose?

   A) by mouth

   B) #30

   C) 1 mg

   D) tablet

   Answers:

   A) Incorrect. *By mouth* is the route of administration.

   B) Incorrect. *#30* indicates the quantity.

   C) Incorrect. The dosage strength is 1 mg.

   D) Correct. *Tablet* indicates the dose.

2. Which of the following is NOT an important reason to get the correct phone number from the patient when he or she drops off a prescription?

   A) to verify the patient's name in the computer system

   B) to be able to reach the patient in case of questions

   C) to sell the patient new OTC products available at the pharmacy store

   D) to let the patient know when a prescription is ready to be picked up

   Answers:

   A) Incorrect. It is important to have a correct phone number for verifying a patient.

   B) Incorrect. It is important to have a number in case a complication arises during the filling process.

   C) Correct. It is not important to call patients on the phone for sales purposes.

   D) Incorrect. It is important to let patients know when their prescriptions are ready.

3. For how long is a non-controlled medication prescription viable after it is written by the physician?

A) a year from the date it is written

B) six months from the date it is written

C) until it runs out of refills

D) A non-controlled medication prescription is only good for one month after it has been written.

Answers:

A) **Correct.** A prescription is good for a year after the date it is written.

B) Incorrect. Certain controlled medication prescriptions are only valid for six months from the date written.

C) Incorrect. Prescriptions may change in strength or be discontinued, so they are only valid for a year.

D) Incorrect. This applies to controlled substances.

4. Why is it important to have the correct physician location entered on the prescription if the physician has multiple offices?

A) This information is required by law.

B) The patient may call the pharmacy to ask for the physician's phone number.

C) The pharmacy may need to call the physician for refills or questions. Calling the wrong office is inconvenient and wastes time.

D) The pharmacy must let the doctor know when the patient's prescription is filled.

Answers:

A) Incorrect. As long as the correct DR and DEA number are entered, the law does not require the correct location of the physician's office to be on the prescription.

B) Incorrect. It is not the pharmacy's responsibility to give the patient the doctor's number, although for customer service purposes, it is helpful to have it.

C) **Correct.** Calling the wrong office can cause confusion and cost time because the office may not have the patient's records at that location.

D) Incorrect. The doctor does not need to be informed when the patient's prescription is ready.

CHECKING FOR ACCURACY

When processing prescription orders, asking specific questions and checking for accuracy is a crucial part of the job of a pharmacy technician. When a patient drops off a prescription, it is very important to study the prescription carefully for any errors or inconsistencies. Mistakes on prescription hard copies can cost both the patient and pharmacy technician valuable time and cause unnecessary stress. Asking the patient specific questions and verifying information before the patient leaves the counter improves accuracy.

If the prescription is written by the physician and not typed, pharmacy technicians must be sure they can read the patient's name. If not, they should ask to verify spelling. Pharmacy technicians should also always ask the patient's date of birth and write it on the prescription, even if the physician added it to the prescription.

If the patient has any drug allergies, these should be written on the prescription or confirmed in the patient's profile, where they may have already been entered. Otherwise, the abbreviation *NKA* must be added to the profile and written on the prescription. **NKA** is the abbreviation for *no known allergies*. Another important question is whether the patient has filled prescriptions at the pharmacy before. If not, pharmacy technicians must obtain all of his or her information: name, address, date of birth, allergies, phone number, and insurance information. It is also the technician's responsibility to check the status of the patient's insurance. If it has changed, the correct information must be entered into the patient's profile before he or she leaves the counter. Errors in information can cause delays when patients return to pick up their medication.

Once this information is confirmed, technicians verify the drug name, dosage, dose form, directions, and quantity. Although the physician usually checks for accuracy, mistakes happen occasionally and can cause delays in processing the prescription if the physician needs to be contacted. In these cases, notifying the patient of the delay will prevent customer frustration.

Finally, pharmacy technicians should respond to any questions patients might have, or refer them to the pharmacist. Pharmacists should be notified if the question is about the medication, how it works, side effects, etc.

If possible, processing prescriptions while the patient is at the counter is optimal. If there are any issues with the third-party payer and reimbursement, such as rejections or the drug not being covered, the patient should be notified that filling the prescription will take extra time to call the insurance and/or doctor for overrides and/or change in medication. This is not always an option if it is busy, but it does save time and stress.

With controlled medication prescriptions, extra vigilance is vital. Pharmacy technicians should be familiar with the handwriting and signatures of local physicians whose patients frequent the pharmacy. Different pen colors, quantities and refills that look altered, or indications that a prescription is copied may indicate problems. Unfortunately, pharmacy technicians sometimes encounter **fraudulent** and **forged** prescriptions. The pharmacist should always be notified of any concerns.

? A patient comes in with a prescription in which the directions and quantity seem to be inaccurate for the drug prescribed. How would you handle this situation?

PRACTICE QUESTION

When processing a controlled medication prescription, which of the following should NOT influence the pharmacy technician when checking to see if the prescription is possibly forged?

A) if the quantity or refills look altered

B) if the physician's handwriting and signature look correct

C) if the prescription looks copied

D) if the patient is acting nervous

Answers:

A)   Incorrect. Always check to see if anything looks altered on the prescription.

B)   Incorrect. If the handwriting or signature of the physician looks wrong, then question whether the prescription was altered.

C)   Incorrect. If it does not look like the prescription was actually written, then question the prescription. One way to determine this is the absence of indentation from pushing the pen on the paper, or if the writing looks faded.

D)   **Correct.** If a patient has a valid prescription for a controlled medication with no signs of forgery or fraud, a pharmacy cannot turn him or her away just because the patient seems nervous. The patient may feel as though he or she is being discriminated against. If the technician feels uncomfortable filling the prescription, the pharmacist must be notified; he or she will decide whether to fill the prescription. Sometimes, patient behavior could even be a symptom of the disease or condition the doctor is treating. For example, if a patient seems nervous, the medication being filled may be for an anxiety disorder.

TRANSFERRING A PRESCRIPTION

When transferring prescriptions, especially when it comes to controlled medications, there are specific federal and state laws that both pharmacists and technicians must abide by. If the medication is not a control and was filled at the same pharmacy, but at a different location, the pharmacy technician can transfer the prescription. For example, chain pharmacies have two different numbers on the prescription label. The first is the **order number** and the second is the **store number.** Chain pharmacy software programs link all the stores in the pharmacy chain. The technician is then able to input the order number and store number into the refill field on the computer screen and bring up the refill. If refills are available, the technician can then refill it on the spot for the patient.

When transferring a medication from one pharmacy to another pharmacy, the pharmacy technician will obtain certain information from the patient; the pharmacist needs this information to call the other pharmacy and manually transfer the prescription refill to the local store. The information needed is: the patient's name, address, phone number, allergies, date of birth, insurance information, as well as the previous pharmacy's phone number, prescription number, and the name of the drug. The pharmacist then calls the pharmacy and retrieves the rest of the prescription information such as the dose, dosage strength, quantity, original date filled, amount of refills left, physician's information, and directions for use. It can then be filled with the information retrieved by the technician.

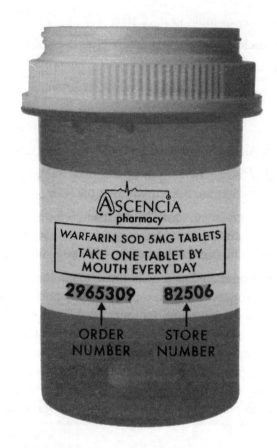

Figure 2.4. Order and Store Numbers on a Prescription Bottle

When transferring controlled substances, laws may differ from state to state. Because CII narcotics require a new prescription each time they are prescribed, this does not pertain to them. But, with CIII to CV controlled substances, some states do allow at least a one-time refill transfer between pharmacies in-state. When it comes to transferring a controlled substance from out of state, it is less common for the state to allow a refill transfer. Even if the state allows a controlled substance to be transferred, it is still up to the pharmacist's discretion to do the transfer.

CONTROLLED SUBSTANCES LISTED IN SCHEDULES III, IV, and V

§1306.25 Transfer between pharmacies of prescription information for Schedules III, IV, and V controlled substances for refill purposes.

(a) The transfer of original prescription information for a controlled substance listed in Schedule III, IV, or V for the purpose of refill dispensing is permissible between pharmacies on a one-time basis only. However, pharmacies electronically sharing a real-time, online database may transfer up to the maximum refills permitted by law and the prescriber's authorization.

(b) Transfers are subject to the following requirements:

(1) The transfer must be communicated directly between two licensed pharmacists.

(2) The transferring pharmacist must do the following:

(i) Write the word *VOID* on the face of the invalidated prescription; for electronic prescriptions, information that the prescription has been transferred must be added to the prescription record.

(ii) Record on the reverse of the invalidated prescription the name, address, and DEA registration number of the pharmacy to which it was transferred and the name of the pharmacist receiving the prescription information; for electronic prescriptions, such information must be added to the prescription record.

(iii) Record the date of the transfer and the name of the pharmacist transferring the information.

(3) For paper prescriptions and prescriptions received orally and reduced to writing by the pharmacist pursuant to §1306.21(a), the pharmacist receiving the transferred prescription information must write the word "transfer" on the face of the transferred prescription and reduce to writing all information required to be on a prescription pursuant to §1306.05 and include:

(i) Date of issuance of original prescription.

(ii) Original number of refills authorized on original prescription.

(iii) Date of original dispensing.

(iv) Number of valid refills remaining and date(s) and locations of previous refill(s).

(v) Pharmacy's name, address, DEA registration number, and prescription number from which the prescription information was transferred.

(vi) Name of pharmacist who transferred the prescription.

(vii) Pharmacy's name, address, DEA registration number, and prescription number from which the prescription was originally filled.

(4) For electronic prescriptions being transferred electronically, the transferring pharmacist must provide the receiving pharmacist with the following information in addition to the original electronic prescription data:

  (i) The date of the original dispensing.

  (ii) The number of refills remaining and the date(s) and locations of previous refills.

  (iii) The transferring pharmacy's name, address, DEA registration number, and prescription number for each dispensing.

  (iv) The name of the pharmacist transferring the prescription.

  (v) The name, address, DEA registration number, and prescription number from the pharmacy that originally filled the prescription, if different.

(5) The pharmacist receiving a transferred electronic prescription must create an electronic record for the prescription that includes the receiving pharmacist's name and all of the information transferred with the prescription under paragraph (b)(4) of this section.

(c) The original and transferred prescription(s) must be maintained for a period of two years from the date of last refill.

(d) Pharmacies electronically accessing the same prescription record must satisfy all information requirements of a manual mode for prescription transferal.

(e) The procedure allowing the transfer of prescription information for refill purposes is permissible only if allowable under existing State or other applicable law.

 Pharmacists have the choice to accept or deny controlled substances at their discretion.

PRACTICE QUESTION

When transferring a prescription from one pharmacy to another, pharmacy technicians can get all the information from the patient and/or patient's prescription bottle for the pharmacist (who then calls for the transfer) EXCEPT for which of the following?

A) patient's name

B) amount of refills left on prescription

C) name of drug

D) pharmacy name

A) Incorrect. The technician can take the patient's name.

B) Correct. The pharmacist confirms the amount of refills left when he or she calls the other pharmacy.

C) Incorrect. The technician can get the name of the drug, but the pharmacist will verify when calling the other pharmacy.

D) Incorrect. The technician can ask the patient for the pharmacy name.

REFILLING PRESCRIPTIONS

There are a few options by which a patient can refill a prescription. Most ambulatory pharmacies have **automated phone systems** that allow a patient to call in refills with the order number on the bottle. When the patient calls the pharmacy, he or she will be prompted by the automated system to input the order number and sometimes the store number (if it is a chain pharmacy). The patient will be asked to verify if the prescription in question is correct. If so, the automated system will then ask the patient for a desired pick-up time. The patient then chooses the pick-up or delivery time. Prompts for this service change depending on the pharmacy.

Most pharmacies also have websites that patients can register with to view their prescription profiles, refill prescriptions, and print out pharmacy records. The patient can sign in to the website, choose the medication to refill, input the pick-up or delivery time, and then the pharmacy can prepare the refill request.

Pharmacies can also refill a patient's maintenance medications automatically a few days before they run out through pharmacy software systems. Then, when the prescription is ready, the automated system will call the patient to advise it is available for pickup. **Maintenance medications** are prescriptions that the patient must take every day to treat a chronic disease or condition.

With advances in technology, patients also have other options they can use to refill prescriptions. For example, some pharmacies have programs that allow patients to use smartphones to photograph the order number on their refill bottles and text the refill request to the pharmacy.

With ambulatory pharmacies, especially community pharmacies, the most important aspect of the job is customer service, including making pharmacy refill services as convenient as possible. So, if the patient would like to speak to the pharmacy staff instead of using the refill services available at the pharmacy, that option is available as well.

Sometimes, a customer will request a refill for a prescription that is out of refills or has passed its expiration date for refills. In these cases, the pharmacy can offer to contact the physician's office on behalf of the patient for a refill. This is asking for a **refill request**. Additionally, patients who also ask for a refill on a prescription that still has refills available is also called a refill request. Refill requests can be faxed to the physician's office, called to the office over the phone, or emailed. Moreover, pharmacies can send refill requests to the physician's office electronically via the Internet. When the physician's office authorizes the refill request, it will send the request back to the pharmacy with the number of refills authorized. This is called a **refill authorization**.

Most refill requests are for maintenance medications. If the medication is a controlled substance, depending on the control class, refills may not be allowed. Also, medications such as antibiotics and cough medications used to treat a temporary ailment most likely will not have refills available. In these cases, the patient may need to contact the doctor's office themselves to request a refill.

When refilling prescriptions, there may be some obstacles. For example, sometimes a patient may have changed physicians or may request a 90-day supply. In these cases, pharmacy technicians may need to send a request to the physician's office with a note stating the changes or call them directly.

Most times, refill requests, once sent through the automated system, will fill automatically. The refill request will be put in a queue and a label will be generated within a specific, designated time period before the patient requested the refill be ready. The **queue** is a file on the pharmacy software system that holds the request until it is due to be refilled. This helps keep an organized workflow in the pharmacy software system. The workflow system helps the pharmacy staff distinguish among prescriptions for patients who are waiting, patients who will soon be coming to pick up a prescription, and patients who requested a refill that will be picked up or delivered in the next couple days.

When a pharmacy technician receives a refill request by phone or in person, he or she will then enter the order number and possibly the store number into the system. For example, using the pharmacy software system, technicians can either manually type the refill number into the appropriate field, or they may use a **scanning system**, scanning barcodes on the labels of bottles directly into the pharmacy software system with a barcode scanner. The way the refill request is inputted in the system depends on the pharmacy and the software system it uses.

When the refill request is pulled up onto the computer screen, the pharmacy technician can then review the information and, if everything is correct, process the refill request. The refill label will then print out.

Telephone communication is an important part of pharmacy customer service. It is important to always remain professional and pleasant when speaking to customers, insurance companies, and physicians' offices. Because of privacy laws (HIPAA), it is also essential for pharmacy technicians to verify with whom they are speaking: directly with the patient or with a person the patient verbally authorizes to receive sensitive information. Verification may include asking patients to identify themselves with specific questions such as name, date of birth, and street address.

PRACTICE QUESTION

Which of the following describes when a prescription has no refills left and the physician's office gives more refills on the prescription?

A) a refill request

B) workflow

C) a refill authorization

D) maintenance medications

Answers:

A) Incorrect. A refill request can either be a patient asking for a refill or the pharmacy calling the physician's office for a refill authorization.

B) Incorrect. Workflow is an organized system in the pharmacy that helps prioritize tasks.

C) Correct. When the physician approves refills for a patient on a prescription that has none left, it is called a refill authorization.

D) Incorrect. Maintenance medications are drugs that the patient needs to take every day for a chronic condition.

DATA ENTRY

When new prescriptions are called in by a physician's office or brought into the pharmacy to be filled, pharmacy technicians input the information through data entry into the patient's profile. Although pharmacy software systems differ, on the screen there will be a field used to look up the patient's profile. This screen may have options such as fields for the patient's name, telephone number, or date of birth. Once the patient's profile is brought up on the screen, the technician can then start entering information needed to fill the prescription.

The most important and first step of this process is **verifying the identity of the patient** by checking the name and date of birth. Then, the software program will prompt the user to add the elements of the prescription into the specific fields. The fields include the name of the drug, strength, dose, refills available, physician's information, and the sig codes. It is very important to understand the sig codes and drug names.

There is also a field for third-party payer adjudication and reimbursement information as well as override codes. When information is placed in this field, the pharmacy can send the prescription request to the third-party payer, along with any override codes such as **DAW (dispense as written)**, used if the doctor does not want the patient to have generic substitutions for medications; the third-party will either accept or deny the request.

Besides entering new and refill prescription requests, pharmacy technicians are also responsible for other tasks that require data entry and computer skills. These tasks will be covered in future chapters. Because there are different software programs used for different pharmacies as well as healthcare settings, technicians are trained upon employment on the software programs the pharmacy uses.

PRACTICE QUESTION

What is the first and most important step taken when inputting new prescriptions for patients?

A) inputting correct prescription information into the correct fields

B) inputting third-party payer information

C) adding override codes

D) being sure to enter the correct information under the correct patient profile

Answers:

A)   Incorrect. While accurately inputting prescription information in the correct fields is important, it is not the first or most important step.

B)   Incorrect. Although important, inputting third-party payer information in the system is not the most important step, nor is it the first.

C)   Incorrect. Pharmacy technicians must be able to code correctly; however, this is not the most important or first step in the process of inputting new prescriptions for patients.

D)   **Correct.** The first and most important step in the process is verifying the accuracy of the information under the patient profile.

THE PATIENT PROFILE

The **patient profile**, in regards to ambulatory pharmacy, serves a few purposes. The first is **identifying the patient.** Using a patient's name, date of birth, address and phone number, the technician can be sure that the correct patient profile is being used. It is important to confirm this personal information with the patient each time he or she comes to drop off or pick up medication. If a patient has moved or changed numbers, the profile must be updated.

The patient profile also contains the patient's **allergy information.** This is a crucial feature of the profile. If the patient is allergic to any drugs, whether prescription or over-the-counter drugs, that information is placed in this field. Additionally, any allergies to vitamins, herbal supplements, topical preparations, eye/ear drops, etc. should be documented in this field as well. Furthermore, it is important to list any foods or dyes the patient has had reactions to. Although not very common, certain drugs derived from food products, such as some kinds of pork and beef insulins, could cause severe allergic reactions. Dyes are important because drug companies use dyes in the binders of drugs for color identification of pills. If a patient does not have allergies, this field would state the patient has no known allergies (NKA).

Current medications are also stored in the patient's profile. Because many drugs interact with one another, knowing the current medications the patient is taking helps the pharmacist recognize any adverse reactions that could be caused by adding a new drug to the patient's drug therapy. Certain drugs can cause very undesirable effects when taken together. Drugs can also interact by reducing or increasing the effectiveness of another drug as well as by altering the amount of the drug in the patient's blood levels. These interactions may require changing the drug or dosage strength. It is critical that over-the-counter medications are recorded as well. Even vitamins and supplements can interact with prescription drugs.

Sometimes, when a patient visits multiple physicians and specialists, he or she may receive a new prescription that can cause either a therapeutic duplication or drug duplication. In these cases it is important that pharmacies keep a record of patients' current medications. **Therapeutic duplications** are when drugs are in the same drug class or have the same function in the body. **Drug duplications** can happen if a drug is prescribed that has an active ingredient that a current medication listed contains as well. For example, if a patient is taking over-the-counter ibuprofen for pain, and a physician prescribes Vicoprofen (a combination of hydrocodone and ibuprofen) there is a drug duplication with the OTC ibuprofen and the ibuprofen in the Vicoprofen. This can also happen with combination drugs. **Combination drugs** are drugs that contain more than one active ingredient.

Medical history is a part of the patient's profile as well. Any medical diseases and conditions can possibly impact the drugs the patient is prescribed. Some of the interactions may be adverse effects. Medical history does not only include the patient; any diseases and condition that could genetically be passed from generation to generation are important to include as well.

Patients with a **history of drug abuse** may be at risk when taking certain prescription drugs. Medications that have a high potential for abuse, such as opioid narcotics, must be monitored by the pharmacist to ensure the patient is taking them as prescribed. The pharmacist may judge it necessary to put certain restrictions on controlled substances such as limiting the quantity distributed.

Any **special considerations** made by the pharmacist, doctor, or patient should also be added to the patent's profile. Here, these could be anything that causes restrictions to the patient such as vision problems, arthritis that causes problems opening bottles, or walking restrictions that may require someone else to pick up a patient's medication and/or delivery options. Language barriers can also be a special consideration. If, for example, a patient speaks and writes only in Spanish, directions can be written in that language.

Insurance carrier information is also added to the patient's profile. This includes the name of the insurance and any third-party payer information needed to process a prescription. Some patients may pay out of pocket for their medications. In this case, it is noted in the profile as a **self-pay**. Other patients may have more than one insurance carrier. For instance, if a patient is on both Medicare and Medicaid, the pharmacy technician could first bill Medicare and then send the remaining copayment to Medicaid for reimbursement. Any other provisions such as copayment information or drugs not covered by the plan can also be added to this area.

On the patient's profile, there will be information on current prescriptions filled and refills available. In this section, information such as date of last refill and copay price at time of service is provided. This information changes with each new fill.

 Keeping the patient profile up-to-date is crucial for the pharmacist's verification process.

PRACTICE QUESTION

Current medications are added to a patient's profile for all EXCEPT which of the following reasons?

A) in case the patient has arthritis and cannot open the bottle

B) to detect therapeutic duplications

C) to detect drug duplications

D) to check for adverse reactions

Answers:

A) **Correct.** Trouble opening bottles is a special consideration.

B) Incorrect. Current medications are noted in a patient's profile to check for therapeutic duplications.

C) Incorrect. Current medications are noted in the patient's profile to check for drug duplications.

D) Incorrect. Current medications are noted in a patient's profile to check for adverse reactions.

MEDICATION THERAPY MANAGEMENT

Medication therapy management (MTM) is a relatively new service in the pharmacy practice and came to be with the passing of the Medicare Modernization Act of 2003. The main concept of MTM is for pharmacists to review a patient's medication history to check for compliance with taking medications, therapeutic duplications, **patient counseling**, and for any other inconsistences in drug therapy. It is used to help reduce healthcare costs by lowering medication costs. Medicare patients should have at least one medication review annually with a pharmacist by phone, face-to-face, or through web-based services.

The most important aspect of MTM is ensuring medication compliance. A patient who is in **compliance** is faithfully taking her or his medication as prescribed. For example, if the patient is prescribed Lisinopril 10mg, to take one tablet by mouth every day, and the patient takes this medication as directed every day, he is in compliance.

If the patient is noncompliant, it means she is not taking medications as directed. She may (either intentionally or unintentionally) be skipping doses, taking another person's medication to avoid copays, or stopping medication altogether. This can be detrimental to a patient's health. The pharmacy technician's role in addressing noncompliance is to refer the patient to the pharmacist for counseling and to help the patient find ways to improve compliance. Some ways to help a patient with noncompliance are calling the physician's office for 90-day supplies on maintenance medications, assisting the patient with delivery and mail-order options, and calling the doctor for refills if no refills are left on maintenance medications.

Pharmacy technicians also assist pharmacists with MTMs by collecting patient information, collecting patient data, and making comprehensive medication review appointments. With MTM, the more information the technician gathers to help the pharmacist counsel the patient, the better. Important information includes income, location, demographics, lifestyle, medical, and pharmaceutical history. Pharmacy technicians also carry out administrative duties associated with MTM. These include collecting copayments for services rendered and documentation of patient records.

Many MTM patients are Medicare recipients who express their opinions about drug therapies, costs, and compliance through comprehensive medication reviews. This gives the pharmacist a chance to intervene for the patient and prevent possible adverse events.

PRACTICE QUESTION

Pharmacy technicians assist pharmacists with all these aspects of MTM EXCEPT which of the following?

A) compliance

B) administrative duties

C) patient counseling

D) collecting patient data

Answers:

A)   Incorrect. Pharmacy technicians assist MTM pharmacists with compliance.

B)   Incorrect. Pharmacy technicians assist with MTM administrative duties.

C)   Correct. Only MTM pharmacists can counsel patients.

D)   Incorrect. Pharmacy technicians assist with collecting patient data.

HEALTH INSURANCE AND THIRD-PARTY PAYERS

Health insurance companies use **third-party payers** for pharmacy billing and reimbursement. Third-party payers are the middle men between the patient and insurance company. They are contracted by insurance companies to collect payments and debts from the patient. The **first-party** is the patient. The patient is the person who is contracted to receive the goods or service. The **second-party** is the health insurance company. The insurance company is providing the service.

For drug benefits, a **pharmacy benefits manager (PBM)** or a **third-party administrator (TPA)** of prescription drug programs for health insurance plans is used by the health insurance company to manage prescription drug benefits. The PBM is an outsourced company and is not the insurance plan itself. When the patient receives a **prescription drug benefit card**, the PBM is listed under the drug benefit section of the card along with information needed for the pharmacy technician to process the claim. Some common PBMs are *Diversified Pharmaceutical Services (DPS)*, *WellPoint Pharmacy Management*, and *Express Scripts*. There are three types of third-party payers. These include:

+ third-party payer full payment groups: **private health insurance companies**
+ third-party contractual payment groups: **Medicare, Medicaid, and Blue Cross Blue Shield**
+ cash payment groups: **self-pay**

With the implementation of the *Affordable Care Act (Obamacare)*, about 84 percent of Americans now have health insurance. There are many companies that offer private health insurance for both individuals and groups. Private health insurance plans are also called **managed care** plans.

Health maintenance organizations (HMOs) usually limit coverage to care from in-network doctors and specialists for a fixed annual fee and/or copayment for services rendered. The patient chooses a primary care doctor from a list of in-network physicians who direct the patient to other services, such as bloodwork, specialist visits, and other therapies needed for personal health and wellness. HMOs normally require prior authorization for services rendered that are not provided by the primary care physician unless in an emergency situation. **Prior authorization** is a referral that authorizes the rendering of goods and services only if the insurance company deems it necessary. HMOs normally have set copayments for each group. Prescription services are listed in a formulary and are normally tiered, which means they have different copayment amounts based on certain factors. **Formularies** are lists of drugs, both brand and generic, that are predetermined by the insurance to be covered based on the level of evidence for its indicated use, cost, and safety considerations. For example:

+ **First Tier Drug:** These are generic drugs. The copay will be the lowest.
+ **Second Tier Drug:** These are preferred brand-name drugs.
+ **Third Tier Drug:** These are non-preferred or **non-formulary** drugs; they have the highest copay.

Preferred provider organizations (PPOs) allow patients to see any in-network physician or specialist without needing a prior authorization, although they need to meet annual deductibles. Benefits are reduced if the patient sees an out-of-network doctor. Depending on the plan prescriptions may be covered as they are by HMOs;

otherwise the patient may pay a percentage of the cost of the prescripti... a deductible.

Point of Service Plans (POS) combine a PPO and an HMO. ... requires an in-network primary care physician, but a patient can get ... services at a higher cost. If a primary care doctor refers a patient for o... ...ork services, the patient is not charged more if the service is authorized. Depending on the prescription coverage, the patient may pay a copayment or a percentage for drugs also based on a formulary.

While the Affordable Care Act made private insurance more accessible for many Americans, millions are covered by government programs.

Medicare is a nationwide, federal program administered by the Centers for Medicare and Medicaid services (CMS). It is the largest medical benefits program in the United States. Medicare became a law in 1965. It provides the same benefits nationally to all citizens sixty-five years of age and older as well as to younger citizens who are blind, widowed, or disabled due to long-term illnesses. Medicare facilitates the **coordination of benefits** to patients for medical and prescription services, helping plans estimate what a patient's payment responsibilities will be and clarify what is covered by the plan for services rendered. Different parts of Medicare help cover specific services.

+ **Medicare Part A** covers hospital services. These services include in-hospital stays, hospice care, long term care, and some home healthcare.

+ **Medicare Part B** helps to cover doctor's appointments and services, outpatient care, medical services, and preventive care.

+ **Medicare Part C** covers Medicare Advantage Plans. These are Medicare benefit health plans managed by private health plans. The private company contracts with Medicare to offer all the benefits from Medicare Part A and B services to the patient. Medicare Advantage Plans can be HMOs, PPOs, Private Fee-For-Service Plans, Special Needs Programs, or Medicare Medical Savings Account Plans. Services are covered by the private plan and are not paid through original Medicare.

+ **Medicare Part D** covers prescription drugs. This is an add-on benefit and can be given through original Medicare or Medicare Advantage Plans. This plan helps to provide better access to important drugs through retail settings.

Also passed in 1965, **Medicaid** is a state and federal medical assistance program for those whose income is below the poverty level. It also supports people who are blind, disabled, or members of a family with dependent children who are only supported by one parent (and financially eligible based on income). State governments choose which services are covered through Medicaid.

There are two types of copay requirements that apply to a Medicaid patient. Some states may require patients to pay providers a small copay when services are rendered. The other requirement is Share-of-Cost. With **Share-of-Cost**, the Medicaid patient may be required to meet a certain monthly payment before Medicaid will start to cover medical services. The amount can change monthly based on a patient's income and other requirements.

The armed services offers **TRICARE**, a health benefits program, to active duty servicemen and servicewomen and to veterans. There are three types of coverage under the TRICARE program.

+ **Standard**: a fee-for-service cost-sharing plan
+ **Extra**: a PPO plan
+ **Prime**: an HMO plan with a POS option

Finally, **worker's compensation** provides insurance to employees who are injured on the job. State law requires that all workers be covered under worker's compensation. Coverage can be limited based on the severity and extent of the injury and is limited to drugs and treatment used to treat the worker's injury. Pharmacy technicians help to call the insurance companies to verify coverage and process prescriptions through online adjudication.

With the introduction of the Affordable Healthcare Act and Medicare Modernization Act, the number of patients who pay out-of-pocket for prescriptions has decreased substantially. However there are cases when a patient's health insurance will not cover a necessary drug, or the patient is underinsured or uninsured. In these cases, the patient is responsible for paying the full amount for their prescriptions. This amount is called the **usual and customary** or the **cash price**.

If a drug is not covered under a patient's drug plan or the patient is uninsured, many drug companies will offer **patient assistance programs (PAPs)**, provided the patient meets certain criteria. These criteria are set by the pharmaceutical drug companies and can vary. Patients fill out an application to the drug company that determines eligibility. If the patient is accepted, the company will then send a 30- or 90-day supply of the drug to the pharmacy and the pharmacist can dispense the medication to the patient at a free or reduced price designated by the drug company.

PRACTICE QUESTIONS

1. Which is NOT a government health plan?

   A) Medicare

   B) private employee group health plans

   C) Medicaid

   D) TRICARE

   Answers:

   A) Incorrect. Medicare is a government plan for Americans over sixty-five years old or who meet certain other criteria.

   B) **Correct.** Private employee group health plans are not government plans.

C) Incorrect. Medicaid is a government health plan for Americans whose income is below the poverty level or who meet certain other criteria.

D) Incorrect. TRICARE is a government health plan for those who presently serve or have served in the military.

2. Which drug tier is for preferred brand names?

A) Tier 1

B) Tier 2

C) Tier 3

D) Tier 4

Answers:

A) Incorrect. Tier 1 is generic drugs.

B) **Correct.** Tier 2 is for preferred drugs.

C) Incorrect. Tier 3 is for non-preferred drugs.

D) Incorrect. Tier 4 is not a category.

3. All of the following are eligible for Medicaid EXCEPT

A) patients who are blind.

B) patients who are disabled.

C) patients whose incomes are below the poverty level.

D) patients above the poverty level who do not work.

Answers:

A) Incorrect. Blind patients are eligible for Medicaid.

B) Incorrect. Disabled patients are eligible for Medicaid.

C) Incorrect. Those patients who live below the poverty level are eligible for Medicaid.

D) **Correct.** Patients who do not work and who live above the poverty level do not qualify for Medicaid.

ONLINE ADJUDICATION AND REIMBURSEMENT

Before a pharmacy technician can bill for a prescription drug, he or she must first collect the insurance card from the patient and enter crucial information from the card into the patient's profile. This information includes:

+ **cardholder's name and ID number:** This is the name of the person, or **beneficiary,** who receives the health insurance; it may differ from that of the patient who brought in the prescription to be filled.

+ **dependent relationship code:** If the patient is not the cardholder, she or he is considered a dependent of the cardholder on a family coverage private group plan. The **dependent** is a family member who is covered under the cardholder's medical benefits. Dependent codes are usually inputted after the cardholder ID number as a two-digit number used to identify the dependent for whom the prescription is being filled. For example, if the cardholder's dependent code is 00, the spouse would be 01, the oldest child would be 02, and so on.

+ **prescription group number:** The group number directs the claim to the specific insurance benefits for that group. The *groups* are a collection of people who have similar benefits packages, such as employee groups.

+ **processor control number (PCN):** This number is used by PBMs for network benefit routing and may change depending on what benefit is being billed.

+ **pharmacy benefit international identification number (BIN):** This number directs the claim to the correct third-party provider. All pharmacy third-party payers have BIN numbers.

+ **date of birth:** The patient's date of birth is used as an identification tool; the date of birth for each person covered is located next to his or her name on the card.

+ **sex code:** The sex code identifies the biological sex of the patient and dependents.

Pharmacies are required to have a NABP number to practice. The **NABP** number is a national identification code that is registered with the National Association of Boards of Pharmacy. Insurance companies and pharmacies use the pharmacy's NABP number for reimbursement purposes. For Medicare, pharmacies must apply for a **national provider identification number (NPI)** through CMS as well. The NPI is used for electronic billing and can be given to a pharmacy as a whole or to the individual pharmacists.

Online adjudication refers to billing third parties for goods and services rendered. It is crucial that information inputted for claim submission is accurate and complete. **Claim submission** is the process of sending a claim to the third-party payer for reimbursement. **Reimbursement** is the compensation given to the pharmacy after collection of the patient's **copay** or **deductible**, a set amount the patient pays for drugs based on the health insurance's **formulary**. The deductible, or **co-insurance**, is the full amount a patient must pay before the health insurance will start charging a copayment and/or covering medications. Reimbursement in the ambulatory settings is usually done as a **retrospective payment**, or **fee-for-service**. The drug is dispensed and later reimbursed through a contractual obligation between the pharmacy and PBMs.

Before sending the claim to the third-party payer, the pharmacy will charge a **dispensing fee** to the claim. The dispensing fee can be a flat fee or a percentage of the selling price that the pharmacy charges for professional services. If the claim is accepted, a **health insurance claim number (HICN)** will be given by the PBM for verification of authorization of the accepted claim.

 If a doctor or patient does not specify a generic substitution, the DAW option must be specified correctly and the prescription must be dispensed as written.

Dispense as written (DAW) codes are specialty codes that are used when a doctor or patient prefers to use a brand name drug even when a generic is available. There are ten codes that can be used, but most insurance companies only recognize a few of them and strictly limit their use. The DAW codes are:

+ **DAW 0**: No product selection is indicated. This code is used when it is acceptable to substitute the generic version of the drug.

+ **DAW 1**: Substitutions are not allowed by the prescriber. This code is used when the doctor deems the brand medication to be medically necessary.

+ **DAW 2**: The patient is requesting the brand-name version of the drug; this code is used when the patient will not take the generic, but the doctor does not deem the brand medically necessary.

+ **DAW 3**: The pharmacist has selected the brand name although substitution is allowed.

+ **DAW 4**: The generic version of the drug is not in stock. Substitution is allowed.

+ **DAW 5**: The brand name version of the drug has been dispensed at generic price; substitution is allowed.

+ **DAW 6**: This is the override code.

+ **DAW 7**: The brand name drug is mandated by law. Substitution is not allowed.

+ **DAW 8**: The generic version of the drug is not available. Substitution is allowed.

+ **DAW 9**: other

The pharmacy technician is responsible for assisting the pharmacist with submitting claims as well as troubleshooting denied and **rejected claims**. Claims can be rejected for a variety of reasons; rejections can often be resolved by contacting the third-party payer. When a claim is rejected, an error code and explanation will appear on the submission screen. Common rejection codes are described below.

+ **Expired coverage**: This occurs if a patient is no longer covered under a certain health plan. Often the patient has changed health insurance plans. This problem can be resolved by asking the patient for his or her new insurance information and updating the information on the patient's profile.

+ **Invalid patient, date of birth, person code, or gender**: This rejection is frequently due to user error either by the technician or insurance company. Technicians can check the patient's profile to see if the correct information has been entered. If information is incorrect, the technician can update the patient's profile with the correct information and resend the claim. In case of further problems, the insurance company may need to be contacted.

+ **Prescribed quantity exceeds limit:** For example, this rejection may occur if the physician writes a prescription for 100 pills for a 100-day supply when the insurance company will only cover a 30-day supply. This error can be fixed by reducing the quantity written to a 30-day supply.

+ **Refill too soon:** This rejection occurs when the prescription is submitted too early for refill; for instance, the patient requests a refill of a 30-day supply of a drug 15 days after it was originally filled. On average, insurance companies allow a grace period to fill refills 5 to 7 days before a prescription is due. If a patient tries to refill earlier, this rejection will come up; normally a date when the prescription can be filled will accompany the rejection. It is important to check with the patient as to why the refill is needed early. In some cases the patient may be taking the medication wrong. The patient should be referred to the pharmacist for patient counseling.

+ **Prescriber not covered:** Occasionally, if a doctor is not a part of an insurance company's in-network group, the rejection *prescriber not covered* may come up on the computer screen. If this is the case, a patient will have to pay out-of-pocket for the medication.

+ **NDC or drug not covered:** Because the NDC number reflects the medication name, the manufacturer, and the packaging, when *NDC not covered* comes up on the rejection screen it normally means that the insurance company will not cover the drug. There are a couple reasons why the drug may not be covered: because it is the brand-name version or because the drug itself is not covered. Brand name prescriptions may need to be replaced by their generic versions. In other cases the patient may need to pay cash for the prescription, or the pharmacy may need to call the doctor to see if the drug can be changed to a therapeutically equivalent drug the company will cover.

+ **Prior authorization required:** Some medications may need special authorization from the doctor; otherwise the insurance company will not cover the medication. In this case, the pharmacy would need to call the doctor to ask that prior authorization be sent to the insurance company for coverage. Once the doctor sends the authorization to the insurance company (and it is approved), the company should remove the rejection so the claim can be submitted.

Sometimes, the insurance company will require **step therapy** before authorizing a prescription. In step therapy, the insurance company requires using a first-line drug, which is a preferred drug, before covering a more expensive alternative.

Codes used to override rejected claims are taught during on-the-job training. Codes can vary depending on the insurance company and/or pharmacy software program.

Health insurance plans will reimburse for drugs based on several formulas. If a generic is available, it is reimbursed by the **maximum allowable cost (MAC)**. The MAC is based upon the lowest cost generic equivalent available.

If a brand name is the only drug available, reimbursement is determined based on either the **average sale price (ASP)** or **the wholesale acquisition cost (WAC)**. The ASP is based on the selling price data from manufacturers as well as volume discounts and price concessions. The WAC is the list price at which the manufacturer sells the drug to the wholesaler. The **average wholesale price (AWP)** is then set at 20 – 25 percent above the WAC and is sold as the **U&C**, or cash, price to **self-pay** customers. Calculating these formulas will be explained in-depth in the pharmacy math chapter of this guide.

The **average manufacturer's price (AMP)** is the average price paid to manufacturers from the wholesalers who only distribute to retail pharmacies. With the introduction of the Affordable Care Act, the government uses the **AMP** to determine the **federal upper limits (FUL)** that are paid through Medicaid. These are the maximum federal matching funds the federal government will pay to state Medicaid programs for eligible drugs. The AMP is 175 percent of the ASP.

Some drugs under Medicare are bundled into an **ambulatory payment classification (APC)** for billing and reimbursement. This normally occurs in ambulatory pharmacy settings such as cancer clinics. APCs are predetermined outpatient payment categories. Biologic or chemotherapy drugs are an example of an APC. In the case of an APC, each drug charge requires a **healthcare common procedure coding system (HCPCS)** code and is billed in service increments. The HCPCS is a federal coding system that uses **Current Procedural Terminology (CPT)**.

> Third-party payer information, including override codes and how the information is entered into the system, can vary between pharmacy software systems and third-party payer companies. The pharmacy setting will train the technician upon hire.

PRACTICE QUESTIONS

1. What is a PCN number on the patient's medical ID card?

   A) a number used by PBMs for network benefit routing; it may change depending on what benefit is being billed

   B) a number that directs the claim to the specific insurance benefits for that group (The groups are collections of people who have similar benefits packages such as employee groups.)

   C) a number that directs the claim to the correct third-party provider

   D) a number that indicates the beneficiary who receives the health insurance (This person may not be the patient who brought the prescription in to be filled.)

Answers:

A) **Correct.** The PCN is used by PBMs for network benefit routing and may change depending on what benefit is being billed.

B) Incorrect. The group number directs the claim to the specific insurance benefits for that group, which is a collection of people with similar benefits packages.

C) Incorrect. The BIN number directs the claim to the correct third-party provider.

D) Incorrect. The cardholder name indicates the beneficiary who receives the health insurance. The patient may not be the beneficiary.

2. Which is NOT a reason for a rejected claim?

A) refill too soon

B) quantity limits exceeded

C) no refills available

D) prior authorization required

Answers:

A) Incorrect. *Refill too soon* is a reason for a rejected claim.

B) Incorrect. Claims may be rejected due to quantity limits exceeded.

C) **Correct.** If there was no refill available on the prescription, the claim would not have been sent in the first place.

D) Incorrect. If prior authorization is required, a claim may be rejected.

3. The WAC is

A) based on the selling price data from manufacturers as well as volume discounts and price concessions.

B) the list price for which the manufacturer sells the drug to the wholesaler.

C) the average price paid to manufacturers by the wholesalers, which only distribute to retail pharmacies.

D) the maximum of federal matching funds the federal government will pay to state Medicaid programs for eligible drugs.

Answers:

A) Incorrect. The ASP is based on the selling price data from manufacturers as well as volume discounts and price concessions.

B) **Correct.** The WAC is the list price that the manufacturer sells the drug to the wholesaler.

C) Incorrect. The AWP is the average price paid to manufacturers from the wholesalers, who only distribute to retail pharmacies.

D) Incorrect. The FUL is the maximum of federal matching funds the federal government will pay to state Medicaid programs for eligible drugs.

4. A retrospective payment is also known as which of the following?

A) the point of service

B) dispensing fee

C) the APC

D) fee-for-service

Answers:

A) Incorrect. Point of service is a type of health insurance plan.

B) Incorrect. Dispensing fees are a fee pharmacies charge for professional services.

C) Incorrect. APC is ambulatory payment classification.

D) **Correct.** Retrospective payments are also fee-for-service.

INSURANCE FRAUD

Health insurance fraud is when a person or organization intentionally misrepresents, deceives, or conceals another person or organization with unauthorized benefits and/or claims. Fraud is considered a felony and can result in severe fines and possible jail time as well as loss of license or certification, and/or disciplinary actions. If a government plan such as Medicare is involved with the fraud, it then becomes a federal offense, and federal laws will apply.

Fraud can be proven by showing intent to practice a fraudulent act or intent to commit a major offense. Some common examples of health insurance fraud include the following:

+ billing for services not rendered
+ altering monetary amounts on claims
+ leaving information deemed important off of an insurance claim
+ using another person's insurance card
+ billing for duplicate payment

Being knowledgeable and staying current on any changes when processing insurance claims helps a pharmacy technician avoid legal and ethical issues. Some important ways to avoid these problems are:

+ keeping updated on changes in state and federal law
+ identifying and double-checking procedures to be sure they are correct
+ ensuring accuracy of coding
+ discussing any concerns or doubts with a supervisor
+ obtaining prior authorization from the doctor if needed

PRACTICE QUESTION

Which is NOT considered an example of fraud?

A) using another person's insurance card

B) billing a claim with correct information on it

C) billing for services not rendered

D) altering monetary amounts on a claim

Answers:

A) Incorrect. Use of another person's card is considered fraud.

B) Correct. Billing a claim with the correct information on it is not fraud.

C) Billing for services not rendered is fraud.

D) Altering monetary amounts on a claim is fraud.

FILLING, PACKAGING, AND LABELING THE PRESCRIPTION ORDER

Once the prescription is entered in the computer and the claim is accepted, a pharmacy label is generated. The **pharmacy label** has the information needed for the patient to correctly take the medication as well as important information for refilling and contacting the pharmacy. The information on the label includes

+ the patient's name and address.
+ the date for prescription refill and the date of the most recent refill.
+ the original prescription date, which indicates the date when the prescription was first filled.
+ the beyond-use date or expiration date (usually a year after the prescription was last filled).
+ the order number, a six-digit number followed by the store number, which is a five-number sequence.
+ the drug manufacturer and NDC number for verification of the drug. Pharmacy technicians use the NDC number to be sure they are filling the prescription with the correct drug by matching the NDC on the label with the NDC on the manufacturer's bottle.
+ the name, dose, and dosage strength of the drug.
+ the dispense quantity of the drug, which is dictated by the patient's insurance. For example, if a prescription is written for 100 pills and the insurance only allows 90 pills at a time, the quantity dispensed would be 90.
+ the signa, or directions for use. The sig code directions from the original prescription will be deciphered into easily understandable directions for the patient.
+ the number of refills available.

+ the pharmacy's name, address, and phone number.

+ the prescribing doctor's name.

+ the initials of the pharmacist who will be verifying the prescription.

+ the initials of the pharmacy technician who entered the prescription in the system.

+ warning or auxiliary labels. These labels are stickers that are placed on the prescription vial to warn against contradictions or indications while taking the medication. For example: "Do not drink alcoholic beverages while taking this medicine."

When the technician receives the label, the first step is to verify the information on the label with the information on the prescription. Always check the drug name, dosage strength, dose, quantity, physician name, patient name, and directions. If there are any issues or questions that arise, always ask the data-entry technician or pharmacist before filling.

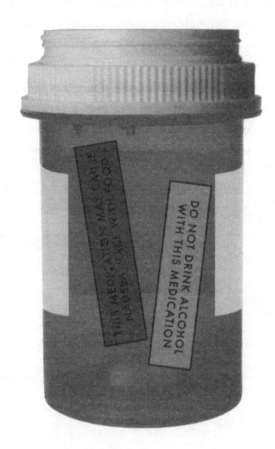

Figure 2.5. Warning Labels

After checking and verifying the prescription with the label, the next step is to find the correct medication on the shelf. The technician then matches the NDC number on the bottle to the NDC number on the label. This is a very important step. By verifying the NDC numbers, the technician is making sure to fill the correct medicine. The **NDC number** is comprised of a group of numbers spaced into three groups: the labeler, product code, and package code. For example, the NDC number for Prozac 20mg capsules in a 100-count bottle would look like this:

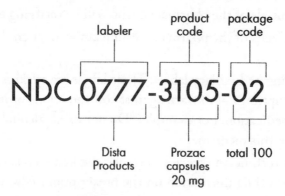

Figure 2.6. NDC Number

For verification purposes, some pharmacies provide a picture of the drug on the label or on the paperwork that accompanies the prescription. Occasionally an issue may arise where, for example, the generic manufacturer the pharmacy normally uses is unavailable, and so a different generic manufacturer must be used. In such cases the label must be changed to reflect the correct drug and NDC number used.

After the correct drug is chosen, the pharmacy technician then checks the quantity to be filled as indicated on the label and uses a **counting tray** to count out the correct number of pills. Again, accuracy is very important; work should be double-checked.

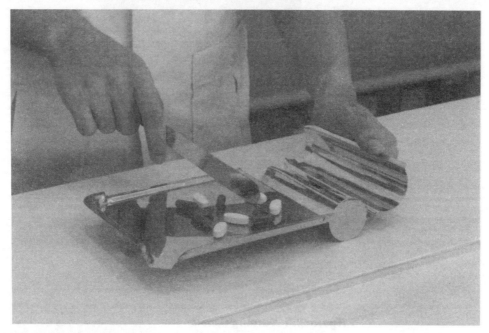

Figure 2.7. Counting Tray

Some pharmacies have **automated counting machines** for commonly used medications. When a label is generated, the machine will count out the correct number of pills. However, automated counting systems can miscount due to technical problems or if they need maintenance, so it is always important to make sure equipment is working properly.

Once the correct number of pills has been counted out to dispense, the technician chooses the correct dram vial or bottle to store the pills or liquid. **Dram vials** are usually amber; this color protects the pills from light degradation. A dram is a unit of English measurement that has been used for centuries. One dram is the equivalent of one-eighth of an ounce. Dram vials come in many different sizes. Some common sizes used in the pharmacy are the 8-, 16-, 20-, 30-, 40-, and 60-dram vials. Bottles are measured in ounces and milliliters. The most common sizes are: 30 ml (1 oz.), 60 ml (2 oz.), 90 ml (3 oz.), 120 ml (4 oz.), 180 ml (6 oz.), and 240 ml (8oz.).

Figure 2.8. Prescription Bottle

Some ambulatory pharmacies that work with nursing home and long-term care facilities use blister packaging for patients. **Blister packaging** helps the patient improve compliance; each dose is marked by date and time, and the medications are easily popped out of the package when the dose is due. Consequently, blister packaging helps not only the patient but also the nurse remember if a dose was taken.

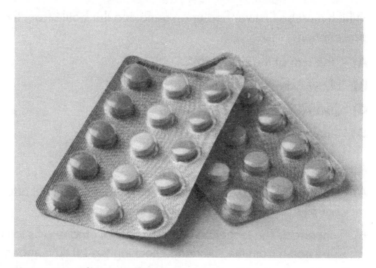

Figure 2.9. Blister Packages

The next step is to place the cap on the dram vial. Most caps can be placed on vials in two ways. In one way, the cap twists on and off easily; in the other, the bottle is childproofed. Due to the Poison Prevention Packaging Act of 1970, caps must be childproofed unless otherwise specified by the patient.

After the cap is placed on the vial, it is then labeled with both the prescription label and any auxiliary labels required. After the technician double-checks his or her work for accuracy, the vial can then be sent to the pharmacist along with the manufacturer's bottle for verification.

> 🔍 It is always important to double-check each step throughout the filling process. Medication errors are one of the leading and most preventable causes of hospitalization and death in the United States. Efficiency is important, but accuracy is crucial.

PRACTICE QUESTIONS

1. Which is not required to be on a prescription label?

A) a picture of the drug

B) the order number

C) directions for use

D) the patient's name

Answers:

A) **Correct.** A picture of the drug is not required on a prescription label.

B) Incorrect. The order number must be displayed on the prescription label.

C) Incorrect. The prescription label must include the directions for use.

D) Incorrect. The patient's name must be on the prescription label.

2. Which must be first verified upon removing the bottle from the shelf when filling a prescription?

A) the size of the dram vial

B) how many pills to count

C) the NDC number

D) the patient's name on the label

Answers:

A) Incorrect. The size of the vial is not determined until after the correct number of pills has been counted out to disperse.

B) Incorrect. The technician determines how many pills to count after removing the bottle from the shelf and checking the NDC number.

C) **Correct.** The NDC number must be checked immediately when removing the bottle from the shelf.

D) Incorrect. The technician verifies the patient's name before taking the bottle off the shelf.

CONTROLLED DRUG DISPENSING

A **controlled substance** refers to a drug that can be habit-forming; these are closely monitored and documented. Although controlled substances will be discussed in depth in chapter three, it is important to specify what is generally expected from the pharmacy technician during the fill process in regard to these medications.

When entering a controlled prescription in the computer, it is important to check the patient's profile for any recently filled controlled medications that may be therapeutically equivalent to the drug prescribed. If any have been recently filled, suggesting the patient is already on a therapeutically equivalent drug, the pharmacy technician should refer the patient to the pharmacist for patient counseling. Controlled medications are filled at the pharmacist's discretion, so the pharmacist should be aware of any issues with them.

Pharmacy technicians should also check the signature of the physician, ink color, number of refills, quantity, and the Drug Enforcement Agency (DEA) number on the hard copy. As explained earlier, any discrepancies on the hard copy of the prescription could signify a forged or fraudulent prescription. Chapter three details a formula that verifies the accuracy of the DEA number on the prescription.

When filling a controlled substance, it is important to double count the medication. After double counting, circle the quantity and then initial next to the quantity of the medication. This is a verification method used by pharmacies to show the medication has been double counted and the quantity is correct. Quantities of controlled substances are closely monitored and recorded, so it is important to be extra vigilant when preparing them.

 If a patient brings in a fraudulent or forged controlled substance prescription, what legal consequences could the patient face?

PRACTICE QUESTION

If pharmacy technicians have any questions about dispensing a controlled substance medication, they should

A) ask the lead pharmacy technician.

B) enter the prescription into the software system and see if the insurance approves or rejects it.

C) dispense the medication at their own risk.

D) ask the pharmacist for guidance.

Answers:

A) Incorrect. Pharmacy technicians should direct questions about controlled substances directly to the pharmacist, not the lead technician.

B) Incorrect. Questions about controlled substances should first be referred to the pharmacist, not to the insurance company.

C) Incorrect. Pharmacy technicians should never fill controlled substances at their own risk.

D) **Correct.** The pharmacist can fill a controlled substance at his or her discretion, so if the technician has any questions about a controlled substance, they should direct it to the pharmacist.

Pharmacist Verification

After the prescription is prepared, the pharmacy technician then gives the prescription to the pharmacist for **verification**. When a pharmacist is verifying a prescription, he or she compares the original hard copy against the bottle label to make sure the information was entered correctly. The pharmacist will also open the bottle to check the pills for the correct color, imprints, and shape as well inspect the drug by checking the NDC number on the stock bottle to the NDC number on the label. It is important that the pharmacist is not interrupted during this process, allowing for a thorough check of the prescription for accuracy.

It is crucial to bring any concerns about the prescription to the pharmacist before the verification process. This way, the pharmacist can investigate and resolve these problems while verifying and is finished before the patient is due to pick up the prescription.

The pharmacist visually checks the prescription for accuracy and then will pull up the patient's profile to check for any therapeutic discrepancies. Many third-party payers have **drug utilization reviews** (DUR) that are sent electronically at the time the claim is sent from the pharmacy to the third-party payer. DURs identify problems such as therapeutic duplications, drug-disease contraindications, incorrect dosages, incorrect duration of treatments, drug allergies, and drug misuse. These indications also have different levels of severity and are resolved in order, based on whether it is a high, moderate or low contraindication. Depending on the DUR, the prescription may not be accepted as a claim by the third-party payer until the pharmacist checks the issue, approves dispensation of the medication, and puts the appropriate override in the correct field on the rejection screen on the computer.

If the prescription cannot be filled because of insurance issues, a need to contact the physician, or any other concerns, the pharmacist will place the information aside until the issue is resolved and/or the patient can be contacted. It is important to contact the patient as soon as possible. Sometimes the patient can clarify information that can help solve the problem. If not, it is important for the pharmacy staff to take the extra steps needed to dispense the medication. This includes calling the physician's office and insurance companies for overrides, changes in therapy, or drug changes.

Once any issues have been resolved and the pharmacist is sure the prescription is filled accurately, the medication is then placed in a bag with paperwork that lists the patient's name and important information about the drug. The bag is then placed alphabetically in bins for patient pick-up.

An ambulatory pharmacist's primary duties include the following: monitoring dosages for patients, assisting customers with OTC medications, signing all medication records counseling patients, providing vaccinations, verifying prescriptions, calling doctors and nurses when necessary, and maintaining perpetual inventory of CII narcotics.

PRACTICE QUESTION

Which of the following does NOT fall under the purview of a DUR?

A) duplicate therapies

B) substitution of a different generic if the usual generic medication is not available

C) drug-disease contraindications

D) drug allergies

Answers:

A) Incorrect. DURs identify drug therapies.

B) **Correct.** The third-party payer will not know if a different generic manufacturer needs to be used.

C) Incorrect. A DUR must account for drug-disease contraindications.

D) Incorrect. Drug allergies would appear in a DUR.

DISPENSING MEDICATION TO PATIENTS

There are several ways patients may receive their medications. Many community pharmacies have a drive-through for picking up and dropping off medications. This is convenient for many reasons. For example, if a patient is sick, has an ill child, or has problems walking, there is no need to enter the store. Patients drive up to the pharmacy, give the same information to the pharmacy as they would if they came in, and come back to the drive-through to pick up at a later time. Other options are delivery or mail order. These are convenient for patients who do not have transportation or are too ill to leave the house.

No matter which way patients pick up their medications, the most important step when dispensing medication is verifying patient identity. Due to the Health Insurance Portability and Accountability Act (HIPAA), which will be discussed at length in chapter three, privacy is crucial; thus ascertaining patient identity must be done as inconspicuously as possible.

Pharmacy technicians follow these steps when dispensing medication:

1. Greet the patient. Always be sure other customers are at a safe distance from the patient you are assisting, so they cannot hear private information.

Most pharmacies ask other patients to stay a certain distance from the pick-up window for this purpose.

2. Determine the type of medication the patient is picking up (new, refill, narcotics, and refrigerated drugs may be stored in different areas based on the pharmacy's operations).

3. Verify the patient's name (other identifiers such as date of birth or phone number confirm identity in cases of common names).

4. Further confirm the patient's identity by verifying address or phone number after collecting the medication.

5. Verify the drug(s) and its price, and determine if the patient has any other prescriptions to pick up. This resolves questions about the medication and cost; it also ensures the patient receives his or her full order.

6. If the medication must be **reconstituted** (i.e., a powdered drug must be mixed with water to make a suspension), the patient should be advised of this and that it will cause a delay. Depending on pharmacy operations, this may need to be done by a pharmacist.

7. Scan or ring up the order and advise the patient of the total price.

8. For any controlled substances, pharmacy technicians must check a valid picture ID and have the patient sign for the medication. Patients may authorize representatives to pick up controlled medications: the representatives must bring the patient's photo ID (as well as their own) and the patient must authorize the representative to sign for the drug. Some states may require patients to sign for other services as well.

9. Determine if the patient has any questions about the medication(s). This is strongly encouraged for new prescriptions. Patients may meet the pharmacist at the consultation window at the pharmacy after payment.

10. Pharmacy technicians must collect payment from the patient. If the patient is paying cash, the correct change must be counted out. If the patient is paying by credit or debit card, the card must be returned and the charge slip signed.

The way pharmacy technicians greet patients reflects upon the pharmacy and store as a whole. The pharmacy staff should display professionalism and courtesy at all times during the dispensing process. Patients with disabilities may need special assistance; however, it is important to ask the patient first if help is needed as many such patients are self-sufficient. The most important aspect of working with patients is to be aware and keep a positive attitude.

? Why is it so important to ask patients if they have any questions or need counseling on a medication when they drop off or pick up a prescription?

OTHER DUTIES ASSIGNED IN AN AMBULATORY SETTING

In addition to assisting in the dispensing process, pharmacy technicians are required to help with other tasks in the ambulatory pharmacy setting. The tasks listed below must be performed regularly to keep the pharmacy efficient and organized. Other tasks may be assigned to the pharmacy technician based on the individual pharmacy's needs.

Daily Tasks

+ returning stock bottles and other medications to shelves
+ maintaining perpetual inventory of controlled substances (Quantities on hand must be verified before, during, and after dispensing.)
+ returning prescriptions to stock that were not picked up by the patient
+ **stocking** and restocking shelves after orders are shipped
+ **filing** hard copy prescriptions (Non-controls are filed numerically by order number and date; controlled substances are filed separately by order number and date.)
+ replenishing supplies such as vials, caps, and liquid bottles
+ **general cleaning up** (wiping down counters, counting trays and spatulas with disinfectants, cleaning up garbage bags, vacuuming)

 Pharmacy trash must be HIPAA compliant. Patient information must be shredded and disposed of separately from regular pharmacy trash.

Monthly Tasks

+ **cycle counts**: counting the medications and medical devices in stock
+ **checking expiration dates** on stock bottles in stock, marking items that are expiring within sixty days, and removing expired items from the shelves (Expired items may be destroyed or returned to the manufacturer for credit.)

PRACTICE QUESTION

Which responsibility is NOT considered a daily task?

A) general clean up

B) filing hard copies of prescriptions

C) cycle counts

D) returning used stock bottles to shelves

Answers:

A) Incorrect. General cleaning up should be done daily.

B) Incorrect. Hard copies of prescriptions are filed every day.

C) **Correct.** Cycle counts are done on a monthly basis.

D) Incorrect. Returning stock bottles is a daily task.

Institutional (Hospital) Pharmacy

Institutional, or hospital, pharmacy refers to an inpatient pharmacy. In this pharmacy setting, pharmacy technicians work in a **health system** environment. Health systems are large settings with many different units and departments that are devoted to patient care. The pharmacy technicians in an institutional setting do not work directly with the patients. Instead, they work with the nurses and doctors on the nursing units delivering medications, stocking medications, processing orders, filling patient-specific unit-dose orders, and making IV admixtures.

In institutional pharmacy, pharmacy technicians do not bill the patient for medication separately from other medical services. Medication billing is done by the hospital billing department by coding and billing all diagnosis-related services given to the patient during the hospital stay into groups called **diagnosis-related groups (DRG)**. This helps determine the payments made to the hospital by the patient's health insurance. DRG was implemented in the 1980s as part of a **prospective payment system (PPS)**, which classifies each hospital case by the type of diagnosis, the patient, the procedures done, complications, and resources used. The hospital stays are then covered for the patient after a deductible is met or a copay has been paid.

To offset high drug costs in the hospital, programs are available that reduce the cost of drugs for covered entities such as hospitals and cancer centers. The **340B program**, established in 1992 as a federal law, reduces costs: drug manufacturers give discounts to hospitals in exchange for putting the drug on the hospital formulary.

PROCESSING A MEDICATION ORDER

The medication order in institutional pharmacy is equivalent to the prescription in ambulatory pharmacy. The medication order starts with the physician. All medications the patient is taking including OTC products are written on a medication order by the physician, and then all of the drugs including any OTC medications are filled in the institutional pharmacy. Once the medication is entered in the pharmacy system, nurses can then access the medication on the **medication administration record (MAR)**. The MAR alerts nurses as to when the medication needs to be administered.

The fill process begins in the pharmacy when a copy of the medication order is sent to the pharmacy from the nursing unit. Due to electronic health records in hospitals, medication orders can be entered electronically by the provider and put in the queue for pharmacists to verify; then the order can be filled by the technician.

Medication orders must contain certain information. All orders require the **patient's name, weight, height, allergies, and date of birth**. Medications in the hospital are more patient specific, especially IV admixtures, so height, weight, and age are used for formulating IV preparations. Orders must also include information about the **patient's medical condition** because knowledge of the medical condition and past conditions is important in case of therapeutic contraindications. For accurate billing and documentation, orders require the **patient's medical record number**; they should also have the **patient's hospital room number and nursing unit floor** to indicate where the order will be sent during delivery.

All medication orders must show the **exact dosage form of the drug**, including solutions, IV admixtures, tablet, etc.; furthermore, the **dosage strength** must be clearly indicated. Certain IV preparation drugs must be exact. For example, a NICU TPN administered to a baby requires very small quantities of vitamins and minerals as based upon the baby's blood work. Medication orders must also indicate the **drug and dosage schedule**. The dosage schedule states how often the drug is to be administered during the hospital stay. It is normally represented in military time for a 24-hour period. For example, if a patient is taking a drug every 6 hours, the times would be written as follows: 6:00, 12:00, 18:00, 24:00. In addition, the order must include **drug preparation instructions**. IV medication orders usually specify the **concentration**—the strength or percentage—of the drug required in the **base solution**, or IV fluid. They also indicate the **volume**, or amount of the IV admixture, needed for one dose. All orders contain **directions for use**, which explain how to take the medication, and the **route of administration**, which specifies whether the drug is taken by mouth, intramuscularly, intravenously, etc.

It is important for the pharmacy technician to distinguish the different orders within a medication order. For instance, physicians will order lab work and tests on the same order as the medication is written on, meaning those orders are meant to be used in a different hospital unit. This is why it is so important to have an understanding of the abbreviations and drugs used in the pharmacy setting. Some common unit acronyms used in the hospital are:

+ **CATH**: Cardiac Catheterization Lab
+ **CCU**: Coronary or Cardiac Care Unit
+ **ED or ER**: Emergency Room
+ **ENDO**: Endoscopy
+ **L & D**: Labor and Delivery
+ **MICU**: Medical Intensive Care Unit
+ **NICU**: Neonatal Intensive Care Unit
+ **OR**: Operating Room
+ **PACU**: Post-Anesthesia Care Unit
+ **PEDS**: Pediatrics
+ **SICU**: Surgical Intensive Care Unit
+ **TCU**: Transitional Care Unit
+ **X-RAY**: Radiology

Besides being able to distinguish between the different orders on a medication order, the pharmacy technician will also encounter different types of medication orders. **Scheduled medication orders** are for medications given on a continuous, around-the-clock schedule. Pharmacy technicians prepare enough of a scheduled order to last for a 24-hour period. **Scheduled intravenous (IV)** or **total parenteral nutrition (TPN) orders** are for injectable medications that be prepared and taken on an around-the-clock schedule. Next, **as-needed (PRN) orders** are orders given when a medication is used in response to a specific parameter or condition. Absent such conditions, the medication is not provided. Finally, **controlled substance medication orders** are given when a narcotic that requires proper documentation of dispensing and administration is being used. In a hospital pharmacy, controlled medications are normally stored in a narcotics room that is occupied by a pharmacist who is scheduled to work with narcotics orders for that workday.

PREPARATION OF ORDERS

When working in institutional pharmacy, pharmacy technicians are responsible for preparing patient-specific medications and IV admixtures in the sterile room. The **sterile room** is where medication is **compounded**, or prepared by hand with one or more ingredients under sterile conditions, for intravenous and/or sterile use. In this section, we will be discussing the procedures used to prepare patient-specific orders. Because preparation of **compounded sterile preparations (CSPs)**, which are also known as **IV admixtures**, is an in-depth procedure that requires extra training, IV admixtures will be covered separately in chapter five.

In a hospital pharmacy, there is the central pharmacy and decentralized pharmacy units. The **central pharmacy** is the center of pharmacy operations in a hospital or healthcare facility. It is where compounding occurs, medications are prepared, medication orders are entered, and drugs are unit-dosed.

In a hospital pharmacy, all medications distributed to the patient are **unit-dosed**. Most of the time, pharmacies order drugs from the manufacturer that are already unit-dosed. This means they are already placed in blister packages where the unit of medication is put in its own package labeled with the lot number, expiration date, NDC

Figure 2.10. Manufacturer-Ordered Unit-Dose Medication

number, and the name of the drug. Unit-dose medications in hospital pharmacy are used for efficiency, making it easier to keep inventory in the automated dispensing machines, and to help control costs. When a medication is only available in a stock bottle, the pharmacy is required to use a unit-dose drug distribution system to make its own unit doses.

Patient-specific medications are prepared in the hospital pharmacy when the order calls for a medication that is not already available in the nursing unit med room in an **automated dispensing machine** such as an Accudose, Suremed, or Pyxis. These areas are **decentralized pharmacies.**

A list of medications required to be filled in the central pharmacy is computed every day. The pharmacy technician will then print out labels for each medication needed within a 24-hour period, fill the medication, label the medication, and put it aside for the pharmacist to verify. Once the pharmacist verifies the order, the pharmacy technician then delivers the medications to the nursing unit and places the prescription in the patient-specific bins in the decentralized pharmacy.

The pharmacy technician is also responsible for filling the medications in the automated dispensing machines when inventory is low. Most hospital pharmacies refill the machines twice daily or when the pharmacy is alerted by the nursing units that they ran out of a medication in the machine. Automated dispensing machines help reduce medication errors because the medication is dispensed from the machine based on the patient's order and time due on the nurse's MAR. Moreover, they are convenient for both the nurses and the pharmacy staff because they keep track of inventory and keep the medication in the machine organized.

Besides patient-specific medications not loaded in the automated drug dispensing machine, STAT drugs are also filled. **STAT drugs** are drugs that are needed as soon as possible; these could be unit-dose medications or IV admixtures. In these cases, a label will print in the pharmacy, the technician will prepare it right away, place the label on the medication, have the pharmacist check the medication, and deliver it as soon as possible directly to the nurse or doctor who needs it.

The IV pharmacy technician also prepares the CSPs needed for the day in the central pharmacy. Every day, CSP labels needed for the patients in the hospital are generated for a 24-hour period, and the IV pharmacy technician prepares them for delivery.

PRACTICE QUESTION

What is NOT a reason that unit-dose medications are used in institutional pharmacy?

A) to cut costs

B) for efficiency

C) so technicians do not need to count out pills

D) for easier inventory in automated dispensing machines

Answers:

A)   Incorrect. Unit-dosing is used to cut costs.

B)   Incorrect. Unit-dosing does improve efficiency.

C)   **Correct.** Although it makes work easier for technicians, unit-dosing in hospital pharmacy is not intended to relieve technicians from counting out pills.

D)   Incorrect. Unit-dosing facilitates inventory in automated dispensing machines.

DELIVERY OF MEDICATION

Pharmacy technicians are responsible for the delivery of medications in the institutional pharmacy setting. When the patient-specific medications are generated and processed, the pharmacy technician delivers the medication to the decentralized pharmacy at the **nursing stations** of the unit. The labels generated tell the technician which nursing unit the patient is in, the **patient's room number**, the patient's name, his or her date of birth, and the **medical record number**.

The same process is used for CSPs. Once the IV pharmacy technician finishes the IV batches for the day, they are placed on a cart and delivered to the patient-specific bin located in the nursing units. The labels generated for CSPs have the same information on them as the labels used for patient-specific medications.

Pharmacy technicians are also required to fill the automated dispensing machines. When a medication in the automated dispensing machine goes below par levels, an alert is generated through the pharmacy software system to the central pharmacy. Unless a medication is completely out in the automated dispensing machine, the technician will print out an order from each nursing unit to see what medication needs to be replenished. The technician will then prepare the medications to be delivered by nursing unit; the pharmacist will compare the drug with what is written on the order generated and verify the medication is correct. Once the pharmacist verifies the order, the technician can then fill the under par medication in the automated dispensing machine in the nursing units.

While delivering medications, technicians carry out a census to check if a patient has been discharged or is still in the hospital. When a patient is discharged, the technician will send unused medications back to the central pharmacy to credit the patient, destroy unused IV medications, and return medications to stock. A **census** shows a count of patients and which ones are still in the hospital. It is important to stress privacy laws and the importance of not allowing other co-workers, patients, and visitors to view the medication cart and census while the technician is making rounds within the hospital.

> It is important for hospital pharmacy technicians to return unused medications from patients' bins to the central pharmacy because the room used by the patient can be filled quickly with a new patient, which may create issues for the nursing staff.

The medication should also be returned so the unused medications can be credited to the patient's account quickly, avoiding unnecessary hospital charges on the patient's bill.

PRACTICE QUESTION

Which of the following is NOT required to be on a label in hospital pharmacy?

A) patient's address

B) patient's name

C) patient's room number

D) patient's medical record number

Answers:

A) **Correct.** The patient's address is not needed on a hospital label.

B) Incorrect. The patient's name is required on a hospital label.

C) Incorrect. The patient's room number must be listed on a hospital label.

D) Incorrect. The hospital label must display the patient's medical record number.

Pharmacy Automation

Pharmacy automation is always growing as new technologies develop. Although **pharmacy automation** is not required to practice pharmacy, the use of pharmacy automation helps improve efficiency and accuracy in both institutional and ambulatory pharmacy settings.

Improving pharmacy efficiency, **carousel technology** reduces technician travel time, bending, and reaching in the fill process. The rotating shelving also allows pharmacies to take advantage of space in the pharmacy that is not being utilized. Meanwhile, **centralized robotic dispensing technology** automatically dispenses medication when the label is generated. **Unit-dose medication repacking systems** are used to unit dose medications in stock bottles in the centralized pharmacy; to facilitate compounding, **IV and TPN compounding devices** are automatic pumping systems that can compound several sterile ingredients into a finished solution dispensed in a single patient bag without being manually touched by the technician. Finally, **pneumatic tube delivery systems** help avoid contamination of products by delivering products in a tube similar to those used at drive-through pharmacies and banks.

Technology also reduces errors. **Barcode administration technology** reduces medication errors by using a barcode on the patient's label that matches the inpatient's barcode and is required to be scanned before medication is administered. **Clinical decision support-based infusion pumps,** also called smart pumps, are used to avoid medication errors by reducing manual programming. The **electronic clinical documentation system** helps to reduce errors in distribution of medications and nurse documentation. **Clinical decision support software** helps reduce medication errors and detect **adverse drug events (ADE)**; similarly, **computerized physician order entry** prevents handwriting mistakes on medication orders and is being implemented in hospitals. **Centralized narcotic dispensing and tracking devices** help keep controlled substance counts accurate; if a problem does arise, the pharmacist is able to track the issue through the pharmacy system to determine the cause of error.

Figure 2.11. Pneumatic Tube Delivery

Finally, technology helps with medication management. **Web-based compliance and disease management tracking systems** help track patient compliance in taking maintenance medications; they also track disease management through software systems connected to physicians' offices, hospitals, and pharmacies.

PRACTICE QUESTION

Which pharmacy automation is used to make CSPs without manual touch by a technician?

A) web-based compliance and disease management tracking systems

B) IV and TPN compounding devices

C) barcode administration technology

D) carousel technology

Answers:

A) Incorrect. Web-based compliance and disease management tracking systems are used for tracking patient compliance and disease management.

B) **Correct.** IV and TPN compounding devices prevent technicians from manually preparing sterile preparations.

C) Incorrect. Barcode administration technology helps prevent medication errors as the nurse must check the barcode on the patient with the barcode on the medication label.

D) Incorrect. Carousel technology reduces a technician's travel time, bending, and reaching in the fill process. The rotating shelving also allows pharmacies to take advantage of space in the pharmacy that is not being utilized.

Investigational Drug Data

Investigational new drugs (IND), when not being used in clinical trials, may sometimes be requested by a physician for a patient when all other medications and treatments have been exhausted. When INDs are used in pharmacy settings, such as ambulatory and institutional, certain **protocols** must be met.

At first, an application for patient use must be completed by the physician and sent to the **Food and Drug Administration (FDA)** for approval. There are two categories for investigational drugs:

+ INDs may be used in an institution as a format protocol.

+ Through authorization by the FDA and the manufacturer, an IND may be used for a single patient on a one-time basis.

Either way, the physician is responsible for ordering the drug; the pharmacy staff will then handle the **special recordkeeping** and inventory management associated with the distribution of the drug to the patient. However when INDs are used for pharmaceutical research, they are managed differently. In those cases clinical trials are used, and the pharmacist would be responsible for ordering, dispensing, and inventory management. **Placebos**, or pills without the drug's active ingredient, are not used in these cases either.

Although not all pharmacies participate in IND protocols, pharmacy technicians who do participate are responsible for preparing, handling, record keeping, perpetual inventory, and inventory management of the IND. Although in these instances dispensing INDs is not considered a clinical trial, data is still collected on patient response to the drug.

PRACTICE QUESTION

The pharmacy technician is responsible for all the responsibilities involving INDs EXCEPT which of the following?

A) inventory management

B) handling

C) preparing

D) ordering

Answers:

A) Incorrect. Technicians are responsible for inventory management.

B) Incorrect. Technicians must handle INDs.

C) Incorrect. Preparing INDs is the responsibility of the technician.

D) Correct. Technicians are not responsible for ordering INDs; physicians are.

THREE: PHARMACY LAW & ETHICS

The pharmacy practice is managed by laws, regulations, and rules that are enforced by both federal and state governments. Pharmacy practice is also regulated by the policies and procedures of the individual healthcare settings where pharmacy technicians are employed. Pharmacy law and regulations were first instituted in the late nineteenth century.

The history of pharmacy law and the FDA will be covered in this chapter along with the laws and regulations that changed the practice of pharmacy. The incidents, acts, and amendments will be listed in chronological order with a basic overview of what each entails. In addition, prescribing authority, controlled substance handling and dispensing, and the ethical responsibilities of the pharmacy technician will be covered.

History

Federal pharmacy laws were first established in the nineteenth century and eventually came under the purview of the Department of Agriculture, which itself was established in 1862. A group of professionals including chemists, physicians, veterinarians, pharmacists, lawyers, and microbiologists made up the department's Division of Chemistry.

Until 1901, the Division of Chemistry was in charge of accepting applications and evaluating new drugs for humans and animals, food additives, medical devices, and infant formulas. Then chief chemist Harvey Wiley changed its name to the Bureau of Chemistry and began regulating and experimenting with the applications. This included exposing hazards, focusing on consumer safety, and researching the chemical effects of drugs and additives. With the new Bureau of Chemistry, Wiley helped pass new legislation which led to the Pure Food and Drug Act of 1906.

In 1927, with increasing demand for chemical insecticides, the agency changed its name again to the Food, Drug, and Insecticides Agency and broadened regulations. In 1930, the name was shortened to the **Food and Drug Administration**, by which it is known today. By 1940 the FDA was placed under the authority of the new Federal

Security Agency; it was transferred to the Department of Health, Education, and Welfare (HEW) in 1953; and in 1968 became part of the US Public Health Service within HEW. When the US Department of Health and Human Services was formed in 1980, the FDA was moved once again and continues to operate to this day, regulating applications for new drugs, medical devices, and other products.

Before federal oversight began with the Pure Food and Drug Act of 1906, the State Boards of Pharmacy, which formed in the mid to late 1800s, developed laws that varied widely from state to state. This caused terrible events to occur due to the interstate transport of unlawful drugs and foods, low standards for strength and quality of food and drugs in certain states, and scientifically unproven uses of drugs and foods for diseases and conditions.

Since 1906, the FDA has investigated the improper use and misbranding of agricultural goods and services used for food and drugs. Over the years, hundreds of bills and acts have been introduced to Congress based upon the FDA's findings as well as to help the FDA regulate and enforce standards on products. With the Food, Drug, and Cosmetic Act of 1938, the **US Pharmacopeia (USP)** and **National Formulary** were developed to meet the guidelines put in place for strength, quality, and purity. Products were then required to be labeled and to list any variations from those guidelines. The law also prohibited adding any chemical or hazardous substance that could cause unnecessary harm and/or conceal any damage or degradation of a product.

Many laws and regulations occur after trial and error. Sometimes, an adverse event occurs that causes a regulation to be placed on a product. Other times, after years of research, a medication may be proven to be habit forming, cause birth defects, or cause harmful long-term side effects. In the next section, the most important acts, amendments, and incidents that changed pharmacy practice will be discussed, along with why the regulation was put in place in the first place.

OVERVIEW OF PHARMACY LAWS AND ETHICS

Before explaining the different laws and regulations in the pharmacy practice, it is important to understand the difference between an act and an amendment. An **act** is a formal decision made by Congress. Before an act is passed into law, it is called a bill. An **amendment** is the altering of a law, motion, or bill that is already in place or being processed. The most common acts, amendments, and incidents relating to pharmacy follow.

According to the **Pure Food and Drug Act of 1906**, all manufacturers are required to properly label a drug with truthful information. In the beginning, the act still allowed many unproven drugs to be marketed; later, it was amended to state that manufacturers must also prove the effectiveness of the drug through scientific methods. In addition, this law prohibited the adulteration and misbranding of food and drugs in interstate commerce.

Because of the trafficking and marketing of highly addictive substances such as opium in 1912, an international meeting called the International Opium Convention limited the recreational use and transport of opium worldwide. In response to international treaties, the United States then implemented the **Harrison Narcotics Tax Act of 1914** to stop recreational use of opium. This act required a prescription to purchase opium. It also allowed the investigation of pharmacists, scientists, and other entities that used or distributed narcotics with their consent; given the widespread demand for opium, investigation was to determine whether its use was legitimately for medical purposes. The act required practitioners to be registered and to document the use and dispensing of narcotics. It also put restrictions and taxes on the sale and distribution of products used to prepare controlled substances such as opium and coca leaves.

About twenty years later, the **Sulfanilamide Tragedy of 1937** occurred when more than 100 people died after the use of sulfanilamide; it led to the passage of the Food, Drug, and Cosmetic Act of 1938. Sulfanilamide was used to treat streptococcal infections and dispensed safely in powder or tablet form. In 1937, a salesman for the S.E. Massengill Company reported a demand for the drug in liquid form. The chief chemist of the company found that the drug dissolved easily in a substance called diethylene glycol. The company only tested the taste, fragrance, and appearance of the drug, and then shipped 633 bottles all over the country. It had not been tested for toxicity and the chemist did not note that he used diethylene glycol, which is used as antifreeze, as the liquid which was mixed with the sulfanilamide. Diethylene glycol is a deadly poison. Once the medication was distributed, reports started to come in about a large number of deaths. The FDA had to track down all sulfanilamide salesmen, the physicians' offices that had purchased the drug, the patients who had received it, and send out urgent warnings across the country by telegram.

In the end, many of those who died were children. They were ill for 7 – 21 days; symptoms included kidney failure, severe abdominal pain, inability to urinate, nausea, vomiting, and convulsions. At the time, there was no treatment for diethylene glycol poisoning.

The **Food, Drug, and Cosmetic Act of 1938** was mainly enacted because of the sulfanilamide tragedy and to add regulations to cosmetics. At the time however, misleading the customer through false claims and exaggeration on the labeling—also known as misbranding—was a common problem. The act banned false claims, required package inserts with directions to be included with products, and required exact labeling on the product. Moreover, the act required that addictive substances be labeled with the statement, *Warning: May be Habit Forming*; it also gave legal status to the FDA. Finally, the Food, Drug, and Cosmetic Act created the US Pharmacopeia and the National Formulary.

Thirteen years later, the **Durham-Humphrey Amendment of 1951** added more labeling requirements for the drug manufacturers, requiring the statement, "*Caution: Federal Law Prohibits Dispensing without a Prescription.*" Following this amendment, certain drugs required a prescription with directions for use and also required that prescription and over-the-counter (OTC) drugs be distinguished.

Sadly, tragedy would strike again leading to more regulations. Thalidomide was first marketed in the 1960s as a sedative and hypnotic used for insomnia, anxiety, and gastritis in West Germany and Europe. Doctors then started to prescribe it to ease morning sickness and nausea in pregnant women. Shortly after the medication was prescribed for pregnant women, 5,000 to 7,000 babies were born in West Germany with a condition called phocomelia, or malformation of the limbs. Only 40 percent of the children survived. In the **Thalidomide Tragedy of 1962**, worldwide over 10,000 children were born with phocomelia; only 50 percent of the children survived. Other effects of thalidomide included deformed eyes, hearts, and urinary tracts as well as blindness and deafness. The thalidomide tragedy led to stricter drug research, development, and regulations.

The **Kefauver-Harris Amendment of 1962** gave the FDA the authority to approve or reject a manufacturer's marketing application before the drug was to become available for consumer or commercial use. This required the manufacturer to prove substantial evidence of safety and efficacy of a drug through adequate and well-controlled studies. The amendment requires informed consent of study subjects and established regulations for clinical drug research and investigations. It also requires all adverse events of a drug be reported to the FDA. Prescription drug advertising authority was also transferred from the Federal Trade Commission (FTC) to the FDA. *Good Manufacturing Practice* (GMP) was placed upon the manufacturing companies to ensure high quality and standards of drugs.

By requiring the evidence of safety and proper clinical research before allowing distribution of a medication, this amendment enabled the FDA to prevent the sale of thalidomide in the United States.

The **Comprehensive Drug Abuse and Prevention Act of 1970** or the **Controlled Substances Act (CSA)** will be discussed in depth with controlled drugs later in this chapter.

The **Poison Prevention Packaging Act of 1970** required manufacturers and pharmacies to secure all medication in containers with childproof caps or packaging. The standard states that the cap or packaging cannot be opened by at least 80 percent of children under the age of five while 90 percent of adults should be able to open the product within 5 minutes. This is required for both prescription and OTC medications. There are exceptions such as if the patient asks for a non-childproof cap, if the patient is hospitalized, or for certain prescription medications.

The act was implemented due to hundreds of deaths of children under the age of five as a result of ingesting drugs and household chemicals and is under the authority of the Consumer Product Safety Commission (CPSC).

The **Occupational Safety and Health Act (OSHA) of 1970** is discussed later with occupational safety and hazardous substances.

In 1972, the **Drug Listing Act** implemented the national drug code number (NDC). Every drug has a ten-digit number divided into three sections. The first section, which consists of five numbers, is the labeler or manufacturer's code and is provided by

the FDA. The second is the product code and it specifies the product or dr[...]
is the package code and represents the size and type of the product. If t[...]
two asterisks (*) at the end of the package number, it means that the prod[...]
raw, or non-formulated controlled substance.

The **Medical Device Amendment of 1976** establishes three regulatory classes for medical devices. Class III devices are the most regulated ones and pose high risks for human use; they require premarket approval applications that are the equivalent to a new drug application. Class II devices are performance-standard devices that are considered moderate risk for human use, and Class I devices are general controlled devices with low risk for human use.

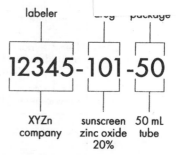

Figure 3.1. NDC Number

The **Resource Conservation and Recovery Act of 1976** gives the Environmental Protection Agency (EPA) complete authority in the disposal of hazardous substances. This includes their generation, transportation, treatment, storage, and disposal.

> NDC numbers are used not only for ordering drugs, but for verifying drugs during the dispensing process and inventory as well.

The **Orphan Drug Act of 1983** regulates orphan drugs, which are pharmaceuticals developed specifically for rare diseases. The Orphan Drug Act was passed to help in the development of treatments for orphan diseases such as Huntington's disease, Tourette's syndrome, muscular dystrophy, and ALS, which only affect a small portion of the population. The designation means that only the sponsor who qualifies as having a rare disease may receive certain benefits from the federal government.

The **Drug Price Competition and Patent Term Restoration Act of 1984** encourages the manufacturing of generic drugs by drug companies and formed the modern system of generic drug regulation in the United States. The act outlines the process for drug companies to file an **abbreviated new drug application (ANDA)** to receive approval of a generic drug by the FDA. The first company that files an ANDA for a generic drug has 180 days of exclusive rights to market the generic alternative to the brand drug. This helps the drug manufacturer by allowing it to market a drug without having to duplicate the clinical studies done by the brand company and avoiding patent infringement damages.

The **Prescription Drug Marketing Act of 1987** helps prevent counterfeit drugs by providing legal safeguards in the chain of distribution of pharmaceuticals. It was designed to prevent the sales of discontinued, counterfeit, misbranded, subpar, and expired prescription drugs.

The **Omnibus Budget Reconciliation Act of 1990** is related to COBRA, which allows for continuing coverage and benefits of group healthcare plans for an employee and family based upon certain qualifying issues and events when benefits would otherwise be terminated.

	FY 2013	FY 2014	FY 2015	FY 2016	FY 2017
Original ANDA	Expedite review of paragraph IV and maintain pre-GDUFA productivity		60% in 15 months	75% in 15 months	90% in 10 months
Tier 1 first major amendment	Maintain pre-GDUFA productivity		60% in 10 months	75% in 10 months	90% in 10 months
Tier 1 minor amendments (1st-3rd)	Maintain pre-GDUFA productivity		60% in 3 months	75% in 3 months	90% in 3 months
Tier 1 minor amendments (4th-5th)	Maintain pre-GDUFA productivity		60% in 6 months	75% in 6 months	90% in 6 months
Tier 2 amendment	Maintain pre-GDUFA productivity		60% in 12 months	75% in 12 months	90% in 12 months
Prior approval supplements	Maintain pre-GDUFA productivity		60% in 6 months	75% in 6 months	90% in 6 months
ANDA, amendment, and PAS in backlog on Oct 1st, 2012	Act on 90% by end of FY 2017				
Controlled correspondences	Maintain pre-GDUFA productivity		60% in four months	75% in two months	90% in two months

Figure 3.2. History of ANDA

In 1990, the **FDA Safe Medical Devices Act** implemented **medical device reporting (MDR)** of serious incidents that occur from the use of medical devices. This is a post-market surveillance tool used by the FDA to monitor performance, potential safety issues, and benefit-risk assessments of the devices. Manufacturers, device-user facilities, and importers are mandatory reporters and are required to report any adverse events and product defects to the FDA.

The **Anabolic Steroids Control Act of 1990** amended the Controlled Substances Act to require penalties for trainers and advisors who recommend anabolic steroid use to individuals. The act also added anabolic steroids as a schedule drug; they are now CIII controlled substances. It also defines anabolic steroids as a drug or hormonal substance that promotes muscle growth in a way similar to testosterone.

The **Americans with Disabilities Act of 1990** is a civil rights law that protects against discrimination based on a disability. It also requires employers to make reasonable accommodations to employees with disabilities.

The **Dietary Supplement Health and Education Act of 1994** defines and regulates dietary supplements under the FDA's Good Manufacturing Practices. The definition of a dietary supplement is a product that supplements the diet or contains one or more of these ingredients: an herb, a vitamin, a mineral, or an amino acid. A dietary supplement can also be a dietary substance used to supplement a diet by increasing dietary intake, a concentrate, metabolite, constituent, extract, or any combination of any of these ingredients.

Dietary supplements must have proper labeling. A dietary supplement label requires:

+ a statement including the words *dietary supplement*
+ net quantity
+ a *Supplement Facts* panel that includes product serving size, amount, and percent daily value
+ for a proprietary blend, the net weight of the blend and a listing of each ingredient in descending order of weight
+ if an herb or botanical, the part of the plant used
+ the name and place of business of the manufacturer, packer, or distributor
+ a complete list of ingredients by their common names in order of prominence or with the dietary ingredient source in *Supplement Facts*
+ safety information
+ the disclaimer on the label, *This statement has not been evaluated by the FDA. This product is not intended to diagnose, treat, cure or prevent any disease.*

The **Health Insurance Portability and Accountability Act (HIPAA) of 1996** established **protected health information (PHI)**. The privacy rules implemented by HIPAA are meant to protect certain health information, including the use and disclosure of a patient's PHI. Example of PHI include any information, oral or recorded, that

+ is created or received by a healthcare provider, health plan, employer, or healthcare clearinghouse.
+ relates to the physical or mental health or condition of an individual.
+ includes the healthcare practicing in regards to an individual.
+ includes the past, present, or future payment for healthcare of an individual that identifies the individual.

Any entities that are defined as providers of PHI must comply with every requirement listed in the privacy rules of HIPAA. HIPAA-covered entities include healthcare workers and providers, health plans, and healthcare clearinghouses. This also includes any health information that is sent and/or received via electronic format or data content.

HIPAA information must be updated annually. Physicians and healthcare facilities must update and display privacy policy and procedures by adding any new standards or changes in regulations. Employers are required to train employees annually and employees are required to comply with the policy and procedures.

Patient confidentiality requires healthcare workers to keep all patients' private and privileged information from being disclosed without the patient's consent. Patients have the right to privacy in regards to their medications, treatment, diseases and conditions, and any other aspect of their healthcare. These laws affect all aspects of healthcare including pharmacy. Obtaining, transferring, and accessing patient information must be done only with the patient's consent.

HIPAA is also included in regards to technology. When sending patient-sensitive information electronically, the information must be converted to a non-readable format through encryption. Access is limited to only the healthcare providers given permission to access a patient's records through databases and the information must be password protected. This means workers must sign in and out of computers with a password each time they use them to access PHI. Any electronic release of information among healthcare providers must be approved by the patient as well.

When it comes to the pharmacy technician, patient information should only be communicated on a need-to-know basis. Because a patient's physician is an entity covered under HIPAA, the physician can call the pharmacy and request information. This is also relevant to the pharmacy staff when speaking to the patient about health coverage or medications. Pharmacy staff must not speak about sensitive information around other customers. If PHI must be discussed with a patient, direct him or her to the patient consultation window and speak quietly to the patient.

Under HIPAA, patients have these specific rights:
+ to obtain a copy of their health records
+ to have corrections amended on their health information
+ to receive a notice stating how their health information may be used and shared
+ to give or rescind permission before health information is used
+ to receive a report stating why their information was shared

If a patient feels their information was used without permission or not protected, the patient can file a complaint with their health insurer or the US government, revoke permission to use PHI at any time, or authorize or not authorize any sharing of their PHI at any time.

> **?** A pharmacy technician is waiting on a patient who is known to abuse narcotics. In front of other customers, the pharmacy technician tells the pharmacist to make sure to check the customer's profile because he is an addict and tries to refill his narcotic prescriptions early. In this scenario, how is the pharmacy technician negligent?

HIPAA privacy laws allow a spouse, family member, or friend to receive PHI about a patient that is directly relevant to a patient's care or payment from health insurance if the patient is present or available before disclosure or if they have legal capacity to make healthcare decisions on behalf of the patient. The patient can also discuss information with a friend or family member under the patient's own recognizance.

A pharmacy technician *cannot* share any personal or medical information to anyone besides the patient unless covered under HIPAA. This includes the pharmacy technician's family members, co-workers, managers, or any other entity that is not covered under HIPAA rules and regulations.

Table 3.1. HIPAA Violation Penalty Tiers

Tier	Violation
First	The covered entity did not know and could not reasonably have known of the breach.
Second	The covered entity "knew, or by exercising reasonable diligence would have known of the violation," though they did not act with willful neglect.
Third	The covered entity "acted with willful neglect," and corrected the problem within a 30-day time period.
Fourth	The covered entity "acted with willful neglect" and failed to make a timely correction.

For controlling disease and for child neglect, public health authorities can, by law, obtain health records. For FDA regulation purposes, records can be obtained for adverse events, product recalls, tracking products, and post-marketing surveillance. When notification is authorized by law, patients who have contracted or may have contracted a communicable disease can be notified. Employers can obtain certain information about an employee who is affected by a work-related illness or injury.

Law enforcement can obtain information based on certain circumstances. The circumstances include, as required by law, court orders; locating or identifying a suspect, fugitive, witness or missing person; obtaining information about a victim; alerting law enforcement of a person's death; using PHI if it is evidence of a crime; or using it in cases of certain medical emergencies.

In 1997, the **FDA Modernization Act** updated the Food, Drug, and Cosmetic Act to include technological, trade, and public health issues more relevant to the twenty-first century.

The **Medicare Prescription Drug Improvement and Modernization Act of 2003** gave low-income patients who need assistance with increasing drug costs the option of a prescription drug discount card. This act helps increase access to medical treatment and reduces unnecessary hospitalizations associated with noncompliance in taking prescription drugs.

The **Dietary Supplement and Nonprescription Drug Act of 2006** amends the Food, Drug, and Cosmetic Act by requiring reporting of adverse events caused by dietary supplements and nonprescription drugs. Reporting includes abuse of the drug, withdrawals from the drug, overdose of the drug, and failure of expected pharmacological action of the drug. Drug manufacturers, packers, distributors, and retailers are required to report adverse events.

The **Patient Protection and Affordable Care Act of 2010** is also known as the Affordable Care Act or Obamacare. It was executed to increase the quality and affordability of healthcare by helping to lower the costs of public and private insurance and lowering the amount of uninsured persons in the United States. Insurance companies are required to cover all individuals with new minimum standards regardless of pre-existing condition or sex. The act also requires an individual to have health insurance or else pay an income tax penalty for each month uninsured.

The Affordable Care Act is the biggest overhaul of the United States healthcare system since Medicare and Medicaid. It gives individuals and business owners coverage options through **health insurance exchanges**, which allow comparisons of policies and prices, keeping insurance rates competitive. Low-income individuals can also receive government subsidies, which will be given as a refundable tax credit, based on a sliding scale if they purchase their policies from an exchange.

Health insurance is more accessible to more people. Insurers are prohibited from imposing lifetime limits on benefits (such as hospital stays); furthermore, they cannot drop policyholders if they get sick. In addition, insurance plans must cover medical screenings and preventative care. They are prohibited from charging copays, co-insurance, or deductibles on these services.

Existing law and programs like the Social Security Act, Medicare, and Medicaid were also affected by the Affordable Care Act. The Hospital Readmissions Reduction Program was implemented under the Social Security Act to help reduce the cost of hospital readmissions by penalizing hospitals that have higher readmission rates with lower Medicare reimbursement rates. Medicare itself has been reformed; the Medicare payment system reformation promotes greater efficiency by restructuring Medicare reimbursement from fee-for-service to bundled payments. The Medicare Part D coverage gap will shrink annually, closing the gap by January 1, 2020. Finally, Medicaid eligibility has been expanded to include incomes up to 133 percent of the federal poverty level which also includes a 5 percent *income disregard*, making income eligibility up to 138 percent of the federal poverty level.

The law has had other effects as well. Dependents can remain on the parent's health insurance plan until their twenty-sixth birthday. Regulations implemented include dependents who are unmarried, not in school, no longer live with their parents, and are not on a parent's tax return.

Finally, any business that employs more than fifty individuals will pay a tax penalty if it does not provide health insurance to full-time employees and if the employee had to subsidize his or her insurance through a government subsidy.

The **Drug Quality and Security Act of 2013** outlines steps to build an electronic tracking system to identify and trace specific prescription drugs distributed in the United States. It will modify the Food, Drug, and Cosmetic Act. Within the next ten years, it will

+ verify the legitimacy of the prescription drug down to the package level.
+ detect and alert to illegitimate prescription drugs in the supply chain.
+ implement more efficient recalls of drug products.

There are regulatory agencies and organizations that work both independently and together to enforce and/or help to regulate the pharmacy laws, acts, and amendments.

Pharmacy law is complex and is constructed of both federal and state requirements. Each agency and organization has a specific role in regulating drugs and the manufacturers, suppliers, and distributors of medication. Other agencies or organizations regulate the licensing, accreditation, and discipline of the pharmacy practice. The combination of pharmacy law and the regulatory agencies and organizations which enforce and regulate it helps deliver consumers the safest products available.

Besides the FDA and the DEA (which will be discussed in-depth later in this chapter) several other agencies and organizations regulate pharmacy or are involved in pharmacy law.

The **Bureau of Alcohol, Tobacco and Firearms (ATF)** is a federal organization within the United States Department of Justice. The ATF combats terrorism, arson and violent crime; it regulates alcohol, tobacco, firearms, arson, and explosives.

 To which agency should adverse events be reported?

The **State Boards of Pharmacy (BOP)** regulate, by state, the practice of pharmacy. State Boards of Pharmacy mainly focus on the public's health and the implementation and enforcement of state pharmacy law. The BOP, in partnership with the state's department of health, also regulates the state's pharmacy personnel. On a broader level, the **National Association of Boards of Pharmacy (NABP)** assists BOPs by developing and implementing uniform standards relating to pharmacy. It also assists in the licensing, certification, and continuing education of pharmacists and pharmacy technicians. The NABP implemented *NABP Interconnect*, which is an internet data exchange platform that allows pharmacists, law enforcement, and state boards to access controlled substance profiles of drug-seeking patients across state lines to prevent drug abuse and drug diversion.

The **Centers for Medicaid and Medicare Services (CMS)** promotes Medicare, Medicaid, and government plans in regards to healthcare coverage. CMS helps to provide effective, modernized coverage with quality healthcare for its beneficiaries.

The **Environmental Protection Agency (EPA)** protects human health and the environment. The EPA has pharmacists who work with public health and sanitation programs that watch for bacteria and viruses in the environment that could become a risk to the human population.

Medwatch is the FDA's safety and adverse event reporting program.

The Joint Commission is a not-for-profit organization; its main function is to enhance patient safety and quality of care in institutional environments. The Joint Commission accredits hospitals through yearly inspections for compliance and national patient safety goals. Hospitals comply with the goals by performing self-assessments, providing action plans, showing compliance by providing data and information through assessments, and undergoing on-site surveys by the Joint Commission.

PRACTICE QUESTIONS

1. Which amendment required the phrase *Caution: Federal Law Prohibits Dispensing without a Prescription* to be placed on all prescription labels?

   A) the Kefauver-Harris Amendment of 1962

   B) the Orphan Drug Act of 1983

   C) the Durham-Humphrey Amendment of 1951

   D) the Pure Food and Drug Act of 1906

   Answers:

   A) Incorrect. The Kefauver-Harris Amendment of 1962 gave the FDA the authority to approve a manufacturer's marketing application before the drug was to become available for consumer or commercial use.

   B) Incorrect. The Orphan Drug Act of 1983 was passed to help development of treatment for orphan diseases such as Huntington's disease, Tourette's syndrome, muscular dystrophy, and ALS, which only affect a small portion of the population.

   C) Correct. The Durham-Humphrey Amendment of 1951 required prescription labels to state *Caution: Federal Law Prohibits Dispensing without a Prescription.*

   D) Incorrect. The Pure Food and Drug Act of 1906 required manufacturers to properly label a drug with truthful information.

2. The Poison Prevention Packaging Act of 1970 required

   A) the manufacturing of generic drugs by drug companies and formed the modern system of regulation of generic drugs in the United States.

   B) that manufacturers and pharmacies must place all medication in containers with childproof caps or packaging.

   C) a prescription to purchase opium; it allowed investigation and required consent to study subjects that use or distribute narcotics.

   D) a ban on false claims, package inserts with directions to be included with products, and exact labeling on the product.

   Answers:

   A) Incorrect. The Drug Price Competition and Patent Term Restoration Act of 1984 required the manufacturing of generic drugs by the drug companies and formed the modern system of regulation of generic drugs in the United States.

   B) Correct. The Poison Prevention Packaging Act of 1970 required that manufacturers and pharmacies must place all medication in containers with childproof caps or packaging.

C) Incorrect. The Harrison Narcotics Tax Act of 1914 required a prescription to purchase opium, allowed investigation of its legitimacy, taxed it, and required consent to study subjects that use or distribute narcotics.

D) Incorrect. The Food, Drug, and Cosmetics Act banned false claims, required that package inserts with directions be included with products, and required exact labeling on the product.

3. The State Boards of Pharmacy

   A) protect human health and the environment.

   B) enhance patient safety and quality of care in institutional environments.

   C) promote Medicare, Medicaid, and government plans in regards to healthcare coverage.

   D) focus on the public's health and the implementation and enforcement of state laws of the pharmacy practice.

   Answers:

   A) Incorrect. The EPA protects human health and the environment.

   B) Incorrect. The Joint Commission is a not-for-profit organization; its main function is to enhance patient safety and quality of care in institutional environments.

   C) Incorrect. CMS promotes Medicare, Medicaid, and government plans in regards to healthcare coverage.

   D) Correct. The State Boards of Pharmacy focus on the public's health and the implementation and enforcement of relevant state laws of the pharmacy practice.

4. Which of the following is NOT true of the Affordable Care Act?

   A) People must purchase healthcare coverage from the government.

   B) Insurers are prohibited from imposing lifetime limits on benefits such as hospital stays.

   C) Insurance plans must cover medical screenings and preventative care.

   D) Dependents can remain on their parent's health insurance plan until their twenty-sixth birthday.

   Answers:

   A) Correct. The ACA does not require consumers to buy healthcare coverage from the government.

   B) Incorrect. The ACA does prohibit insurers from imposing lifetime limits on benefits such as hospital stays.

   C) Incorrect. The ACA does require insurance plans to cover medical screenings and preventative care.

D)   Incorrect. The ACA does require that dependents be permitted to remain on the parent's health insurance plan until their twenty-sixth birthday.

PRESCRIBING AUTHORITY

Prescribing authority is defined as the authority to prescribe certain prescription drugs according to established protocol. It was established by the Durham-Humphrey Amendment of 1951. In the United States, prescribing authority regulations vary from state to state, so it is important to verify which professionals are able to prescribe medications within your state of practice.

The drugs the professional can prescribe also vary by state and profession as well. This is called the professional's **scope of practice**. The scope of practice defines whether the practitioner can diagnose or treat a condition and if so, how that determines per state law what prescriptive authority the practitioner has. For example, although a nurse practitioner has prescribing authority, the scope of practice of the nurse practitioner does not allow him or her to prescribe controlled substances.

Pharmacy technicians have no prescribing authority, but pharmacists do have some limited authority in certain circumstances. Independent prescriptive authority is not given to pharmacists in any state, but most states do allow pharmacists to initiate or adjust drug therapies in collaboration with physicians. This normally happens in inpatient settings. Recently in Oregon and California pharmacists have been given prescriptive authority to fill oral contraceptives.

Several professions have prescribing authority based on their scope of practice in the United States, depending on their state:

+ advanced practice registered nurse
+ chiropractor
+ certified RN anesthetist
+ dentist
+ doctor of homeopathy
+ doctor of osteopathy
+ doctor of veterinary medicine (DVM)
+ emergency medical technician
+ licensed certified social worker (LCSW)
+ medical physician
+ neuropathic MD
+ nurse midwife
+ nurse practitioner
+ OB/GYN nurse
+ optometrist
+ pediatric RN practitioner
+ pharmacist
+ physician assistant
+ psychiatric RN practitioner
+ psychologist

PRACTICE QUESTION

The scope of practice of a practitioner depends on

A) whether the practitioner can fill prescriptions.

B) how many prescriptions the practitioner can fill.

C) whether the practitioner can diagnose or treat a condition.

D) how long the practitioner has been practicing.

Answers:

A) Incorrect. Scope of practice is determined by whether the practitioner can diagnose or treat a condition. If the practitioner cannot treat or diagnose a condition, he or she cannot write prescriptions at all.

B) Incorrect. If the practitioner's scope of practice does not allow him or her to write prescriptions, then there would be no prescriptions to fill in the first place.

C) **Correct.** Scope of practice is determined by whether the practitioner can diagnose or treat a condition.

D) Incorrect. If a practitioner does not treat or diagnose a condition, his or her years of experience are irrelevant.

RESPONDEAT SUPERIOR

The **Respondeat Superior,** in Latin, is defined as "let the master answer." In regards to pharmacy, the respondeat superior is a legal doctrine meaning the pharmacist is responsible, in certain circumstances, for the acts of the pharmacy technician or any other employee working under her or him. In other words, the pharmacist trusts that the pharmacy technician will work ethically and responsibly within the scope of his or her own practice.

This does not state that there will not be any consequences for the pharmacy technician who has been negligent; it just means that if the pharmacy technician was negligent, the pharmacist may be held responsible as well. As an example, the technician is filling a prescription for hydrochlorothiazide 25mg tablets. The technician negligently grabs a bottle of alprazolam 0.5 mg tablets instead and fills the prescription. As the pills are both peach colored and the pharmacist was rushed, the pharmacist does not catch the mistake during verification and dispenses it to the patient. The patient then ends up at the emergency room due to the side effects of the medication. The patient sues the pharmacy. Under the respondeat superior doctrine, the pharmacy, the pharmacist, and the pharmacy technician would all be held responsible.

> **?** A pharmacy technician is filling two prescriptions for one individual patient. The technician mistakenly labels the bottles wrong, placing the labels on the opposite bottles. The pharmacist verifies the medication, failing to note the mistake. The patient then takes the medication incorrectly because the directions are wrong, even though he has been taking the medications for years. Who is responsible for the mistake?

Within the pharmacy, a **ratio** is established so that the pharmacist can responsibly carry out his or her duties even while managing the pharmacy technicians. The ratio required in most states is three technicians to each pharmacist. This is important because if the pharmacist has the correct amount of technicians to help, it will free the pharmacist to thoroughly verify orders. Furthermore, the proper ratio prevents the technicians from being overworked and making negligent mistakes.

PRACTICE QUESTION

A pharmacy technician negligently filled the wrong strength of a medication and the pharmacist did not catch the mistake while verifying. The patient did not read the paperwork that came along with the prescription and took it anyway; she ended up in the hospital from an overdose and sues the pharmacy.

Under the respondeat superior doctrine, who or which of the following would NOT be responsible for the mistake?

A) the pharmacist

B) the patient

C) the pharmacy technician

D) the place of business

Answers:

A) Incorrect. The pharmacist would be responsible.

B) **Correct.** The patient trusted that the pharmacy filled the correct medicine; she would not be responsible for the error.

C) Incorrect. The pharmacy technician is responsible.

D) Incorrect. The place of business is held responsible.

PHARMACY TECHNICIAN CODE OF ETHICS

What exactly is *the practice of pharmacy?* The general definition is the scope of professional acts the pharmacist is allowed to perform within the practice of that specific state. Consequently the pharmacy technician assists the pharmacist in the practice of pharmacy. The pharmacy technician is responsible for completing the tasks that do not require the pharmacist's professional judgment. Carrying out any other actions means the pharmacy technician is working outside of his or her scope of practice.

Ethics is defined as a set of moral principles. **Principles** are a guiding sense of obligations. Most individuals have a set of standards and principles they abide by that they believe are a personal rule or law of professional conduct. **The American Association of Pharmacy Technicians (AAPT)**, an organization dedicated to supporting and educating pharmacy technicians, developed a **Pharmacy Technician Code of Ethics**. Just like the PTCB Code of Conduct that was discussed in the introduction, this document delineates, from an ethical point of view, what is expected of the pharmacy technician.

Code of Ethics for Pharmacy Technicians

Preamble

Pharmacy Technicians are healthcare professionals who assist pharmacists in providing the best possible care for patients. The principles of this code, which apply to pharmacy technicians working in any and all settings, are based on the application and support of the moral obligations that guide the pharmacy profession in relationships with patients, healthcare professionals, and society.

Principles

A pharmacy technician's first consideration is to ensure the health and safety of the patient, and to use knowledge and skills to the best of his/her ability in serving others.

1. A pharmacy technician supports and promotes honesty and integrity in the profession, which includes a duty to observe the law, maintain the highest moral and ethical conduct at all times, and uphold the ethical principles of the profession.

2. A pharmacy technician assists and supports the pharmacist in the safe, efficacious, and cost effective distribution of health services and healthcare resources.

3. A pharmacy technician respects and values the abilities of pharmacists, colleagues, and other healthcare professionals.

4. A pharmacy technician maintains competency in his/her practice, and continually enhances his/her professional knowledge and expertise.

5. A pharmacy technician respects and supports the patient's individuality, dignity, and confidentiality.

6. A pharmacy technician respects the confidentiality of a patient's records and discloses pertinent information only with proper authorization.

7. A pharmacy technician never assists in the dispensing, promoting, or distribution of medications or medical devices that are not of good quality or do not meet the standards required by law.

8. A pharmacy technician does not engage in any activity that will discredit the profession, and will expose, without fear or favor, illegal or unethical conduct in the profession.

9. A pharmacy technician associates with and engages in the support of organizations which promote the profession of pharmacy through the utilization and enhancement of pharmacy technicians.

CONTINUE

OT one of a pharmacy technician's ethical duties?

armacy technician never assists in the dispensing, promoting, or distribution dications or medical devices that are not of good quality or do not meet the ards required by law.

B) A pharmacy technician supports and promotes honesty and integrity in the profession, which includes a duty to observe the law, maintain the highest moral and ethical conduct at all times, and uphold the ethical principles of the profession.

C) A pharmacy technician associates with and engages in the support of organizations which promote the profession of pharmacy through the utilization and enhancement of pharmacy technicians.

D) A pharmacy technician helps the pharmacist by counseling patients to free up time when the pharmacist is backed up verifying prescriptions.

Answers:

A) Incorrect. Working only with those medications and devices approved by the law and of good quality is part of the pharmacy technicians' code of ethics.

B) Incorrect. It is the duty of the pharmacy technician to observe the law, behave morally and ethically, and uphold ethical principles.

C) Incorrect. Networking with relevant organizations is part of the code of ethics.

D) **Correct.** Only the pharmacist counsels patients.

Controlled Drugs

Controlled drugs are drugs that are strictly regulated by the government; prescribers must follow specific rules when prescribing them that differ from non-controlled drugs. In this section, the information required to safely and accurately dispense controlled substances will be discussed. The Controlled Substances Act, DEA registration, accurate dispensing, inventory, and the ordering and receiving process of controlled substances will be covered.

CONTROLLED SUBSTANCES ACT

The Controlled Substances Act (CSA) is a federal drug policy that was passed in 1970. The policy strictly controls the manufacture, importation, possession, use, and distribution of certain controlled substances. The substances it covers are narcotics, stimulants, depressants, hallucinogens, anabolic steroids, and other regulated chemicals.

> **?** When a state controlled-substance law is more stringent than a federal law, the state board of pharmacy will require pharmacies to adhere to the stricter state requirements.

The DEA, the Department of Health and Human Services, and the FDA are in charge of regulating the Controlled Substances Act. The DEA is responsible for enforcing the CSA and can prosecute any violators on a domestic and international level. Any individual who handles, stores, orders, or distributes controlled substances must be registered with the DEA and given a DEA number. Controlled substances must be inventoried and recorded accurately.

> On the stock bottles of controlled substances, the schedule of the drug is imprinted. As an example, a stock bottle for alprazolam 0.5mg tablets will have a CIV imprinted on it.

The CSA implemented a scheduled class of narcotics based on abuse potential and safety. The schedules range from CI – CV. These are called **schedule drugs**.

Schedule I (CI) are illegal drugs and are considered not to have any medical value or use. They also pose severe safety concerns and have the most abuse potential. Drugs included in this class are heroin, LSD, Ecstasy, mescaline, MDMA, GHB, psilocybin, methaqualone, khat, and bath salts. Marijuana is still considered, on a federal level, to be a Class I narcotic although some state laws have changed to allow marijuana to be used for medical and/or recreational use.

Schedule II (CII) are legal drugs, but they have a high potential for abuse. CII drugs do have medical value and use, but are used under severe restrictions. Opioids and amphetamines are in this schedule. Examples of drugs in this class include cocaine, oxycodone, hydrocodone, amphetamines, methadone, methamphetamine, methylphenidate, amobarbital, pentobarbital, morphine, opium, fentanyl, and glutethimide.

Schedule III (CIII) are legal drugs that have the potential for abuse, but are less abused and safer than CII narcotics. These drugs have low to moderate potential for physical abuse but high potential for psychological abuse. Anabolic steroids are in this schedule. Examples of drugs in this class include benzphetamine, phendimetrazine, Depo-Testosterone, buprenorphine, and anabolic steroids.

Schedule IV (CIV) are legal drugs that have a low potential for physical abuse and a moderate level of psychological abuse. Tranquilizers and sleeping medicines are in this schedule. Drugs in this class include alprazolam, clonazepam, diazepam, triazolam, tramadol, and carisoprodol.

Schedule V (CV) are legal drugs that have a low potential for abuse both physically and psychologically. Examples of CV drugs are cough medicines with codeine, marinol, ezogabine, and lonox.

CONTINUE

PRACTICE QUESTION

Which drug is NOT considered a CII drug?

A) cocaine

B) marijuana

C) oxycodone

D) hydrocodone

Answers:

A)   Incorrect. Cocaine is a CII drug.

B)   Correct. Marijuana is still considered a CI drug.

C)   Incorrect. Oxycodone is a CII drug.

D)   Incorrect. Hydrocodone is considered a CII drug.

DEA REGISTRATION FOR CONTROLLED SUBSTANCES

The **Drug Enforcement Agency (DEA)** is part of the US Department of Justice. The DEA enforces the Controlled Substances Act to prevent the diversion and abuse of both controlled substances and chemicals regulated by the FDA. The DEA is involved in every aspect of the handling and distribution of controlled substances and regulated chemicals. They require accurate recordkeeping and compliance from pharmacies, wholesalers, and distributors of controlled substances.

The DEA restricts access to controlled substances and requires all entities that prepare, handle, or distribute controlled substances to fill out an application for **DEA registration**. When the DEA approves registration, it will then give the entity a DEA registration number. Entities that require DEA registration include physicians, drug distributors, drug importers, drug exporters, drug manufacturers, and pharmacies. The application form for DEA registrants is **DEA Form 224**. DEA registration forms are available at www.deadiversion.usdoj.gov/drugreg.

Once the entity registers with the DEA, it then receives a unique DEA number. The **DEA number** is necessary to allow for the dispensing and distribution of controlled substances. DEA numbers are also used in pharmacy billing; some insurance claims may be denied if the DEA number is incorrect.

Pharmacy technicians must know how to verify a DEA number. There are several indicators involved; a DEA formula can also be calculated to be sure the number is correct. For example, a patient has just dropped off a prescription for a controlled substance. The prescription states that the patient needs morphine IR 30 mg tablets.

Form-224   **APPLICATION FOR REGISTRATION**   Supplementary Instructions and Information

SECTION 1. APPLICANT IDENTIFICATION - Information must be typed or printed in the blocks provided to help reduce data entry errors. A physical address is required in address line 1; a post office box or continuation of address may be entered in address line 2. Fee exempt applicant must list the address of the federal or state fee exempt institution.

Applicant must enter a valid social security number (SSN), or a tax identification number (TIN) if applying as a business entity. *Debt collection information is mandatory pursuant to the Debt Collection Improvement Act of 1996.*

The email address, point of contact, national provider id, date of birth, year graduated, and professional school are new data items that are used to facilitate communication or as required by inter-agency data sharing requirements.

Practitioner must enter one degree from this list: DDS, DMD, DO, DPM, DVM, or MD.
Mid-level practitioner must enter one degree from this list: DOM, HMD, MP, ND, NP, OD, PA, or RPH.

SECTION 2. BUSINESS ACTIVITY - Indicate only one. Practitioner or mid-level practitioner must enter the degree conferred, and are requested to enter the last professional school of matriculation and the year graduated.

> Automated dispensing system (ADS) must provide current DEA registration number of parent retail pharmacy or hospital, and attach a **notarized** affidavit in accordance with 21 CFR Part 1301.17. Affidavit must include:
>
> 1) Name of parent retail pharmacy or hospital and complete address
> 2) Name of Long-term Care (LTC) facility and complete address
> 3) Permit or license number(s) and date issued of State certification to operate ADS at named LTC facility
> 4) Required statement:
>   *This affidavit is submitted to obtain a DEA registration number. If any material information is false, the Administrator may commence proceedings to deny the application under section 304 of the Act (21 USC 8224a). Any false or fraudulent material information contained in this affidavit may subject the person signing this affidavit, and the named corporation/partnership/business to prosecution under section 403 of the Act (21 USC 843).*
> 5) Name of corporation operating the retail pharmacy or hospital
> 6) Name and title of corporate officer signing affidavit
> 7) Signature of authorized officer

SECTION 3. DRUG SCHEDULES - Applicant should check all drug schedules to be handled. However, applicant must still comply with state requirements; federal registration does not overrule state restrictions. Check the order form box only if you intend to purchase or to transfer schedule 2 controlled substances. Order forms will be mailed to the registered address following issuance of a Certificate of Registration. The following list of drug codes are examples of controlled substances for narcotic and non-narcotic schedules 2, 3, 4, and 5. Refer to the CFR for a complete list of basic classes.

SCHEDULE 2 NARCOTIC	BASIC CLASS
Alphaprodine (Nisentil)	9010
Anileridine (Leritine)	9020
Cocaine (Methyl Benzoylecgonine)	9041
Codeine (Morphine methyl ester)	9050
Dextropropoxyphene, bulk	9273
Diphenoxylate	9170
Diprenorphine (M50-50)	9058
Ethylmorpine (Dionin)	9190
Etorphine HCL (M-99)	9059
Glutethimide (Doriden, Dorimide)	2550
Hydrocodone (Dihydrocodeinone)	9193
Hydromorphone (Dilaudid)	9150
Levo-alphacetylmethadol (LAAM)	9648
Levorphanol (Levo-Dromoran)	9220
Meperidine (Demerol, Mepergan)	9230
Methadone (Dolophine, Methadose)	9250
Morphine (MS Contin, Roxanol)	9300
Opium, powdered	9639
Opium, raw	9600
Oxycodone (Oxycontin, Percocet)	9143
Oxymorphone (Numorphan)	9652
Opium Poppy/ Poppy Straw	9650
Poppy Straw Concentrate	9670
Thebaine	9333

SCHEDULE 2 NON-NARCOTIC	BASIC CLASS
Amobarbital (Amytal, Tuinal)	2125
Amphetamine (Dexedrine, Adderall)	1100
Methamphetamine (Desoxyn)	1105
Methylphenidate (Concerta, Ritalin)	1724
Pentobarbital (Nembutal)	2270
Phencyclidine	7471
Phenmetrazine (Preludin)	1631
Phenylacetone	8501
Secobarbital (Seconal)	2315

SCHEDULE 3 NARCOTIC	BASIC CLASS
Buprenorphine (Buprenex, Temgesic, Subutex)	9064
Codeine combo product 90mg/du (Empirin)	9804
Dihydrocodeine combo prod 90mg/du (Compal)	9807
Ethylmorphine combo product 15 mg/du	9808
Hydrocodone combo product (Lorcet, Vicodin)	9806
Morphine combo product 50 mg/100 ml or gm	9810
Opium combo product 25 mg/du (Paregoric)	9809

SCHEDULE 3 NON-NARCOTIC	BASIC CLASS
Anabolic Steroids	4000
Benzphetamine (Didrex, Inapetyl)	1228
Butalbital (Fiorinal, Butalbital w/aspirin)	2100/2165
Dronabinol in sesame oil w/soft gelatin capsule	7369
Gamma Hydroxybutyric Acid preps (Zyrem)	2012
Ketamine (Ketaset)	7285
Methyprylon (Noludar)	2575
Pentobarbital suppository du & noncontrolled active ingred (FP-3, WANS)	2271
Phendimetrazine (Plegine, Bontril, Statobex)	1615
Secobarbital suppository du & noncontrolled active ingredients	2316
Thiopental (Pentothal)	2100/2329
Vinbarbital (Delvinal)	2100/2329

SCHEDULE 5	BASIC CLASS
Codeine Cough Preparation (Cosanyl, Pediacof)	9050
Difenoxin Preparation (Motofen)	9167
Dihydrocodeine Preparation (Cophene-S)	9120
Diphenoxylate Preparation (Lomotil, Logen)	9170
Ethylmorphine Preparation	9190
Opium Preparation (Kapectolin PG)	9809

SCHEDULE 4	BASIC CLASS
Alprazolam (Xanax)	2882
Barbital (Veronal, Plexonal, Barbitone)	2145
Chloral Hydrate (Noctec)	2465
Chlordiazepoxide (Librium, Libritabs)	2744
Clorazepate (Tranxene)	2768
Dextropropoxyphene du (Darvon)	9278
Diazepam (Valium, Diastat)	2765
Diethylpropion (Tenuate, Tepanil)	1610
Difenoxin 1 mg/25ug ATSO4/du (Motofen)	9167
Fenfluramine (Pondimin, Dexfenfluramine)	1670
Flurazepam (Dalmane)	2767
Halazepam (Paxipam)	2762
Lorazepam (Ativan)	2885
Mazindol (Sanorex, Mazanor)	1605
Mebutamate (Capla)	2800
Meprobamate (Miltown, Equanil)	2820
Methohexital (Brevital)	2264
Methylphenobarbital (Mebaral)	2250
Midazolam (Versed)	2884
Oxazepam (Serax, Serenid-D)	2835
Paraldehyde (Paral)	2585
Pemoline (Cylert)	1530
Pentazocine (Talwin, Talacen)	9709
Phenobarbital (Luminal, Donnatal)	2285
Phentermine (Ionamin, Fastin, Zantryl)	1640
Prazepam (Centrax)	2764
Quazepam (Doral)	2881
Temazepam (Restoril)	2925
Triazolam (Halcion)	2887
Zolpidem (Ambien, Ivadal, Stilnox)	2783

NEW INST · Page 3

Figure 3.3. DEA Form 224

The physician's name is Dr. May Long and her DEA number is AL2455562. To verify that the DEA number is correct, follow this **DEA formula**:

1. A valid DEA number will consist of two letters, six numbers, and one check digit.

2. Check to verify the first letter of the DEA number. This is the **DEA registrant** type. As shown by the list of different registrant types, some have authorization to only distribute or manufacture. Other registrants are only allowed to use controlled substances for use in research and labs. Still others, such as practitioners, can write prescriptions for patients. As

a pharmacy technician, you will normally encounter DEA numbers that begin with an *A*, *B*, *C*, or *M*. A complete list of registrant types follows.

A: deprecated (used by older entities)

B: hospital or clinic

C: practitioner

D: teaching institution

E: manufacturer

F: distributor

G: researcher

H: analytical lab

J: importer

K: exporter

L: reverse distributor

M: mid-level practitioner

P to U: narcotic treatment program

X: Suboxone/Subutex prescribing program

3. The second letter is the first letter of the last name of the practitioner. In the example, this would be **L**.

4. To verify the number, the next step is to add the first, third and fifth numbers in the DEA number. In the example, this would be $2 + 5 + 5 = 12$.

5. The next step is to add the second, fourth, and sixth number together and multiply by 2. Here, the arithmetic would be $4 + 5 + 6 = 15$; $15 \times 2 = 30$.

6. Finally, the 12 and 30 are added together. The last number should match the last digit in the DEA number. In this example, $12 + 30 = 42$. 2 is the last digit in the DEA number: AL2455562.

? Practice the DEA formula by using these samples: AW3284065, AG4342793, FN5623740, AR5472612, and BN6428521.

PRACTICE QUESTIONS

1. Which DEA registrant type is used for a hospital or clinic?

   A) B

   B) M

   C) L

   D) A

   Answers:

   A) **Correct.** *B* is used for a hospital or clinic.

   B) Incorrect. *M* is used for a mid-level practitioner.

   C) Incorrect. *L* is used for reverse distributor.

   D) Incorrect. *A* is used for older entities.

2. Which is NOT a step to verifying a DEA number using the DEA formula?

A) Add the second, fourth, and sixth numbers and multiply by 2.

B) Make sure the second letter of the DEA number is the first letter of the practitioner's last name.

C) Add the first, third, and fifth numbers together and multiply by 2.

D) Make sure the first number is a DEA registrant type that is able to prescribe medications to patients.

Answers:

A) Incorrect. This arithmetic is a step in the DEA formula.

B) Incorrect. The first letter of the practitioner's last name should match the second letter in the DEA number.

C) **Correct.** The first, third, and fifth numbers should be added together, but not multiplied by 2.

D) Incorrect. The first letter of the DEA number must delineate a DEA registrant type that is able to write prescriptions.

DISPENSING OF CONTROLLED SUBSTANCES

The dispensing of controlled substances must comply with both federal and state regulations. As mentioned in chapter two, the process of dispensing controlled substances is much more complex than that of non-controlled drugs. It is important that the pharmacist, pharmacy technician, and even the prescriber follow the protocols of their state in this matter.

Because of the criminal and/or civil actions the pharmacy could be subject to if a controlled substance is dispensed incorrectly, it is important to discuss each step of the dispensing process of these drugs in depth. When the patient drops off the controlled prescription, it is crucial to obtain certain information from the patient. It is crucial to verify the information listed below—especially with CII drugs—to be sure the prescription is correctly written by the physician.

+ date the prescription was written
+ patient's full name and address
+ practitioner's name, full address, phone number, and DEA number
+ directions for use
+ quantity
+ number of refills (if allowed)
+ manual signature of prescriber

After the technician receives a controlled prescription, the next step is to verify the DEA number and inspect the prescription for any of the red flags explained in chapter 2. If there are any discrepancies or questions as to the validity of the prescription, or if the DEA number is not verifiable, the pharmacist should be notified. He or she will then take steps, like calling the prescriber, to verify the prescription.

Next, the technician checks the patient's profile. It is essential to look for duplicate drug therapies when dispensing controlled substances. Sometimes a patient may unknowingly be prescribed a medication similar to the drug prescribed from a recent dental or emergency room procedure. Other times, a patient may have dependency issues; he or she may be trying to fill multiple prescriptions from different physicians. Any questionable circumstances should always be brought to the attention of the pharmacist.

Data Entry

When entering information into the pharmacy software system, it is important to be familiar with the schedule of controlled medications. CII prescriptions must be signed manually in ink. Seven days after the prescription is written, it becomes invalid and the prescriber must submit a new prescription. CII prescriptions can only be written for a 30-day supply and cannot have refills. The prescriber must write a new prescription for additional fills.

For schedules CIII – CV, the original prescription must be manually signed by the physician. When refilling CIII – CV drugs, the physician can write up to 6 months of additional refills (the original fill plus five refills), but if the patient needs a refill and none are left on the original prescription, the patient must have a new prescription written by the doctor. It is important to check the date of the last refill on a controlled substance. If the patient is trying to refill the prescription too early, that patient may be abusing the medication and not complying with the directions for use. Oral prescriptions are only allowed in emergencies.

Fill Process of Controlled Substances

CII narcotics are stored in a locked narcotics cabinet that can only be accessed by the pharmacist. Depending on state and business-related policies, most pharmacists fill CII narcotics themselves to avoid any counting discrepancies. On the other hand, pharmacy technicians can fill prescriptions for CIII – CV narcotics. Most pharmacy practices require the pharmacist and technicians to double-count and initial the quantity of controlled substances on the label, verifying the medication was counted twice to avoid count discrepancies and inventory issues.

Controlled substances labels have specific requirements under state and federal law. Besides the pharmacy name, address, and phone number, the label must also include the date of fill, prescriber's name, NDC number of drug, patient's name, patient's address, order number, directions for use, and any auxiliary labels. Federal guidelines require all controlled substance labels to state *Caution: Federal Law Prohibits the Transfer of This Drug to Any Person Other Than the Patient for Whom It was Prescribed.*

Most prescription pads are tamper-resistant, meaning if an individual attempts to copy a prescription, *VOID* will show up on the background of the prescription.

Perpetual Inventory

Perpetual inventory is required for all CII drugs. Although most inventory in pharmacies is done electronically, perpetual inventory of CII drugs must still be handwritten and signed by a pharmacist when a CII drug has been received into inventory, dispensed to a patient, or when the CII has been disposed of. Perpetual inventories must be reconciled and verified every ten days to avoid counting discrepancies. CIII – CV drugs may be estimated unless the bulk container contains more than 1,000 units; then it must have an exact count.

On a CII perpetual inventory log, the name of the drug, the item number of the drug, and sheet number are listed on top of the page. The sheet is then divided into three sections that state when the drug is ordered, received, and sold. Under the order section, the pharmacist is required to state the date ordered, the order number, the vendor, and the quantity. When the order is received, under the received section, the pharmacist marks the date received and the quantity. If the drug is backordered, the pharmacist marks the backorder and/or states the date the vendor is expecting the drug to be available. In the *sold* section, the pharmacist writes the date, order number, and the quantity dispensed. After each function has been added, the pharmacist must calculate the quantity balance, sign, and add any comments necessary.

Perpetual Inventory Control

ITEM				ITEM NO				SHEET NO		

Ordered				Recieved				Sold		
Date	Order No	Vendor	Qty	Date	Qty	Backorder	Due Date	Date	Order No	Qty

Figure 3.4. Perpetual Inventory Control Form

Filing Controlled Substances

As stated in chapter two, hard copies of prescriptions must be kept on file in the pharmacy for at least two years. Non-controlled and controlled prescriptions can be filed with one of three separate prescription file systems.

+ **three-file system:** In this system, the pharmacy keeps three files. One file is used exclusively for CII prescriptions, one for CIII – CV prescriptions, and one for non-controlled prescriptions.

+ **the two-file system:** One file only contains CII prescriptions and the other contains all other prescriptions. Because the second file contains both controlled and non-controlled medications, the DEA requires that, with this system, the controlled drugs are identified with a red C stamp placed on the lower right-hand corner of CIII – CV prescriptions.

+ **alternative two-file system:** With this system all controlled substances are placed in one folder and non-controls in another folder. The CIII – CV prescriptions must still have the C stamp placed on the prescription.

PRACTICE QUESTIONS

1. Which information does NOT need to be checked on a controlled prescription when the patient drops it off?

   A) the manual signature of prescriber

   B) the date the prescription was written

   C) the patient's full name and address

   D) the patient's signature

   Answers:

   A) Incorrect. The physician should have manually signed the prescription.

   B) Incorrect. The original date of the prescription is important because a controlled prescription is only valid for a limited time.

   C) Incorrect. The patient's full name and address is required on a controlled prescription.

   D) Correct. The patient's signature is not required on a controlled prescription.

2. What is NOT documented on a perpetual inventory log?

   A) CII drug information when ordered from the drug manufacturer

   B) the patient to whom the CII drug was prescribed

   C) CII drugs received by the drug manufacturer

   D) the balance of the quantity for the specific CII drug after each CII drug transaction is recorded

Answers:

A) Incorrect. The CII drug order information is recorded on a CII perpetual inventory log.

B) Correct. Patient names are not listed on the perpetual inventory log.

C) Incorrect. The CII drug order should be recorded on the log when received from the manufacturer.

D) Incorrect. The balance of the quantity is always logged after each drug transaction carried out for the specific CII drug.

3. What should always be placed on CIII – CV prescriptions when filing hard copies in a two-file system?

A) a red X stamped in the lower left-hand corner

B) a red C stamped in the lower left-hand corner

C) a red C stamped in the lower right-hand corner

D) a red X stamped in the lower right-hand corner

Answers:

A) Incorrect. A red X in the lower left-hand corner is not required.

B) Incorrect. A red C in the lower left-hand corner is not correct.

C) Correct. A red C in the right-hand corner is required.

D) Incorrect. A red X in the lower right-hand corner is incorrect.

EMERGENCY DISPENSING

The physician may only call in an oral prescription in place of a written one in an emergency, and this requires special circumstances. Emergency dispensing is used when a physician determines that the need for a CII drug is required as soon as possible and there is no other alternative treatment available for the patient. An example of an incident where emergency dispensing may be considered is if a patient is on hospice and is terminally ill. The pharmacist will then fill the prescription *In Good Faith*, meaning the pharmacist expects the physician to send a written and signed prescription within 7 days or less, depending on state laws.

Other guidelines for emergency dispensing follow.

+ Emergency dispensing can be used if a physician is out of the area and cannot give the pharmacist a written prescription.

+ The physician must give the pharmacist the patient's name, address, drug name, drug dosage, drug strength, dosage form, route of administration, physician's name, address, phone number, and DEA number. The pharmacist must document the information manually and in written form.

+ The quantity dispensed can only be enough to sustain the patient during the emergency time period. It should not pass three days.

+ The pharmacist must document on the prescription that it was dispensed in an emergency.

+ The pharmacist must verify the physician's authority.

+ When the hard copy is received, if the statement *Authorization for Emergency Dispensing* is not written on the prescription by the physician, the DEA must be informed.

+ The hard copy must be attached and filed with the oral prescription.

+ Additional requirements might be implemented by BOP regulation of the state in which the CII drug was dispensed.

With CIII – CV prescriptions, if the pharmacy does not have enough of a drug in stock to fill the full quantity of the prescription, the pharmacist can give the patient a **partial fill** to hold the patient over until the rest of the prescription can be filled. In these cases, the pharmacist may prorate the price of the prescription and the patient can call in a refill when needed; otherwise, the pharmacy may owe the additional quantity to the patient and, when the drug is available, the patient can pick up the additional quantity at no charge. In this event, the pharmacist must mark on the label the amount of pills given and the amount owed to the patient.

With CII prescriptions, the pharmacist may also partially fill for a patient. If the pharmacist is unable to dispense the remaining quantity within 72 hours, the physician must be notified and a new prescription must be written for the additional quantity. Partial fills must be noted on the hard copy along with the amount filled.

PRACTICE QUESTION

Which is NOT a guideline for the emergency dispensing of a CII prescription?

A) The quantity dispensed can only be enough to sustain the patient during the emergency time period.

B) A physician cannot ask the pharmacist to dispense a CII prescription in an emergency if the physician is out of town.

C) The pharmacist must document on the prescription that it was dispensed in an emergency.

D) The hard copy must be attached and filed with the record of the oral prescription.

Answers:

A) Incorrect. One guideline for emergency dispensing is that the quantity dispensed may only sustain the patient during the emergency time period.

B) **Correct.** A physician can emergency dispense a CII prescription if he or she is out of town.

C) Incorrect. The pharmacist must document on the prescription that it is an emergency situation.

D) Incorrect. The hard copy must be attached to the record of the oral prescription.

ELECTRONIC PRESCRIPTIONS

Transmitting an **electronic prescription** is called e-prescribing. **E-prescribing** allows pharmacies, nurses, and physicians to communicate and send prescriptions through computer-based transmission and helps provide error-free, accurate prescriptions and information to other healthcare entities.

Although there are many benefits to e-prescribing, problems arise when it comes to controlled substances. In 2010, the DEA issued new rules on e-prescribing controlled substances. This included the allowance for CII – CV prescriptions to be able to be transmitted electronically *only if* both the physician and pharmacy software systems were certified to do so by a third-party auditor.

> Because of potential new developments in regards to controlled drug e-prescribing, for more information and updates on electronic prescriptions for controlled substances please visit http://www.deadiversion.usdoj.gov/ecomm/e_rx/index.html.

Although it is believed that the use of e-prescribing for controlled prescriptions in the future will help in the prevention of medication errors, many pharmacies and physicians' offices still do not have required software and have not met DEA requirements to allow controlled prescriptions to be transmitted electronically.

Besides not meeting requirements, transmission of electronic controlled prescriptions also depends on the laws and regulations of the individual state's BOP. With prescription drug abuse on the rise, some BOPs still require patients to receive new written prescriptions of certain CII drugs from the physician's office monthly. Therefore, currently e-prescribing controlled substances is voluntary based on whether both the physician office that e-prescribes and the pharmacy that dispenses the controlled substance meet federal and state requirements.

If either the physician or pharmacy do not meet the software requirements and are not certified to e-prescribe controlled substances, the transmission will be rejected and the controlled substance prescription will not be sent. The physician can still use electronic software to print out a prescription and can manually sign the prescription if this is the case. Controlled prescriptions can be computer generated from the patient's electronic health record (EHR), but it is required that the physician manually signs the prescription.

Security concerns, when it comes to the transmission and manipulation of e-prescribing controlled substances, have kept some practitioners from using the software. As technology progresses, so will new developments in controlled substance e-prescribing software.

CONTINUE

PRACTICE QUESTION

According to the DEA, what is the main requirement for a pharmacy or physician's office to e-prescribe controlled substances?

A) a manual signature from the physician

B) The patient must have an ER.

C) Both entities (the pharmacy and doctor's office) must be certified and audited to do so by a third-party auditor.

D) Both entities (the pharmacy and doctor's office) must be authorized by the state BOP.

Answers:

A) Incorrect. The prescription is signed electronically if e-prescribe is allowed.

B) Incorrect. The patient can have an EHR, but the physician still may not have certification to e-prescribe controlled substances.

C) **Correct.** The entities (pharmacy and doctor's office) must be certified and audited to allow controlled substance e-prescribing by a third-party auditor.

D) Incorrect. Even if permitted by the state BOP, both the pharmacy and doctor's office must have the correct authorization and certification from a third-party auditor in order to e-prescribe.

STORAGE AND SECURITY REQUIREMENTS

All controlled substances are stored in a way to obstruct theft or drug diversion. The higher the class of the controlled substance, the more stringent the storage and security requirements of the drug.

CI substances, although very rarely used, must be securely locked and placed in a cabinet with controlled accessibility. **Controlled accessibility** refers to the use of security features that control access to a certain resource. CI drugs are only used in scientific and clinical studies and research.

CIII – CV drugs must also be stored securely. These drugs are stored in pharmacies, clinical research clinics, and scientific labs. Although the drugs can be placed alongside non-controlled drugs, the healthcare setting itself is secured through strict regulations to prevent diversion. Some regulations include keeping the healthcare setting accessible only to authorized personnel who need keys or passwords to enter the facility.

> The DEA provides more information and updates on storage and security of controlled substances at www.deadiversion.usdoj.gov/21cfr/cfr/1301/1301 _71.htm.

CII drugs are more strongly secured within the healthcare setting. As with CI drugs, they are closely monitored under lock and key in specially constructed safety cabinets. Some ways to prevent theft and ensure the security of the healthcare setting include:

+ electronic alarm systems
+ self-closing and automatic locking doors
+ key- and/or password-control systems
+ allowing authorized personnel only
+ possible use of security officers in high-crime areas

PRACTICE QUESTION

Which of the following is NOT a way to control theft and drug diversion?

A) keeping CII drugs alongside non-control drugs

B) controlled accessibility

C) self-locking doors

D) electronic alarm systems

Answers:

A) **Correct.** CII drugs must be kept in a safety cabinet under lock and key or password protected.

B) Incorrect. Controlled accessibility is one way to prevent theft and diversion of drugs.

C) Incorrect. Self-locking doors help prevent theft and diversion.

D) Incorrect. Electronic alarm systems help prevent theft and diversion.

ORDERING, RECEIVING, DISTRIBUTING, AND RETURNING CONTROLLED SUBSTANCES

CII ordering requires **DEA Form 222**. Pharmacists are responsible for ordering CII drugs because only individuals who have a DEA number can order them. When filling out DEA Form 222, the pharmacist must include specific information.

+ company name and address
+ order date
+ name of drug
+ order number of the item (up to ten items per form)
+ quantity of packages of the item needed
+ package size of the item needed
+ purchaser's (pharmacist's) signature
+ pharmacist's DEA number

The **distributor,** or the business that stores and sells the drugs to the pharmacies, receives DEA Form 222 and processes the order. When preparing the order in the

warehouse, the distributor must add the NDC number of each drug, the packages shipped, and the date of shipment. If the form is filled out incorrectly, the distributor cannot process the order.

BLANK DEA FORM-222
U.S. OFFICIAL ORDER FORM - SCHEDULES I & II

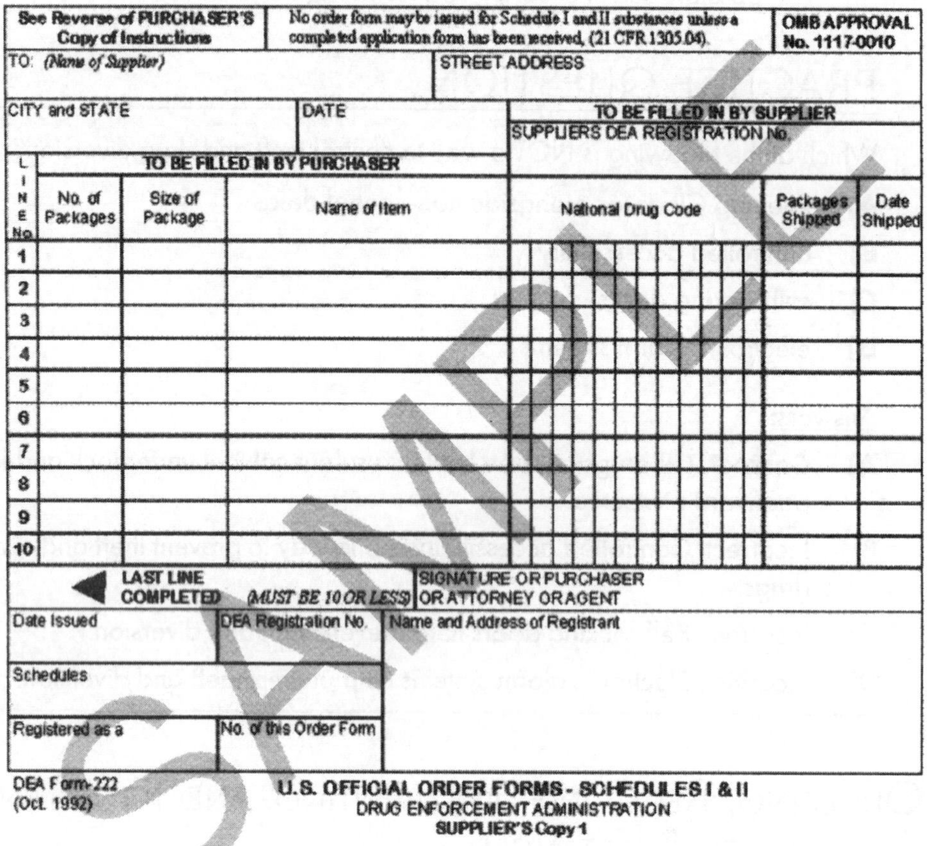
See Reverse of PURCHASER'S Copy of Instructions | No order form may be issued for Schedule I and II substances unless a completed application form has been received, (21 CFR 1305.04). | OMB APPROVAL No. 1117-0010

TO: (Name of Supplier) | STREET ADDRESS

CITY and STATE | DATE | TO BE FILLED IN BY SUPPLIER | SUPPLIERS DEA REGISTRATION No.

LINE No.	No. of Packages	Size of Package	Name of Item	National Drug Code	Packages Shipped	Date Shipped
1						
2						
3						
4						
5						
6						
7						
8						
9						
10						

LAST LINE COMPLETED (MUST BE 10 OR LESS) | SIGNATURE OR PURCHASER OR ATTORNEY OR AGENT

Date Issued | DEA Registration No. | Name and Address of Registrant

Schedules

Registered as a | No. of this Order Form

DEA Form-222 (Oct. 1992)

U.S. OFFICIAL ORDER FORMS - SCHEDULES I & II
DRUG ENFORCEMENT ADMINISTRATION
SUPPLIER'S Copy 1

Note: The graphic illustrated above is only a depiction of the DEA Form-222. It is not intended to be used as an actual order form.

Figure 3.5. DEA Form 222

The distributor is only able to send the order to the address specified on both the order form and DEA registration form of the pharmacist. If the distributor can only partially fill an order, the remaining balance of the order must be shipped within 60 days of the original order date.

Pharmacists are also required to receive the CII orders. When the order is received, the pharmacist verifies that the order is complete and logs the order in the perpetual inventory book. Recordkeeping of CII drugs must be complete, accurate, and be kept on record for two to five years, depending on the state where the pharmacy is located. CII records are kept separately from all other records.

 DEA Form 222 is now available online for convenience. Information is available at https://www.deadiversion.usdoj.gov/webforms/orderFormsRequest.jsp.

When returning CII drugs, pharmacists also use the DEA Form 222. The order can only be returned from one DEA registrant to another. Each drug is labeled separately and must state the drug description and name, quantity, product size, strength, NDC number, and the name of the manufacturer.

Occasionally, a pharmacy may distribute a CII drug to another pharmacy or healthcare setting. In these cases, certain restrictions apply. The pharmacy or healthcare setting must be a DEA registrant and must use DEA Form 222. The pharmacy must record the distribution, and the recipient must record the receipt of the substance. Finally, the dosage units of the drug must not exceed more than 5 percent of the amount that the pharmacy dispenses during the one-year period in which it registered. Any more than 5 percent requires the pharmacy to have a separate registration as a distributor.

CIII – CV orders can be placed when ordering non-controlled drugs. However when the order is received, the pharmacy technician must verify the drug and the amount sent, sign the invoice to document the order was correct, mark the invoice with the red C stamp used when filing controlled hard copies, and make a duplicate copy for the pharmacy records. State laws and individual business requirements may differ. Some require the pharmacist to sign the invoices as well as the technician, and others require the pharmacist to receive all controlled substances, not just CII drugs.

PRACTICE QUESTION

Which is NOT required on DEA Form 222 when a pharmacist is ordering CII drugs?

A) order number

B) number of packages

C) size of package

D) doctor's DEA number

Answers:

A)   Incorrect. The order number is required.

B)   Incorrect. The number of packages must be specified on the form.

C)   Incorrect. The form must include the size of the package.

D)   Correct. The purchaser's (pharmacist's) DEA number is required, not the doctor's.

HANDLING OUTDATED CONTROLLED SUBSTANCES

When handling outdated controlled substances, a pharmacy must fill out **DEA Form 41** with a cover letter stating why it is requesting permission to destroy the drugs. The information required on DEA Form 41 includes the name of the drug; the number of packages; the quantity in the package (contents); the DEA number; the pharmacy name, address, and phone number; and the signature of the DEA registrant. If a representative from the State Board of Pharmacy witnesses the destruction of the drugs, approval is not needed from the DEA.

OMB Approval No. 1117-0007	U.S. Department of Justice/Drug Enforcement Administration **REGISTRANTS INVENTORY OF DRUGS SURRENDERED**	PACKAGE NO.

The following schedule is an inventory of controlled substances which is hereby surrendered to you for proper disposition.

FROM: (Include Name, Street, City, State and ZIP Code in space provided below.)

Signature of applicant or authorized agent

Registrant's DEA Number

Registrant's Telephone Number

NOTE: CERTIFIED MAIL (Return Receipt Requested) IS REQUIRED FOR SHIPMENTS OF DRUGS VIA U.S. POSTAL SERVICE. See instructions on reverse (page 2) of form.

NAME OF DRUG OR PREPARATION	Number of Containers	CONTENTS (Number of grams, tablets, ounces or other units per container)	Controlled Substance Content (Each Unit)	FOR DEA USE ONLY		
				DISPOSITION	QUANTITY	
Registrants will fill in Columns 1,2,3, and 4 ONLY.					GMS.	MGS.
1	2	3	4	5	6	7
Example: Methadone HCL Tablets, 10mg	1	100mg	10			
Example: Methadose 960 ml, 10mg/ml	1	960ml	10			
1						
2						
3						
4						
16						

> **Note: The graphic illustrated above is only a depiction of the DEA Form-41. It is not intended to be used as an actual Drug Disposal form.**

Figure 3.6. DEA Form 41

Permission to destroy outdated drugs can be sent once a year up to two weeks prior to destruction date. Destruction of the drugs must be witnessed by two people.

Approved witnesses include pharmacists, nurses, practitioners, and law enforcement officers. Many pharmacies are also a part of a product-return program that allows the pharmacy to send back the outdated controlled substances for partial reimbursement.

PRACTICE QUESTION

Which is NOT required on DEA Form 41?

A) drug name

B) package content

C) pharmacy technician's signature

D) DEA number

Answers:

A)   Incorrect. The drug name is required on the form.

B)   Incorrect. The package content must be indicated on the form.

C)   Correct. The DEA registrant must sign the form, not the pharmacy technician.

D)   Incorrect. The DEA number is required.

THEFT OR LOSS

Any theft or loss of a controlled substance must be documented and the pharmacist must contact his or her local DEA office. Significant losses must be reported immediately. For smaller losses or thefts of controlled substances, pharmacists fill out **DEA Form 106**. The form includes the pharmacy's name, address, phone number, DEA number, date of loss or theft, list of items stolen or lost, local police department information, and information about the container and labels with a description and costs. Copies of DEA Form 106 are then sent to the BOP, the local police, and the DEA.

PRACTICE QUESTION

Whom should the pharmacist contact first if the theft or loss of a controlled substance occurs?

A) the local police

B) the DEA

C) the BOP

D) the company CEO

Answers:

A)   Incorrect. The local police should be contacted, but they are not the first contact.

B)   Correct. The pharmacist should immediately contact the DEA before anyone else.

C) Incorrect. The BOP should be contacted but not before the DEA.

D) Incorrect. The company CEO should not be contacted.

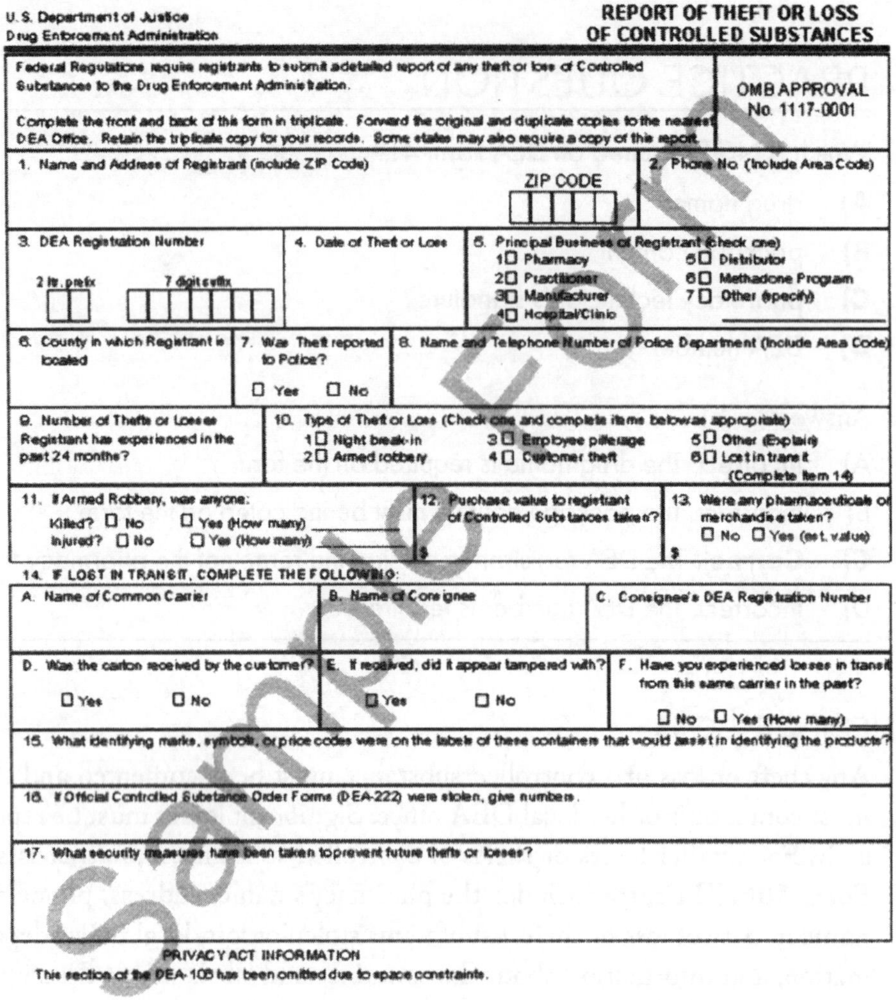
U. S. Department of Justice
Drug Enforcement Administration

REPORT OF THEFT OR LOSS OF CONTROLLED SUBSTANCES

Federal Regulations require registrants to submit a detailed report of any theft or loss of Controlled Substances to the Drug Enforcement Administration.

Complete the front and back of this form in triplicate. Forward the original and duplicate copies to the nearest DEA Office. Retain the triplicate copy for your records. Some states may also require a copy of this report.

OMB APPROVAL No. 1117-0001

1. Name and Address of Registrant (include ZIP Code) ZIP CODE

2. Phone No. (Include Area Code)

3. DEA Registration Number 2 ltr. prefix 7 digit suffix

4. Date of Theft or Loss

5. Principal Business of Registrant (check one) 1 Pharmacy 2 Practitioner 3 Manufacturer 4 Hospital/Clinic 5 Distributor 6 Methadone Program 7 Other (specify)

6. County in which Registrant is located

7. Was Theft reported to Police? Yes No

8. Name and Telephone Number of Police Department (Include Area Code)

9. Number of Thefts or Losses Registrant has experienced in the past 24 months?

10. Type of Theft or Loss (Check one and complete items below as appropriate) 1 Night break-in 2 Armed robbery 3 Employee pilferage 4 Customer theft 5 Other (Explain) 6 Lost in transit (Complete Item 14)

11. If Armed Robbery, was anyone: Killed? No Yes (How many) Injured? No Yes (How many)

12. Purchase value to registrant of Controlled Substances taken? $

13. Were any pharmaceuticals or merchandise taken? No Yes (est. value) $

14. IF LOST IN TRANSIT, COMPLETE THE FOLLOWING:

A. Name of Common Carrier

B. Name of Consignee

C. Consignee's DEA Registration Number

D. Was the carton received by the customer? Yes No

E. If received, did it appear tampered with? Yes No

F. Have you experienced losses in transit from this same carrier in the past? No Yes (How many)

15. What identifying marks, symbols, or price codes were on the labels of these containers that would assist in identifying the products?

16. If Official Controlled Substance Order Forms (DEA-222) were stolen, give numbers.

17. What security measures have been taken to prevent future thefts or losses?

PRIVACY ACT INFORMATION
This section of the DEA-106 has been omitted due to space constraints.

Note: The graphic illustrated above is only a depiction of the DEA Form-106. It is not intended to be used as an actual Theft or Loss report.

Figure 3.7. DEA Form 106

DEA Inspections

DEA inspections are mandated by the Controlled Substances Act and require administrative search warrants. Before entering a DEA-registered business, the inspectors must state the purpose of the inspection and identify themselves. During consensual inspections, the DEA checks for the accuracy of DEA- and BOP-required controlled substances recordkeeping. DEA inspections are usually performed with a representative of the BOP. The inspectors also check for correct and up-to-date DEA registrants, certifications, and registrations.

The controlled substance records, discussed in the previous chapters, help the inspectors to find important records easily and make the inspection quick and efficient. Records checked include all invoices and receipts for orders, receiving, distribution, inventory, DEA Form 222s, and the file systems for those CII and CIII – CV prescriptions filled. Records are kept on file for at least 2 years—sometimes longer depending on state requirements.

> When a DEA inspector identifies him- or herself, the pharmacy technician must refer the DEA agent to the pharmacist-in-charge; otherwise the DEA agent will give the pharmacy a negative mark for noncompliance during the DEA inspection.

In emergencies, dangerous health situations, or if the inspection is of a special state statute category, DEA agents may not have an administrative search warrant but still must identify themselves and their purpose. Pharmacy technicians are required to refer the DEA agent immediately to the pharmacist-in-charge.

PRACTICE QUESTION

What must the pharmacy technician immediately do if DEA agents identify themselves for an inspection?

A) retrieve all records needed for the inspection

B) allow the agents into the pharmacy and start showing them around

C) show the inspectors where the file system is located

D refer the agents to the pharmacist-in-charge

Answers:

A) Incorrect. Pharmacy technicians do not retrieve records for the inspectors.

B) Incorrect. Pharmacy technicians do not show the inspectors around the pharmacy.

C) Incorrect. Pharmacy technicians do not show the inspectors where the files are located.

D) **Correct.** Pharmacy technicians should immediately refer the inspectors to the pharmacist-in-charge.

PRESCRIPTION MONITORING

Many states now participate in **prescription drug monitoring programs (PDMP)**. These programs are used to identify possible abuse and diversion of controlled substances. The statewide electronic database is used by statewide regulatory, administrative, and law enforcement agencies. The DEA is not involved in state monitoring programs. The monitoring programs not only identify discrepancies within a patient's controlled prescription history, but can also find discrepancies with prescribers and pharmacies in the dispensing of controlled drugs as well. For more information about PDMPs, visit www.pmpalliance.org.

The **National Alliance for Model State Drug Laws (NAMSDL)** states that PDMPs

+ support access to legitimate medical use of controlled substances.
+ identify and deter or prevent drug abuse and diversion.
+ facilitate and encourage the identification, intervention with, and treatment of persons addicted to prescription drugs.
+ inform public health initiatives by outlining use and abuse trends.
+ educate individuals about PDMPs and the use, abuse and diversion of, and addiction to prescription drugs.

Besides state monitoring programs, some states have begun to participate in nationwide monitoring programs that can monitor the prescription histories of potential drug abusers across state lines. Briefly mentioned above, the program is called **NABP PMP Interconnect**. States that participate include:

+ Alaska	+ Kentucky	+ Ohio
+ Arizona	+ Louisiana	+ Oklahoma
+ Arkansas	+ Maryland	+ Rhode Island
+ Colorado	+ Michigan	+ South Carolina
+ Connecticut	+ Minnesota	+ South Dakota
+ Delaware	+ Mississippi	+ Tennessee
+ Idaho	+ Nevada	+ Utah
+ Illinois	+ New Jersey	+ Vermont
+ Indiana	+ New Mexico	+ Virginia
+ Iowa	+ New York	+ Wisconsin
+ Kansas	+ North Dakota	

PRACTICE QUESTION

Which is NOT a purpose of the PDMP?

A) to track and deter patients from taking narcotics who have chronic pain

B) to support access to legitimate medical use of controlled substances

C) to identify and deter or prevent drug abuse and diversion

D) to inform public health initiatives through outlining use and abuse trends

Answers:

A) **Correct.** PDMP is not used to track and/or deter patients who have chronic pain from taking narcotics.

B) Incorrect. PDMP supports access to legitimate medical use of controlled substances.

C) Incorrect. PDMP is used to identify and deter or prevent drug abuse and diversion.

D)   Incorrect. PDMP does inform public health initiatives through outlining use and abuse trends.

RESTRICTION ON SALES OF PRODUCTS CONTAINING EPHEDRINE AND PSEUDOEPHEDRINE

The Combat Methamphetamine Epidemic Act of 2005 (CMEA) regulates the over-the-counter sales of **ephedrine** and **pseudoephedrine**, chemicals commonly used in the production of **methamphetamine**. In retail pharmacy, enforcing the CMEA requirements is an important task of the pharmacy technician.

 Mississippi and Oregon require prescriptions for ephedrine and pseudo ephedrine.

CMEA is an amendment to the CSA. The act ensures there is a sufficient supply of these drugs for medical purposes, while it still deters the use of the drugs for illegal purposes. Besides ephedrine and pseudoephedrine, the act also gives the DEA the ability to regulate other chemicals used in the manufacturing process of methamphetamine. The act requires retailers to place the products out of direct customer access. Customers must purchase these products at the pharmacy counter; employees must ask for customer photo ID verification and signatures and keep sales logbooks. Furthermore, sellers of ephedrine and pseudoephedrine must obtain self-certification; employees must receive required training.

? If each Sudafed pill contains 30 mg of pseudoephedrine, how many pills could a patient buy every 30 days if the limit is 9 grams?

A daily supply of these products is limited to 3.6 grams. Sales of these products are limited to every 30 days, and these supplies are limited to 7.5 grams if sold by mail-order and 9 grams in retail environments such as drug stores. Prescription drugs are exempt from logbook requirements.

PRACTICE QUESTION

Which of the following is NOT a requirement of the CMEA?

A)   A 30-day supply of medication containing ephedrine or pseudoephedrine is limited to 9 grams per 30-day supply in retail environments.

B)   Sellers must obtain self-certification.

C)   Patients are required to have a prescription to receive ephedrine and pseudoephedrine.

D)   Selling products containing ephedrine or pseudoephedrine requires employee training.

<u>Answers:</u>

A)   Incorrect. 30-day supplies are limited to 9 grams in retail environments.

B)   Incorrect. It is true that sellers must obtain self-certification.

C)   Correct. Patients do not need a prescription to purchase products containing ephedrine or pseudoephedrine in most states.

D)   Incorrect. Selling products containing ephedrine or pseudoephedrine requires employee training.

FOUR: ADMINISTRATION & MANAGEMENT OF THE PHARMACY

Pharmacy technicians play a vital role in assisting the pharmacist with administrative and management duties. Technicians help ensure that the pharmacy runs efficiently by participating in protocols used to prevent medication errors, assuring safety in the workplace, and through vigilant recordkeeping. In this chapter, these tasks as well as inventory control, purchasing, hazardous materials, and reference materials will be discussed.

Medication Errors

Medication errors are the third-leading cause of preventable death and injuries in the United States. A **medication error** is any healthcare action or decision that causes an unintended consequence. Each year, nearly 1.5 million medication errors occur in the United States. In hospitals alone, over 400,000 people die annually due to medication errors. Medication errors also cause higher healthcare costs due to ER visits, extra drug and medical therapies, and resulting disabilities. As for pharmacy, it is estimated that nearly 2 percent of all written prescriptions contain some form of medication error.

Although most medication errors reported do not cause any serious harm to the patient, the fact that an error occurred at all puts a patient at risk of an adverse reaction or death. It also inconveniences patients and lowers their level of care. For example, if a nurse administers pain medications to a patient later than the scheduled time of dosage, the patient is inconvenienced and suffers unnecessary pain and discomfort. While the error did not cause an adverse reaction, it did make the patient uncomfortable.

Pharmacy technicians play an important role in medication safety. By being extra attentive to detail when monitoring prescriptions for errors, the pharmacy technician helps to prevent them from occurring. Medication errors can be varied and complex, so it is crucial for technicians to be well informed so they can work effectively and efficiently.

Medication errors are not only associated with pharmacy mistakes. Medication errors are a top education and training priority for all healthcare professionals including doctors and nurses.

There are several classifications of medication errors. Due to the many systems for prescribing and dispensing medication, sometimes it can be difficult to ascertain exactly when or how the medication error occurred. For instance, in the hospital the physician prescribes the drug, the pharmacy prepares and dispenses the drug, and the nurse administers the drug. Because so many healthcare providers are involved in patient care, an error could occur through a miscommunication between one or more of the entities involved or even just within an individual entity.

Through evaluating medication error reports, it has been found that most errors occur from prescribing errors, omission errors, and wrong dose errors. In combination, these errors account for 68 percent of all reported medication errors. The causes of these errors include not following procedures, miscommunication, and poor performance.

A pharmacy technician is preparing a drug that requires 2.5 ml of magnesium sulfate in 100 ml normal saline. Magnesium sulfate comes in a 2 mg/ml in a 20 ml vial. The technician misreads the medication order as 25 ml of magnesium sulfate and prepares the drug this way. What type of medication error did the technician make?

Other common drug errors include:

+ **prescribing errors**: Prescribing errors occur when any action during the writing or dispensing of a prescription causes either a decrease in the efficacy of the treatment or an increased risk of harming the patient compared to the general accepted use of the drug.

+ **omission errors**: The prescribed dose is not administered as ordered.

+ **wrong time errors**: The prescribed dose is not administered at the correct time.

+ **unauthorized drug errors**: The wrong drug is administered to the patient.

+ **improper dose errors**: The patient receives a lower dose, a higher dose, or extra doses of the drug than what was originally prescribed.

+ **wrong dosage form errors**: The prescribed route of administration of the drug is incorrect.

+ **wrong drug preparation errors**: The drug is not prepared as prescribed.

+ **wrong administration technique errors**: These are mistakes in administering the drug. Errors may be due to improperly following protocols, a performance deficit, or lack of knowledge.

+ **deteriorated drug errors**: An expired drug is used, or the chemical or physical potency and integrity of the drug has been compromised.

+ **monitoring errors**: Healthcare workers incorrectly monitor drugs that require specific laboratory values for medication and dose selections.
+ **compliance errors**: The patient is not correctly complying with drug therapy.

PRACTICE QUESTIONS

1. A wrong dosage form error happens when

A) the drug was not prepared as prescribed by the physician.

B) the patient is not correctly complying with drug therapy.

C) the prescribed route of administration of the drug is incorrect.

D) the prescribed dose is not administered as ordered.

Answers:

A) Incorrect. Wrong drug preparation errors happen when the drug was not prepared as prescribed by the physician.

B) Incorrect. Compliance errors happen when the patient does not correctly comply with drug therapy.

C) Correct. A wrong dosage form error occurs when the prescribed route of administration of the drug is incorrect.

D) Incorrect. Omission errors occur when the prescribed dose is not administered as ordered.

2. What percentage of medication errors occur due to prescription errors?

A) 5 percent

B) 2 percent

C) 10 percent

D) 20 percent

Answers:

A) Incorrect. Less than 5 percent of medication errors occur due to prescription errors.

B) Correct. Only 2 percent of medication errors are caused by prescription errors.

C) Incorrect. Less than 10 percent of medication errors are caused by prescription errors.

D) Incorrect. Less than 20 percent of medication errors are caused by prescription errors.

CAUSES OF MEDICATION ERRORS

Besides the errors listed in the previous section, certain errors may also occur because of the patient's own response to the drug. Unfortunately, adverse reactions to drugs cannot be predicted and can only be determined after the patient ingests the drug.

In some cases, a patient's **physiological makeup** can cause a drug to metabolize differently from other patients. This can occur due to a patient's age, organ function, or abnormal levels of enzymes used for drug metabolism in the body. For example, a patient with a dysfunctional liver may be unable to metabolize a drug properly and thus require a different drug dosage than a healthy patient. In such a case, a physician should know to adjust the drug dosage accordingly and prevent a medication error.

Social causes of medication errors can occur when the patient is not under the direct care of a physician in an inpatient setting. In an inpatient setting, the healthcare staff provides medication on a regular schedule. The staff also reviews a patient's OTC medication history and medical history. Yet problems still occur. For example, if an elderly outpatient who has cognitive difficulties is prescribed a drug to treat hypertension, the patient is responsible for taking the medication as prescribed when he leaves the clinic no matter what his condition. If the patient lives alone and has no family or other supporters to remind him to take his medications, he could forget to take his medication every day and end up in the hospital due to his blood pressure problems. This would be a compliance error because the patient did not follow the doctor's orders, but it has a social cause: the patient needs a helper to remind him to take his medication every day.

Calculation errors occur when drug doses and compounded drugs are miscalculated. Unfortunately, in these cases children are the most commonly affected. Because children's doses must be calculated based on their weight and body surface area (BSA), calculations require extra attention to ensure accuracy. Making an error as small as the location of a decimal point could kill a child. If a physician prescribes 5.25 g of a medication and the technician unintentionally enters the quantity as 52.5 g, the child would receive ten times more of the drug than what was intended, with potentially fatal results.

> **?** A patient with liver failure receives a prescription for Vicodin 5/325 mg (a combination drug of hydrocodone and acetaminophen). Acetaminophen can be toxic to the liver. The prescriber did not know of the patient's condition and prescribed the drug with directions normally given to a healthy patient. The patient had to be rushed to the emergency room due to liver toxicity caused by the acetaminophen. What was the cause of this medication error?

Although using abbreviations in the pharmacy saves time and improves efficiency, **abbreviation errors** can also result in misinterpretations, especially if two abbreviations are similar. As in the example above, the placement of a decimal point could change the abbreviation or definition. If unsure of an abbreviation or calculation, technicians should always ask the pharmacist. The Joint Commission has created an official *Do Not Use* list of abbreviations that can cause medication errors, which applies to all orders and all medication-related documentation that is handwritten (including free-text computer entry) or on pre-printed forms.

Table 4.1. Official *Do Not Use* Abbreviation List

Do Not Use	Potential Problem	Use Instead
U, u (unit)	Mistaken for *0* (zero), the number *4* (four), or *cc*	Write *unit*
IU (international unit)	Mistaken for *IV* (intravenous) or the number *10* (ten)	Write *international unit*
Q.D., QD, q.d., qd (daily) Q.O.D., QOD, q.o.d, qod (every other day)	Mistaken for each other Period after the Q mistaken for *I* and the O mistaken for *I*	Write *daily* Write *every other day*
Trailing zero (X.0 mg)* Lack of leading zero (.X mg)	Decimal point is missed	Write *X mg* Write *0.X mg*
MS MSO$_4$ and MgSO$_4$	Can mean morphine sulfate or magnesium sulfate Confused for one another	Write *morphine sulfate* Write *magnesium sulfate*

*Exception: A trailing zero may be used only where required to demonstrate the level of precision of the value being reported, such as for laboratory results, imaging studies that report size of lesions, or catheter tube sizes. It may not be used in medication orders or other medication-related documentation.

Table 4.2. Additional Abbreviations, Acronyms, and Symbols*

Do Not Use	Potential Problem	Use Instead
> (greater than) < (less than)	Misinterpreted as the number *7* (seven) or the letter *L* Confused for one another	Write *greater than* Write *less than*
Abbreviations for drug names	Misinterpreted due to similar abbreviations for multiple drugs	Write drug names in full
Apothecary units	Unfamiliar to many practitioners Confused with metric units	Use metric units
@	Mistaken for the number 2 (two)	Write *at*
cc	Mistaken for *U* (units) when poorly written	Write *mL, ml,* or *milliliters* (*mL* is preferred)
µg	Mistaken for *mg* (milligrams)	Write *mcg* or *micrograms*

*For POSSIBLE future inclusion in the *Do Not Use* Abbreviation List

In institutional settings, there are **high-alert medications** that may cause significant harm to a patient if they are used in error. Although the drugs are not consistently prescribed wrong, when they are, the results can be much more devastating for the patient. The following drugs are high-alert medications:

+ heparin
+ opioids
+ potassium chloride injections
+ insulin
+ chemotherapeutic agents
+ neuromuscular blocking agents

In the pharmacy, a medication error can occur at any point in the dispensing process: data entry, filling, selection of the drug, verification, administering, or monitoring of drug therapy. Pharmacy technicians assist in enforcing these safeguards by assessing the patient at the time of drop-off or pick-up. By reviewing the patient's profile, the technician is able to update important information and alert the pharmacist when questions or concerns arise. The pharmacist will then counsel the patient on compliance and proper use and contact the physician when necessary.

PRACTICE QUESTIONS

1. Which of these drugs is NOT a high-alert medication?

A) neuromuscular blocking agents

B) heparin

C) insulin

D) penicillin

Answers:

A) Incorrect. Neuromuscular blocking agents are high-alert medications.

B) Incorrect. Heparin is a high-alert medication.

C) Incorrect. Insulin is a high-alert medication.

D) **Correct.** Penicillin is not a high-alert medication.

2. Which of the following is NOT a cause of medication errors?

A) a patient's physiological makeup

B) the end of a medication's course of therapy

C) calculation errors

D) social causes

Answers:

A) Incorrect. The patient's physiological makeup can cause a medication error.

B) **Correct.** The end of a course of medication therapy is not a medication error.

C) Incorrect. Calculation errors may result in medication errors.

D) Incorrect. Medication errors may be due to social causes.

LOOK-ALIKE SOUND-ALIKE DRUG NAMES

According to the **US Pharmacopeia (USP)**, look-alike sound-alike drugs—or **SALAD** drugs—are increasingly a problem for healthcare professionals. Due to the amount of brand and generic drugs available and in development, some drug names can sound or be spelled similarly. These similarities can cause healthcare professionals to mistakenly dispense or administer the wrong drug.

 Complete and current lists of SALAD drugs are available at these websites: www.usp.org, www.ismp.org, and www.fda.org/medwatch.

Some contributing factors to misreading SALAD drugs include similar packaging, interruptions while preparing the drug, bad lighting, and incorrect placement of the stock bottles on the shelf. To resolve these factors and avoid confusion, the FDA and the Joint Commission developed strategies and requirements.

+ Tallman lettering should be used on labels. When drugs have similar names, they are differentiated by capitalizing the dissimilar letters. As an example; ClomiPHENE and ClomiPRAMINE.

+ The Joint Commission requires keeping all SALAD medications, along with chemicals and reagents that can be mistaken for drugs, away from other products.

+ The Joint Commission also requires that a written policy be displayed in the healthcare setting specifying necessary precautions and procedures when ordering SALAD drugs.

+ Healthcare facilities must define which drugs and products used in the facility qualify as high-risk and develop policies and procedures needed to address the drug or product throughout the dispensing process.

+ Finally, healthcare settings must identify and produce an annual review of all SALAD drugs used in the facility.

Pharmacy staff can be proactive in preventing SALAD errors by following a few tips.

+ Pharmacy staff must not store SALAD drugs alphabetically with other drug products; they should place SALAD drugs on a separate shelf or in another area of the pharmacy.

+ Pharmacy staff must undergo training on the precautions taken with SALAD drugs to avoid prescribing errors.

+ Pharmacy staff should change the appearance of SALAD drugs by using techniques such as bold typing, color codes, highlighting, circling, or

Tallman lettering to emphasize dissimilar parts of the drug name. The same method must be used throughout the chosen medication management system including the computer system, MARs, and in nursing unit med rooms and bins.

+ Pharmacy staff must apply auxiliary labels that warn about SALAD drugs.
+ Pharmacy staff must avoid abbreviations when entering, filling, or dispensing SALAD drugs.
+ Pharmacy staff must add a prompt in the pharmacy computer system that warns when SALAD drugs are dispensed.

Table 4.3. Common SALAD Drugs (Generic)

Drug One	Drug Two
acetaZOLAMIDE	acetoHEXAMIDE
ALPRAZolam	LORazepam
amantadine	amiodarone
ARIPiprazole	RABEprazole
ARIPiprazole	proton pump inhibitors that end with AZOLE
azaTHIOprine	azaCITIdine
buPROPion	busPIRone
captopril	carvedilol
ceFAZolin	cefTRIAXone
cyclophosphamide	cycloSPORINE
cetirizine	sertraline
cetirizine	stavudine
chlordiazePOXIDE	chlorproMAZINE
carBAMazepine	OXcarbazepine
Disopyramide	desipramine
dimenhyDRINATE	diphenhydramine
DOPamine	DOBUtamine
DULoxetine	FLUoxetine
FLUoxetine	PARoxetine
fomepizole	omeprazole
hydrALAzine	hydrOXYzine
HYDROcodone	oxyCODONE
hydromorPHONE	morPHINE

Drug One	Drug Two
lamoTRIgine	levETIRAcetam
lamoTRIgine	lamiVUDine
lanthanum carbonate	lithium carbonate
lithium	Ultram (brand name for tramadol)
leucovorin calcium	Leukeran (brand name for chlorambucil)
methylphenidate	methadone
metolazone	methimazole
metroNIDAZOLE	metFORMIN
misoprostol	miFEpristone
naloxone	Lanoxin (brand name for digoxin)
OLANZapine	QUEtiapine
OXcarbazepine	carBAMazepine
oxaprozin	OXcarbazepine
penicillAMINE	penicillin
PHENObarbital	PENTObarbital
piroxicam	PARoxetine
prednisoLONE	predniSONE
risperiDONE	rOPINIRole
roxanol	roxicet
roxicet	roxycodone
sandIMMUNE	sandoSTATIN
sertraline	cetirizine
sitaGLIPtin	SUMAtriptan
sulfaDIAZINE	sulfiSOXAZOLE
sulfaSALAzine	sulfADIAZINE
tiZANIdine	tiaGABine
TOLAZamide	TOLBUTamide
traMADol	traZODone
zolpidem	Zyloprim (brand name for allopurinol)

Table 4.4. Common SALAD Drugs (Brand Name)

Drug One	Drug Two
ADacel	DAPTacel
Amaryl	Reminyl
AVINza	INVanz
Axert	Antivert
AVINza	EVIsta
CeleBREX	CeleXA
Cymbalta	Symbyax
CeleXA	ZyPREXA
CeleXA	CeleBREX
Depo-Medrol	Solu-MEDROL
Diprivan	Ditropan
Diprivan	Diflucan
Diovan	Zyban
Dynacin	Dynacirc
Effexor	Enablex
Farxiga	Fetzima
Femara	Femhrt
Fioricet	Fiorinal
Flonase	Flovent
Foradil	Toradol
HumuLIN	NovoLIN
HumuLIN	HumaLOG
NovoLIN	NovoLOG
Lanoxin	levothyroxine
Lantus	latuda
Lodine	codeine
Micronase	Microzide
Microzide	Maxzide
Motrin	Neurontin
MS Contin	Oxycontin

Drug One	Drug Two
Neulasta	Lunesta
Oxycontin	oxycodone
Paxil	Plavix
Pradaxa	Paxil
Precare	Precose
PriLOSEC	PROzac
Procet	Percocet
Rifampin	Rifadin
Rifampin	rifamate
Sinemet	Janumet
Tambocor	Pamelor
Taxol	Paxil
Tenex	Xanax
Tobrex	Tobradex
Virammune	Viracept
ZyPREXA	ZyrTEC
Ziac	Tiazac
Zestril	Zetia
Yaz	Yasmin
Zantac	Xanax

PRACTICE QUESTIONS

1. Which is NOT considered a SALAD drug?

A) metformin

B) clonidine

C) amoxicillin

D) hydromorphone

Answers:

A) Incorrect. Metformin is a SALAD drug.

B) Incorrect. Clonidine is a SALAD drug.

C) **Correct.** Amoxicillin is not a SALAD drug.

D) Incorrect. Hydromorphone is a SALAD drug.

2. Which is NOT a contributing factor to misreading SALAD drugs?

   A) similar packaging

   B) Tallman lettering

   C) bad lighting

   D) placing product on the shelf incorrectly

Answers:

   A)   Incorrect. Pharmacy technicians could confuse SALAD drugs because of similar packaging.

   B)   Correct. Tallman lettering helps differentiate SALAD drugs from each other.

   C)   Incorrect. Bad lighting may cause confusion among SALAD drugs.

   D)   Incorrect. Placing products on the shelf incorrectly could cause pharmacy technicians to mix up SALAD drugs.

DETERIORATED MEDICATIONS

The pharmacy technician is responsible for ensuring medications on the shelf are safe, secure, and effective before they are dispensed to the patient. Expired or improperly stored drugs may lose **potency** and effectiveness. The technician must maintain the inventory of stocked drugs on the shelf by consistently checking for **expired medications** to ensure the patient is receiving a quality product.

Three months before the drug is due to expire, the pharmacy technician marks the stock bottle, based on the pharmacy's procedure, to alert the staff the drug will be expiring soon. Many pharmacies use a bright color sticker with the date of expiration. When checking expiration dates, if the date on the stock bottle states 5/20, the medication will expire on the last day of May in the year 2020. If the expiration date states 5/15/20, the medication will expire on May 15, 2020. Expired medications must be completely removed from the shelf a month before the expiration date.

Although pharmacies may have different inspection policies and procedures, pharmacy technicians must check the inventory for expired medications monthly. While they are checking for expired drugs to pull, technicians also ensure that the stock is rotated correctly. This task includes making sure the stock bottle with the earliest expiration date is placed in front of the other stock bottles on the shelf and that open bottles are marked so the staff does not open a new bottle before the open bottle is finished.

Once expired drugs are pulled from the shelves, they are then stored separately from other active drugs in the pharmacy to prevent the pharmacy staff from accidently dispensing them. Dispensing a deteriorated drug could cause an adverse event to occur—a potentially dangerous dispensing error. The drugs are then disposed of based on the policy of the pharmacy. Many pharmaceutical companies give credit to the pharmacy in exchange for expired drugs. Other times the drugs are sent out to be properly destroyed.

PRACTICE QUESTION

With regard to expiring medications, stock bottles are removed from the shelf

A) one month before expiring.

B) two months before expiring.

C) three months before expiring.

D) two weeks before expiring.

Answers:

A) **Correct.** Expiring medications should be removed from the shelf one month before their expiration date.

B) Incorrect. Expiring medications are not removed from the shelf two months before their expiration date.

C) Incorrect. Expiring medication stock bottles are marked three months before expiration date; they are not yet removed.

D) Incorrect. Expiring medications should have already been removed from the shelf two weeks before their expiration date.

PREVENTION OF MEDICATION ERRORS

Preventing medication errors is one of the pharmacist's highest priorities. Pharmacy technicians play a crucial role in preventing errors by assisting the pharmacist with routine tasks so the pharmacist can focus on verification of prescription orders.

Pharmacy technicians also help the pharmacist by being vigilant and checking their work through **multiple check systems.**

The first check system is at **prescription drop-off.** Technicians stationed at the drop-off window work with the patient. They create a checklist of important information needed to accurately enter the prescription and alert the pharmacist to any issues requiring the pharmacist's attention.

During **order entry,** technicians who enter the prescription information into the pharmacy software system use their knowledge of pharmacy terminology and drug names to prevent medication errors and enhance patient safety. **Computerization and automation** also help technicians by increasing accuracy and decreasing errors, but these are only tools. Technicians are alerted to possible warnings that include interaction, allergies, and duplications. Technicians must work with the pharmacist to decide if the warning can be overridden or if the doctor must intervene.

It is important to point out that in some cases, computerization can actually decrease accuracy and patient safety if not used correctly. For example, warnings can be excessive; a technician may be compelled to override an alert to avoid interrupting the pharmacist during a busy time of the day. However all alerts that involve interactions, allergies, duplications, or any other clinical warning must be reported to the pharmacist.

Depending on the pharmacy's **policies and procedures**, some technicians may be allowed to carry out certain overrides—for instance, if a patient is going on vacation and an early refill is needed. If the technician gets an authorization code from the third-party payer allowing the early fill, the policies and procedures of the pharmacy may allow the technician to override the prescription.

During the **dispensing process**, another check system, medication errors can occur in a few ways. First, it is important for the fill technician to check the hard copy against the prescription label that was generated by the order entry technician. This way, the fill technician is double checking the order entry technician's work for errors and possibly preventing a dispensing error.

Another error can happen if the fill technician incorrectly reads the label: one consequence could be choosing the incorrect SALAD drug from the shelf, for example. Furthermore, a technician could be rushed and choose the correct drug, but not the correct strength. In these cases, it is crucial to check the NDC number and the illustration placed on the label. Tools like barcode technology and vial-filling systems that count out the amount of pills needed when the label is generated are also available to the technician to help prevent errors.

The next check system is the **pharmacist verification process**. The pharmacist thoroughly checks the prescription order from order entry through the dispensing process. Through scanning and barcode technology, the pharmacy software system will alert the pharmacist to any issues that require reconciliation. The pharmacist will then check the NDC number with the stock bottle, check the labeling for accuracy, and make sure the drug is correct by verifying the illustration image.

The last check system—**point of sale**—is at the check-out counter. Prevention of errors at this stage includes using a second identifier in addition to the name at the point of sale. The technician will ask the patient for an address, phone number, or date of birth. This ensures that the medication was filled for the correct patient, especially if the prescription was called in or sent electronically to the pharmacy.

Verifying the quantity of prescriptions for pick-up is important, too. Many patients pick up more than one prescription at a time; failure to distribute all their medications at once is poor customer service. Sometimes a medication may be overlooked or not yet filled. In these cases, the technician should check the patient's profile in the computer system to determine the problem. For example, the pharmacist may be waiting for the patient's doctor to call in a new prescription, or the patient may have called in a refill too soon.

Furthermore, pharmacies have systems to refer patients to the pharmacist for high-risk medications or alert to changes in dosages or strengths of medications. Some pharmacies place notes on the bag or use other internal protocols directing technicians to refer patients to a pharmacist for counseling.

? It is a very busy day in the pharmacy and the fill technician is behind in the dispensing process. While filling a prescription for Warfarin 2.5 mg tablets, the technician

These checks and balances help prevent errors, but pharmacy technicians also need **education and training** to prevent medication errors. Most states **require by law** that pharmacy technicians complete at least two continuing education credits on medication errors every two years to re-register. PTCB now requires one patient safety continuing education credit every two years to become recertified.

Failure mode and effects analysis (FMEA) is an ongoing quality multi-disciplinary improvement process carried out by healthcare organizations. FMEA helps to inspect new products and services to determine points of possible failure and the effects of the failure before any error can actually happen. FMEA is a proactive process determining steps that can be taken to avoid errors before the product or service is purchased. For example, to reduce medication errors, a multidisciplinary team will use FMEA to assess new drugs before considering placement of the drug in the healthcare organization's formulary. To complete the process, a series of steps must be taken.

+ **Step One:** The multidisciplinary team will first determine how the product is to be used. This will be deliberated thoroughly, from purchasing to administering the drug. Questions that would be considered include: What type of patient needs the drug? Who would prescribe the drug? How is the drug stored? How is the drug prepared and administered?

+ **Step Two:** While discussing how the drug is used, the team would then examine possible failures of the drug including whether the labeling of the drug could be mistaken for another similarly packaged drug, if the drug could be mistaken for another drug, or if errors could occur during the administration of the drug.

+ **Step Three:** After identifying any failures in the process, the team then determines the likelihood and consequences of the mistake. What adverse events could happen if the patient receives the drug at the wrong time, dose, route of administration, or rate?

+ **Step Four:** The team factors in any pre-existing conditions of the patient and any processes already in place that may cause an error before the drug reaches the patient. Then, team members use their individual, specialized knowledge to account for human factors to determine the effectiveness of the drug.

+ **Step Five:** If any significant errors occur during the evaluation, the team takes actions to detect, prevent, or minimize the consequences. Some examples include using a different product, requiring dosing and concentration methods, using warning systems such as auxiliary labels or computer alerts, requiring specific drug preparations in the pharmacy, and requiring specific data in the software systems before processing orders.

> 🔍 The FMEA helps to **identify trends** in potential errors with drug products and services based on past use experience and informational media tools such as *ISMP Medication Alerts!* This can be viewed online at https://www.ismp.org/newsletters/.

Although companies outside of medicine have more advanced scoring systems available, using the FMEA process is a proactive risk management tool in healthcare organizations and pharmacy services.

PRACTICE QUESTIONS

1. Which stage of FMEA consists of identifying any failures in the process and determining why the failure is occurring?

    A) Stage 1

    B) Stage 4

    C) Stage 3

    D) Stage 2

    Answers:

    A) Incorrect. In Stage 1 the multidisciplinary team first determines how the product is to be used.

    B) Incorrect. Stage 4 is when the team considers the patient's pre-existing conditions, if any, and any processes already in place that may cause an error before the drug reaches the patient.

    C) Correct. In Stage 3 the team identifies any failures in the process and determines why those failures are occurring.

    D) Incorrect. Stage 2 is when the team examines possible failures of the drug, including whether the drug could be mistaken for another one, if the labeling of the drug could be confused with another, or if errors could easily occur during the administration of the drug.

2. A pharmacy technician incorrectly reads a prescription label. Which multiple-check system has failed?

    A) data entry

    B) verification

    C) drop-off

    D) dispensing

    Answers:

    A) Incorrect. During data entry, pharmacy technicians focus on accurately entering patient data.

B) Incorrect. Pharmacists, not pharmacy technicians, are responsible for verification.

C) Incorrect: Pharmacy technicians work with the patient to accurately enter information during drop-off and alert the pharmacist to any valid concerns.

D) Correct. Pharmacy technicians may incorrectly read the prescription label during the dispensing process when selecting the drug.

WHAT TO DO IF AN ERROR OCCURS

As a pharmacy technician, being knowledgeable and proficient, keeping up with required continuing education and training, and following all policies and procedures will help prevent or reduce the risk of errors occurring in the dispensing process. But, despite all efforts, mistakes may still happen.

If an error does occur, it is important to focus on its cause and how to improve the work habits that contributed to the problem. Technicians should take pride and personal responsibility in the work they do. A technician who cannot learn from mistakes may become a **liability** to the practice.

By using systemic reviews to identify common factors that lead to errors, pharmacies can develop and implement strategies that improve the quality of pharmacy workflow while limiting mistakes. Because pharmacy staff must work as a team, **continuous quality improvements (CQI)** should be discussed among coworkers. The team can acknowledge the pros and cons of current systems and implement improvements effectively.

> **?** Despite safeguards to avoid confusion among SALAD drugs, a technician entered the wrong drug. The pharmacist catches the mistake during the verification process. What can the technician do in the future to avoid making the same mistake again?

Methodologies such as FMEA and **root cause analysis (RCA)** can also improve quality and reduce errors in the pharmacy. RCA helps to identify the cause of an error after the error occurs. When initiating a CQI project, another cycle called **FOCUS-PDCA** can be used as well.

FOCUS stands for:

+ **Find** the improvement opportunity.
+ **Organize** a group to help in the improvement process.
+ **Clarify** current knowledge of the process.
+ **Understand** the cause and effect in the process.
+ **Select** which improvement needs to take place.

PDCA stands for:

+ **Plan** the action needed to solve the problem.
+ **Do** the action needed to solve the problem.

+ **Check** to be sure the action works properly by studying the results.
+ **Act** on the action: proceed with implementing the solution.

PRACTICE QUESTION

Which is NOT a methodology used by pharmacies for continuous quality improvement?

A) root cause analysis

B) suggestion boxes

C) FMEA

D) FOCUS-PDCA

Answers:

A) Incorrect. Root cause analysis is used by pharmacies for CQI.

B) Correct. Suggestion boxes are not used for CQI.

C) Incorrect: FMEA is used for CQI.

D) Incorrect: FOCUS-PDCA is used for CQI.

Reference Materials

In the pharmacy, technicians have access to a variety of reference materials. These materials are available in several different formats; some can be accessed on the Internet. Because reference materials are often consulted during pharmacy work, it is important for technicians to familiarize themselves with this information.

+ *American Drug Index*: Available in print and online, the *American Drug Index* is a reference source that identifies and describes thousands of prescription drugs in a dictionary format.

+ *American Hospital Formulary Service Drug Information*: This publication provides drug information with therapeutic guidelines and off-label uses. It is written and published by pharmacists and is also available online.

+ *Drug Facts and Comparisons*: A book that compiles information on 22,000 prescription and 6,000 OTC products, it lists products by therapeutic categories. *Drug Facts and Comparisons* includes actions of drugs, warnings and precautions, interactions, adverse reactions, administration and dosage, contraindications and indications, dosages, and brand and generic names. It is also available online.

+ *Geriatric Dosage Handbook*: Written by Todd P. Semla, this dictionary-formatted source gives geriatric-sensitive dosing information as well as information about drug interactions and dosing in the elderly. In addition, it includes a risk assessment of drugs that should be avoided or used with caution in older adults. It is also available in PDF format.

- **Goodman and Gilman's *The Pharmacological Basis of Therapeutics*:** This pharmacology textbook, nicknamed the *Blue Bible*, was first published in 1941 and emphasizes the relationship between pharmacotherapy and pharmacodynamics. It is also available in PDF format.

- ***Handbook of Nonprescription Drugs*:** This book contains information on nonprescription drugs and self-care. It includes pharmacotherapy, medical foods, nutritional supplements, nondrug and preventative measures, and therapies unrelated to the use of prescription drugs. It is available in PDF format, too.

- ***Ident-A-Drug*:** This online and print pill identifier presents drugs by shape, imprints, and color. The site provides an illustration of the drug including the brand and generic name, manufacturer, and purpose.

- **Martindale's *The Complete Drug Reference*:** This is an unbiased and evaluated resource book on drugs used internationally. It also provides international disease reviews and drug preparations.

- ***Micromedex Healthcare Evidence and Clinical Xpert*:** This online database includes evidence-based, referenced information on drugs, diseases, acute care, toxicology, and alternative medicines for healthcare professionals.

- ***Orange Book: Approved Drug Topics with Therapeutic Equivalence Evaluations*:** Also known as the *List*, the *Orange Book* identifies approved drug products along with evaluations of therapeutic equivalents (generic drugs). The *Orange Book* is approved by the FDA, updated daily, and available online.

- ***Pediatric and Neonatal Dosage Handbook*:** Because pharmacodynamics and pharmacokinetics change extensively through infancy to adolescence, this handbook by Jane Hodding and Donna M. Kraus gives important dosing information and evaluations for the management of pediatric patients by healthcare professionals.

- ***The Pharmacy Technician's Pocket Drug Reference*:** This small, portable book provides brand and generic drug names, illustrations, therapeutic class, dosage forms and strengths, and therapeutic uses.

- ***The Physician's Desk Reference (PDR)*:** The PDR is a compilation of annually updated manufacturers' prescribing information (package inserts) on prescription drugs. The PDR is also available online.

- ***Red Book: Pharmacy's Fundamental Reference*:** Available in print and online, the *Red Book* is a resource on drug pricing. It includes information about prescription pricing and order entry, forecasting, competitive analysis, formulary development management, claims adjudications, processing, reimbursement information, and AWP policies.

- **Remington's *The Science and Practice of Pharmacy*:** This reference and textbook on the science and practice of pharmacy includes pharmacy curriculum and professional pharmacy practice guidelines.

+ Trissel's *Handbook on Injectable Drugs*: This reference book gives extensive information on injectable drugs available in the US and internationally. It explains in detail how to prepare, store, and administer injectable drugs. The handbook also gives information on drug stability and compatibility.

+ **The United States Pharmacopeial Convention's** *Pharmacopeia (USP)*: A body of information on the standards of strength, purity, and quality of drugs, this publication was made a legal standard in 1907 and is revised periodically. It is also available online.

+ *United States Pharmacopeia-National Formulary (USP-NF)*: This is a compilation of both the *USP* and the *National Formulary*; it includes standards for botanicals, excipients, and other similar products. In 1975 the *USP* and *NF* were combined into one book.

PRACTICE QUESTIONS

1. When was the USP made a legal standard?

   A) 1901

   B) 1938

   C) 1907

   D) 1975

   Answers:

   A) Incorrect. The USP was not made a legal standard in 1901.

   B) Incorrect. The USP was not made a legal standard in 1938.

   C) Correct. The USP was made a legal standard in 1907.

   D) Incorrect. The USP was not made a legal standard in 1975.

2. Which reference material identifies approved drug products and includes evaluations of therapeutic equivalents (generic drugs)?

   A) the *Red Book*

   B) *Ident-A-Drug*

   C) the *Orange Book*

   D) *The Physician's Desk Reference*

   Answers:

   A) Incorrect. The *Red Book* is a resource on drug pricing.

   B) Incorrect. *Ident-A-Drug* is a pill identifier.

   C) Correct. The *Orange Book* identifies approved drug products and includes evaluations of therapeutic equivalents (generic drugs).

D) Incorrect. *The Physician's Desk Reference* is a compilation of annually updated manufacturers' prescribing information (package inserts) on prescription drugs.

RESEARCHING A DRUG

There are several reasons that pharmacy technicians may need to research a drug in the pharmacy setting. Generally pharmacy technicians assist the pharmacist in drug research for patient-specific reasons. For instance, a patient may ask the pharmacist for specific information about the effects of a prescribed drug on the usage of an OTC drug. In this case, the technician would assist by finding the correct resource to respond to the question. Pharmacy technicians also assist pharmacists in clinical research and drug information centers.

Pharmacy technicians also research for self-study when they are not knowledgeable about a specific drug and would like to learn additional information. As stated in the previous section, many technicians carry a drug reference book for easy access to information.

Technicians research numerous issues. A **monograph** is a detailed written study about the drug. **Drug classification** describes the group of drugs, by chemical structure, the medication is grouped with. **Chemical structure** is the structural determination of a drug based on molecules and chemical compounds. The **brand or trade name** of a drug is the patented name of the drug given by the manufacturer that developed it, while the **generic or chemical name** is the name that was given to the drug based on its chemical makeup and not the advertised brand name. Chemically equivalent to the brand name, it has the same active ingredient, although bindings of the drug can differ. Essentially, the generic version of a drug is the cheaper version of the brand name. Technicians also research **indications**, or the purpose of the drug—how it is used to treat a particular disease or conditions. Likewise, technicians must know drug **interactions**, or situations in which another substance or occurrence can affect the activity of a drug when used simultaneously. Finally, technicians should be aware of **warnings and adverse effects**, undesired and harmful effects that are the result of another drug or specific occurrence contraindicating with the desired drug therapy.

When pharmacy technicians need to research information on a drug, they must recognize that all reference sources have advantages and disadvantages. Technicians should be able to differentiate between reputable and unreliable resources. There are three types of resource categories: tertiary, secondary, and primary resources.

Tertiary resources are general resources. These include package inserts, textbooks, databases, and review articles. Tertiary resources are useful as general information for self-study about a medicine or condition, or when first initiating a search strategy. The disadvantage of tertiary resources is they can be out-of-date at the time they are researched. These sources are most commonly sought by pharmacy technicians.

Package inserts are the most common tertiary source. Before a drug is available for public use, the drug is evaluated for efficacy and safety. The FDA will then grant approval to the manufacturer to market the drug. The package insert is a data compilation of premarket studies and prescribing information. The package insert also provides drug labeling, product information, pharmacology, pharmacokinetics, pharmacodynamics, clinical studies, indications, contraindications, adverse effects, warnings, drug and administration, overdose precautions, supply information, preparation information, and patient information. Package insert information is also available online through the manufacturer's website as well as in the *PDR*.

Trissel's *Handbook of Injectable Drugs*, the *American Drug Index*, the *Red Book*, *The PDR*, and *Ident-A-Drug* are all examples of tertiary resources.

Secondary resources are indexing services or abstracts of publications that require a subscription. These resources are available online and link to primary literature. Pharmacy technicians require extra training to properly research secondary resources. Some examples of secondary resources follow.

+ *MEDLINE (www.pubmed.gov)*
+ *International Pharmaceutical Abstracts (IPA)*
+ *Journal Watch*

Other frequently referenced websites used as secondary resources include:

+ *www.cdc.gov*
+ *www.cms.gov*
+ *www.drugs.com*
+ *www.medscape.com*
+ *www.health.NIH.gov*
+ *www.medicare.gov*
+ *www.PDRhealth.com*
+ *www.Rxlist.com*
+ *www.webmd.com*
+ *www.FDA.gov*
+ *www.mayoclinic.org*

Primary resources are publications in their original form; these include technical reports, theses and dissertations, conference papers, and monographic series. These refer to new ideas, discoveries, and results. These resources are usually united with existing research and undergo peer reviews by experts for evaluation before publication. Primary resources are accessed by pharmacists and clinical research experts.

1. Which of the following is NOT among the information most commonly researched by pharmacy technicians?

   A) monographs

   B) brand name or generic name of a drug

   C) drug interactions

   D) peer reviews by experts

   Answers:

   A) Incorrect. Technicians frequently research monographs.

   B) Incorrect. Technicians often seek out more information about the brand or generic names of drugs.

   C) Incorrect. Technicians commonly research drug interactions.

   D) Correct. Pharmacists, not technicians, usually research peer reviews by experts.

2. Which type of source is MOST commonly used in research by pharmacy technicians?

   A) tertiary sources

   B) secondary sources

   C) primary sources

   D) none of the above

   Answers:

   A) Correct. Pharmacy technicians usually use tertiary sources in research.

   B) Incorrect. While technicians do use secondary sources, these sources are not consulted as frequently as tertiary sources are.

   C) Incorrect. Pharmacy technicians do not generally use primary sources for research.

   D) Incorrect. Tertiary, secondary, and primary resources denote sources of information used in research.

Hazardous Materials and Safety in the Workplace

Safety in the workplace is essential for all workers in every profession. Hazards exist in all workplace settings, and employees must know and understand the policies and procedures put in place at their workplaces in order to protect themselves and others.

In pharmacies, policies and procedures are put in place by OSHA, the BOP, and the individual pharmacy practice. Such policies and procedures address safety precautions, the safe handling of hazardous substances, and proper infection control practices; they also offer guidelines for required responses to unsafe or hazardous situations occurring in the pharmacy setting.

OSHA is the Occupational Safety and Health Administration. Established in 1970 to ensure safe working conditions in the United States through the Occupational Health and Safety Act, OSHA is part of the US Department of Labor and establishes mandatory workplace safety regulations. OSHA also monitors the workplace to ensure compliance with these regulations. Employers must keep the workplace free of all recognized hazards that can cause serious injury and/or death. Employees are required to abide by health and safety standards that apply to their job specifications and were agreed to at the time of hire.

Pharmacy technicians have to abide by specific safety guidelines as well.

+ Technicians must observe warning labels on biohazard packaging and containers.

+ Workers must bandage any breaks in the skin or lesions on hands before gloving.

+ Technicians must not recap, bend, or break contaminated needles or other sharps.

+ Technicians must minimize splashing, spraying, or splattering of drops of hazardous chemicals or infectious materials.

+ If exposed skin comes in contact with body fluids, workers should scrub with soap and water as soon as possible. If the eyes have been contaminated, workers should flush with water, preferably at an eye station.

+ Technicians should decontaminate contaminated materials before reprocessing or place in biohazard bags and dispose of according to policies and procedures.

+ Workers may not keep food or drink in refrigerators, freezers, countertops, shelves, or cabinets that can be exposed to blood, bodily fluid, or hazardous chemicals.

+ Technicians must not use mouth pipetting or suck blood or other harmful chemicals from tubing.

+ Pharmacy technicians must use hemostats to attach or remove scalpel blades from handles.

Besides enforcing safety standards, OSHA provides information, training, and education to help in the implementation and continuity of required policies and procedures. Emergency and fire safety plans and the proper removal of hazardous materials are also enforced by OSHA. Furthermore, OSHA provides the training guidelines needed for treating and reducing physical and biological hazards that could occur in the workplace.

In addition to the safety guidelines put in place for pharmacy technicians, OSHA requires that employers follow certain steps to ensure the safety and health of their employees. OSHA may inspect any workplace to ensure proper steps and protocols are being followed. It can cite or discipline any place of business that does not comply with safety standards.

OSHA enforces fire safety and emergency plans and environmental standards, among others. It also addresses latex allergies, work-related musculoskeletal injuries, ergonomics, and violence in the workplace. OSHA regulations that are applicable to the pharmacy setting include the Hazard Communication Standard and the Bloodborne Pathogens Standard.

PRACTICE QUESTION

Which is NOT a safety guideline required by OSHA for pharmacy technicians?

A) Technicians may recap, bend, or break contaminated needles or other sharps if necessary.

B) Technicians must minimize splashing, spraying, or splattering of drops of hazardous chemicals or infectious materials.

C) Technicians must observe warning labels on biohazard packaging and containers.

D) Technicians may not keep food or drink in refrigerators, freezers, countertops, shelves, or cabinets that can be exposed to blood, bodily fluid, or hazardous chemicals.

Answers:

A) **Correct.** Technicians may not recap, bend, or break contaminated needles or other sharps.

B) Incorrect. This is a safety guideline.

C) Incorrect. This is a safety guideline.

D) Incorrect. This is a safety guideline.

HAZARD COMMUNICATION PLAN

A **hazard communication plan** must be established to educate and train employees on labeling requirements and keeping and maintaining a **material safety data sheet (MSDS)**. The MSDS is an inventory list of all hazardous materials that may be found in the pharmacy setting. The fields on the MSDS must list the chemical name of the hazardous substance, accompanying warnings, and name and address of its manufacturer. An MSDS outlines the structure of the chemical substance and also documents its potential hazards. Also supplied in the MSDS are the substance's chemical composition, characteristics, **physical data**, health hazards data, **fire and explosion data**, and guidelines for safe handling and correct disposal. Some **chemical materials** located in the pharmacy include inks, toners, cleaners, glues, lubricants, controlled substances, radiopharmaceuticals, gases, alcohol, and certain prescription drugs. Special hazards require warning labels on the packaging.

Ascencia Pharmacy
4894 S. Westbury St.
Akron, OH 33327, 1-800-683-5822
www.AscenciaPharmacy.com
After Hours Emergency: (800) 631-5483

MATERIAL SAFETY
DATA SHEET
ETHYL CHLORIDE

TRADE NAME SYNONYM	ETHYL CHOLRIDE	REVISION DATE	9/2001 BY S. WOJCIK
CHEMICAL NAME SYNONYMS	ETHYL CHOLRIDE. CHLOROETHANE HYROCHLORIC ETHER	CASE NO.	75-00-3
CHEMICAL FAMILY	HALOGENATED HTDROCARBON	FORMULA	C_2H_5Cl

II. HAZARDOUS INGREDIENTS

PRINCIPLE HAZARDOUS COMPONENTS	CAS NO.	%	EXPOSURE LIMITS
ETHYL CHOLRIDE	75-00-3	100	OSHA PEL: 1000PPM

NPCA-HMIS RATINGS | EPA HAZARD CAT: | LISTS: | | ACGIH TWA: 100PPM SKIN; SEE SECTION V.
HEALTH 1 | CHRONIC HEALTH NO | EXTREMELY HAZARDOUS
FLAMMABILITY 4 | ACUTE HEALTH YES | SUBSTANCE NO
REACTIVITY 0 | FIRE HAZARD YES | CERCLA HAZARDOUS
PERSONAL See Sec. | PRESSURE HAZZARD YES | SUBSTANCE YES
PROTECTION VIII. | REACTIVITY HAZARD NO | TOXIC CHEMICALS YES

III. PHYSICAL DATA

BOILING POINT: 54.1°F (12.3°C)	FREEZING POINT: -213.5°F (-136.4°C)	EVAPORATION RATE: GREATER THAN 1 (BUTYL ACETATE = 1
VAPOR PRESSURE: at68°F (20°C)=20.1psia (5.4pslg)	LIQUID DENSITY at68°F (20°C)=0.8950 g/ml	
VAPOR DENSITY: (AIR=1) at BP 2.2 at 77°F (25°C)	PERCENT VOLATILE BY VOLUME: 100	
SOLUBILITY IN WATER:	SOLUABLE IN WATER AT CONCENTRATIONS OF 0.57g/108g WATER AT 68°F (20°C)	
APPEARANCE AND ODOR:	COLORLESS LIQUID WITH A PUNGENT, ETHER-LIKE ODOR, LIQUID IS WATER WHITE	

IV. FIRE AND EXPLOSION HAZARDS

FLASH POINT (METHOD USED): -45°F (-42.8°C) OC 1 -58°F (-50°C)	AUTO-IGNITION TEMPERATURE: 966°F (519°C)
FLAMMABLE OR EXPLOSIVE LIMITS IN AIR BY% VOLUME: LOWER: 3.8	UPPER: 15.4
EXTINGUSHING MEDIA: DRY CHEMICAL OR CARBON DIOXIDE FOR SMALL FIRES	ELECTRICAL CLASSIFICATION: Group C. NFPA No.70

SPECIAL FIREFIGHTING PROCEDURES:
STOP FLOW OF GAS, FROM A SAFE DISTANCE, USE WATER TO KEEP FIRE-EXPOSED CONTAINERS COOL. ALLOW FIRE TO BURN ITSELF OUT. USE A POSITIVE PRESSURE SELF-CONTAINED BREATHING APPARATUS. RESCUE PERSONNEL SHOULD AVOID UNNECESSARY EXPOSURE.

UNUSUAL FIRE AND EXPLOSION HAZARDS:
UPON COMBUSTION, ETHYL CHORIDE FORMS TOXIC GASES SUCH AS HYDROGEN CHLORIDE, CARBON DIOXIDE AND TRACES OF PHOSGENE. EXTREME HAZARD OF FIRE OR EXPLOSION MAY RESULT FROM STATIC ELECTRIC DISCHARGE OR OTHER IGNITION SOURCES. VAPOR ID HEAVIER THAN AIR AND MAT TRAVEL A CONSIDERABLE DISTANCE TO A SOURCE OF IGNITION AND FLASHBACK. VAPOR MAY EXPLODE IF IGNITED IN ENCLOSED AREAS.

Figure 4.1. MSDS Sheet

Some characteristics of chemical materials that pose a risk to humans and the symbols used to identify them follow.

Flammable: can easily catch fire

Caustic: can burn or corrode through a chemical action

Poisonous: a substance that can cause illness or death if ingested

Carcinogenic: cancer-causing

Figure 4.2. Warning Symbols

Teratogenic: may be harmful to, cause defects, or cause death of a fetus or embryo

Biohazard: poses a risk to human health or the environment; usually caused by a microorganism

Radioactive: indicates the spontaneous emission of alpha, beta, or neutron particles and/or radiation

Figure 4.2. Warning Symbols (continued)

Safety signs must be posted appropriately in the pharmacy and an **exposure control plan** should be implemented in case of chemical **contamination**.

The hazard communication plan should review the hazards that exist in the workplace and the location. It should also include the location of MSDS as well as the location of all hazard-related information. The plans should review how to read and understand chemical labels and hazard signs. It must provide information about personal protection equipment used and where the equipment is stored, including the location of cleaning equipment. Finally, it should describe management of chemical spills and **decontamination** procedures.

PRACTICE QUESTION

Which is NOT included in the hazard communication plan?

A) the location of MSDS

B) the location of hazard-related information

C) the location of cleaning equipment

D) how to fill out a worker's compensation claim

Answers:

A) Incorrect. The hazard communication plan should include the location of the MSDS.

B) Incorrect. The hazard communication plan should include the location of hazard-related information.

C) Incorrect. The hazard communication plan should include the location of cleaning equipment.

D) **Correct.** The hazard communication plan does not need to discuss worker's compensation claims.

Exposure Control Plan

The Bloodborne Pathogens Standard reduces work-related cases of HIV and hepatitis infections. Through an exposure control plan, exposure determination, and universal precautions, the standard helps to limit exposure and treat healthcare workers who are exposed to blood, bodily fluids, and other infectious agents in the workplace setting.

The **exposure control plan** outlines how the pharmacy must handle exposure to blood, bodily fluids, or other infectious agents. The plan is revised and updated annually with employee input and training and must be provided to all employees. The plan must be posted in a visible area and available at all times to employees.

Exposure controls defined by OSHA include **engineering** and **work practice controls.** Engineering controls refer to devices such as eyewash stations, biohazard symbols, needleless systems, and proper handwashing facilities that reduce exposure to microorganisms. Work practice controls are defined by OSHA as the use of universal precautions for infection control, proper disinfection procedures, and proper handling of spills.

Exposure determination refers to defining the risk to employees. There are three levels of risk.

1. Exposure is anticipated (doctors and nurses).
2. Occasional exposure is anticipated (pharmacist, pharmacy technician).
3. No expected exposure.

Universal precautions include methods and standards that are implemented and used to avoid the risk of exposure in the pharmacy setting. These precautions include aseptic technique, aseptic handwashing, the use of personal protective equipment (PPE) with **barrier precautions,** standards for handling sharps, spill clean-up, equipment disinfection, disposal of biohazards, and housekeeping. Barrier precautions are designed to protect the skin from exposure to blood and bodily fluids. Gloves and masks are examples of barrier precautions.

PRACTICE QUESTION

Which is NOT a work practice control as defined by OSHA?

A) universal precautions

B) biohazard symbols

C) proper disinfection procedures

D) proper handling of spills

Answers:

A) Incorrect. Work practice controls include universal precautions.

B) Correct. Biohazard symbols are engineering controls.

C) Incorrect. Work practice controls include proper disinfection procedures.

D)   Incorrect. Work practice controls include proper handling of spills.

SAFE HANDLING AND PREPARATION OF HAZARDOUS MATERIALS

Pharmacy technicians do not only encounter hazardous conditions in the pharmacy setting; some of the drugs prepared in the pharmacy are **cytotoxic** and require special handling procedures. Cytotoxic drugs are drugs that can be toxic to certain cells in the human body. Most cytotoxic drugs are used to treat cancer; touching or inhaling these chemical agents can be hazardous to the technician's health.

When preparing cytotoxic drugs, pharmacy technicians must abide by strict procedures in regard to the storage, labeling, and transport of these hazardous agents. Use of PPEs, the use of biological safety cabinets, and special handling of spills and clean-ups all help keep the technician safe while preparing cytotoxic drugs.

For regular preparation of cytotoxic drugs, engineering controls such as **sharps containers** for contaminated needles and cytotoxic **disposal guidelines** help prevent accidental exposure to these agents. These cover **cytotoxic waste**, waste generated by a hazardous agent over the course of its use.

Cytotoxic drugs and waste are indicated by a capital C with the word *cytotoxic* underneath. Cytotoxic waste must be contained in a container impervious to leaks and tears marked with the cytotoxic symbol. For cytotoxic waste that leaks, the container must have a pad on the bottom that absorbs the waste. Other waste, such as tubing and PPEs, must also be placed in leak-proof and tear-resistant containers identified with the cytotoxic symbol. This waste includes incontinence briefs used by patients taking cytotoxic drugs. Unless waste is being disposed of, lids must remain closed. Automatic locks ensure bins with foot pedals and lids remain secure when full; storage areas for cytotoxic waste must be secure, too. Similarly, sharps used for cytotoxic drugs must be disposed of in a red sharps container with a leak-proof lid. Finally, the waste must be incinerated at a temperature between 800 and 1200 degrees Celsius.

Figure 4.3. Cytoxic Symbol

Workers who handle cytotoxic waste must have disposal gloves and a spill kit readily available at all times, and cytotoxic disposal containers must be available where any cytotoxic drugs are handled. Those responsible for the transport of cytotoxic waste must be properly trained. Cytotoxic waste must be separated from biohazardous waste; hazardous chemicals are disposed in containers with the biohazard symbol.

Biohazardous waste such as bodily fluids, sharp objects, and blood must be disposed of separately from other waste. Sharps containers are used for glass vials, needles, scalpel blades, and any broken glass to avoid accidental punctures. Any biohazardous materials are placed in special red bags with the biohazard symbol imprinted on them. To avoid leakage, items should be double bagged before disposal. Disposal of waste must be carried out by trained waste management workers.

🔍 More information about preparing hazardous drugs is available at the *ASHP's Guidelines on Handling Hazardous Drugs* at www.ashp.org/DocLibrary/BestPractices/PrepGdlHazDrugs.aspx and from the US Nuclear Regulatory Commission (www.nrc.gov).

Workplace controls, such as using proper gowning techniques for cytotoxic preparations, help prevent hazardous chemicals from touching the skin. Technicians require special training in these techniques. Besides universal precautions such as the use of **isopropyl alcohol** and **handwashing techniques**, when preparing hazardous drugs technicians are required to keep all skin surfaces covered. Some ways technicians prevent accidental inhalation or absorption of hazardous agents are by tucking the cuffs of their lab coats into high-quality **hypoallergenic gloves**, using eye shield safety glasses, and using chemotherapy respirator masks.

PRACTICE QUESTION

Which is NOT a cytotoxic disposal guideline?

A) Cytotoxic waste must be incinerated at a temperature of 400 to 800 degrees Celsius.

B) A spill kit must be readily available where hazardous and cytotoxic agents are stored and prepared.

C) Cytotoxic waste must be separated from biohazardous waste.

D) Waste such as tubing and PPEs must be placed in leak-proof and tear-resistant containers identified with the cytotoxic symbol.

Answers:

A) **Correct.** Cytotoxic waste must be incinerated at a temperature of 800 to 1200 degrees Celsius, not 400 to 800 degrees Celsius.

B) Incorrect. It is true that a spill kit must be readily available where hazardous and cytotoxic agents are stored and prepared.

C) Incorrect. One guideline for cytotoxic waste disposal is that it must be separated from biohazardous waste.

D) Incorrect. Waste such as tubing and PPEs must be placed in leak-proof and tear-resistant containers identified with the cytotoxic symbol.

SPILLS AND CLEANUPS

When a spill occurs during the preparation of hazardous agents, important guidelines and training must be used to ensure the spill is safely contained and does not cause health hazards. Any workplace area that handles, prepares, or disposes of cytotoxic agents must be equipped with a readily available spill kit. The spill kit includes several items:

+ written directions for use
+ warning signs to indicate the hazard and to isolate the contaminated area
+ use of proper PPEs
+ a pair of large-sized gloves that are specifically used for cytotoxic handling, or two pairs of regular gloves
+ a plastic broom and dustpan
+ a spill mat to absorb small volumes of the spill
+ numerous swabs to absorb and clean liquid spills
+ concentrated alkali detergent solution. With a pH higher than 7, **alkali**-based detergent is water soluble and neutralizes **acidic** spills (spills of substances with a pH lower than 7).
+ a clearly labeled cytotoxic container
+ a spill incident form
+ a spill pillow to absorb liquid, possibly in large amounts

Pharmacies maintain clean-up procedures in case of spills. Technicians should

+ announce the spill and use warning signs to secure the area.
+ garb up with PPEs.
+ in case of liquid spills, use swabs, spill mat, or pillow (depending on the volume of liquid to absorb the liquid). Dissolve spilled powders into the mat and swabs by placing them over the powder and wetting the area with water.
+ remove the contaminated clean-up materials; sweep up broken glass.
+ repeat the process until the spill is cleared. Be sure to place waste into a cytotoxic container.
+ add alkali detergent to water.
+ wash the spill area thoroughly, discarding any waste into the cytotoxic container.
+ use clean water to rinse the area thoroughly.
+ dry thoroughly to avoid accidentally slipping on a wet floor.
+ dispose of the cytotoxic container per company procedures.
+ wash hands thoroughly.
+ have housekeeping re-clean the area.
+ complete the spill report card.
+ prepare another spill kit.

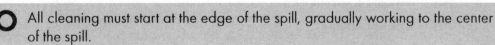 All cleaning must start at the edge of the spill, gradually working to the center of the spill.

PRACTICE QUESTION

In the event of a spill, which of the following is NOT a required step?

A) rinse area well with clean water

B) add acidic detergent to water

C) garb up with PPEs

D) complete the spill report card

Answers:

A) Incorrect. Pharmacy technicians must use clean water to rinse the area thoroughly.

B) **Correct.** Alkali, not acidic, detergent should be added to water.

C) Incorrect. Garbing with PPEs is required.

D) Incorrect. It is essential to complete a spill report.

IMMUNIZATIONS

Pharmacy technicians who choose to work in institutional pharmacies may be required to take or offered certain immunizations based on the practice. **Immunizations** help technicians protect themselves against certain diseases and conditions that they could encounter in the hospital pharmacy setting.

Policies and procedures differ among institutional settings depending on state, federal, and company-based guidelines about immunizing healthcare workers. Policies are based on how closely the technician works with patients. For institutional pharmacy technicians, tuberculosis testing is required during the pre-employment hiring phase. Many hospitals suggest all pharmacy staff receive flu and pneumonia shots and **hepatitis B** vaccinations. Although most immunizations are voluntary, the hospital will give free immunizations and other incentives to encourage immunization to keep the staff healthy.

PRACTICE QUESTION

Which of the following immunizations is NOT likely to be offered to an institutional pharmacy technician?

A) flu shot

B) pneumonia shot

C) hepatitis B vaccination

D) HPV vaccination

Answers:

A) Incorrect. It is likely that an institutional pharmacy would require technicians to get a flu shot.

B) Incorrect. Many hospitals suggest all pharmacy staff receive pneumonia shots.

C) Incorrect. An institutional pharmacy technician may be asked to receive a hepatitis B vaccination.

D) Correct. An institutional pharmacy technician would not be asked to receive an HPV immunization.

OCCUPATIONAL MUSCULOSKELETAL INJURIES

There are physical hazards in the pharmacy setting that could cause occupational musculoskeletal injuries. These hazards include trips, slips, and falls; moreover, **ergonomic** hazards result from incorrect workplace design that causes awkward positioning and repetitive motion. Pharmacy technicians are also required to lift up to fifty pounds or more at times; improper lifting of heavy objects can cause back injuries.

Ergonomic hazards that occur from computer use and workplace design can be controlled through ergonomically designed workstations, taking breaks to stand and stretch, and rotation of job tasks. Hazards caused by repetitive motion, awkward positioning, and compression can be controlled by the use of ergonomically correct carts, trolleys, and job rotation.

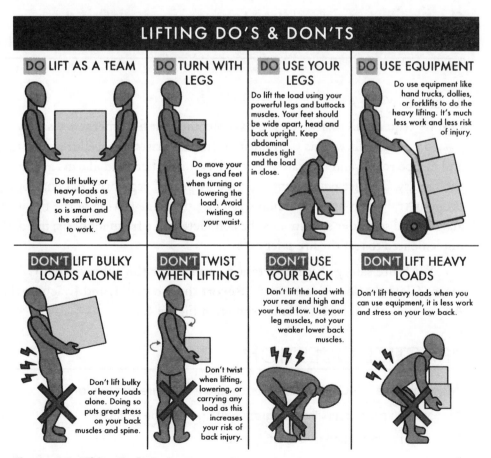

Figure 4.4. Lifting Techniques

Falling hazards such as trips, slips, and falls can be controlled with slip-resistant flooring, adequate lighting, regular maintenance, proper spill clean up, good house-keeping, education, and the use of appropriate footwear with gripping soles and good support.

Proper lifting technique is also a way to control back injuries. Lifting injuries can be prevented by following the illustration in Figure 4.4.

PRACTICE QUESTION

Which is considered an ergonomic hazard?

A) incorrect shoes without slip-resistant soles

B) incorrect lifting technique

C) incorrect workplace design

D) incorrect spill clean up

Answers:

A)   Incorrect. Shoes that have no slip-resistant soles are a physical hazard.

B)   Incorrect. Incorrect lifting is physically hazardous.

C)   Correct. Incorrect workplace design is an ergonomic hazard.

D)   Incorrect. Failure to properly clean up a spill would result in a physical hazard.

FIRE SAFETY PLAN

OSHA requires all pharmacies to have a compliant fire emergency safety plan clearly posted in the facility. This plan must consist of written procedures that diagram exit and escape routes and indicate where fire extinguishers and alarms are present within the facility. The fire equipment must be inspected regularly. All employees must be properly trained in fire prevention strategies. Routine testing of the fire alarm, smoke alarms, and sprinkler system must be conducted on a frequent basis; fire drills must be implemented to test the fire safety plan.

With fire safety, it is important to remember the abbreviation *CARE*. **CARE** means Close the door, Alert others, Report the fire to 911, and Evacuate the building. An example of a fire safety plan is shown in Figure 4.5.

PRACTICE QUESTION

Which of these is NOT an OSHA requirement for a fire safety plan?

A) written procedures that diagram exit and escape routes

B) regular inspection of fire equipment

C) proper training for all employees in fire prevention strategies and fire drills

D) safety plans may be distributed to staff

<u>Answers:</u>

A) Incorrect. OSHA requires that pharmacies develop written procedures that diagram exit and escape routes.

B) Incorrect. OSHA does require that all fire equipment be regularly inspected.

C) Incorrect. OSHA requires that all employees be properly trained in fire prevention strategies and fire drills.

D) Correct. Staff may receive copies of safety plans, but OSHA requires that safety plans are visibly posted.

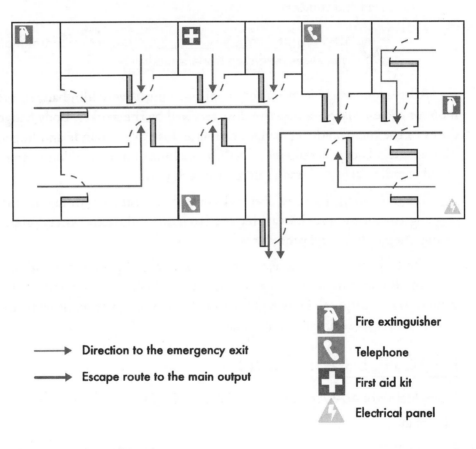

→ Direction to the emergency exit

→ Escape route to the main output

🧯 Fire extinguisher

📞 Telephone

➕ First aid kit

⚡ Electrical panel

Figure 4.5. Fire Safety Plan

EXPOSURE TO RADIATION

It is very important that pharmacy technicians avoid exposure to radiation while working with radiopharmaceuticals. The handling, preparation, storage, dispensing, and transport of radioactive drugs require specialized training. The concept of *ALARA* is an important procedure in the nuclear pharmacy practice. ALARA is the practice of keeping exposure to **radioactive materials As Low As Reasonably Achievable**. Three major factors help the technician achieve ALARA: time, distance, and shielding.

+ **Time** refers to using time wisely when preparing radiopharmaceuticals. The less time technicians spend preparing, the less exposure they have to radiation.

+ **Distance** reminds that the greater the pharmacy technician's distance from the radiopharmaceutical, the less chance he or she has of **radiation exposure**. Using remote handling devices and tongs puts distance between the technician and radiation.

+ **Radiation shields** form an impenetrable barrier that protects the technician from radioactive emissions. Effective shields must be made out of lead and tungsten.

 The website http://www.nrc.gov/ has more information on NRC guidelines regarding nuclear medicine.

All persons working in nuclear pharmacy must wear film badges. **Film badges** monitor the estimated radioactive dose received by the worker. Body badges estimate doses to the torso, and ring badges estimate dose in the hands and fingers. The US Nuclear Regulatory Commission (NRC) sets limits on the maximum amount of permissible radioactivity a person can receive each year.

The most important radioactivity controls are safety training, monitoring, and ongoing assessment. Facilities are required to have a radioactive safety program in place among their policies and procedures.

The disposal of radioactive materials is a crucial part of any radioactive safety program. Radioactive waste is segregated by radiation type and stored until it is decayed sufficiently for disposal. Only highly trained radiation waste management workers are qualified to dispose of radioactive wastes.

PRACTICE QUESTION

Major factors of ALARA consist of all of these EXCEPT

A) time.

B) distance.

C) weight.

D) shielding.

Answers:

A) Incorrect. Time is a factor in ALARA.

B) Incorrect. Distance is a factor in ALARA.

C) Correct. Weight is not a factor in ALARA.

D) Incorrect. Shielding is a factor in ALARA.

Inventory

Inventory management is required to run an efficient pharmacy practice. Properly managing the inventory in the pharmacy ensures that needed medications and supplies are always on hand for the patient. On the other hand, inventory management also helps to minimize cost and increase profits. Inventory management consists of maintaining stock, proper **inventory storage**, repackaging, disposal of products, and distribution.

Pharmacies develop a **periodic automatic replenishment (PAR) level** which consists of keeping track of the minimum and maximum level of a particular drug to be available at all times. **Level adjustments** are done periodically depending on the supply and demand of the drug. PAR levels are maintained in the pharmacy through the use of inventory systems. The type of inventory system depends on the pharmacy; some examples follow.

Barcode technology refers to handheld scanning systems that scan the barcode on the stock bottle, which consists of the NDC number. The scanning system then shows the estimated quantity of the drug available in the pharmacy and how much of the drug should be ordered to replenish the stock. The scanning systems are connected to the pharmacy software system and a report is then generated for ordering.

Pareto ABC Systems use a system also called the 80/20 rule or ABC analysis. This classifies drugs based on their importance and stocks them into groups based on the total annual cost of each drug. The first step in **cost analysis** in regard to ABC analysis is to create a PAR level to **control cost** by weighing the use and value of the item. For fast-moving drugs with a high unit value, close control is implemented. For

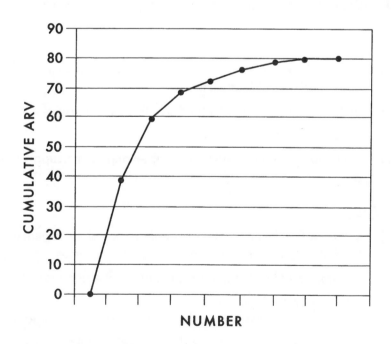

Figure 4.6. Pareto Curve

slow-moving items with low unit value, the cost of the drug may exceed the value; methods of controlling the stock should be used.

These factors are then used to create an annual requirement value (ARV) which is an estimate of total annual usage. The drugs are listed in descending order with the most commonly used and profitable drugs on top. When the cumulative ARV is plotted against the amount of drugs, a Pareto curve is determined.

Just-in-time inventory systems are management systems in which drugs are only ordered as demand requires. These help control costs while still keeping up with consumer demand, even while avoiding situations in which inventory exceeds demand. Excessive inventory causes increased cost due to storage and management costs.

PRACTICE QUESTIONS

1. Inventory management consists of all of the following tasks EXCEPT
   A) distribution.
   B) disposal of products.
   C) proper inventory storage.
   D) ringing up customers.

   Answers:
   A) Incorrect. Distribution is part of inventory management.
   B) Incorrect. Product disposal is part of inventory management.
   C) Incorrect. Proper inventory storage is part of inventory management.
   D) **Correct.** Ringing up customers is not part of inventory management.

2. PAR levels
   A) consist of keeping track of the minimum and maximum level of a particular drug to be available at all times.
   B) are not maintained in the pharmacy through the use of inventory systems.
   C) classify drugs based on importance.
   D) cannot be adjusted periodically depending on the supply and demand of the drug.

   Answer:
   A) **Correct.** PAR levels consist of keeping track of the minimum and maximum level of a particular drug to be available at all times.
   B) Incorrect. PAR levels can be maintained in the pharmacy through the use of inventory systems.
   C) Incorrect. PAR levels do not classify drugs based on importance.
   D) Incorrect. PAR levels can be adjusted periodically depending on the supply and demand of the drug.

DRUG RECALLS

Sometimes a manufacturer will issue a recall of a particular drug batch because the product has been determined to be harmful. This could happen for a few reasons including defective products, contamination, incorrect labelling, FDA interference, or improper production.

In these cases, **recall notices** will be sent to the pharmacy. The pharmacy must act on these immediately to prevent the consumer from encountering the recalled drug. Notices identify specific information on the drug product including the drug name, lot number, and the reason for recall. Lot numbers are crucial to the recall because they identify the defective batch of the drug. Pharmacy practices have specific policies and procedures in place to ensure that the recalled drug is pulled from the shelves, documented, and returned based on recall procedures. This includes sending notification to the manufacturer and the FDA of compliance with the removal of the recalled drug.

Recalled medications should be removed from inventory and placed in a designated area until they are returned or disposed of as required by the recall notice. Technicians must check all inventory including the shelving in the pharmacy as well as the med units and automated drug dispensing systems located in the institutional pharmacy. If the recalled product is not in stock, the recall form must still be sent back to the FDA and manufacturer stating so. It is also required to contact affected patients if the recalled product may have been dispensed by the pharmacy. In these cases, the pharmacy or doctor's office may contact the patient to check the lot number of the dispensed medication. If the patient receives a recalled product, the patient is asked to return the medication and it is replaced. The pharmacy then must contact the manufacturer for replacement of the drug.

 A current listing of drug recalls is available at http://www.fda.gov/Drugs/Drugsafety/DrugRecalls.

There are three levels of recalls. They can be conducted by the FDA or the manufacturer. The levels are determined by the urgency and severity of the recall.

+ **Class I recall:** There is a probability that use of or exposure to the product could cause an adverse event, health consequences, or death.
+ **Class II recall:** The product may cause temporary health problems, and there is a remote probability of an adverse health event.
+ **Class III recall:** The product is not likely to cause an adverse event but has violated FDA regulations.

FDA market withdrawals can happen when a product has a minor violation that does not require legal action, but the product still must be removed from the market to correct the violation.

CONTINUE

PRACTICE QUESTION

A Class II recall occurs when

A) the product is not likely to cause an adverse event but has violated FDA regulations.

B) a product has a minor violation that does not require legal action, but the product still must be removed from the market to correct the violation.

C) the product may cause temporary health problems, and there is a remote probability of an adverse health event.

D) there is a probability that the use of or exposure to the product could cause an adverse event, health consequences, or death.

Answers:

A) Incorrect. This describes a Class III recall.

B) Incorrect. This describes an FDA market withdrawal.

C) Correct. A Class II recall is when the product may cause temporary health problems, and there is a remote probability of an adverse health event.

D) Incorrect. This describes a Class I recall.

DRUG SHORTAGES

Drug shortages can negatively impact the pharmacy practice for a few reasons. Shortages may result when **supply does not meet demand**; they may also be due to natural disasters, lack of availability of raw materials, manufacturing difficulties, regulatory issues, recalls, and changes in formulation of the product.

Drug shortages have been on the rise for the past few years and can be very frustrating for the pharmacy staff. When shortages occur, the FDA will send a report stating when the product may be available again. The product will then be placed on back order by the wholesaler. The **back order** keeps the order request on file with the vendor, but states the date when the manufacturer believes the product should be available and can be sent to the pharmacy for replenishment of stock. Wholesalers may also inform pharmacies of alternative manufacturers of the product that may have it available for purchase.

 More information about current and resolved drug shortages is available at www.ashp.org/drugshortages.

Drug shortages can be time consuming and costly for the affected pharmacy, but they can be effectively managed. Contacting the wholesaler for other available options and discussing therapeutically equivalent drugs with the physician are just a few ways to manage drug shortages. If a patient must use a recalled drug, pharmacies can call other facilities to see if they can allocate the quantity needed for the patient until the drug becomes available again.

PRACTICE QUESTION

Which of the following is NOT a reason for drug shortages?

A) The vendor does not want to stock the drug anymore.

B) natural disasters

C) changes in the formulation of the drug

D) regulatory issues

Answers:

A) **Correct.** Drug shortages do not occur because the vendor voluntarily refuses to stock a drug.

B) Incorrect. Natural disasters can cause drug shortages.

C) Incorrect. Formulation changes can cause drug shortages.

D) Incorrect. Regulatory issues can cause drug shortages.

COUNTERFEIT PHARMACEUTICALS

Although the Prescription Drug Marketing Act helped address counterfeit pharmaceuticals and established legal guidelines to discourage the sale of counterfeit, **sub-potent**, adulterated, and misbranded pharmaceuticals, counterfeit pharmaceuticals are still making their way into the United States drug market.

Counterfeit pharmaceuticals are any drug that has been made by someone other than the manufacturer. This is done by copying or imitating a drug without permission, and it is used to defraud the patient. **The International Medicinal Products Anti-Counterfeiting Taskforce (IMPACT)** states that an estimated 10 – 30 percent of medicines sold in developing countries are counterfeit. The value of the counterfeit pharmaceutical industry is $200 billion annually, and 80 percent of counterfeit drugs purchased in the United States come from overseas.

 More information on counterfeit pharmaceuticals is available at the World Health Organization's IMPACT website: http://apps.who.int/impact/en/.

Many of these drugs have become available with the rise of online drug sellers. Consumers are tempted to buy drugs online to decrease the cost of medication, only to receive drugs that have the incorrect ingredients, are misbranded, or are dangerously adulterated. Most online drug sellers are illegal or are not compliant with the pharmacy laws and standards developed by the FDA.

The **World Health Organization (WHO)** developed a checklist to educate and caution consumers before they order drugs online.

The following are indicators of counterfeit retailers.

+ spam emails advertising medicines

+ lack of authentic certification on the website

- poor grammar and spelling mistakes on the website
- websites that do not have a phone number or address posted
- websites that offer prescription drugs without requiring a prescription
- suspiciously low-priced medications

If a consumer purchases a drug online, upon receiving it the consumer should check to be sure that

- the medication is exactly what was ordered.
- the dosage is correct.
- the packaging is in good condition.
- the medicine smells, looks, and feels as it should.
- the seals show no signs of tampering.
- the lot number and expiration date on the outside packaging match that on the inside packaging.
- there is no unauthorized activity on the credit card used to purchase the drug.

PRACTICE QUESTION

A consumer should not purchase drugs from an online seller if

A) the website requires a prescription from a doctor before dispensing.

B) the website has accurate contact information available.

C) authenticity is validated in regard to certification of the website.

D) the website contains poor grammar and other mistakes.

Answers:

A) Incorrect. An online seller that requires a prescription from a doctor before dispensing drugs is more reputable.

B) Incorrect. An online retailer is more trustworthy if its website has accurate contact information available.

C) Incorrect. It may be safer for a consumer to purchase drugs from an online seller if authenticity is validated in regard to certification of the website.

D) Correct. A consumer should not purchase drugs from an online seller if the website contains poor grammar and other mistakes.

PURCHASING PHARMACEUTICALS

Pharmacy technicians are responsible for purchasing non-controlled substances in the pharmacy. Depending on the pharmacy, there may be different types of ordering systems available. Many pharmacies use a **want book**. The want book keeps track of drugs that are running low or that have prematurely run out before the regular weekly order will be delivered, uncommon drugs the pharmacy does not usually stock but that a particular patient needs, and special orders. The technician will write the drug name, the quantity needed, and the vendor order number, if available, in the book. The inventory technician or pharmacy buyer then checks the want book at the time of ordering to make sure the order is placed for next-day delivery.

There are three types of **drug procurement** in the pharmacy. These include direct purchasing through the manufacturer, purchasing from the wholesaler, and purchasing from the prime vendor.

Direct purchasing is less costly, eliminating intermediary and handling fees, but it requires more time and dedication to purchasing from multiple vendors.

Wholesaler purchasing is when many products are purchased from one vendor source. The vendor is normally located close to the pharmacy and delivers to the pharmacy daily. The wholesaler maintains most of the inventory, reducing inventory costs. The personnel required for inventory is lower, but the cost of pharmaceuticals is higher.

With pharmacy automation, **order generation software** and **barcode scanning technology** produce a medication fill list that is reviewed by the pharmacy buyer or inventory technician. The technician then creates a **purchase order** and sends it to the wholesaler for delivery.

In **prime vendor purchasing**, the pharmacy and a single wholesaler establish a contractual relationship. The practice will then commit to a certain volume of purchases; the vendor will guarantee a delivery schedule, competitive fee, and quick transactions. Prime vendor agreements can be done through an independent agreement or through a **general purchasing organization (GPO)**. GPOs are normally used by a chain of hospitals and are based upon the **formulary selection** of the hospitals. The prime vendor offers the hospital chain competitive rates for drugs on the hospital formulary in return for its commitment to high-volume orders.

Special ordering is used for specific drugs needed by the pharmacy. These drugs include investigational drugs, controlled substances, cytotoxic drugs, and hazardous substances. Besides special ordering, these drugs require special documentation, storage, handling, and return policies. Because special ordering is subject to federal and state regulations, it is important for pharmacy technicians to remain current and knowledgeable about regulations that apply to the pharmacy practice.

When the order is delivered, the pharmacy will receive an **invoice**, or a summary of the individual drugs ordered and their cost, to document and store for its records.

CONTINUE

PRACTICE QUESTIONS

1. Which is a system of purchasing in which the pharmacy and a single wholesaler establish a relationship?

    A) prime vendor purchasing

    B) special ordering

    C) wholesaler purchasing

    D) direct purchasing

    Answers:

    A) **Correct.** Prime vendor purchasing is a system of purchasing in which a relationship is established between the pharmacy and a single wholesaler.

    B) Incorrect. Pharmacies use special ordering to obtain specific drugs such as investigational drugs, controlled substances, cytotoxic drugs, and hazardous substances.

    C) Incorrect. In wholesaler purchasing, many products are purchased from one vendor source.

    D) Incorrect. Direct purchasing eliminates the need for intermediary and handling fees for drug procurement.

2. Want books are used for all of the following EXCEPT

    A) special ordering.

    B) uncommon drugs not normally stocked in the pharmacy but needed for a specific patient.

    C) in situations when the pharmacy prematurely runs out of the drug due to high demand, and regular order day is still a few days away.

    D) when the drug is running low and the regular weekly order will not be delivered until the next morning.

    Answers:

    A) Incorrect. Want books are used for special order items.

    B) Incorrect. Want books are used for such drugs.

    C) Incorrect. Want books are used in these situations.

    D) **Correct.** Want books are not used in these situations.

RECEIVING DRUGS

When the order is received by the pharmacy, the first step is **verification** of the order. Verifying the order requires checking each individual drug and **comparing the invoices and statements** received with what was sent from the vendor. This includes the quantity, the order number of the drug, and the NDC number to be sure the drug ordered is the same as the drug received. If a specific generic drug was ordered and the vendor substituted a different version of the generic, the invoice should state so.

Stickers accompanying the order are marked with the drug order number. Each stock bottle should have the correct sticker placed on the bottle for future ordering and/or returning to the vendor. Once the technician is sure all the correct drugs and quantities have been received, the technician signs and dates the **wholesaler's recorded invoices** and files them according to the pharmacy's policies and procedures.

Figure 4.7. Wholesaler's Recorded Invoice

RETURNING DRUGS

Drugs to be destroyed or returned should always be separated based on the reason they were pulled from stock and placed in a designated area. Besides **expired stock** and **drug recall stock**, which were discussed in earlier sections, drugs to be returned include unneeded, defective, or damaged medication.

If items were ordered that need to be returned, the drugs must be separated from the order being used. Some pharmacies use bins to separate defective and **damaged stock** received from a vendor from the regular order. Once the order has been resolved, the technician must then use the appropriate return forms to return the drugs not being used. Required fields on these forms indicate order purchase number, item number, quantity, and reason for the return. The vendor is then contacted and advised about the return; returned items are picked up at the next delivery.

PRACTICE QUESTIONS

1. When returning a drug to the vendor, all of the following information is required on the return form EXCEPT

    A) the item order number.

    B) the reason for returning the item.

    C) the pharmacy technician's certification number.

    D) the order purchase number.

    Answers:

    A) Incorrect. The item order number is required on the return form.

    B) Incorrect. The return form must include the reason for returning the item.

    C) Correct. The pharmacy technician's certification number is not required on the return form.

    D) Incorrect. The return form must contain the order purchase number.

2. Which is NOT required after receiving an order from a vendor?

    A) checking each individual drug ordered and comparing the invoices and statements received with what was sent from the vendor

    B) having the pharmacist sign the invoices on non-controlled drugs

    C) placing the correct vendor stickers that state the item number on the correct stock bottle for future ordering

    D) signing and dating the invoices and filing them accordingly

    Answers:

    A) Incorrect. Pharmacy technicians must check each individual drug ordered and compare the invoices and statements received with what was sent from the vendor.

    B) Correct. Pharmacists do not need to sign invoices for non-controlled drugs.

    C) Incorrect. Pharmacy technicians must place the correct vendor stickers stating the item number on the correct stock bottle for future ordering.

    D) Incorrect. Pharmacy technicians must sign and date the invoices and file them accordingly.

STOCKING

When receiving pharmaceuticals, pharmacy technicians must store the medication in the proper areas. Proper storage means adhering to the manufacturer's recommendations on proper lighting, temperature, and exposure. Any **refrigerated items** received by the pharmacy should be stocked in the refrigerator as soon as possible to avoid damaging the product.

When **shelf stocking**, technicians must be knowledgeable about the arrangement of the drug supply. For safety purposes, drugs are separated by their routes of administration. For example, **stock bottles** are normally separated from injectable drugs, while injectable drugs would be separated from liquids. In addition, drug stock should be rotated while stocking. Opened bottles and bottles with earlier expiration dates should be placed in the front, while those with later expiration dates are placed in the back.

Once medications are separated by their routes of administration, the drugs are then arranged alphabetically. Retail pharmacies normally order medications by brand name, while institutional pharmacies arrange them by generic name.

As previously discussed, some drugs are separated from others. Controlled substances are stored in locked areas away from non-controlled drugs, and SALAD drugs are separated from drugs they may be confused with. Cytotoxic drugs are stored in a biological safety cabinet or isolator to prevent them from contaminating other drugs.

It is important to understand the differences between drug packaging in hospital and retail pharmacies, too. Because hospital pharmacies develop individual doses of medications for individual patients, drugs are repackaged in unit-dose blister packaging; on the other hand, retail pharmacies fill higher quantities of medication and therefore use stock bottles. Repackaging of pharmaceuticals is discussed in chapter two.

Upon hiring, pharmacy technicians must familiarize themselves with the pharmacy setup. Storage and shelving organization keeps the pharmacy in compliance with regulations and running efficiently.

PRACTICE QUESTION

Which of the following is NOT true about stocking drugs?

A) Technicians must be knowledgeable about the arrangement of the drug supply.

B) Drugs are separated by their routes of administration.

C) All pharmacies arrange drugs on the shelf alphabetically by brand name.

D) Refrigerated drugs must be stored in the refrigerator as soon as possible.

Answers:

A) Incorrect. It is true that technicians must be knowledgeable about the arrangement of the drug supply.

B) Incorrect. Drugs are indeed separated by their routes of administration.

C) Correct. Not all pharmacies arrange drugs alphabetically by brand name. Some pharmacies arrange drugs by generic name.

D) Incorrect. Refrigerated drugs must be properly stored as soon as possible.

FIVE 5: COMPOUNDING PHARMACEUTICALS

The art and science of compounding pharmaceuticals dates back to the origins of humanity. Early practitioners practiced through experimentation by collecting and mixing different plant extracts. These practitioners became known as apothecaries, people who prepare and sell medicines. Now, most refer to this practice as pharmacy. The practice of modern pharmaceutical compounding has changed over the years. In the 1930s, around 60 percent of pharmaceuticals were compounded. During the 1950s and 1960s, with the influx of manufacturing, compounding waned and pharmacists began to dispense more medications.

Compounding pharmaceuticals is considered an advanced role of the pharmacy technician. It is defined as the personalized preparation, from one or more ingredients, of a prescribed medication that is not commercially available. There are a wide range of medications that can be compounded. Some can be as simple as adding **product flavoring** to a child's antibiotic to improve taste, while other product formulations need to be precisely calculated into patient-specific **customized dosage forms**.

> **?** Break down the following terms to their Latin roots and find their definitions: neurologic, ophthalmologic, oncologic, homeopathic, and podiatric.

Although compounding is commonly practiced in retail and hospital settings, there are specialty pharmacies and clinics that compound as well. **Veterinary** clinics prepare medications for non-human animals. Cancer centers develop patient-specific **oncologic**, or **radiopharmaceutical**, infusions. **Sports medicine** clinics compound creams for joint and muscular ailments, in addition to pain injections. Research clinics develop and track **investigational** drugs for experimentation purposes. Holistic centers use a **homeopathic** philosophy, the practice and belief in the body's ability to heal itself, to develop patient-specific natural medicines and **vitamins** and **supplements**. Other examples of compounded pharmaceuticals are **ophthalmologic**, **podiatric**, and **neurologic** medications.

Which is NOT considered a compounding facility?

A) sports medicine centers

B) veterinary clinics

C) physical therapy centers

D) cancer centers

Answers:

A)   Incorrect. Sports medicine centers compound creams and injections for joint and muscle ailments.

B)   Incorrect. Veterinary clinics compound medications for non-human animals.

C)   Correct. Physical therapy relates to exercises and massages for physical disabilities without the use of medications.

D)   Incorrect. Cancer centers make oncology infusions and injections for cancer patients.

Non-Sterile Compounding

Non-sterile compounding refers to the compounding of two or more ingredients that a patient can swallow, drink, insert, or apply topically, under the federal and state laws of an accredited pharmacy in accordance with a licensed practitioner's prescription or medication order. Many independent pharmacies and clinics that participate in non-sterile compounding join organizations such as the **PCCA (Professional Compounding Centers of America)**. Being a part of an organization like PCCA helps the pharmacy stay on top of new guidelines and provides it with resources on ordering, continuing education, and compounding equipment.

Due to the standards pharmacy technicians are required to maintain, when compounding pharmaceuticals it is important to have a strong **work ethic**. Work ethic refers to the ability to make sound judgments, act professionally at all times, and demonstrate a positive attitude. A technician should also have above-average **mathematical skills**. Pharmaceutical math entails performing calculations with precise formulas and requires accuracy. Another goal in the pharmacy is to dispense medication in a swift and precise manner. Accuracy is the most important goal. In a pharmacy compounding environment, excellent **written and oral communication skills** and **attention to detail** are crucial to providing the best and safest service possible to the patient.

Circumstances that would require compounding are:

+   when a product is commercially unavailable. Topical hormonal therapies, veterinary preparations, specialty dermatologic products that are applied topically, and patient-specific rectal or vaginal compounds all may require compounding.

- specialized dosage strengths. If a patient-specific dosage or strength of a preparation is needed that is not commercially available, the pharmacy technician may need to compound it.
- product flavoring. If the taste of a medication affects compliance, compounding may be necessary.
- if a different dosage form is needed. If a patient cannot take capsules or tablets, then a liquid formulation may be compounded.

The FDA requires that non-sterile compounding must adhere to the standards of **USP Chapter 795** and the State Boards of Pharmacy. The **US Pharmacopeial Convention (USP)** is a nonprofit organization that sets standards for the strength, purity, quality, and identity of medicines, dietary supplements, and food. Although the guidelines are not as strict as with sterile compounding, the USP does set the minimum standards of education and training of pharmacy personnel, facilities, equipment, documentation, policies and procedures, records and reports, and patient counseling needed to safely and accurately prepare non-sterile compounds. It also sources information on strength, quality, and purity of compounded products and proper manufacturing practices. When compounding controlled substances, DEA guidelines must be met as well. The DEA requires specific compounding record logs for narcotics, a recording of inventory after each batch, and a record kept by the pharmacist regarding any waste. Other important reference guides for non-sterile compounding are the **FCC (Food Chemical Codex)** and publications of the **ACS (American Chemical Society)**.

When compounding, it is important to know the FDA **grades**, or standards, for products that may be consumed or used for cosmetic or topical purposes. **Spectroscopic grade** is for measuring purity of light. This is important when working with substances that may be degradable in light. Such substances may require processes to protect them from light, such as amber packaging. **Food grade** refers to the regulations on purity of food, and **cosmetic grade** refers to regulations on colors, dyes, and perfumes. Some compounded products also require specific grade levels to define how **purified**, or how free of contamination, the finished product is. These levels include **technical grade**, or commercial quality, **chemically pure (CP)**, which is more refined than technical grade, and **HPLC**, which is of very high purity.

Reagents are substances or mixtures used in chemical reactions. An **analytical reagent (AR)** confirms the presence of another substance. A **primary standard** is a reagent that is extremely pure, stable, has a high molecular weight, and lacks waters of hydration.

Non-Sterile Compounding Techniques

To ensure that the proper purity standards are met while compounding, pharmacy technicians are required to use aseptic technique. **Aseptic technique** puts safeguards in place to avoid contamination. The safeguards consist of using a sterile work area, good personal hygiene, sterile reagents, sterile handling, and **aseptic handwashing** using an **antiseptic** agent, or a solution free of contamination.

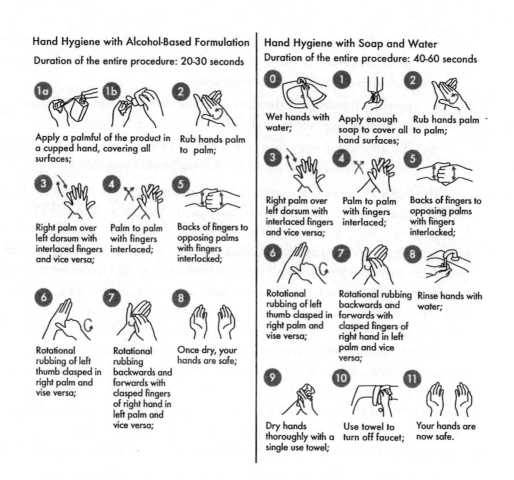

Hand Hygiene with Alcohol-Based Formulation
Duration of the entire procedure: 20-30 seconds

1a 1b Apply a palmful of the product in a cupped hand, covering all surfaces;

2 Rub hands palm to palm;

3 Right palm over left dorsum with interlaced fingers and vice versa;

4 Palm to palm with fingers interlaced;

5 Backs of fingers to opposing palms with fingers interlocked;

6 Rotational rubbing of left thumb clasped in right palm and vise versa;

7 Rotational rubbing backwards and forwards with clasped fingers of right hand in left palm and vice versa;

8 Once dry, your hands are safe;

Hand Hygiene with Soap and Water
Duration of the entire procedure: 40-60 seconds

0 Wet hands with water;

1 Apply enough soap to cover all hand surfaces;

2 Rub hands palm to palm;

3 Right palm over left dorsum with interlaced fingers and vice versa;

4 Palm to palm with fingers interlaced;

5 Backs of fingers to opposing palms with fingers interlocked;

6 Rotational rubbing of left thumb clasped in right palm and vise versa;

7 Rotational rubbing backwards and forwards with clasped fingers of right hand in left palm and vice versa;

8 Rinse hands with water;

9 Dry hands thoroughly with a single use towel;

10 Use towel to turn off faucet;

11 Your hands are now safe.

Figure 5.1. Aseptic Handwashing

Although the aseptic requirements for non-sterile compounding are not as stringent as those for sterile compounding, depending on the State Board of Pharmacy and the healthcare facility other **personal protection equipment (PPE)**, or contamination barriers, may be required as well. These include sterile gloves, masks, sterile gowns, bouffant caps, gloves, goggles, and shoe covers.

Non-Sterile Compounding Tools and Terms

Non-sterile compounding is also called **extemporaneous compounding**. According to USP 795, any equipment or supplies used to compound MUST

+ reduce ingredients to the smallest particle size.
+ ensure the solution has no visible undissolved matter when dispensed.
+ make sure preparations are similarly structured to ensure uniform final distribution.

Common preparations that can be made by extemporaneous compound follow.

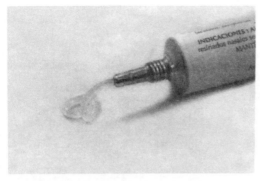

Figure 5.2. Ointment: an oily preparation that is normally medicated and applied topically

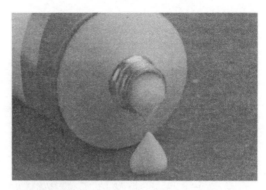

Figure 5.3. Cream: a thick or semisolid preparation applied topically

Figure 5.4. Paste: a thick, soft, and moist substance usually produced by mixing dry ingredients with a liquid (pictured: mustard)

Figure 5.5. Oil-in-Water Emulsion: a diffusion (droplets) of one liquid in another impassible liquid (pictured: mayonnaise)

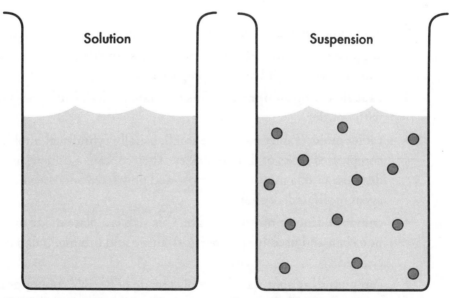

Figure 5.6. Solution: a liquid preparation of one or more soluble chemical substances that are usually dissolved in water, vs. suspension: a preparation of finely divided, undissolved drugs or powders distributed in a liquid medium

Figure 5.7. Lotion: a thick, smooth, liquid preparation designed to be applied to the skin for medicinal or cosmetic purposes

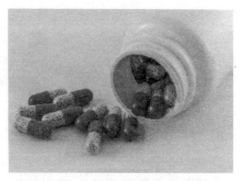

Figure 5.8. Capsule: a solid encapsulated in gelatin

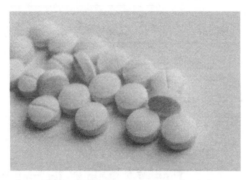

Figure 5.9. Tablet: a compressed solid dosage unit

Figure 5.10. Suppository: a solid preparation in either conical or cylindrical shape that is inserted into the rectum or vagina to dissolve

Some common tools and equipment used for extemporaneous compounding are:

+ **suppository molds:** Plastic or metal, these molds are used to form the suppository after it has been prepared.

+ **capsule-filling equipment:** This mechanical device fills the gelatin capsules with powder.

+ **tablet mold:** Tablet molds are small, usually cylindrical, molded or compressed disks of different sizes. They contain a diluent, usually made of dextrose or of a mixture of lactose and powdered sucrose and a moistening agent or diluted alcohol.

+ **compounding or ointment slab:** This slab is a plate made of glass or porcelain and used for geometric dilution and mixing. It can be easily cleaned.

+ **compounding spatula:** This tool is made of flexible rubber or metal and is used to mix and shear ointments and creams.

+ **blenders and mixers:** These common devices can be used for mixing as well.

A **mortar and pestle** is a tool that has been used for centuries in pharmacy. It is used to grind and crush, or **levigate**, ingredients into a fine paste. These tools are usually made of wood, ceramics, or stone.

Figure 5.11. Mortar and Pestle (ceramic)

Trituration is to pulverize or reduce to a fine particle by rubbing or grinding into a powder. **Geometric dilution** is the process by which a **homogenous**, or similarly structured, combination or delivery of two or more substances is achieved.

For measuring and weighing, technicians use different tools. **Class A balances** are required in all pharmacies and must be inspected and meet the requirements of the National Bureau of Standards (NBS). A Class A balance is a two-pan torsion type with internal and external weights. It has a capacity of 120 mg and has a sensitivity of 6 mg. **Counter balances** are less accurate than Class A balances. They have a limit of 5 kg and a sensitivity of 100 mg.

Figure 5.12. Counter Balance

Figure 5.13. Class A Balance

In addition, **weighing boats** and **glassine paper** are flexible containers used for holding liquids and solids for weighing on the balances.

Weights are usually made of brass or polished metal and must be maintained and handled properly. Sets generally contain cylindrical weights ranging from 1 to 50 grams and fractional weights of 10 to 500 mg. The weights should be calibrated annually to ensure accuracy. **Forceps** should be used when picking up weights so as to not damage them.

Figure 5.14. Weights

Figure 5.15. Forceps

Conical graduated cylinders are used for measuring liquids and allow easy pouring due to their circular design. **Cylindrical graduated cylinders** are also used for measuring liquids but have a narrow design. The **meniscus** is the curved upper surface of a liquid in a container: it is curved in if the liquid wets the walls and curved out if it does not.

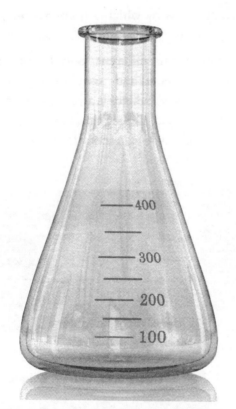

Figure 5.16. Conical Graduated Cylinder

Figure 5.17. Cylindrical Graduated Cylinder

Some preparations are made to the patient's order, while other formulations may be commonly prescribed by a physician. If the latter is the case, the pharmacy has a **master**

formula record, or recipes of frequently used compounding formulas and recordkeeping. Some formulations that are frequently prescribed may be made in bulk so the product can be dispensed to the patient in a timely manner. Any time a compounded medication is prepared, it must be verified by a pharmacist. It also must be recorded in a **compounding log** with the name of products used, lot numbers, expiration and beyond-use dates, quantity made, and amount of ingredients used (lot numbers and expiration dates on packaging are always grouped together). The initials of the technician who prepared the medication and the pharmacist who verified it are required as well. It is then filed as a permanent record.

> The beyond-use date is different from the expiration date. When a medication is compounded, due to degradation it is only good for a limited amount of time. For example, Vancomycin may have an expiration date of 5/19 on the vial, but once it is reconstituted and added to a solution, it must be used within 7 days. So the BUD for this compound made on 7/10/2018 would be 7/17/2018.

Proper labeling is important when compounding is complete. If a bulk preparation is used for stock, the label must include the preparation name, date prepared, lot numbers, names and amounts of the compounded medications, and the expiration date or the beyond-use date. If the compounded medication is patient specific, proper labeling

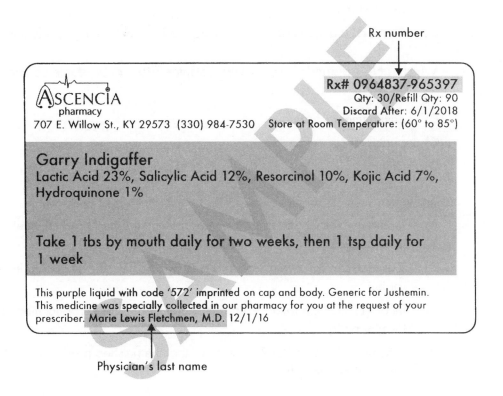

Figure 5.18. Proper Labeling

with name, address, physician information, prescription number, and directions for use is required as well.

> In retail pharmacy settings, medications are usually recognized by the brand names, while in institutional settings, even if there is no generic available, medications are always recognized in generic form.

PRACTICE QUESTIONS

1. Which is NOT a circumstance that may require non-sterile compounding?

    A) when a product is commercially unavailable

    B) product flavoring

    C) if a different dosage form is needed

    D) if a medication has been recalled

    Answers:

    A) Incorrect. Compounding is available for specialized compounds such as patient-specific hormonal creams and veterinary products.

    B) Incorrect. Flavoring is added to medications to improve taste.

    C) Incorrect. If a patient cannot take a tablet, medication can be compounded to make a liquid.

    D) Correct. If a medication is recalled, then it may be temporarily unavailable.

2. Which is NOT a standard set by USP Chapter 795 for non-sterile compounding?

    A) quality

    B) environmental testing

    C) purity

    D) strength

    Answers:

    A) Incorrect. USP Chapter 795 requires that the finished product meet a certain level of quality.

    B) Correct. Environmental testing is part of USP 797 for air quality in the clean room.

    C) Incorrect. USP Chapter 795 requires that the finished product meet a certain level of purity.

    D) Incorrect. USP Chapter 795 requires that the finished product be at the appropriate strength.

3. Which of the following is NOT considered personal protection equipment (PPE)?

A) bouffant caps

B) tennis shoes

C) goggles

D) masks

Answers:

A) Incorrect. Bouffant caps are used as PPE. Caps keep hair from contaminating compounded products.

B) **Correct.** Tennis shoes are not considered PPE.

C) Incorrect. Goggles are PPE. They protect the eyes from irritants and backsplash.

D) Incorrect. Masks prevent contamination with bodily fluid and stop the preparer from inhaling irritants.

4. Aseptic technique consists of all of the following EXCEPT

A) good personal hygiene.

B) a sterile work area.

C) wearing scrubs.

D) proper hand washing technique.

Answers:

A) Incorrect. Keeping clean is essential to avoid microbe contamination.

B) Incorrect. A sterile work area keeps the compounded product pure.

C) **Correct.** Wearing scrubs can still contaminate a sterile environment.

D) Incorrect. Proper handwashing is the best way to avoid contamination.

5. The definition of *triturate* is

A) to grind or crush into a fine paste.

B) to dissolve one or more chemical liquid substances in water.

C) to diffuse a liquid into another impassable liquid.

D) to rub or crush into a fine powder.

Answers:

A) Incorrect. Grinding or crushing into a paste is levigating.

B) Incorrect. Dissolving one or more chemical liquid substances in water results in a solution.

C) Incorrect. Diffusing a liquid into another impassable liquid results in an oil-in-water emulsion.

D) **Correct.** To rub or crush into a fine powder is to triturate.

6. Which compound can be made using a mold?

A) a capsule

B) a tablet

C) a solution

D) a lotion

Answers:

A) Incorrect. A capsule is encapsulated gelatin that is filled with medication.

B) Correct. A tablet can be made using a mold.

C) Incorrect. A solution is a liquid.

D) Incorrect. A lotion is a topical solution.

Sterile Compounding

Sterile compounding is the manipulation of a sterile or non-sterile product to create a patient-specific sterile finished product for intravenous or parenteral use. Sterile compounding is highly regulated and requires a specific skill set.

USP Chapter 797 refers to the standards and guidelines that are required for performing the highest quality sterile compounding measures. These are policies and procedures that are scientifically recognized to produce clean air quality, clean facilities and equipment, knowledge of stability and sterilization techniques, and specialized training. **Compounded sterile preparations**, or **CSPs**, and the spaces in which they are prepared must comply with USP 797 due to the nature of these products. Proper training is required by those of all disciplines involved in the sterile compounding process including pharmacy personnel, nurses, and physicians. Because products prepared as a CSP have the greatest risk of contamination, they must be manipulated in a highly controlled environment.

 Non-sterile compounding routes of administration are oral, rectal, and topical, while sterile compounding is intravenous and parenteral.

Quality control, continuous improvement procedures and safeguards in pharmacy compounding, is required in sterile compounding environments. The technician must abide by the regulations implemented by USP 797 to keep microbial contamination risk low. This is done by creating a system of checks and balances called **quality assurance**. Quality assurance includes proper aseptic technique, air particulate testing, use of the appropriate technique while preparing CSPs, and continuing education. This system ensures that the manufactured product adheres to a defined set of criteria. Frequent audits and evaluations of the sterile room ensure that the patients receive a quality medication with low risk to their overall health. The most important aspects of quality control in sterile compounding are cleaning and sanitizing, environmental monitoring, and sterility testing of equipment. All processes are logged, initialed, and kept on file as a permanent record.

PRACTICE QUESTIONS

1. What is a route of administration for sterile compounding?

   A) oral

   B) rectal

   C) sublingual

   D) intravenous

   Answers:

   A) Incorrect. Sterile compounding is not necessary for compounds taken by mouth.

   B) Incorrect. Suppositories are taken rectally; this is not a sterile route.

   C) Incorrect. Sublingual administration, in which a medication is dissolved under the tongue, does not require sterile compounding.

   D) Correct. Medications administered intravenously are injected into a vein and go directly into the bloodstream, so they require sterile compounding.

2. Which is NOT covered by standard guidelines in USP Chapter 797?

   A) complying with the FDA requirements

   B) air quality

   C) stability and sterilization

   D) proper continuing education

   Answers:

   A) Correct. Although the FDA is involved in non-sterile compounding due to the routes of administration, sterile compounding is considered a part of pharmacy practice and does not fall under the agency's authority.

   B) Incorrect. Air quality is an important part of USP 797 because particulates in the air must not contaminate the sterile environment.

   C) Incorrect. USP 797 provides very stringent guidelines on the stability and sterilization of CSPs.

   D) Incorrect. Because USP 797 is revised often, continuing education is needed to keep personnel up to date on policies and procedures.

CONTINUE

MICROORGANISMS AND METHODS OF INFECTION TRANSMISSION

Basic knowledge of the microorganisms that can be transmitted by improperly preparing CSPs is an important safeguard in sterile compounding. A **microorganism**, or **microbe**, is a single-celled organism that is so small to the naked eye it is considered microscopic. These microorganisms can be found everywhere by the millions. They are on clothing, in cosmetics, on skin, and on the surfaces people touch every day. Although microorganisms can never be fully contained, when working with medication that will be entering directly into a person's bloodstream, pharmacy technicians must be mindful of the critical importance of keeping them contained to a safe level.

There are three main microorganisms in sterile compounding. **Bacteria** are common, widespread microorganisms that can multiply by the thousands very quickly. If introduced into the bloodstream, bacteria can become **pyrogens**, causing fever and infection. A **virus** is an infective agent capable of multiplying in the cells of a living host. Finally, **fungi** live by decomposing and absorbing organic material as they grow.

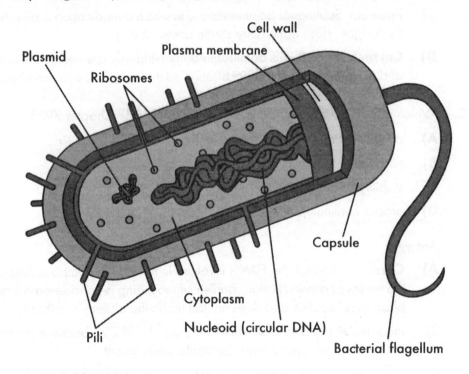

Figure 5.19. Bacteria

Under normal conditions, proper handwashing, covering the mouth and nose while coughing and sneezing, and avoiding skin contact all keep people relatively healthy. In sterile compounding, however, medications are administered **parenterally**, or through an injection or infusion—subcutaneously, intravenously, or intramuscularly. Because other contact barriers are bypassed, if a sterile preparation is not prepared under proper conditions, harmful microorganisms could easily be transmitted directly into a patient's bloodstream.

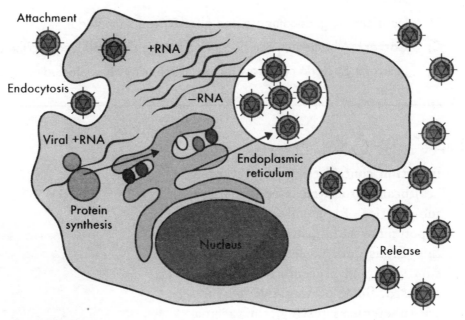

Figure 5.20. Virus

A sterile compounding technician should always be aware of his or her personal, environmental, and surface area surroundings to keep microbe contamination under control in the clean room.

+ **personal surroundings:** Workers should limit makeup and hair products, refrain from wearing jewelry, maintain personal hygiene, and always use aseptic technique.

+ **environmental surroundings:** Air quality must be controlled in the clean room.

+ **surface area surroundings:** The surface areas used while preparing CSPs and the **instruments**, or common tools and equipment, used while compounding should be kept cleaned and sterilized at all times.

PRACTICE QUESTION

What is a characteristic of bacteria?

A) It is an infective agent capable of multiplying in the cells of a living host.

B) It can decompose and absorb organic material as it grows.

C) It can become a pyrogen if introduced into the bloodstream.

D) It cannot grow on soft surface areas.

A) Incorrect. A virus is an infective agent capable of multiplying in the cells of a living host.

B) Incorrect. Fungi decompose and absorb organic material.

C) Correct. A bacterium can become a pyrogen if introduced into the bloodstream.

D) Incorrect. Bacteria can grow by the millions anywhere, including on soft surface areas.

INFECTION CONTROL

Infection control refers to preventing healthcare-associated infection. It is a sub-practice of epidemiology and very important to the infrastructure of healthcare. In institutional settings, employee education and preventative measures are used. Some preventative measures are tuberculosis testing, flu vaccinations, hepatitis vaccinations, and MRSA education. The number one preventative measure in infection control is **hand hygiene** as discussed previously.

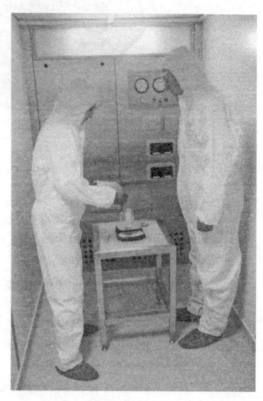

Figure 5.21. Lab Suits

In sterile compounding, aseptic technique is critical. Within a sterile compounding environment, infection control becomes more complex. To keep microorganisms in the clean room at a safe level, it is necessary to follow a step-by-step procedure known as gowning up, or **garbing. Personal protection equipment (PPE)** must be worn according to specific guidelines.

How to gown up, or garb:

+ Only **lab coats or suits** that are specifically made for the clean room may be used. Lab coats worn outside of the anteroom and clean room area may not be brought into the anteroom; if the clean room coat is worn outside of the anteroom, it must be discarded.

+ **Shoe covers** must be put on before feet touch the floor in the clean room.

+ **Masks** should only be put on right before working at the laminar airflow bench and should be discarded each time workers leave the compounding area.

- Only latex, Nitrile, or vinyl **gloves** may be worn. Gloves should be sprayed down with 70 percent isopropyl alcohol before compounding. They must be changed when punctured or torn and between batches.

Figure 5.22. Shoe Covers

- Depending on the product being prepared, **goggles** or **shields** may be worn. They are not required for low risk CSPs, but they are required when compounding toxic preparations and eye irritants.

- **Bouffant caps** keep hair covered to avoid contamination.

Figure 5.23. Bouffant Cap

Garbing always takes place in the anteroom. Workers begin by putting on shoe covers, then a hair cover or bouffant cap and mask. Then they wash their hands, gown, and enter the clean room. At that point, workers once again clean their hands, this time using an alcohol-based cleanser, then don gloves. Workers should be sure that their gloves go over the sleeves of the gown. Aside from shoe covers, garb should never touch the floor.

> When garbing up, always start from the dirtiest to the cleanest areas. Put on shoe covers and cap; wash hands; don gown and mask. Then enter the clean room, cleanse hands with an alcohol solution, and put on gloves.

When de-gowning, everything should be thrown away. The garbing-up process begins again when workers re-enter the anteroom unless the facility's policies state otherwise. If workers can re-wear any garments that have been in the anteroom, they must be sure that none of these garments leave the clean area or touch the floor.

It is always the pharmacy technician's responsibility to properly garb and de-garb per the facility's policies and procedures.

PRACTICE QUESTION

Infection control is a sub-practice of

A) epidemiology.

B) biology.

C) immunology.

D) ecology.

Answers:

A) **Correct.** Epidemiology is the branch of medicine that addresses disease control.

B) Incorrect. Biology is the study of life.

C) Incorrect. Immunology is the study of the immune system.

D) Incorrect. Ecology is a branch of biology that deals with the relations of organisms to one another.

CLEAN ROOM

The **clean room** is a room that is free from dust and other contaminants. Every compounding area consists of two rooms: the anteroom and the clean room.

The **anteroom** is where preparation takes place. It has a label generator, a faucet, **antiseptic** (or antibacterial solution for handwashing), CSP labeling, PPEs, staging of components, order entry, a storage area, and a gowning area. It is also where other high particulate activities are performed. Compounding is never actually done in the anteroom.

The air quality in the anteroom should be at least ISO 6 to ISO 8 standard, which is 3,520,000 particles or less. The air quality depends on the facility and what at risk levels it compounds. The anteroom should have smooth walls with locked and sealed panels. Floors are covered in vinyl, with seals soldered together. All joints and junctures must be caulked with no visible cracks.

The clean room is where the laminar airflow workbench (LAFW) is located. The LAFW is where preparers compound the CSPs. Its physical characteristics are the same as those of the anteroom. A positive room air pressure must be maintained and checked on a regular basis. If the facility only compounds low- and medium-risk CSPs, the clean room and anteroom do not need to be separated. However they must be separated at high-risk facilities. The area immediately next to the LAFW is called the **buffer area**.

PRACTICE QUESTION

What is NOT performed in the anteroom?

A) label preparation

B) compounding under the laminar airflow workbench

C) garbing up

D) order entry

Answers:

A) Incorrect. Labels can be prepared in the anteroom.

B) **Correct.** The laminar airflow workbench is in the clean room.

C) Incorrect. Garbing up is done in the anteroom.

D) Incorrect. Order entry is done in the anteroom unless the facility puts a specialized computer in the clean room.

CLEAN AIR ENVIRONMENTS

The most important piece of equipment used in the sterile room is the **laminar airflow workbench**. Nonhazardous CSPs are made in a **horizontal laminar airflow hood**, which pushes positive pressure toward the preparer. The **vertical laminar airflow hood**, which pushes negative air pressure away from the preparer, is used for hazardous CSPs such as radiopharmaceuticals. While preparing CSPs, all products used must be at least 6 inches from the sides and front of the hood. This is important so that the CSPs are not contaminated by the preparer. It also prevents disturbances of the airflow current in the buffer area. Some pharmacies use **barrier isolators**, or glove boxes, to avoid contamination as well. The preparer can avoid touching the CSPs altogether by putting his or her hands inside gloves within an isolator enclosure in order to compound.

By using **HEPA (high efficiency particulate abstractor)** filters, air is filtered into the clean room while removing all but the finest particulates. The amount of air is also much greater and at a higher pressure than required for normal ventilation and comfort. It is important to check the filters every 6 months to prevent contamination by air from other rooms and keep the air filter clean.

A clean room environment must not allow more than 3,500 airborne particles or **air particulates**, of no larger than 0.5 microns each, per square meter into the area. They are classified as Class 100 or Class A environments. Air is cycled through at 90 to 100 feet per minute. This is called an ISO 5 environment.

An anteroom environment must not allow more than 35,200 to 3,520,000 airborne particles in and is considered either a Class 1,000 to 100,000 environment. The environment must be between ISO 6 and 8. The higher the risk level the facility compounds, the lower the environment should be in the anteroom. **Pressure differentiation**, or changes in pressure between the anteroom and clean room, helps keep the larger particulates from the anteroom out of the clean room.

Air quality is implemented by controlling the environment, workforce, product, and processes in the room. Some other controls used to maintain clean air environments are the room temperature and humidity, fixtures, fittings, flat surfaces, strict cleaning schedules, and routine testing. All of the processes are recorded and documented. Keeping this documentation helps the facility comply with the guidelines of USP 797 and keep a record of any changes in equipment or environment.

PRACTICE QUESTIONS

1. What is the definition of pressure differentiation?
    A) control of the environment
    B) any environment that takes in more than 35,200 particulates
    C) change in pressure between the clean room and anteroom
    D) an ISO 5 environment

    Answers:
    A) Incorrect. This term refers to air quality.
    B) Incorrect: The anteroom environments permit 35,200 to 3,520,000 airborne particles in.
    C) **Correct.** Pressure differentiation refers to the change in pressure between the anteroom and the clean room. This change keeps air particles out of the clean room.
    D) Incorrect. This term describes the clean room.

2. A clean room environment must not allow more than how many particles in?
    A) 3,520,000
    B) 35,200
    C) 352
    D) 3,500

    Answers:
    A) Incorrect. This number describes the highest amount of particles allowed in an anteroom environment.
    B) Incorrect. This number also refers to the anteroom environment.
    C) Incorrect. This number is too low. Some particulates will always come through even in the lowest ISO environment.

D) **Correct.** The maximum amount of particles allowed in a clean room environment is 3,500.

STERILE COMPOUNDING EQUIPMENT

Much of the equipment used to compound CSPs is unique to the practice of sterile compounding. In this section, the main components used in sterile compounding will be defined. Several examples follow.

+ **alcohol pads**: small, individually wrapped pads soaked with isopropyl alcohol and used to disinfect tops of vials and ports when compounding

+ **ampule breaker**: a plastic device placed over a glass ampule to make it safer to open

+ **ampules**: glass medication containers with concave, narrow, breakable necks

+ **autoclave**: a pressure chamber used to carry out sterilization by using elevated temperature and pressure different to ambient air pressure

+ **catheters**: 1- to 5-inch pieces of fine plastic tubing attached to a hub that itself is attached to an administration set or syringe

Figure 5.24. Ampules

+ **compounding log**: documents used for recording CSPs; include name of medication, date made, beyond-use date, lot numbers of ingredients, quantity made, and initials of preparer and verifying pharmacist

+ **depth filter**: a filter that traps particles as fluid moves through its channels

+ **drip chamber**: a hollow area where IV fluid drips in the plastic tubing without letting air bubbles pass

+ **filters**: screens that remove unwanted particles from a solution

+ **filter needles**: needles that come in 10, 5, 1, and 0.45 micrometer sizes and remove unwanted particles from a solution

+ **filter straws**: straw-like needles that withdraw a large amount of fluid quickly

+ **flexible bag**: polyvinyl (PVC) bags for intravenous fluid

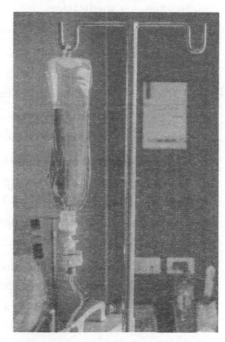

Figure 5.25. Flexible Bag

- **isopropyl alcohol 70 percent**: the strength required for disinfecting in the pharmacy
- **IV administration set**: the length of plastic tubing with a spike on one end, a needle adaptor on another, and a clamp in the middle of tubing to stop the flow of fluid; used to transfer medication from one IV bag or vial to another
- **heparin lock**: a flush for an IV line that keeps a vein open due to its anti-blood clotting properties
- **infusion pump**: a device that applies a set amount of pressure to control the flow rate of an IV medication
- **large volume parenteral (LVP)**: IV bags that contain 250 ml or more of solution
- **male and female adapters**: cover ends of syringes; are used to mix contents
- **membrane filter**: a device that filters a solution as it is expelled from a syringe
- **mini-bag**: an IV piggyback that holds under 100 ml of IV fluid.
- **mini-bag plus**: an IV piggyback that contains under 100 ml of fluid and has an adaptor that can "snap" and spike a vial of medication without the need to reconstitute
- **multi-dose vial**: a vial of medication that contains multiple doses and can be used more than once
- **needle adapter**: a plastic adapter on an IV administration set where a needle is attached
- **roll clamp**: a clamp that pinches the tubing of an IV administration set to regulate the flow rate
- **single-dose vial**: a medication vial that contains only one dose of medication
- **small-volume parenteral (SVP)**: a prepackaged product given directly to the patient or added to another parenteral formulation
- **transfer needle**: a needle designed with a hollow cut that transfers medication from one medication vial or container to another
- **vial**: a small glass or plastic bottle that holds medication protected by a metal-enclosed rubber seal

One common specialized tool is the syringe. A **syringe** is sterile, prepackaged, **non-pyrogenic** or endotoxin-free, and ready to use. Syringes are available in 1 ml, 3 ml, 5 ml, 10 ml, 20 ml, 30 ml, 40 ml, and 60 ml sizes, and they are calibrated for measuring. When dosing with a syringe, always use the next size higher than the measurement needed. There are four parts to a syringe: the plunger, barrel, flange, and tip.

The **plunger** is the movable cylinder that inserts into the barrel. It draws the medicine into the barrel or pushes it out. The **barrel** is the part of the syringe that holds the medication; it indicates the calibrations for measuring. The **flange** is where the barrel is inserted, and the **tip** is where the needle is attached. A **syringe cap** screws onto the tip of a syringe to stop the fluid in the syringe from coming out when a needle is not being used.

Figure 5.26. Sterile, Packaged Syringes   Figure 5.27. Syringe Needle

Syringe needles are sterilized and individually wrapped. They draw medication from a vial and push medication out into an IV bag. They are screwed onto the syringe and have four parts:

+ **hub**: the end of the needle that attaches to the syringe
+ **shaft**: the long, slender stem of the needle
+ **bevel**: the sharp, pointed tip
+ **lumen**: the hollow bore of the needle shaft

One type of needle, a **spike**, is a large plastic needle that attaches to the end of a syringe, can screw onto a syringe, and allows the solution to come out of the vial quicker.

Solutions are essential in compounding. **Irrigation Solution** is a sterile water or normal saline solution used for irrigation of a wound or body cavity. **Normal Saline (NS) 0.9 percent** is also known as sodium chloride, a sterile, isotonic solution, manufactured in plastic containers, and almost equivalent to human tears. It is used intravenously for fluid replacement as well as irrigation of wounds. **Dextrose 5 percent** is a sterile solution used for fluid replacement and caloric supply. **D5NS (Dextrose 5 percent** and **Normal Saline)** is a combination of Dextrose 5 percent and NS that is used intravenously for fluid and electrolyte replacement and caloric supply. **0.45 percent Normal Saline (1/2 NS)** is a sterile, hypotonic solution, manufactured in plastic containers, and used intravenously for fluid and electrolyte replacement. **Lactated Ringer's Solution** is a sterile, isotonic (acidity-lowering) solution, manufactured in plastic containers and used intravenously for fluid and electrolyte replacement. **IVPB (IV piggy back)** is a secondary IV solution, usually smaller than the primary solution that uses a different type of tubing. Sometimes this is called a rider. **Potassium Chloride 10, 20, 40 MEQ solution** is a sterile solution used for treatment of potassium deficiencies. It comes in plastic containers as a piggy back and is also combined with Normal Saline for intravenous use.

Bacteriostatic water is sterile water mixed with 0.9 percent benzoyl alcohol that is used to dilute or dissolve medications. It comes in a multi-dose vial. **Sterile water** is water that is sterilized and contains no antimicrobial agents. It is used for irrigation only.

Some abbreviations commonly used for IV fluid in sterile compounding: LR or RL (Lactated Ringer's), NS (Normal Saline 0.9 percent), D5 (Dextrose 5 percent), D10 (Dextrose 10 percent), KCL (Potassium Chloride), SW (sterile water). When combined, numbers are added to indicate the strength. For example: D10LR is Dextrose 10 percent with Lactated Ringer's Injection, while KCL20NS would be Potassium Chloride 20meq with 0.9 percent Normal Saline.

PRACTICE QUESTIONS

1. What is the lowest strength of isopropyl alcohol required for sterilization in the clean room?

    A) 70 percent

    B) 90 percent

    C) 50 percent

    D) 80 percent

    Answers:

    A) **Correct.** The lowest strength of isopropyl alcohol permitted for sterilization in the clean room is 70 percent.

    B) Incorrect. Although 90 percent is available and can be used, the lowest strength permissible is 70 percent.

    C) Incorrect. Isopropyl alcohol 50 percent would not effectively disinfect in the clean room; this percentage is too low.

    D) Incorrect. There is no such strength as 80 percent isopropyl alcohol.

2. Which fluid is considered an isotonic solution?

    A) 0.45 percent Normal Saline (1/2NS)

    B) Dextrose 5 percent (D5)

    C) Lactated Ringer's (LR)

    D) bacteriostatic water

    Answers:

    A) Incorrect. 1/2NS is considered hypertonic.

    B) Incorrect. Dextrose 5 percent is used for caloric replenishment and is hypotonic.

    C) **Correct.** Lactated Ringer's is an isotonic solution.

    D) Incorrect. Bacteriostatic water is not used for IVs.

FACTORS THAT AFFECT STERILE COMPOUNDING

During compounding, certain factors can affect the quality of the finished sterile product. Some issues can be as simple as the order in which the preparer adds ingredients to a solution. For example, when preparing a TPN (total parenteral solution), adding calcium gluconate before adding potassium phosphate can cause crystallization and sometimes precipitation. Therefore, preparers generally wait until the end of the preparation to add calcium gluconate. Other problems, such as a mistake in calculation or dosage form, can cause serious effects. It is always important to check and double-check the products used during the preparation, the final preparation of the product, and the label for strength, dosage, or quantity discrepancies. Mistakes can happen; reference books should be accessible and the pharmacist should be consulted in case of any doubts. Mistakes may cost not only money, but even lives.

Chemical degradation is the most common issue that a sterile compounding technician will encounter. After a period of time, the chemical components in a compounded solution will start to reduce, making the solution less potent. All medications have diverse rates to which they will degrade. It is important for technicians to know the expiration dates of the CSPs they compound. Other factors that can cause degradation are changes in pH, drug structure, and temperature.

If a drug is incompatible with another ingredient in a solution or if it is kept at the wrong temperature, **drug precipitation** may occur. Consequently, the drug may become inactive or adhere to the container. Technicians should visually inspect the final compounded product to observe any changes such as clouding of the solution or any other irregularities.

Some CSPs are sensitive to lighting conditions. If the CSP is not protected by amber coverings, **photo degradation** may result, causing potency and stability issues. These reactions are due to **oxidation-reduction**. **Oxidation** is a chemical reaction between two or more ingredients. **Reduction** is the end result of the reaction. The chemical reaction causes cloudiness, crystallization, or a change in potency. **Instability** in the CSP may result.

> **?** If calcium gluconate is pushed into a TPN solution before potassium phosphate, crystallization will occur. However this reaction will not happen if the calcium gluconate is added later in the process. Why?

The conditions in the clean room can also cause undesirable effects when compounding medications. Therefore it is crucial to keep work areas sterilized and decontaminated. The upkeep of the air quality and temperature requirements must be recognized as well. Because of the importance of the environment in the clean room, USP 797 has requirements for working with CSPs of certain **risk levels.**

+ **Risk level 1** covers all medications and procedures used in compounding CSPs. This includes sterile medications, needles, syringes, aseptic technique, and a Class 5 laminar airflow workbench (LAFW). This level is for performing only minimal preparations under the LAFW.

Technicians must garb up with PPE. Risk level 1 requires proper testing of the technicians annually with a **media fill** (performance of an aseptic manufacturing procedure using a microbe growth medium in place of a drug solution) and safety measures including certification of the LAFW.

✦ **Risk level 2** covers bulk compounding. This includes multiple CSPs prepared for several patients or multiple CSPs to be used by one patient over several days. All guidelines listed in level 1 are included as well as a more rigid testing of technicians, including an evaluation of how a CSP is manipulated. In addition, a more stringent media fill is required.

✦ **Risk level 3** covers all requirements of levels 1 and 2 as well as additional guidelines. Level 3 products are susceptible to contamination because of the handling of non-sterile products and/or delayed purification. Requirements include semiannual certification of aseptic compounding. Technicians must demonstrate they can compound and ensure sterility of these products. All patches over 25 units require pyrogen testing to ensure the batch is free of contamination.

 Explain the process of a media fill and what factors would cause a media fill to fail.

PRACTICE QUESTIONS

1. Which risk level covers preparing multiple CSPs for one specific patient?

   A) Level 2

   B) Level 1

   C) Level 3

   D) There is no risk associated with this task.

   Answers:

   A) **Correct.** Level 2 covers bulk compounding, which consists of preparing multiple CSPs for one patient.

   B) Incorrect. Level 1 covers minimal preparations.

   C) Incorrect. Level 3 does cover all levels, but focuses on CSPs that are susceptible to contamination.

   D) Incorrect. Preparing multiple CSPs for one specific patient falls under risk level 2.

2. Which is NOT a factor in chemical degradation?

   A) change in pH

   B) change in quantity

   C) change in temperature

   D) change in drug structure

Answers:

A)   Incorrect. One factor in degradation may be change in pH.

B)   Correct. A change in quantity will not affect degradation of a CSP.

C)   Incorrect. Change in temperature can cause cloudiness, crystallization, and change in potency.

D)   Incorrect. Degradation can cause drug structure to become unstable.

INTRAVENOUS ORDERS AND LABELING

Medication orders for IV admixtures differ depending on certain factors specific to the patient. The physician uses bloodwork, disease states, other drug therapies, and weight of the patient to determine the order. This important information will ensure that the correct dosage, strength, and solution are used.

The physician will then compile all these factors and write the medication order, which will include the information the physician collected, the type of medication needed, the IV fluid used (NS, D5NS, LR, etc.) and the **volume**, or quantity needed. The **IV fluid** used will consist of what is needed to maintain and replenish the patient's electrolyte and fluid levels. The physician will choose the IV fluid that will best maintain proper homeostasis and compatibility with the compounded medication. The order will either be marked as a one-time fill or will be put on a schedule. For example, if the IV admixture needs to be given every 6 hours, it would be written in military time as 6:00–12:00–18:00–24:00.

 In an institutional setting, all times are in military time. For example, the label for a medication due at 6:00 p.m. will read 18:00.

To prepare labeling for nurses, the pharmacy will need to calculate the infusion rate of the IV. The **infusion rate** refers to the dosing rate: the rate at which the drug should be administered to achieve the steady, therapeutically effective state of a fixed dose. To accurately administer an IV infusion, the **flow rate**—drops per minute or per hour of infusion, infusion time, and total volume needed—must be determined.

After the medication order is completed, the pharmacist will check the patient's history for any drug **incompatibilities**, or undesirable reactions or interactions, assess storage requirements, and add any **special instructions** to the order. Specifying **storage requirements** is crucial because some medications require refrigeration or other special care. Errors could result in instability in the finished product causing clouding, crystallization, and degradation of the medication.

Finally, a label will be generated for sterile compounding. The label provides the sterile-compounding technician with specific information for preparation: the patient's name, identification number, hospital room, IV solution (NS, D5, etc.) and volume, medication, strength needed, and instructions. After the CSP is prepared, the preparer initials it, adds auxiliary labels (*Do Not Refrigerate*, etc.), the **beyond-use date (BUD)**, or date the compounded medication will expire, and places it in a specific area based on the facility for pharmacist verification. The pharmacist will verify the medication and solution used and add it to the compounding log. It is then ready to send to the nursing floor.

PRACTICE QUESTIONS

1. What is the flow rate of an IV infusion?

    A) medication drops per minute or per hour

    B) the quantity needed for infusion

    C) the dosing rate

    D) the therapeutic dose

    Answers:

    A) **Correct.** The flow rate is the drops per minute or per hour during which a medication is infused.

    B)   Incorrect. The quantity of a medication needed for infusion is its total volume.

    C)   Incorrect. The dosing rate is the infusion rate, not the flow rate.

    D)   Incorrect. The therapeutic dose is the dose of medication that would be effective to treat the disease state.

2. What is beyond-use dating?

    A) the expiration date on the medication vial

    B) the expiration date on the IV fluid

    C) the expiration date after the CSP has been prepared per manufacturer's instructions

    D) the expiration date after the CSP has been prepared if not refrigerated

    Answers:

    A)   Incorrect. After the vial is punctured and reconstituted it starts to degrade; the expiration date changes as a result.

    B)   Incorrect. IV fluid also starts to degrade after it has been punctured; again, the expiration date changes.

    C) **Correct.** The beyond-use date indicates when the medication expires once the medication is compounded per the manufacturer's instructions.

    D)   Incorrect. Whether a CSP is refrigerated depends on the medication. The wrong temperature may cause a medication to become unstable, so it is crucial to read the instructions for the CSP in question.

SIX: PHARMACY MATH

Successful pharmacy technicians need an extensive understanding of the math skills they must perform on a daily basis. Moreover, it is crucial for pharmacy technicians to be confident in the accuracy of their calculations. Drugs can be integral in disease treatment and management, but they are also very potent and sometimes dangerous chemicals. In pharmacy math, misplaced decimals, inaccurate measuring, improper dosage strengths, and incorrect calculations are unacceptable due to the harm medication errors can cause.

This chapter will review basic math skills, crucial terminology used in pharmacy math, calculations of medication doses, math equations and conversions, and business math.

Fundamentals of Pharmacy Math

Because pharmacy has been practiced for centuries, some concepts are calculated or written in different systems; they even use different numerals. For example, the label on a bottle of aspirin might state that the drug measures 325 mg and/or 5 grains. One measurement (mg) uses the metric system, whereas the other (grains) uses the apothecary system. Aspirin has been used in the form of salicylic acid for centuries and was originally measured in grains. When the metric system became the more common form of measurement, grains were converted to milligrams, although they are not exactly equivalent. This section covers translating and understanding the difference between arabic and roman numerals, along with metric, apothecary, and household systems and terminology.

Roman Numerals

The roman numeral system uses letters to represent numerical values, as shown below.

Table 6.1. Roman Numerals

Roman Numeral	Value
I	1
V	5
X	10
L	50
C	100
D	500
M	1000

These seven numerals are combined to form numbers (arabic numerals). Numerals are always arranged from greatest to least in value starting with the largest possible number. For example, the number 157 would be written as: 100 + 50 + 5 + 1 + 1 = CLVII, and the number 3,621 is written as 1000 + 1000 + 1000 + 500 + 100 + 10 + 10 + 1 = MMMDCXXI.

To avoid adding four of the same numeral in a row, subtraction is used. If a numeral with a smaller value is placed before a numeral with a larger value, the smaller number is subtracted from the bigger number. For example, the number 9 is written as IX (10 – 1 = 9). Since I has a value of 1 and it is placed before X, which has a value of 10, the number is found by subtracting 1 from 10.

Metric System

You are expected to memorize some units of measurement. These are given in tables 6.2 and 6.3. When doing unit conversion problems (i.e., when converting one unit to another), find the conversion factor, then apply that factor to the given measurement to find the new units.

Table 6.2. Unit Prefixes

Prefix	Symbol	Multiplication Factor
tera	T	1,000,000,000,000
giga	G	1,000,000,000
mega	M	1,000,000
kilo	k	1,000
hecto	h	100
deca	da	10
base unit	--	--

Prefix	Symbol	Multiplication Factor
deci	d	0.1
centi	c	0.01
milli	m	0.001
micro	μ	0.0000001
nano	n	0.0000000001
pico	p	0.0000000000001

Table 6.3. Units and Conversion Factors

Dimension	American	SI
length	inch/foot/yard/mile	meter
mass	ounce/pound/ton	gram
volume	cup/pint/quart/gallon	liter
force	pound-force	newton
pressure	pound-force per square inch	pascal
work and energy	cal/British thermal unit	joule
temperature	Fahrenheit	kelvin
charge	faraday	coulomb

Conversion Factors

1 in. = 2.54 cm

1 yd. = 0.914 m

1 mi. = 1.61 km

1 gal. = 3.785 L

1 oz. = 28.35 g

1 lb. = 0.454 kg

1 cal = 4.19 J

$1°F = \frac{5}{9} (°F - 32°C)$

$1 \text{ cm}^3 = 1 \text{ mL}$

1 hr = 3600 s

APOTHECARY SYSTEM

The apothecary system addresses small units, measuring them in **minims**, **drams**, and **grains**. It then progresses to units used in the household system such as **ounces**, **pints**, **quarts**, **gallons**, and **pounds**. Although this system is no longer frequently used, it still sometimes appears in older medication dosages and in some vials and bottles in the pharmacy setting. The apothecary system does not exactly correlate to the metric system. For instance, 1 grain is equivalent to 60 – 65 mg. Whether to use 60 or 65 mg to equal 1 grain depends on the manufacturer.

Weight and mass are measured in grains, scruples, and pounds. **Scruples** are equivalent to 20 grains; however they are rarely used. Some medications are still measured in grains, but for calculation purposes, grains are normally converted to the metric system. Liquid is measured in minims, drams, ounces, pints, quarts, and gallons.

Table 6.4. Apothecary System Terminology and Equivalents

Common Measure	Conversion Factor	Common Use
Volume		
min.= minim	i min. = 1 drop xv or xvi min. = 1 ml	calibration on syringes for small dose parenteral medications
dr. = dram	i dr. = 4 or 5 ml	cough medicine
oz. = ounce	i oz. = 30 ml	antacids
Note: the volume of a dram is smaller than the volume of an ounce; it is rarely used.		
Weight		
gr. = grain	i gr. = 60–65 mg	solid medications (like ibuprofen)

PRACTICE QUESTIONS

1. What is 5 grains equivalent to?

    A) 600 – 650 mg

    B) 300 – 325 mg

    C) 225 – 250 mg

    D) 60 – 65 mg

    Answers:

    A) Incorrect. This range is too high.

    B) Correct. Five grains is equal to 300 – 325 mg.

    C) Incorrect. This range is too low.

    D) Incorrect. This range is too low.

2. What is 6 drams equivalent to?

    A) 2 ounces

    B) 4 ounces

    C) 1 ounce

    D) $\frac{1}{2}$ ounce

    Answers:

    A) Incorrect. Two ounces does not equal 6 drams.

    B) Incorrect. Four ounces does not equal 6 drams.

    C) Correct. An ounce does equal 6 drams.

    D) Incorrect. Half an ounce is less than 6 drams.

3. One-half grain is equal to what?

    A) 65 mg

    B) 25 mg

    C) 35 mg

    D) 32.5 mg

Answers:

    A) Incorrect. Half a grain does not equal 65 mg.

    B) Incorrect. Half a grain is not equal to 25 mg.

    C) Incorrect. Half a grain is not equal to 35 mg.

    D) **Correct.** Half a grain is equivalent to 32.5 mg.

4. Which of the following is equivalent to 2 ounces?

    A) 30 ml

    B) 60 ml

    C) 120 ml

    D) 240 ml

Answers:

    A) Incorrect. This number is too low.

    B) **Correct.** Two ounces is equivalent to 60 ml.

    C) Incorrect. This number is too high.

    D) Incorrect. This number is too high.

HOUSEHOLD SYSTEM

Another form of measurement that is commonly used in a pharmacy setting is the **household system.** As with the apothecary system, all systems are converted to the metric system when performing calculations. The most commonly used household measurements include **teaspoonful, tablespoonful, fluid ounce, cup, pint, quart,** and **gallon.** A complete list of terminology and conversions of the household system includes:

Table 6.5. Household System Terminology and Equivalents

Metric	Apothecary	Household
5 mL	1 fl dr	1 teaspoonful*
10 mL	2 fl dr	1 dessertspoonful
15 mL	4 fl dr	1 tablespoonful $\left(\frac{1}{2}\text{ fl oz}\right)$
30 mL	8 fl dr	2 tablespoons (1 fl oz)
60 mL	2 fl oz	1 wineglassful

Table 6.5. Household System Terminology and Equivalents (continued)

Metric	Apothecary	Household
120 mL	4 fl oz	1 teacupful
240 mL	8 fl oz	1 tumblerful
480 mL	16 fl oz	1 pint
960 mL	32 fl oz	1 quart

*Official U.S.P. teaspoon is 5 mL.

PRACTICE QUESTIONS

1. What is 1.5 quarts equivalent to?

    A) 1440 ml

    B) 960 ml

    C) 1240 ml

    D) 2500 ml

Answer:

$\dfrac{1\text{ quart}}{960\text{ mL}} = \dfrac{1.5\text{ quarts}}{x\text{ mL}}$	Set up a proportion with quarts on top and mL on bottom. Recall that 1 quart = 960 mL.
$x = 1.5 \times 960$ $x = \textbf{1440 mL (A)}$	Cross-multiply and solve for x.

Note: This can also be solved using Dimensional Analysis, multiplying by conversion ratios to cancel out units until finding the needed units. Here, ratios are set up so that unwanted units cross out on top and bottom:

$1.5\ \cancel{\text{quarts}} \times \dfrac{960\text{ mL}}{1\ \cancel{\text{quart}}} = 1440\text{ mL}$

2. What quantity is 3 tablespoonsful equivalent to?

    A) 60 ml

    B) 5 ml

    C) 30 ml

    D) 45 ml

Answers:

    A)   Incorrect. This number is too high.

    B)   Incorrect. This number is too low.

    C)   Incorrect. This number is also too low.

    D)   **Correct.** These quantities are equivalent.

3. 2.5 pints is equivalent to:

A) 1500 mL

B) 960 mL

C) 1200 mL

D) 480 mL

Answers:

A) Incorrect. 2.5 pints does not equal 1500 mL.

B) Incorrect. 2.5 pints does not equal 960 mL.

C) Correct. 2.5 pints does equal 1200 mL.

D) Incorrect. 2.5 pints does not equal 960 mL.

4. Which of the following is 24 drams approximately equivalent to?

A) 2 teaspoonsful

B) 8 tablespoonsful

C) 4 tablespoonsful

D) 8 teaspoonsful

Answers:

A) Incorrect. This quantity is too low.

B) Correct. Since 1 dram can be 4 or 5 mls, 8 tablespoonsful can be converted to 24 drams.

C) Incorrect. This quantity is too low.

D) Incorrect. This quantity is too high.

Fractions and Decimals

FRACTIONS

Fractions are made up of two parts: the **numerator**, which appears above the bar, and the **denominator**, which is below it. If a fraction is in its simplest form, the numerator and the denominator share no common factors. A fraction with a numerator larger than its denominator is an **improper fraction**; when the denominator is larger, it's a **proper fraction**.

Improper fractions can be converted into proper fractions by dividing the numerator by the denominator. The resulting whole number is placed to the left of the fraction, and the remainder becomes the new numerator; the denominator does not change. The new number is called a **mixed number** because it contains a whole number and a fraction. Mixed numbers can be turned into improper fractions through the reverse process: multiply the whole number by the denominator and add the numerator to get the new numerator.

Adding and subtracting fractions requires a **common denominator**. To find the common denominator, you can multiply each fraction by the number 1. With fractions, any number over itself is equivalent to 1, so multiplying by such a fraction can change the denominator without changing the value of the fraction. Once the denominators are the same, the numerators can be added or subtracted.

To add mixed numbers, you can first add the whole numbers and then the fractions. To subtract mixed numbers, convert each number to an improper fraction, then subtract the numerators.

To multiply fractions, convert any mixed numbers into improper fractions and multiply the numerators together and the denominators together. Reduce to **lowest terms** if needed.

To divide fractions, first convert any mixed fractions into single fractions. Then, invert the second fraction so that the denominator and numerator are switched. Finally, multiply the numerators together and the denominators together.

 Inverting a fraction changes multiplication to division. $\frac{a}{b} \div \frac{c}{d} = \frac{a}{b} \times \frac{d}{c} = \frac{ad}{bc}$.

PRACTICE QUESTIONS

1. Simplify the fraction $\frac{121}{77}$.

$\frac{121}{77} = \frac{11}{11} \times \frac{11}{7} = \mathbf{\frac{11}{7}}$	121 and 77 share a common factor of 11. So, if we divide each by 11 we can simplify the fraction.

2. Simplify the expression: $\frac{2}{3} - \frac{1}{5}$.

$\frac{2}{3} - \frac{1}{5} = \frac{2}{3}\left(\frac{5}{5}\right) - \frac{1}{5}\left(\frac{3}{3}\right)$ $= \frac{10}{15} - \frac{3}{15}$	First, multiply each fraction by a factor of 1 to get a common denominator. How do you know which factor of 1 to use? Look at the other fraction and use the number found in that denominator.
$\frac{10}{15} - \frac{3}{15} = \mathbf{\frac{7}{15}}$	Once the fractions have a common denominator, simply subtract the numerators.

3. Find $2\frac{1}{3} - \frac{3}{2}$.

$2\frac{1}{3} = \frac{2 \times 3}{3} + \frac{1}{3} = \frac{7}{3}$	This is a fraction subtraction problem with a mixed number, so the first step is to convert the mixed number to an improper fraction.

$$\frac{7}{3} \times \frac{2}{2} = \frac{14}{6}$$

$$\frac{3}{2} \times \frac{3}{3} = \frac{9}{6}$$

Next, convert each fraction so they share a common denominator.

$$\frac{14}{6} - \frac{9}{6} = \frac{5}{6}$$

Now, subtract the fractions by subtracting the numerators.

4. Find the sum of $\frac{9}{16}$, $\frac{1}{2}$, and $\frac{7}{4}$.

$$\frac{1}{2} \times \frac{8}{8} = \frac{8}{16}$$

$$\frac{7}{4} \times \frac{4}{4} = \frac{28}{16}$$

$$\frac{9}{16} + \frac{8}{16} + \frac{28}{16} = \frac{45}{16}$$

For this fraction addition problem, we need to find a common denominator. Notice that 2 and 4 are both factors of 16, so 16 can be the common denominator.

5. Sabrina has $\frac{2}{3}$ of a can of red paint. Her friend Amos has $\frac{1}{6}$ of a can. How much red paint do they have combined?

$$\frac{2}{3} \times \frac{2}{2} = \frac{4}{6}$$

To add fractions, make sure that they have a common denominator. Since 3 is a factor of 6, 6 can be the common denominator.

$$\frac{4}{6} + \frac{1}{6} = \frac{5}{6} \textbf{ of a can}$$

Now, add the numerators.

6. What is the product of $\frac{1}{12}$ and $\frac{6}{8}$?

$$\frac{1}{12} \times \frac{6}{8} = \frac{6}{96} = \frac{1}{16}$$

Simply multiply the numerators together and the denominators together, then reduce.

$$\frac{1}{12} \times \frac{6}{8} = \frac{1}{12} \times \frac{3}{4}$$

$$= \frac{3}{48} = \frac{1}{16}$$

Sometimes it's easier to reduce fractions before multiplying if you can.

7. Find $\frac{7}{8} \div \frac{1}{4}$.

$$\frac{7}{8} \div \frac{1}{4} = \frac{7}{8} \times \frac{4}{1} = \frac{28}{8}$$

$$= \frac{7}{2}$$

For a fraction division problem, invert the second fraction and then multiply and reduce.

8. What is the quotient of $\frac{2}{5} \div 1\frac{1}{5}$?

$$1\frac{1}{5} = \frac{5 \times 1}{5} + \frac{1}{5} = \frac{6}{5}$$

This is a fraction division problem, so the first step is to convert the mixed number to an improper fraction.

$$\frac{2}{5} \div \frac{6}{5} = \frac{2}{5} \times \frac{5}{6} = \frac{10}{30}$$

$$= \frac{1}{3}$$

Now, divide the fractions. Remember to invert the second fraction, and then multiply normally.

DECIMALS

When adding and subtracting decimals, line up the numbers so that the decimals are aligned. You want to subtract the ones place from the ones place, the tenths place from the tenths place, etc.

When multiplying decimals, start by multiplying the numbers normally. You can then determine the placement of the decimal point in the result by adding the number of digits after the decimal in each of the numbers you multiplied together.

When dividing decimals, you should move the decimal point in the divisor (the number you're dividing by) until it is a whole. You can then move the decimal in the dividend (the number you're dividing into) the same number of places in the same direction. Finally, divide the new numbers normally to get the correct answer.

PRACTICE QUESTIONS

1. Find the sum of 17.07 and 2.52.

$$\begin{array}{r} 17.07 \\ +\ \ 2.52 \\ \hline = \textbf{19.59} \end{array}$$

Line up the decimals and add the numerals together.

2. Jeannette has 7.4 gallons of gas in her tank. After driving, she has 6.8 gallons. How many gallons of gas did she use?

$$\begin{array}{r} 7.4 \\ -\,6.8 \\ \hline = \textbf{0.6 gal.} \end{array}$$

Line up the decimals and subtract the numerals.

3. What is the product of 0.25 and 1.4?

$25 \times 14 = 350$

There are 2 digits after the decimal in 0.25 and one digit after the decimal in 1.4. Therefore the product should have 3 digits after the decimal: **0.350** is the correct answer.

4. Find 0.8 ÷ 0.2.

$0.8 \div 2$

Change 0.2 to 2 by moving the decimal one space to the right.

$8 \div 2 = \mathbf{4}$	Next, move the decimal one space to the right on the dividend. 0.8 becomes 8. Now, divide 8 by 2.

5. Find the quotient when 40 is divided by 0.25.

$40 \div 25$	First, change the divisor to a whole number: 0.25 becomes 25.
$4000 \div 25 = \mathbf{160}$	Next, change the dividend to match the divisor by moving the decimal two spaces to the right, so 40 becomes 4000. Now divide.

Ratio, Proportions, and Percentage

RATIOS

A ratio tells you how many of one thing exists in relation to the number of another thing. Unlike fractions, ratios do not give a part relative to a whole; instead, they compare two values. For example, if you have 3 apples and 4 oranges, the ratio of apples to oranges is 3 to 4. Ratios can be written using words (3 to 4), fractions $\left(\frac{3}{4}\right)$, or colons (3:4).

In order to work with ratios, it's helpful to rewrite them as a fraction expressing a part to a whole. For example, in the example above you have 7 total pieces of fruit, so the fraction of your fruit that are apples is $\frac{3}{7}$, and oranges make up $\frac{4}{7}$ of your fruit collection.

One last important thing to consider when working with ratios is the units of the values being compared. You may be asked to rewrite a ratio using the same units on both sides. For example, you might have to rewrite the ratio 3 minutes to 7 seconds as 180 seconds to 7 seconds.

PRACTICE QUESTIONS

1. There are 90 voters in a room, and each is either a Democrat or a Republican. The ratio of Democrats to Republicans is 5:4. How many Republicans are there?

$5 + 4 = 9$ Democrats: $\frac{5}{9}$ Republicans: $\frac{4}{9}$	We know that there are 5 Democrats for every 4 Republicans in the room, which means for every 9 people, 4 are Republicans.
$\frac{4}{9} \times 90 = \mathbf{40\ Republicans}$	If $\frac{4}{9}$ of the 90 voters are republicans, then multiply the fraction by the whole number.

2. The ratio of students to teachers in a school is 15:1. If there are 38 teachers, how many students attend the school?

$\frac{15 \text{ students}}{1 \text{ teacher}} \times 38$ teachers = **570 students**	To solve this ratio problem, we can simply multiply both sides of the ratio by the desired value to find the number of students that correspond to having 38 teachers.

PROPORTIONS

A proportion is an equation which states that 2 ratios are equal. Proportions are usually written as 2 fractions joined by an equal sign $\left(\frac{a}{b} = \frac{c}{d}\right)$, but they can also be written using colons (a : b :: c : d). Note that in a proportion, the units must be the same in both numerators and in both denominators.

Often you will be given 3 of the values in a proportion and asked to find the 4th. In these types of problems, you can solve for the missing variable by cross-multiplying —multiply the numerator of each fraction by the denominator of the other to get an equation with no fractions as shown below. You can then solve the equation using basic algebra.

$$\frac{a}{b} = \frac{c}{d} \rightarrow ad = bc$$

PRACTICE QUESTIONS

1. A train traveling 120 miles takes 3 hours to get to its destination. How long will it take for the train to travel 180 miles?

$\frac{120 \text{ miles}}{3 \text{ hours}} = \frac{180 \text{ miles}}{x \text{ hours}}$	Start by setting up the proportion (note that it doesn't matter which value is placed in the numerator or denominator, as long as it is the same on both sides).
120 miles × x hours = 3 hours × 180 miles	Now, solve for the missing quantity through cross-multiplication.
$x = \frac{(3 \text{ hours}) \times (180 \text{ hours})}{120 \text{ miles}} =$ **4.5 hours**	Now solve the equation.

2. One acre of wheat requires 500 gallons of water. How many acres can be watered with 2600 gallons?

$\frac{1 \text{ acre}}{500 \text{ gal.}} = \frac{x \text{ acres}}{2600 \text{ gal.}}$	Set up the equation.
$x \text{ acres} = \frac{1 \text{ acre} \times 2600 \text{ gal.}}{500 \text{ gal.}}$ $x = \frac{26}{5}$ or **5.2 acres**	Then solve for x.

3. If 35 : 5 :: 49 : x, find x.

$\dfrac{35}{5} = \dfrac{49}{x}$	This problem presents two equivalent ratios that can be set up in a fraction equation.
$35x = 49 \times 5$ $x = \textbf{7}$	You can then cross-multiply to solve for x.

PERCENTAGE

A percent is the ratio of a part to the whole. Questions may give the part and the whole and ask for the percent, or give the percent and the whole and ask for the part, or give the part and the percent and ask for the value of the whole. The equation for percentages can be rearranged to solve for any of these:

$$\text{percent} = \frac{\text{part}}{\text{whole}} \qquad \text{part} = \text{whole} \times \text{percent} \qquad \text{whole} = \frac{\text{part}}{\text{percent}}$$

In the equations above, the percent should always be expressed as a decimal. In order to convert a decimal into a percentage value, simply multiply it by 100. So, if you've read 5 pages (the part) of a 10-page article (the whole), you've read $\dfrac{5}{10}$ = 0.5 or 50%. (The percent sign (%) is used once the decimal has been multiplied by 100.)

Note that when solving these problems, the units for the part and the whole should be the same. If you're reading a book, saying you've read 5 pages out of 15 chapters doesn't make any sense.

PRACTICE PROBLEMS

1. 45 is 15% of what number?

$whole = \dfrac{part}{percent} = \dfrac{45}{0.15} = \textbf{300}$	Set up the appropriate equation and solve. Don't forget to change 15% to a decimal value.

2. Jim spent 30% of his paycheck at the fair. He spent $15 for a hat, $30 for a shirt, and $20 playing games. How much was his check? (Round to nearest dollar.)

$whole = \dfrac{part}{percent} = \dfrac{15 + 30 + 20}{.30}$ $= \textbf{\$217.00}$	Set up the appropriate equation and solve.

3. What percent of 65 is 39?

$percent = \dfrac{part}{whole} = \dfrac{39}{65} = 0.6$ or **60%**	Set up the appropriate equation and solve.

4. Greta and Max sell cable subscriptions. In a given month, Greta sells 45 subscriptions and Max sells 51. If 240 total subscriptions were sold in that month, what percent were NOT sold by Greta or Max?

$percent = \dfrac{part}{whole} = \dfrac{(51 + 45)}{240}$ $= \dfrac{96}{240} = 0.4$ or 40%	You can use the information in the question to figure out what percentage of subscriptions were sold by Max and Greta.
$100\% - 40\% = $ **60%**	However, the question asks how many subscriptions weren't sold by Max or Greta. If they sold 40%, then the other salespeople sold the rest.

5. Grant needs to score 75% on an exam. If the exam has 45 questions, at least how many does he need to answer correctly?

$part = whole \times percent =$ $45 \times 0.75 = 33.75;$ **34 questions**	Set up the equation and solve. Remember to convert 75% to a decimal value.

Liquid Measures

Pharmacy technicians must be able to accurately measure solutions and suspensions with the most precise devices available. For small volumes of less than 10 ml, a syringe or small graduated cylinder should be used. These devices measure by unit, so the measurement will be much more accurate. For larger volumes, it is important that the device used for measuring is the closest possible size to the volume that needs to be measured. Volumes below 20 percent of the graduated cylinder's capacity will not be accurately measured. As the device gets larger, the markings and graduations on the device become less accurate. For example, a 60 ml graduate will not accurately measure volumes below 20 ml.

Measurements should also be made at eye level. Measurement should be taken at the bottom of the meniscus. The **meniscus** is the concave bottom of the curve on the top portion of a liquid in a graduated measuring device.

Proper technique is required when measuring liquids. Pharmacy technicians must

+ hold the graduate at the bottom with a thumb and finger and use the little finger to support its underside.
+ grasp the bottle with the right hand, keeping the label against the palm of the hand, to avoid defacing the label.
+ raise the graduate to eye level while pouring the liquid.
+ place the graduate on a flat surface, taking readings at eye level. This prevents the graduate from tilting, avoiding an incorrect reading.
+ pour liquid until the bottom of the meniscus is at the required mark.

DENSITY AND SPECIFIC GRAVITY

Some ingredients must be converted before from solid to liquid form when calculating and compounding liquids in the pharmacy. In these cases, the technician may have to determine the density, or specific gravity, of the substance. In a pharmacy setting, **specific gravity** and **density** are used interchangeably.

Every substance has a number unique to it called **specific gravity**. Specific gravity is defined as the ratio of the weight of the compound to the weight of the same amount of water. Basically a substance's specific gravity describes how heavy it is compared to water. For instance, the specific gravity of ethanol is 0.787 g/mL, meaning that ethanol is about 21 percent lighter than water.

 The specific gravity of water is 1 g/mL, meaning 1 mL of water always weighs 1 gram.

When converting between weight and volume it is useful to know a particular compound's specific gravity. The equation for finding the specific gravity of a substance follows.

$$\text{specific gravity} = \frac{\text{weight (g)}}{\text{volume (mL)}}$$

PRACTICE QUESTION

In a compound, the weight of a solid is 45 grams and volume of the solution used to dissolve it is 500mL. What is the specific gravity?

A) 0.09 g/mL

B) 11.1 g/mL

C) 0.05 g/mL

D) 12.5 g/mL

Answer:

specific gravity = weight (g)/volume (mL) weight = 45 g volume = 500 mL	Identify the formula and variables.
specific gravity = 45 g/500 mL = **0.09 g/mL (A)**	Solve for specific gravity.

Concentrations

Concentration refers to the amount of a particular substance in a given volume, or the substance's strength. The more of a substance in a given volume, the higher the concentration of the solution. On the other hand, the lower the amount of a substance in the given volume, the lower the concentration.

The substance dissolved in a solution is called the solute. The substance the solute is dissolved into is called the solvent.

Concentrations can be expressed as a fraction (mg/mL), a ratio (1:1000), or a percentage (60%). When a pharmacy technician receives an order to prepare a solution, the following terms are used to determine what is required to compound:

+ **final strength (FS):** the strength of the final solution
+ **final volume (FV):** the volume of the final solution
+ **initial strength (IS):** the strength of the original product used to prepare the final solution
+ **initial volume (IV):** the volume of the original product used to prepare the final solution
+ **final weight (FW):** for solids, the strength of the final solution
+ **initial weight (IW):** for solids, the strength of the original product used to prepare the final solution

The formula for compounding is: *IV* (or *IW*) × *IS* = *FV* (or *FW*) × *FS*.

The initial strength (IS) must be larger than the final strength (FS); the initial volume (IV) must be less than the final volume (FV). The FV, minus the IV, equals the amount of diluent that needs to be added.

? The pharmacist asks a technician to compound calcium gluconate 5.58 mEq in sodium chloride 0.9 percent solution 250 mL. The calcium gluconate is stocked in calcium gluconate 0.465 mEq/mL 10 mL vials. Which is the initial volume (IV) of the solution?

PRACTICE QUESTION

C_1 = concentration of stock solution (actual drug) = 0.465 mEq/mL	
V_1 = volume of stock solution needed to make new solution = x mL	Identify variables.
	x = volume of initial solution
C_2 = final concentration of new solution = 0.9% × 5.58 mEq/mL	
V_2 = final volume of new solution = 250 mL	
$C_1V_1 = C_2V_2$	Plug the values into the appropriate formula.
0.465x = 0.009 × 5.58 × 250	
0.465x = 12.555	
$x = \frac{12.555}{.465}$ = **27 mL**	Isolate x to get solution.

CALCULATING CONCENTRATION

Three formulas are used to calculate concentrations by percentages. Percentages are changed to equivalent decimal fractions by dropping the percent sign (%) and dividing the expressed numerator by a fraction. The formulas are:

+ **Weight/Weight ($\frac{w}{w}$%)** is the number of grams of a mass solute dissolved in 100 grams of a total mass solution, or vehicle base. The weight—not the volume—of each chemical is determined.

    $\frac{w}{w}$% = (weight of solute/weight of solution) × 100

+ **Volume/Volume ($\frac{v}{v}$%)** is the number of milliliters of volume solute dissolved in 100 milliliters of volume solution, or vehicle base. The volume of each chemical—not the weight—is determined.

    $\frac{v}{v}$% = (volume of solute in mg/volume of solution in mL) × 100

+ **Weight/Volume ($\frac{w}{v}$%)** is the number of grams of mass solute dissolved in 100 milliliters of a volume solution, or vehicle base. This formula is used when a solid is dissolved into a liquid.

    $\frac{w}{v}$% = (weight of solute/volume of solution) × 100

Note that grams and mLs are used for $\frac{w}{v}$% problems.

PRACTICE QUESTIONS

1. What is the w/v% if 42 g of Potassium is added to 1 L of Sodium Chloride?

    A) 42%

    B) 420%

    C) 4.2%

    D) 0.42%

    Answer:

weight of solute = 42 g volume of vehicle base (in mL) = 1 L = 1000 mL $\frac{w}{v}$% = $\dfrac{\text{weight of solute (g)}}{\text{volume of vehical base (mL)}}$ × 100	Identify variables and formula. Note that the solute is the Potassium and the vehicle base is the Sodium Chloride. By definition of this formula, weight must be in **grams** and volume in **mL**.
$\frac{w}{v}$% = $\dfrac{42\ g}{1000\ mL}$ × 100 = 0.042 × 100 = **4.2% (C)**	Solve for $\frac{w}{v}$%.

CONTINUE

2. If 10 mL of glycerin is dissolved in enough water to make a 200 ml solution, what is the $\frac{v}{v}\%$ of the glycerin?

A) 50%

B) 500%

C) 0.50%

D) 5%

Answer:

volume of solute = 10 mL volume of vehicle base = 200 mL $\frac{v}{v}\% = \dfrac{\text{volume of solute}}{\text{volume of vehicle base}} \times 100$	Identify variables and formula. Note that the solute is the glycerin and the vehicle base is the water.
$\frac{v}{v}\% = \dfrac{10 \text{ mL}}{200 \text{ mL}} \times 100 = 0.05 \times 100 = \textbf{5\% (D)}$	Solve for $\frac{v}{v}\%$.

3. 15 g of hydrocortisone is added to 120 g of cold cream. What is the $\frac{w}{w}\%$ of hydrocortisone?

A) 12.5%

B) 125%

C) 1.25%

D) 0.125%

Answer:

volume of solute = 15 g volume of vehicle base = 120 g $\frac{w}{w}\% = \dfrac{\text{volume of solute}}{\text{volume of vehicle base}} \times 100$	Identify variables and formula. Note that the solute is the hydrocortisone and the vehicle base is the cold cream.
$\frac{w}{w}\% = \dfrac{15 \text{ g}}{120 \text{ g}} \times 100 = 0.125 \times 100 = \textbf{12.5\% (A)}$	Solve for $\frac{w}{w}\%$.

RATIO STRENGTH

Many solutions require only a very tiny amount of a drug in order to be effective. When this happens, the **ratio strength** will be indicated on the product labeling; it is also known as strength-to-weight ratio. It is written using a slash (/) or colon (:). For example, ratio strength may be expressed in three concentrations: 1 mL/100 mL, 1 mL/1000 mL, and 1 mL/10,000 mL. Ratio strength may also be described as 1:100, 1:1000, and 1:10,000.

In calculations, ratio strength is expressed as 1 in x, the corresponding fraction having a numerator of 1.

Remember that with ratio strength, the "1" in the ratio must correspond to the drug (active ingredient), not the solution.

To calculate ratio strength in percentage, it's easiest to set up a proportion with the active ingredient on top and the inactive ingredient on the bottom.

For $\frac{w}{v}$ ratio strengths, volume is expressed in mL and weight in grams.

PRACTICE QUESTIONS

1. 5 g of a product contains 250 mg of Sodium Chloride. What is the ratio strength?

   A) 1:10

   B) 1:20

   C) 1:25

   D) 1:5

   Answer:

250 mg = 0.25 g $$\frac{0.25\ g}{5\ g} = \frac{1}{x}$$	Remember that with ratio strength, the "1" in the ratio must correspond to the drug (active ingredient), not the solution. First convert the 250 mg of Sodium Chloride (the active ingredient) into grams, so the units will match. Next set up a proportion with the drug on the top and the Sodium Chloride solution on the bottom.
0.25x = 5 x = 20 **1:20 (B)**	Cross-multiply and solve for the ratio strength, which will be a number greater than 1. Then describe ratio strength in a ratio with "1" corresponding to the active ingredient amount.

2. 2000 mL of a solution contains 2500 mg of vancomycin. What is the ratio strength?

   A) 1:800

   B) 1:400

   C) 1:200

   D) 1:100

   Answer:

2500 mg = 2.5 g $$\frac{2.5\ g}{2000\ mL} = \frac{1}{x}$$	Remember that with ratio strength, the "1" in the ratio must correspond to the drug (active ingredient), not the solution. First convert the 250 mg of vancomycin into grams. With $\frac{w}{v}\%$ ratio strength, g/mL must be used. Next set up a proportion with the drug (vancomycin) on the top and the solution on the bottom.

2.5x = 2000 x = 800 **1:800 (A)**	Cross-multiply and solve for the ratio strength, which will be a number greater than 1. Then describe the ratio strength in a ratio with "1" corresponding to the drug amount.

3. What is the ratio strength of a 1500 ml Sodium Chloride solution with 2500 mg of Magnesium?

    A) 1:450

    B) 1:300

    C) 1:250

    D) 1:600

    Answer:

2500 mg = 2.5 g $\dfrac{2.5\ g}{1500\ mL} = \dfrac{1}{x}$	Remember that with ratio strength, the "1" in the ratio must correspond to the drug (active ingredient), not the solution. First convert the 2500 mg of Magnesium into grams. With $\frac{w}{v}\%$ ratio strength, g/mL must be used. Next set up a proportion with the drug (Magnesium) on the top and Sodium Chloride solution on the bottom.
2.5x = 1500 x = 600 **1:600 (D)**	Cross-multiply and solve for the ratio strength, which will be a number greater than 1. Then describe ratio strength in a ratio with "1" corresponding to the drug amount.

Dilutions

Pharmacy technicians should be familiarized with dilutions because many stock solutions require diluting before they can be sold to patients. When solutions are diluted, it decreases the concentration of the drug and increases the volume. In this chapter, stock solutions, liquid and solid dilutions, and alligations will be discussed.

Stock Solutions and Solids

Stock solutions are solutions that have already known concentrations and are prepared for stock by the pharmacy staff for ease in dispensing. Rather than keeping large amounts of a solution in the pharmacy, concentrated amounts are kept. Then, the stock solutions can be diluted to the desired concentration needed for the preparation of the final product. They are prepared on a **weight-in-volume basis**, in which other weaker solutions can be made from them. Weight-in volume is normally expressed as a percentage or ratio strength and is calculated with this formula:

IV (or IW) × IS = FV (or FW) × FS.

PRACTICE QUESTION

Using the correct formula, what volume must 500 mL of a 10% w/v solution be diluted to produce a 2.5% solution?

A) 1,000 mL

B) 1,500 mL

C) 2,000 mL

D) 2,500 mL

<u>Answer:</u>

C_1 = concentration of stock solution (actual drug) = 10%	Identify variables.
V_1 = volume of stock solution needed to make new solution = 500 mL	x = volume of sterile water to be added
C_2 = final concentration of new solution = 2.5%	Notice that for final volume, include original amount (500 L) and what is being added (x).
V_2 = final volume of new solution = $(500 + x)$L	
$C_1V_1 = C_2V_2$	
$0.10 \times 500 = 0.025(500 + x)$	Plug the values into the appropriate formula.
$50 = 12.5 + 0.025x$	Isolate x to get the solution.
$0.025x = 50 - 12.5 = 37.5$	
$x = \frac{37.5}{0.025} = $ **1500 mL (B)**	

Liquid Dilutions

Liquid solutions are normally diluted with water or saline solutions. These **solvents** are called **diluents**. **Dilutions** represent the parts of the concentrate in total mass or volume.

The formula for dilution is $C_1 V_1 = C_2 V_2$ where

+ C_1 = concentration of stock solution
+ V_1 = volume of stock solution needed to make the new solution
+ C_2 = final concentration of new solution
+ V_2 = final volume of new solution

So, for all dilution problems, C_1 is greater than C_2 and V_1 is less than V_2 (note: This formula can apply to weight instead of volume).

CONTINUE

PRACTICE QUESTIONS

1. Mary has 40 L of a 5 g/L solution. To this solution, she adds 10 L. What is the final concentration of the solution? Hint: The unknown is C_2.

   A) $C_2 = 1$ g/L

   B) $C_2 = 3$ g/L

   C) $C_2 = 4$ g/L

   D) $C_2 = 2.5$ g/L

   Answer:

C_1 = concentration of stock solution (actual drug) = 5 g/L	Identify variables.
V_1 = volume of stock solution needed to make new solution = 40 L	x = volume of sterile water to be added
C_2 = final concentration of new solution = x g/L	Notice that for final volume, include original amount (40 L) and what is being added (10 L).
V_2 = final volume of new solution = 40 L + 10 L = 50 L	
$C_1 V_1 = C_2 V_2$	Plug the values into the appropriate formula.
$5 \times 40 = x \times 50$	
$200 = 50x$	Isolate x to get solution.
$x =$ **4 g/mL (C)**	

2. Bob has 20 L of a 2 g/1 L solution. He dilutes it and makes 3 L of a 1 g/ L solution. How much of the original solution was needed to make the diluted solution? (Hint: we are looking for V_1.)

   A) 1.5 L

   B) 1 L

   C) 2 L

   D) 3 L

   Answer:

C_1 = concentration of stock solution (actual drug) = 2 g/L	
V_1 = volume of stock solution needed to make new solution = x	Identify variables.
C_2 = final concentration of new solution = 1 g/L	x = volume of original solution
V_2 = final volume of new solution = 3 L	

$$C_1V_1 = C_2V_2$$
$$2 \times x = 1 \times 3$$
$$2x = 3$$
$$x = \frac{3}{2} = \textbf{1.5 L (A)}$$

Plug the values into the appropriate formula.

Isolate x to get the solution.

---

3. Mark has 5 L of a 10 g/L solution. He needs to add 15 L to this solution to make the needed concentration. What is the final concentration of the solution? Hint: we are looking for C_2.

A) 7.5 g/L

B) 15 g/L

C) 1.25 g/L

D) 2.5 g/L

Answer:

C_1 = concentration of stock solution (actual drug) = 10 g/L

V_1 = volume of stock solution needed to make new solution = 5L

C_2 = final concentration of new solution = x

V_2 = final volume of new solution= 5L + 15L = 20L

Identify variables.

x = volume of original solution in g/L

Notice that for final volume, add original amount (5 L) to additional (15 L).

$$C_1V_1 = C_2V_2$$
$$10 \times 5 = 20 \times x$$
$$50 = 20x$$
$$x = \frac{50}{20} = \textbf{2.5 g/L (D)}$$

Plug the values into the appropriate formula.

Isolate x to get the solution.

SOLID DILUTIONS

Solids, such as ointments, creams, and lotions, can also be diluted with another solid. This is normally done with the **trituration method**. In trituration a potent drug powder is diluted with an inert diluent powder. The dilution occurs proportionally by weight; usually lactose is used as the diluent. By then removing a weighable portion, or **aliquot**, of the mixture containing the desired amount of substance, you can maintain an acceptable range of accuracy. By using ratio and proportion, the weight of the drug and lactose can then be determined to triturate the compound and the weight of the aliquot can also be used to fill the prescription.

 When triturating, it is important to keep in mind that any substance weighed on the balance must be at least 120mg.

The formula used for dilution of solids by trituration is:

$$\frac{\text{weight of drug in trituration}}{\text{weight of trituration}} = \frac{\text{weight of drug aliquot}}{\text{weight of aliquot}}$$

PRACTICE QUESTIONS

1. Which is the lowest amount of milligrams that must be used with a weight balance to allow for accurate weighing?

    A) 500 mg

    B) 100 mg

    C) 250 mg

    D) 120 mg

    Answers:

    A) Incorrect. 500mg is not the lowest amount of milligrams that must be used with a weight balance for accurate weighing.

    B) Incorrect. 100mg is not the lowest amount of milligrams that must be used with a weight balance for accurate weighing.

    C) Incorrect. 250mg is not the lowest amount of milligrams that must be used with a weight balance for accurate weighing.

    D) **Correct.** 120mg is the lowest amount of milligrams that must be used with a weight balance for accurate weighing.

2. To determine the weight of the diluent needed to prepare the trituration after solving the formula, a pharmacy technician must

    A) subtract the weight of the drug being used for trituration by the trituration weight.

    B) multiply the weight of the drug being used for trituration by the trituration weight.

    C) divide the weight of the drug being used for trituration by the trituration weight.

    D) add the weight of the drug being used for trituration by the trituration weight.

    Answers:

    A) **Correct.** Subtracting the weight of the drug being used for trituration by the trituration weight will determine the weight of the diluent.

    B) Incorrect. Multiplying the weight of the drug being used for trituration by the trituration weight will not determine the weight of the diluent.

    C) Incorrect. Dividing the weight of the drug being used for trituration by the trituration weight will not determine the weight of the diluent.

    D) Incorrect. Adding the weight of the drug being used for trituration by the trituration weight will not determine the weight of the diluent.

ALLIGATIONS

Pharmacy alligations are also known as **Tic-Tac-Toe Math** and is a short-cut method used for solving algebra problems. It is mainly used as an alternative to standard algebra when calculating the volumes for a compound made from different strengths of a similar chemical (note that the standard algebraic method is shown as well).

The easiest way to learn how to use alligation is to work through a sample problem:

A prescription order has arrived for **500ml of a 12% solution**. The pharmacy stocks the solution needed in **1 gallon of 30% solution** and **1 gallon of 10% solution**. You must mix together the two solutions to prepare a custom compound of the ordered volume. How much of the **30% solution** will you need?

The information needed to solve the question is:

+ 500ml of a 12% solution

+ 10% and 30% solutions are available

Alligation:

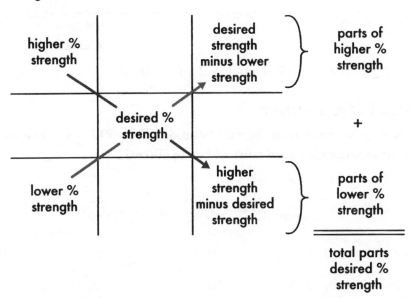

Figure 6.1. Alligations

Alligation Solution

Step 1: Draw a tic-tac-toe grid and put **higher % strength** in the top left square, **desired % strength** in the middle square, and **lower % strength** in the bottom left square:

30		
	12	
10		

Step 2: Calculate the difference between the bottom left number and the middle number going up diagonally, and also the difference from the top left and middle number going down diagonally (ignore any negatives). Then add up those two numbers to get 20. This sum becomes the "parts" needed to work with.

30		
	12	
10		

2 + 18 = 20 parts

Step 3: Now, divide the needed volume into the total parts: 500 mL ÷ 20 parts, getting 2 5mL per part.

Step 4: On the grid, go back up to the parts and write the volume for each part.

30		2 × 25 = 50mL
	12	
10		18 × 25 = 450mL

So 25 parts of the 30% solution × 2 mL = **50 mL**.

Algebraic Solution

Let x = the amount of the 30% solution. Then $500 - x$ = the amount of the 10% solution, since they both must add up to 500 mL.

Now fill out this chart:

	Amount	%	Total	
30% Strength	x	0.30	0.3x	**Multiply across**
10% Strength	$500 - x$	0.10	0.10(500 − x)	**Multiply across**
Total (What we want)	500	0.12	60	**Multiply across**
	Add Down		**Add Down: 0.3x + 0.10 (500 − x) = 60; solve.**	

Now solve:

$$0.3x + 0.10(500 - x) = 60$$
$$0.3x + 50 - 0.10x = 60$$
$$0.2x = 10$$
$$x = 50 \text{ mL}$$

Solve for x, which is the amount of the 30% solution.

🔍 With formulas requiring more than one step, it is important to work through each step thoroughly and not switch between steps to be sure you calculated correctly and avoid confusion in future steps.

PRACTICE QUESTION

A prescription for a 30 g tube of 2% hydrocortisone needs to be made from a 1% solution and a 2.5% solution. Using allegation, how much of each available product is needed to prepare this prescription?

A) 1 g of 1% and 2.5 g of 2%

B) 10 g of 1% and 20 g of 2.5%

C) 15 g of 1% and 15 g of 2.5%

D) 20 g of 1% and 10 g of 2.5%

<u>Answer:</u>

Alligation Solution

Step 1: Draw a tic-tac-toe grid and put higher % strength in the top left square, desired % strength in the middle square, and lower % strength in the bottom left square:

2.5		
	2	
1		

Step 2: Calculate the difference between the bottom left number and the middle number going up diagonally, and also the difference from the top left and middle number going down diagonally (ignore any negatives). Then add up those two numbers to get 1.5. This sum becomes the "parts."

2.5		1
	2	
1		0.5

0.5 + 1 = 1.5 parts

Step 3: Now, divide the needed volume into the total parts—30 g/1.5 parts—to get 20 g per part.

Step 4: On the grid, go back up to the parts and write the volume for each part.

2.5		$1 \times 20 =$ 20 g
	2	
1		0.5×20 $= 10$ g

So 0.5 parts of the 1% solution × 20 g = **10 g**, and 1 part of the 2.5% solution × 20 g = **20 g (B)**.

Algebraic Solution

Let x = the amount of the 1% solution. Then $30 - x$ = the amount of the 2.5% solution, since they both have to add up to 30 g.

Now fill out this chart:

	Amount	%	Total	
1% Strength	x	0.01	0.01x	**Multiply across**
2.5% Strength	$30 - x$	0.025	0.025(30 − x)	**Multiply across**
Total (desired quantity)	30	0.02	0.6	**Multiply across**
	Add Down			**Add Down: 0.1x + 0.025 (30 − x) = 0.6; solve.**

$0.01x + .75 - 0.025x = 0.6$

$-0.015x = -0.15$

$x = 10$ g

$30 - x =$ **20 g (B)**

Solve for x, which is the amount of the 1% solution. Then, to get the 2.5% solution, subtract this from 30.

DOSING

Calculating medication **dosage** is one of the most commonly used math concepts done by the pharmacy technician. Accuracy and verification that **dosage regimens** are safe become more crucial when it comes to special age populations. Geriatric and pediatric patients are more at risk because of how these populations break down and absorb medications.

In this chapter, identifying factors that affect absorption, distribution, metabolism, and elimination of drugs in special populations, explaining why **doses** for geriatrics and pediatrics must be calculated based on the individual patient, and identifying medication limitations in dosage regimens will be discussed. Also, how to calculate dosages based on the patient's body surface area (BSA) and weight as well as age will be covered.

It is important to stress the importance of clarifying confusing orders, verifying safe doses, and calculating with extreme accuracy when it comes to these populations. When calculating medication dosages, it is always important to consider all the relevant factors involved in preparing a specific dose for a patient. In case of any doubts, the pharmacist should always be consulted before providing the patient with the product.

GERIATRICS

Geriatric refers to patients who are age sixty-five or older. Pharmacy technicians will encounter this population the most, especially in retail and other ambulatory pharmacy settings. It is important to stress being respectful, encouraging, and attentive when working with the geriatric population. Because the geriatric patient's health concerns can change at any time, pharmacy technicians must remain current on relevant diseases, conditions, and medications including OTC drugs. Any questions or situations that may require pharmacy counseling should be directed to the pharmacist.

When it comes to geriatric dosages, an important issue is diseases or conditions that affect any part of the ADME (absorption, distribution, metabolism, and excretion) process. The function of the body systems may change in geriatric patients, which may require changes in the dosage of certain medications. For example, if a patient has kidney disease, the body may develop problems eliminating the drug. Or, if a patient has liver disease, the dose of the drug may need to be decreased due to problems metabolizing the drug.

The Geriatric Dosage Handbook is one resource used to help with calculating medication dosages in geriatric patients. When a problem arises with a geriatric patient based on a disease or condition that affects the ADME process, the pharmacist will base the dosage on the doctor's considerations, weight, age, and body surface area (BSA).

The pharmacy technician's role in geriatric dosing is to be vigilant and aware of concerns with the prescription order and to alert the pharmacist to any questions in regards to the accuracy of dosing regimens of the order. The pharmacist may ask the technician to calculate dosage based on the patient's weight or BSA. The rules and calculations will be covered below with pediatric dosing.

PRACTICE QUESTION

Which does NOT need to be considered when calculating medication dosages for geriatric patients?

A) their age

B) the function of the body systems in the geriatric patient

C) diseases or conditions that may affect the ADME process

D) whether the patient is married

Answers:

A)   Incorrect. Age is a consideration when calculating dosages for geriatric patients.

B)   Incorrect. The function of the body systems in the geriatric patient must be considered when calculating dosages.

C)   Incorrect. Diseases or conditions that may affect the ADME process must be considered when calculating dosages.

D)   Correct. The marital status of the patient does not matter.

PEDIATRICS

Pediatric refers to any patient eighteen years old or younger. Because infants and children cannot tolerate adult doses of drugs, drugs given to pediatric patients are dosed based on the child's age and weight. There are several methods for calculating pediatric dosages. The most accurate way is by weight: kilogram or pound. Pediatric dosages can also be calculated by BSA and age. Charts called **nomograms** are used to determine **BSA** by square meters according to height and weight.

It is important to emphasize that not all drugs can be given to children, even with change in dosage strength. Because of severe side effects or because the drug has not been tested on children, certain drugs are not to be given to children at all. It is also important to stress how crucial it is to be accurate in calculating dosage strengths for children. Most medication errors occur due to mistakes made in pediatric dosing. A single mistake in the placement of a decimal point can cause injury or death in children.

The Pediatric Dosage Handbook is one reference tool used in the pharmacy setting for resources on pediatric dosing; it includes **manufacturer packaging** and labeling information and requirements. It is also important to state that if the technician has any questions, he or she should ask the pharmacist-in-charge or a supervisor for verification of correct dosing.

 For Clark's Rule, always use the weight of the child in pounds, not kilograms.

Three formulas are used for calculating dosage for infants and children. The formulas are Clark's Rule, Young's Rule, and Fried's Rule. Fried's Rule is the least common calculation as it is only used for pediatric patients under twenty-four months of age.

+ Clark's Rule (child's dose): $\dfrac{\text{weight of the child}}{150} \times$ average adult dose

+ Young's Rule (child's dose): adult dose $\times \dfrac{\text{age}}{\text{age} + 12}$

+ Fried's Rule (pediatric dose): $\dfrac{\text{child's age in months}}{150} \times$ adult dose

 The most commonly used rule is Clark's Rule.

When calculating pediatric and geriatric dosing, in hospital settings weight is frequently documented in kilograms (kg) and need to be converted to pounds (lbs.) or vice versa. This requires an extra step before the technician is able to calculate medication doses by body weight.

+ 2.2 lbs. = 1 kg
+ To convert kg to lbs.:
+ Amount of weight in kg × 2.2
+ To convert lbs. to kg:
+ Amount of weight in lbs./2.2

Another way to calculate dosage strengths is by using a nomogram. A nomogram is a graphic representation of several lines that connect two known values on two lines and an unknown value at the point of intersection with another line. In pharmacy, nomograms show height, weight, and BSA in graph form with a graphic value of dosage values based on children of the same height and weight. Doses are then calculated based on normal adult doses by multiplying the BSA in square meters by the dose ordered. The formula for calculation using a nomogram is:

$$\text{weight per dose} \times \text{BSA} = \text{desired dose}$$

Example for a child who is 52 inches tall and weighs 90 pounds

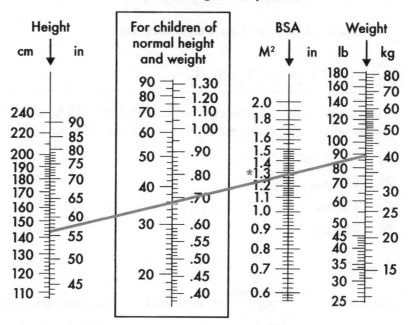

Figure 6.2. Pediatric Nomogram

CONTINUE

Body Surface Area Nomogram
Body Surface Area from Height and Weight
$$BSA = W^{0.425} \times H^{0.725} \times 71.84$$

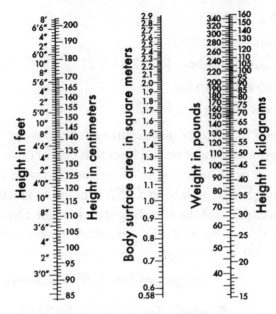

In the above formula, weight is in kgm
and height is in cm, giving body surface area in cm².

Figure 6.3. Body Surface Area Nomogram

PRACTICE QUESTIONS

1. Using Clark's Rule, if a physician orders Cefzil for a 38 lb. child, what would be the pediatric dose given if the adult dose is Cefzil 600 mg q 24 h?

A) 150.2 mg

B) 85.4 mg

C) 152 mg

D) 250 mg

Answer:

child's dose = $\frac{\text{weight of the child}}{150} \times$ "adult dose"	Identify the formula and variables.
weight of the child = 38 lb	Note that the child's weight is already in pounds.
adult dose = 600 mg	

child's dose = $\frac{38}{150} \times$ 600 mg = **152 mg (C)**	Solve for child's dose.

2. A physician orders Zyrtec 0.1 mg/kg daily for a child who weighs 70 lbs. What is the correct pediatric dose for the patient?

  A) 3.18 mg daily

  B) 2.75 mg daily

  C) 1.25 mg daily

  D) 5.5 mg daily

Answer:

$$\frac{0.1\ mg}{kg} \times \frac{1\ kg}{2.2\ lb} \times 70\ lb = \textbf{3.18 mg (A)}$$

Use Dimensional Analysis to get the pediatric dose for the patient. In Dimensional Analysis, multiply by conversion ratios to cancel out units until arriving at the needed units. Recall that 1 kg ≈ 2.2 lb.

3. A physician writes a prescription for valproic acid for a nine-year-old child who weighs 45 lbs. The adult dose is valproic acid 250 mg/5ml. Using Young's Rule, what is the correct dosage for the pediatric patient?

  A) 45.2 mg

  B) 210.15 mg

  C) 156.43 mg

  D) 107.14 mg

Answer:

child's dose = adult dose × $\frac{age}{age + 12}$

age of the child = 9 years

adult dose = 250 mg

Identify the formula and variables. Ignore the child's weight since it's not in the formula.

child's dose = 250 mg × $\frac{9}{9 + 12}$ = **107.14 mg (D)**

Solve for child's dose.

4. If a child weighing 42 lbs. is given Zarontin 20 mg/kg, what is the correct pediatric dose in mg?

  A) 240 mg

  B) 381.8 mg

  C) 189.25 mg

  D) 275.69 mg

CONTINUE

<u>Answer:</u>

$$\frac{20 \text{ mg}}{\text{kg}} \times \frac{1 \text{ kg}}{2.2 \text{ lb}} \times 42 \text{ lb} = \textbf{381.8 mg (B)}$$

Use Dimensional Analysis to get the pediatric dose for the patient. Dimensional Analysis is where we multiply by conversion ratios to cancel out units until we get the units we need.

Use the fact that 1 kg ≈ 2.2 lb.

CHEMOTHERAPY

Special considerations are required when calculating **chemotherapy** doses in cancer patients. Chemotherapy drugs are very potent and hazardous chemicals that cause cell death. It is crucial that doses are correctly calculated. Chemotherapy drugs are normally calculated based on BSA and breakdowns in the ADME process—especially kidney failure—must be considered before dosing.

Kidney failure is measured based on chemotherapy patients' creatinine levels. **Creatinine** is the byproduct of muscle metabolism. The lab values are then used in a formula that determines the patient's creatinine clearance. This formula determines the calculations for dosing of the chemotherapy drugs. A normal creatinine value ranges from 0.7 – 1.5 mg/dL. If it is above 1.5 dL, the patient has decreased renal function; if it is under 0.7 mg/dL, the patient has increased renal function. Depending on the level, the medicine will then be either dosed higher for an increase and lower for a decrease.

Although technicians do not use the formula often, it is important for them to know the formula for creatinine clearance if they are working with chemotherapy agents. Note that weight in these formulas is in kilograms. The Cockcroft-Gault equation is below:

The formula for male patients is:	The formula for female patients is:
$CrCl = \dfrac{(140 - \text{age})(\text{weight})}{72 \times \text{Scr}}$	$CrCl = \dfrac{(140 - \text{age})(\text{weight})(0.85)}{72 \times \text{Scr}}$

Admixture Calculations

This chapter will focus on the formulas and calculations used to prepare and administer **IV admixtures**. Intravenous medications will be discussed more in-depth as well as measurement conversions used with compounded sterile products (CSPs). Formulas used to make TPN solutions and to calculate flow rates and drip rates of IV admixtures will also be covered.

INTRAVENOUS MEDICATIONS

Intravenous medications are liquid or liquid-like drugs that are administered through a syringe or a needle. The routes of administration of intravenous medications follow below.

+ **subcutaneous**: under the first layer of skin; such as insulins
+ **intravenous**: through the vein
+ **intramuscularly**: through the muscle

The medications themselves may be taken by:

+ **bolus**: a single-dose given all at once
+ **IV drip solution**: a drip that is administered directly into the venous circulation
+ **IV push**: a bolus medication administered through an open venous line
+ **parenteral IV solution**: an intravenous or central line solution used to administer nutrients into the body

The drugs are normally in bulk packaging; calculations must be used to dilute the product into a specified solution. Some solutions used in the preparation of IV medications include:

+ **salt solutions**: lactated ringers and normal saline
+ **sugar solutions**: dextrose
+ **potassium solutions**: different strengths of potassium which may or may not be combined with a salt or sugar solution
+ **irrigation solutions**: made for surgical preparations

PRACTICE QUESTIONS

1. Which is NOT a route of administration for IV solutions?

    A) subcutaneous

    B) transdermal

    C) intravenous

    D) intramuscular

    Answers:

    A) Incorrect. IV solutions are administered subcutaneously.

    B) **Correct.** IV solutions are not administered transdermally.

    C) Incorrect. IV solutions are administered intravenously.

    D) Incorrect. IV solutions are administered intramuscularly.

2. Which is considered a salt solution?

A) Lactated Ringer's

B) Dextrose

C) Potassium IVPB solution

D) insulin

Answers:

A) **Correct.** Lactated Ringer's is a salt solution.

B) Incorrect. Dextrose is a sugar solution.

C) Incorrect. Potassium is a potassium solution.

D) Incorrect. Insulin is not an IV solution.

MILLIEQUIVALENTS, EQUIVALENTS, AND INTERNATIONAL UNITS

Common conversions used in the preparation of CSPs are **milliequivalents (mEq)**, **equivalents (eq)**, and **international units (IU)**. Milliequivalents and equivalents are used mainly with electrolytes. Minerals such as calcium, sodium, phosphates, and potassiums are all mEqs. A mEq or Eq is a ratio between a molecule's weight and its valence electrons. When calculating conversions, they are treated no differently than milligrams or grams in the way they are expressed. Milliequivalents are noted as mEq/ml.

Another unit of measurement frequently seen in the preparation of CSPs is international units (IUs) and units. Some examples of drugs measured in units are insulin, heparin, and penicillin. Units are based on the unit of measure of a drug's activity based on a testing system for that particular medication. These are biological assays that are created to define a specific drug's unit of activity. Each drug is measured differently based on its particular effect on the body based on the drug's use.

Because insulin is measured in units on insulin syringes, the measurement is in units as well. So if the standard concentration of insulin is 100 units/mL, then insulin is also ordered by unit based on the patient's glucose level.

mEq problems can be solved using either proportions or Dimensional Analysis, where you multiply by conversion ratios to cancel out units until getting the units needed.

PRACTICE QUESTIONS

1. A physician orders Sodium Chloride 20 mEq. The pharmacy only has Sodium Chloride 40 mEq/20 mL available. How many mLs are needed to make the solution?

A) 2 mL

B) 6 mL

C) 10 mL

D) 12 mL

Answer:

$$\frac{40\text{ mEq}}{20\text{ mL}} = \frac{20\text{ mEq}}{x\text{ mL}}$$

Set up a proportion with mEq on top and mL on the bottom.

$40x = 400$

$x = \textbf{10 mL (C)}$

Cross-multiply and solve for x.

2. A physician requires a patient to take 40 units of insulin SQ qam and 60 units SQ of insulin qpm. How much insulin is needed in mL for each dose if the insulin is available in a 100 units/mL vial?

A) 0.4 mL and 0.6 mL

B) 0.04 mL and 0.06 mL

C) 4 mL and 6 mL

D) 40 mL and 60 mL

Answer:

$$\frac{40u}{x} = \frac{100}{1\text{ mL}}; \, x = \textbf{0.4 mL}$$

$$\frac{60u}{x} = \frac{100}{1\text{ mL}}; \, x = \textbf{0.6 mL (A)}$$

Set up proportions with units on the top and mL on the bottom.

Solve for each amount.

TPN Solutions

Total parenteral nutrition (TPN) is a solution that delivers nutrition to a patient through a **peripheral vein** or **central line**. A dose of lipids (**fat solution**) may be given separately from the TPN to maintain the needed fats in the patient's diet. The additives in a TPN are mainly multivitamins and minerals used to deliver nutrients the patient is lacking in the body due to **malnutrition**. The solution used in TPNs has a mixture of dextrose and amino acids. This solution delivers the amount of **sugar** (dextrose) and **proteins (amino acids)** needed to maintain a nutritionally balanced diet. TPNs can sometimes include insulins, **electrolytes, salts, minerals**, and a H_2 antagonist used for decreasing stomach acid as well.

Examples of TPN orders include:

✦ amino acids 8.5% 500 mL

✦ dextrose 50% 500 mL

✦ potassium chloride (KCl) 40 mEq (stock solution = 2 mEq/mL)

✦ sodium chloride (NaCl) 24 mEq (stock solution = 4 mEq/mL)

✦ calcium gluconate 1 g (stock solution = 1g/10 mL)

✦ insulin 24 units (stock solution = 100 units/mL)

Usually the amino acids and dextrose solutions come in the doses that the physician orders. They can come in separate bottles or in a premix solution that keeps the amino acids and dextrose solution separated until the TPN is ready to be prepared. The premix solution separates the products with a perforated closure that is broken by the pharmacy technician to mix the solution together.

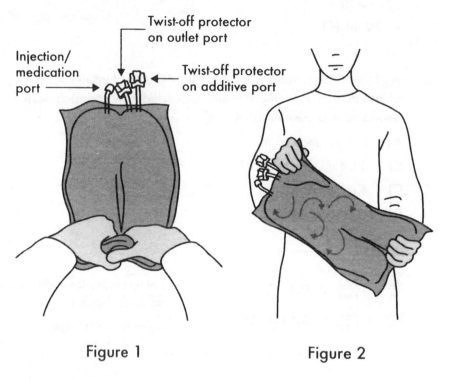

Figure 1   Figure 2

Figure 6.4. Using a Premix Solution

The additives are then shot into the bag through the medication injection port of the bag. The pharmacy technician will calculate the needed doses of each additive based on the stock solutions available.

TPNs are usually ordered on a 12- or 24-hour cycle. Methods of preparing the TPN will be based on the facility's policies and procedures, but they usually involve a step-check procedure in which the pharmacist checks the additives and calculations of the TPN before the pharmacy technician injects the medication into the dextrose/amino acid solution.

> TPNs are also used for nutrition in neonatal units. When preparing TPNs for neonates, much larger, more specified amounts of vitamins and minerals are prepared in very small quantities. This makes the preparation of the TPN more complex, but also requires much more precision in calculating on the part of the technician. One misplacement of a decimal when measuring could cause serious adverse effects.

PRACTICE QUESTIONS

1. If a TPN required potassium phosphate 15 mEq and the stock solution is 4.4 mEq/mL, how many mL will be needed to prepare the solution?

    A) 1.54 mL

    B) 2.5 mL

    C) 3.41 mL

    D) 2.95 mL

    Answer:

$\dfrac{4.4 \text{ mEq}}{1 \text{ mL}} = \dfrac{15 \text{ mEq}}{x \text{ mL}}$	Set up a proportion with mEq on top and mL on the bottom.
$4.4x = 15$ $x = \textbf{3.41 mL (C)}$	Cross-multiply and solve for x.

2. A TPN order calls for sodium acetate 20 mEq. The stock solution available is 4 mEq/mL. How many mL are need to prepare the order?

    A) 8.5 mL

    B) 5 mL

    C) 7.5 mL

    D) 10 mL

    Answer:

$\dfrac{4 \text{ mEq}}{1 \text{ mL}} = \dfrac{20 \text{ mEq}}{x \text{ mL}}$	Set up a proportion with mEq on top and mL on the bottom.
$4x = 20$ $x = \textbf{5 mL (B)}$	Cross-multiply and solve for x.

IV FLOW RATES

All IV solution orders have a rate of administration; they are infused over a specified amount of time and/or at a continual rate. This is called an **IV flow rate.** IV piggybacks (IVPB) are solutions under 250 mL that are normally delivered through a main line over a specific period of time. Large volume solutions, which are 500 mL or more, are normally infused at a continual rate.

By knowing the rate of administration, the pharmacy technician is able to calculate how many IV bags must be prepared for a patient to last a specific amount of time (usually a 24-hour period). For example, if a patient is on a solution that is being delivered at 125 mL/hr., and the volume of the bag is 1,000 mL, then the patient would require three bags to last a 24-hour period:

$$\frac{125 \text{ mL}}{\text{hr.}} \times 24 \text{ hr.} \times \frac{1 \text{ bag}}{1000 \text{ mL}} = 3 \text{ bags}$$

Flow rates can be calculated either by mL/min. or mL/hr., depending on the volume of the IV solution or the amount of time needed to infuse it. The formula for calculating flow rates is:

$$\frac{\text{volume of IV solution}}{\text{hours}} \quad \text{or} \quad \frac{\text{volume of IV solution}}{\text{minutes}}.$$

The formula to calculate how many hours it will take for an IV solution to be infused is:

$$\text{volume in mL/rate} = \text{hours}$$

Again, these problems may be solved using either proportions or Dimensional Analysis, where multiplying by conversion ratios cancels out units until arriving at the units needed.

PRACTICE QUESTIONS

1. If a 1000 ml solution is being infused over an 8-hour period of time, how many mL are infused each hour?

A) 75 mL/hr.

B) 150 mL/hr.

C) 100 mL/hr.

D) 125 mL/hr.

Answer:

$\frac{1000 \text{ mL}}{8 \text{ hr.}} = \frac{x \text{ mL}}{1 \text{ hr.}}$	Set up a proportion with mL on top and hours on the bottom.
$8x = 1000$ $x = \textbf{125 mL (D)}$	Cross-multiply and solve for x.

2. If a 500 mL solution is being infused over a 4-hour period of time, what is the mL/min. (flow rate) of the solution?

A) 2.08 mL/min.

B) 4.14 mL/min.

C) 3.25 mL/min.

D) 1.37 mL/min.

Answer:

flow rate (mL/min.) = $\dfrac{\text{volume of IV solution}}{\text{time minutes}}$

volume = 500 mL

time = 4 hours = 240 minutes

Identify the formula and variables.

Note that **flow rate** is the volume of the IV solution divided by the time it takes to infuse it.

Since the time is provided in hours, multiply it by 60 to convert it into minutes.

---

flow rate (mL/min.) = $\dfrac{500 \text{ mL}}{240 \text{ minutes}}$ = **2.08 mL/min. (A)**

Multiply out. Notice that the units turn out correctly!

---

3. If a 1000 mL solution is being infused at 3.75 mL/min., approximately how many bags of the solution will be needed in a 24-hr period?

A) 4.5

B) 2.8

C) 3.7

D) 5.4

Answer:

$\dfrac{3.75 \text{ mL}}{1 \text{ min.}} = \dfrac{x}{60 \text{ min.}}$

x = 3.75 × 60 = 225

225 × 24 = 5400 mL

First compute how many mL will flow during this 24-hour period. Given a flow rate of 3.75mL/min, it is possible to set up a proportion to see how much is infused in 60 minutes, or 1 hour.

In 1 hour, 225 mL of the solution will be infused. So in 24 hours, 225 × 24 = 5400 mL will be infused.

5400 mL/1000 mL= **5.4 bags (D)**

Since each bag contains 1000mL of solution, divide the total by 1000 to get the number of bags.

DROP RATES

IV solutions are administered through IV tubing referred to as drip sets or drop sets, which deliver a specific number of drops per minute or number of drops per mL. Depending on the drop set, the **drops per mL (gtt/mL)** may differ based on the length of tubing. Some standard drip rates for different IV tubing sets are 10, 15, 20, or 60 gtts/mL. While the physician or nurse normally calculates the **drip rate**, or **drop rate** of an IV solution, pharmacy staff calculate drop rates as well to double check the volume given is correct.

The formula to calculate drip rates or drop rate from a given flow rate (mL/hr) is:

$$\text{gtts/min.} = \frac{\text{full volume of solution}}{60 \text{ min.}} \times \text{gtt/min. of IV tubing}$$

(gtt/min. of IV tubing is the drop factor)

If the mL/hr. is not available, and the order asks for a specific volume to be delivered over a set time, by knowing the drip rate of the tubing used, the gtts/min. can still be calculated.

$$\text{gtts/min.} = \text{volume of solution in ml} \times \frac{\text{drops per minute}}{\text{drops per mL of IV tubing} \times 60 \text{ min.}} = \text{hours}$$

The amount of drug being delivered and the volume of the solution needed over a set period of time can also be calculated if the gtts/min is known as well as the size of IV tubing used.

$$\text{mL per minute} = \frac{\text{gtts}}{1\text{mL}} \times \frac{1\text{mL}}{\text{size}} \text{ of IV tubing}$$

> 🔍 Drip rates and flow rates can be confusing due to the fact that with drip rates, the technician is calculating gtt/min and with flow rates, the calculation is mL/min or mL/hr. Be sure to check these terms when preparing to calculate.

PRACTICE QUESTIONS

1. A 1500 mL Lactated Ringer's solution is being infused at 100 mL/hr. What is the gtts/min. if the nurse is using a 20 gtt/mL tubing?

   A) 25.75 gtts/min.

   B) 33.3 gtts/min.

   C) 38.27 gtts/min.

   D) 17.25 gtts/min.

   Answer:

	Identify the formula and variables.
drip rate (gtt/min.) = $\frac{\text{volume}}{\text{time (minutes)}} \times$ drop factor volume = 100 mL time = 1 hour = 60 minutes drop factor = 20 gtts/mL	Note that drip rate (or drop rate) is the number of drops per minute to be infused (gtt/min) and drop factor (expressed in gtt/mL) is the drops per volume, based on length of tubing. Since the rate of mL/hr. is already provided, there is no need to use the 1500 mL.
drip rate (gtt/min.) = $\frac{100 \text{ mL}}{60 \text{ minutes}} \times 20 \frac{\text{gtt}}{\text{mL}}$ = **33.3 gtts/min. (B)**	Multiply out. Notice that the units turn out correctly!
$\frac{100 \text{ mL}}{1 \text{ hr.}} \times \frac{1 \text{ hr.}}{60 \text{ min.}} \times \frac{20 \text{ gtt}}{1 \text{ mL}} = \mathbf{33.3 \frac{gtts}{min.}}$	Note: It might be easier to solve this using Dimensional Analysis, multiplying by conversion ratios to cancel out units until obtaining the needed units.

2. An IV solution is running 175 mL/hr. through 20 gtts/mL tubing. What is the gtts/min.?

    A)   42.35 gtts/min.

    B)   25 gtts/min.

    C)   58.3 gtts/min.

    D)   32.5 gtts/min.

Answer:

$$\frac{175 \text{ mL}}{1 \text{ hr.}} \times \frac{1 \text{ hr.}}{60 \text{ min.}} \times \frac{20 \text{ gtt}}{\text{mL}} = \textbf{58.3 gtts/min. (C)}$$

This is a good problem for Dimensional Analysis, since there are a lot of different units.

Start with the existing units, and use conversion factors to get to the needed units.

3. If a 500 mL IV solution is being administered at 125 mL/hr, what is the gtts/min for a 20 gtt/mL tubing?

    A)   4 gtts/min

    B)   72 gtts/min

    C)   37.5 gtts/min

    D)   41.7 gtts/min

Answer:

$$\frac{125 \text{ mL}}{1 \text{ hr.}} \times \frac{1 \text{ hr.}}{60 \text{ min.}} \times \frac{20 \text{ gtt}}{\text{mL}} =$$

41.7 gtts/min. (D)

This is a good problem for Dimensional Analysis, since there are a lot of different units.

Note that we don't need to use the 500 mL, since the mL/hr rate is already provided.

Start with the given units, and use conversion factors to get to the needed units.

Business Math

The pharmacy setting is a business. As with any business, one goal of the practice is to make a profit so the company can continue to do more business with its customers. The pharmacy technician plays a crucial role in keeping the pharmacy running smoothly financially. In this section, a basic understanding of calculating turnover rates, inventory-based math, discounts and markups, profit, and insurance reimbursement will be reviewed.

INVENTORY

As discussed in chapter 4, pharmacy technicians have a crucial role in the upkeep of the inventory in the pharmacy. Because the technician is responsible for thousands of dollars in drugs yearly, it is important for the technician to keep track of the inventory to determine which drugs should be ordered and which drugs are not used as often.

By determining the **turnover rate** of the inventory in the pharmacy, the technician can calculate the overall effectiveness of the purchasing and inventory control systems put in place in the pharmacy. Inventory turnover rate is calculated by dividing the total dollars spent on **annual inventory purchased** by the actual value of the pharmacy at any given point in time (the inventory at hand). By doing so, an estimated **average inventory** can be determined. The more turnovers, the more profit the pharmacy makes.

Because pharmacies must keep a specific amount of drug in their inventory, they often set goals to lower inventory to increase profit margins. One way to do this is to set goals based on the **days' supply of inventory**. This is done by making the value of the inventory equivalent to the amount of products sold within a specific amount of days. To calculate the days of inventory supply, we can use the following formula:

$$\text{days of inventory supply} = \frac{\text{actual inventory} \times 7 \text{ days}}{\text{cost of products sold in a week}}$$

PRACTICE QUESTIONS

1. Bob's pharmacy has an inventory value of $650,000. The last quarterly report states that Bob's pharmacy made inventory purchases of $812,500 for that quarter. What is Bob's turnover rate?

    A) 2

    B) 3

    C) 4

    D) 5

    Answer:

    $$\text{turnover rate} = \frac{\text{cost of goods sold for a year}}{\text{total inventory}}$$

    total inventory = $650,000

    inventory purchases = cost of goods sold for a year

    = $812,500 × 4 = $3,250,000

    $$\text{turnover rate} = \frac{\$3,250,000}{\$650,000} = \textbf{5 (D)}$$

    Identify the formula and variables.

    Multiply the quarterly purchases by 4 to get the yearly amount.

    Note that *turnover rate* refers to the number of inventory turns in a year.

2. A pharmacy has a value of $270,000 in actual inventory, and the previous week's sales were $95,000 with the cost to the pharmacy of products sold being $65,000. What is the pharmacy's number of days of inventory supply?

A) about 20 days

B) about 29 days

C) about 15 days

D) about 22 days

Answer:

$days = \dfrac{actual\ inventory \times 7\ days}{cost\ of\ products\ sold\ in\ a\ week}$	Identify the formula.
$days = \dfrac{\$270,000 \times 7}{\$65,000} = \textbf{29 days (B)}$	Add variables and solve.

Profit

To stay in business, the pharmacy must make a profit each year to keep inventory in stock, pay rent or lease, pay for utilities, and to employ other pharmacists and pharmacy technicians. **Gross profit** refers to the sales of the pharmacy minus all the costs that are directly related to the sales. The formula for gross profit is:

selling price – acquisition price = gross profit

Net profit is the gross profit minus the sum of all costs that are associated with dispensing the prescription. The cost of dispensing the medication is referred to as the **dispensing fee** or professional fee. Net profit is determined by using this formula:

gross profit – dispensing fee = net profit

The dispensing fee the pharmacy charges depends on the policies and procedures of the pharmacy. Some pharmacies have a standard dispensing fee, while others may charge a higher dispensing fee for more expensive medications and lower dispensing fees on cheaper medications.

> Although dispensing fees are added to the final price of a medication, they are still subtracted from the net profit of the pharmacy because they are not profits; rather, they reflect the costs of preparing the medication.

CONTINUE

PRACTICE QUESTIONS

1. If a pharmacy purchases 100 tablets of Levaquin 500 mg for $550.00 and sold 20 pills to a patient for $125.00, what was the gross profit for each 100 pills of Levaquin sold?

   A) $50

   B) $75

   C) $125

   D) $150

   Answer:

gross profit = selling price − acquisition fee (cost) selling price = $\frac{\$125}{20 \text{ pills}}$ = $6.25/pill cost = $\frac{\$550}{100 \text{ pills}}$ = $5.50/pill	Identify the formula and variables. Find the selling price and cost for each pill.
profit/pill = $6.25 − $5.50 = $0.75/pill $0.75 × 100 pills = **$75 (B)**	Now find the profit for each pill, and multiply it by 100 pills that are sold.

2. A pharmacy charges a dispensing fee of $4.00 for all prescriptions. A patient acquires a prescription for Zithromax 250 mg #7 tablets. The pharmacy bought the Zithromax for $25.00 and charged the patient $38.00. What is the net profit of the sale?

   A) $9

   B) $20

   C) $15

   D) $9

   Answer:

gross profit = selling price − acquisition fee (cost) net profit = gross profit − dispensing fee selling price = $38 cost = $25 gross profit = $38 − $25 = $13	Identify the formula and variables. First get the gross profit.
net profit = gross profit − dispensing fee = $13 − $4 = **$9 (D)**	To get the net profit, subtract the dispensing fee.

SELLING PRICE

The **selling price** begins in the pharmacy when the drug is purchased from the wholesaler. When it is purchased, the pharmacy receives the drug at the **cost price** or average wholesale price (AWP). The pharmacy increases the price of the medication by a certain percentage and the drug is then at its selling price. The percentage amount between the cost price and the selling price is called the **markup rate**.

After the price is fixed, the next part of the selling price comes from the dispensing fee system. As stated in the last section, the pharmacy charges a professional fee, which is a standard or percentage fee for costs associated with running a pharmacy. It may also charge a **compounding fee** for drugs that take extra time and cost. Compounding fees could be calculated by hour or percentage depending on the policies and procedures of the pharmacy. The fees are then calculated into the net profit the same way dispensing fees are.

> If a compounding pharmacy charges a compounding fee of $60/hour for preparation costs, and the technician compounded a medication for a patient that took 20 minutes, what would be the compounding fee added to the final cost to the patient?

PRACTICE QUESTIONS

1. A pharmacy gives a 10% discount on its glucose monitoring machines. A patient buys one for $89.00 before the discount. What is the discounted price of the glucose machine?

   A) $74.50

   B) $77.00

   C) $80.10

   D) $83.40

   Answer:

   discounted price =

   $$\text{retail price} - \frac{\text{retail price} \times \% \text{ discount}}{100}$$

   retail price = $89

   % discount = 10

   discounted price = ?

   | Identify the formula and variables. Prepare to solve for the discounted price. |

   $$\text{discounted price} = 89 - \frac{89 \times 10}{100} = \textbf{\$80.10 (C)}$$

   Solve for discounted price.

   Note it is also possible to multiply the retail price by 0.90 (which is 1.00 – 0.10) to get $80.10.

2. There is a 300% markup on a drug that the pharmacy paid $28.00 for at cost. What is the final price?

A) $112.00

B) $84.00

C) $120.00

D) $68.00

Answer:

retail price = wholesale price + $\dfrac{\% \text{ markup} \times \text{wholesale price}}{100}$ wholesale price = $28.00 % markup = 300	Identify the formula and variables. The final price is the retail price.
retail price = $28 + $\dfrac{300 \times \$28}{100}$ = **$112.00 (A)**	Solve for the retail price.

3. What is the markup of a drug that was acquired at cost for $30.00 and sold for $88.00?

A) 19%

B) 1.9%

C) 0.19%

D) 193%

Answer:

retail price = wholesale price + $\dfrac{\% \text{ markup} \times \text{wholesale price}}{100}$ wholesale price = $30.00 % markup = ? retail price = $88.00	Identify the formula and variables.
$88 = \$30 + x \times \dfrac{\$30}{100}$ $88 = \$30 + \dfrac{30x}{100}$ $30x = (88 - 30) \times 100$ $x = $ **193% (D)**	Solve for the % markup.

4. What is the discount price of a drug that normally costs $48.00, but is on sale for 25% off?

  A) $42.00

  B) $43.00

  C) $36.00

  D) $38.00

Answer:

discounted price = retail price − $\dfrac{\text{retail price} \times \% \text{ discount}}{100}$ retail price = $48 % discount = 25 discounted price = ?	Identify the formula and variables. Solve for the discounted price.
discounted price = $48 - \dfrac{48 \times 25}{100}$ = **$36 (C)**	Solve for discounted price. Note that it is also possible to multiply the retail price by 0.75 (which is 1.00 − 0.25) to get $36.

5. If a drug was acquired for $25.00 and sold for $44.00, what percentage is the markup?

  A) 70%

  B) 65%

  C) 81%

  D) 76%

Answer:

retail price = wholesale price + $\dfrac{\% \text{ markup} \times \text{wholesale price}}{100}$ wholesale price = $25.00 % markup = ? retail price = $44.00	Identify the formula and variables.
$44 = \$25 + \dfrac{x \times \$25}{100}$ $44 = \$25 + \dfrac{25x}{100}$ $25x = (44 - 25) \times 100$ $x =$ **76% (D)**	Solve for the % markup.

6. If a drug was originally priced at $82.00 and was marked down by 28%, what is the discounted price?

A) $45.99

B) $59.04

C) $52.00

D) $47.88

Answer:

discounted price = $$\text{retail price} - \frac{\text{retail price} \times \% \text{ discount}}{100}$$ retail price = $82 % discount = 28 discounted price = ?	Identify the formula and variables. Solve for the discounted price.
discounted price = $82 - \frac{82 \times 28}{100}$ discounted price = **$59.04 (B)**	Solve for the discounted price. Note that it is also possible to multiply the retail price by 0.72 (which is 1.00 − 0.28) to get $59.04.

INSURANCE REIMBURSEMENT

Insurance reimbursement is based on how insurance companies pay the pharmacy for services rendered. Reimbursement rates change depending on the insurance company. However, because the average warehouse price (AWP) is priced lower than the usual and customary price (U&C), insurance companies will reimburse based on the AWP. Insurance companies also know that some pharmacies may offer drugs below AWP, so they will only reimburse at whichever price is less. A typical reimbursement formula for third party reimbursement would be similar to this:

87% of AWP or 100% of the U&C (whichever is less) + a $3.50 dispensing fee

Capitation fees are another concept used for third-party reimbursement. The individual or institutional provider pays a fixed fee without regard to the amount of services rendered for each patient. For example, a long-term care facility would use this service because it receives a fixed amount of money from the patient each month to pay for the services. The amount the patient pays does not change whether the patient received no drugs that month or if the cost of the drugs he or she received goes beyond the amount allotted by the capitation fee.

? A patient receives a prescription for 30 Crestor 20 mg tablets. The U&C price for 30 tablets is $45.12, whereas the AWP for 100 tablets is $76.88. Based on the insurance reimbursement formula, what would be the reimbursement charge for this medication?

PRACTICE QUESTION

Which is NOT true about insurance reimbursement?

A) Insurance companies will reimburse for AWP or U&C, depending on which costs less.

B) Capitation fees change month to month.

C) Reimbursement formulas may change depending on the provider.

D) If a patient goes over his or her allotted amount for capitation fees, the patient must pay the difference to the pharmacy.

Answers:

A) Incorrect. Insurance companies will reimburse for AWP or U&C, depending on which costs less.

B) **Correct.** Capitation fees do not change month to month.

C) Incorrect. It is true that reimbursement formulas may change depending on the provider.

D) Incorrect. If a patient goes over her or his allotted amount for capitation fees, the patient does have to pay the difference to the pharmacy.

1.
A) Incorrect. The suffix –*olol* refers to beta blockers.

B) Incorrect. The suffix –*pril* refers to ACE inhibitors.

C) **Correct.** The suffix –*tidine* is used for histamine-2 blockers.

D) Incorrect. The suffix –*artan* is used for angiotensin 2 receptor blockers.

2.
A) Incorrect. A class A balance does not weigh this much.

B) **Correct.** The weight limit of a class A balance is 120 mg.

C) Incorrect. Class A balances can weigh 100 mg, but they may weigh even more.

D) Incorrect. Class A balances weigh far less than 360 mg.

3.
A) Incorrect. Using cc instead of mL can be an abbreviation error.

B) Incorrect. Using apothecary units instead of metric units can be an abbreviation error.

C) **Correct.** Using STAT instead of as soon as possible is acceptable.

D) Incorrect. Using MS in an unclear manner may be an abbreviation error.

4.
A) **Correct.** Barcode administration technology reduces medication errors by using a barcode on the patient's label that matches the inpatient's bar code on their wristband to verify the correct patient is being scanned before medication is administered.

B) Incorrect. Web-based compliance and disease management tracking systems helps to track patient's compliance with taking maintenance medications and tracking disease management through software systems connected to physician's offices, hospitals, and pharmacies.

C) Incorrect. Unit-dose repacking systems are used to unit dose medications in stock bottles in the centralized pharmacy.

D) IV and TPN compounding devices are automatic pumping systems that can compound several sterile ingredients into a finished solution dispensed in a single patient bag without being manually touched by the technician.

5.
A) Incorrect. Ondansetron is not used for pain.

B) Incorrect. Ondansetron is not used to treat diabetes.

C) Incorrect. Ondansetron does not treat stomach acid.

D) **Correct.** Ondansetron is used for nausea.

6.
A) Incorrect. Leukemia is a disease of the immune system.

B) Incorrect. Cystitis is a disease of the urinary system.

C) Incorrect. Angina affects the circulatory system.

D) **Correct.** Osteoarthritis is a musculoskeletal condition.

7.
A) Incorrect. Less than 3 million medication errors occur in the United States each year.

B) Incorrect. There are not 5 million medication errors in the United States each year.

C) **Correct.** Nearly 1.5 million medication errors occur each year.

D) Incorrect. Less than 2.5 million medication errors occur in the United States each year.

8.
A) Incorrect. The PCN number is used by PBMs for network benefit routing and may change depending on what benefit is being billed.

B) **Correct.** The BIN number directs the claim to the correct third-party provider.

C) Incorrect. The group number directs the claim to specific insurance benefits for that group.

D) Incorrect. The patient's date of birth is used as an identification tool; an insurance card displays the dates of birth for each person covered next to his or her name.

9. B)

Break up the arabic number:

2014 = 2000 + 10 + 4

Plug in the roman numeral values.

2000 = MM, 10 = X, 4 = IV (5 – 1), since I is before V.

= MMXIV

10. A) Incorrect. The root word *hepat/o* refers to the liver.

B) **Correct.** The root word *lapar/o* refers to the abdomen.

C) Incorrect. The root word *hist/o* refers to body tissue.

D) Incorrect. The root words *mamm/o* or *mast/o* refer to the breast.

11. A) Incorrect. The patient's name is required on a non-control hard copy.

B) **Correct.** Although it is normally pre-printed on the hard copy, the DEA number is not required on a non-control.

C) Incorrect. The patient's phone number must be included on a non-control hard copy.

D) Incorrect. A non-control hard copy must display the prescriber's name.

12. A) **Correct.** Salmeterol prevents asthma attacks and bronchospasms.

B) Incorrect. Salmeterol does not lower fevers or treat inflammation.

C) Incorrect. Salmeterol is not used to treat autoimmune disorders.

D) Incorrect. Salmeterol is not an estrogen modulator.

13. A) **Correct.** USB chapter 795 discusses the standards required for non-sterile compounding.

B) Incorrect. There is no USB 799.

C) Incorrect. USB chapter 797 addresses sterile compounding.

D) Incorrect. USB chapter 796 does not reference non-sterile compounding.

14. A)

Find equivalent fractions with the common denominator 40.

$\frac{3}{8} = \frac{15}{40}, \frac{2}{5} = \frac{16}{40}$

Add the numerators of the fractions and leave the denominator. This fraction cannot be reduced.

$\frac{3}{8} + \frac{2}{5} = \frac{15}{40} + \frac{16}{40} = \mathbf{\frac{31}{40}}$

15. A) **Correct.** Harvey Wiley helped to pass the Pure Food and Drug Act of 1906.

B) Incorrect. The Food, Drug, and Cosmetic Act of 1938 was separate from the Pure Food and Drug Act.

C) Incorrect. Harvey Wiley did not lead efforts to pass the Poison Prevention Packaging Act.

D) Incorrect. Harvey Wiley was not a driver of the Harrison Narcotics Tax Act of 1914.

16. A) Incorrect. The suffix *–tomy* refers to an incision.

B) Incorrect. The suffix *–plasia* refers to a formation.

C) Incorrect. The suffix *–osis* refers to an abnormal condition.

D) **Correct.** The suffix *–stomy* refers to an artificial opening.

17. A) Incorrect. POS plans are managed care plans

B) Incorrect. HMOs are managed care plans.

C) Incorrect. PPOs are managed care plans.

D) **Correct.** PAPs are for self-pay patients.

18. A) Incorrect. Medication errors are a primary cause of preventable death and injuries, but they are not the leading one.

B) Incorrect. Medication errors are not the fifth leading cause of preventable death and injuries.

C) Incorrect. Medication errors are not the fourth leading cause of preventable death and injuries.

D) **Correct.** Medication errors are the third leading cause of preventable death and injuries in the United States.

19. **C)**

Set up a proportion with mL on top and L on bottom. Recall that 1000 mL = 1 L.

$$\frac{1000\ mL}{1\ L} = \frac{3600\ mL}{x\ L}$$

Cross-multiply and solve for x.

$1000x = 3600$

$x = \mathbf{3.6\ L}$

Note: This can also be solved using Dimensional Analysis, multiplying by conversion ratios to cancel out units until finding the needed units. Here, ratios are set up so that unwanted units cross out on top and bottom:

$$3600\ mL \times \frac{1\ L}{1000\ mL} = 3.6\ L$$

20. **A) Correct.** Pharmacodynamics is how the action, effect, and breakdown of drugs happens in the body.

B) Incorrect. The difference in quantity of medication between the effective dose and the amount that causes adverse side effects is called the therapeutic window.

C) Incorrect. Bioequivalence is when two drugs have the same bioavailability.

D) Incorrect. Pharmacodynamics does not address what happens if a patient decides not to take a drug the physician prescribes.

21. **A) Correct.** The FDA was formed in 1906.

B) Incorrect. The FDA did not form in 1938.

C) Incorrect. The US Department of Agriculture was formed in 1862.

D) Incorrect. The Bureau of Chemistry was formed in 1901.

22. A) Incorrect. Wrong dosage form errors occur when the prescribed route of administration of the drug is incorrect.

B) Incorrect. Improper dose errors occur when the patient receives a lesser dose, a higher dose, or extra doses of the drug than what was prescribed.

C) **Correct.** Omission errors occur when the prescribed dose is not administered as ordered.

D) Incorrect. Compliance errors occur when the patient does not take the drug the way the doctor prescribes it.

23. A) Incorrect. The tip is where the needle is attached.

B) Incorrect. The plunger is the cylinder that inserts into the barrel of the syringe.

C) **Correct.** The lumen is part of the syringe needle.

D) Incorrect. The barrel is the part that holds the medication and displays the calibrations.

24. **A) Correct.** Third-party payers are contracted by insurance companies to collect payments and debts from patients.

B) Incorrect. Patients are first-party payers.

C) Incorrect. Insurance companies are second-party payers.

D) Incorrect. PBMs manage prescription drug benefits for health insurance companies.

25. A) Incorrect. The Harrison Narcotics Tax Act of 1914 was passed because of the International Opium Convention.

B) **Correct.** The Food, Drug and Cosmetic Act of 1938 was passed because of the Sulfanilamide tragedy.

C) Incorrect. The Kefauver-Harris Amendment of 1962 was passed because of the Thalidomide Tragedy.

D) Incorrect. The Poison Prevention Packaging Act was passed because of the hundreds of deaths of children under the age of five as a result of ingesting drugs and household chemicals.

26. A) Incorrect. Monitoring errors are due to incorrectly monitored drugs that require specific laboratory values for medication and dose selections.

B) **Correct.** Deteriorated drug errors are caused by using expired drugs or drugs whose chemical or physical potency and integrity has somehow been compromised.

C. Incorrect. These situations are called wrong administration technique errors.

D.) Incorrect. These instances are wrong time errors.

27. A) Incorrect. Scheduled medication orders are for those medications given around the clock.

B) Incorrect. PRN is a type of medication order; these medications are provided on an as-needed basis.

C) **Correct.** Blood testing is not a type of medication order.

D) Incorrect. Medication orders include controlled substances.

28. **D)**

Multiply numerators across and denominators across.

$$\frac{4}{5} \times \frac{7}{8} = \frac{4 \times 7}{5 \times 8} = \frac{28}{40}$$

Reduce (simplify) answer to simplest terms.

$$\frac{28}{40} = \frac{7 \times 4}{10 \times 4} = \frac{7}{10}$$

29. A) Incorrect. Pancreatic amylase is a digestive enzyme that passes to the small intestine.

B) Incorrect. Trypsin is a digestive enzyme that passes to the small intestine.

C) Incorrect. Pancreatic lipase is a digestive enzyme that passes to the small intestine.

D) **Correct.** Insulin is not a digestive enzyme.

30. A) Incorrect. Workers may only garb in the anteroom.

B) Incorrect. No paper is permitted in the clean room, so labels must be generated in the anteroom.

C) **Correct.** CSPs are prepared in the sterile room under the laminar airflow hood.

D) Incorrect. Workers can use an antibacterial solution to sterilize their

hands in the clean room, but aseptic handwashing is done at the faucet in the anteroom.

31. **A)** **Correct.** The Food, Drug and Cosmetic Act of 1938 developed the USP.

B) Incorrect. The Controlled Substance Act controls the manufacture, importation, possession, use, and distribution of certain controlled substances.

C) Incorrect. The Orphan Drug Act supports the development drugs to treat rare, or orphan, diseases.

D) Incorrect. The Pure Food and Drug Act of 1906 required manufacturers to properly label a drug with truthful information.

32. A) Incorrect. Alprazolam is not a SALAD drug.

B) Incorrect. Meloxicam is not considered a SALAD drug.

C) Incorrect. Hydrochlorothiazide is not considered a SALAD drug.

D) **Correct.** Clomiphene is a SALAD drug.

33. **A)** **Correct.** Drug duplications happen if a patient is prescribed a new drug that contains an active ingredient shared by a medication he or she already takes.

B) Incorrect. Therapeutic duplication refers to situations when drugs are in the same drug class or have the same function in the body.

C) Incorrect. Drugs have more than one active ingredient in them that are used for separate conditions are called combination drugs.

D) Incorrect. Special conditions could be anything that causes restrictions on the patient.

34. **A)**

Set up a proportion with ounces on top and tablespoons on the bottom. Recall that $\frac{1}{2}$ fl.ounce = 1 tablespoon.

$$\frac{\frac{1}{2} \text{ fl.ounce}}{1 \text{ tablespoon}} = \frac{2 \text{ fl.ounce}}{x \text{ tablespoons}}$$

Cross-multiply and solve for x.

$$\frac{1}{2}x = 2$$

x = **4 tablespoonsful**

Note: This can also be solved using Dimensional Analysis, multiplying by conversion ratios to cancel out units until finding the needed units:

$$2\text{ fl.ounces} \times \frac{1\text{ tablespoon}}{\frac{1}{2}\text{ fl.ounce}} = 4\text{ tablespoonsful}$$

35. A) Incorrect. The Food, Drug, and Cosmetic Act of 1938 required a ban on false claims, required package inserts with directions to be included with products, and required exact labeling on the product.

B) Incorrect. The Kefauver-Harris Amendment gave the FDA the authority to approve a manufacturer's marketing application before the drug was to become available for consumer or commercial use.

C) **Correct.** The Durham-Humphrey Amendment required the phrase, "Caution: Federal Law Prohibits Dispensing without a Prescription" be placed on prescription labeling.

D) Incorrect. The Controlled Substance Act controls the manufacture, importation, possession, use, and distribution of certain controlled substances.

36. A) **Correct.** Diarrhea is not a side effect of montelukast.

B) Incorrect. Headaches are a side effect of montelukast.

C) Incorrect. Flu symptoms are a possible side effect of montelukast.

D) Incorrect. One side effect of montelukast is a sore throat.

37. A) **Correct.** POS plans still require an in-network primary care physician, but a patient can get out-of-network services at a higher cost.

B) Incorrect. HMO plans usually limit coverage to care from in-network doctors and specialists for a fixed annual fee and/or copayment for services rendered.

C) Incorrect. PPO plans allow patients to see any in-network physician or specialist without needing a prior authorization, although they need to meet annual deductibles.

D) Incorrect: Worker's Compensation provides coverage to people injured on the job.

38. A) Incorrect. Class A balances are not calibrated twice a year.

B) Incorrect. Class A balances require more frequent upkeep.

C) Incorrect. Class A balances do not need to be calibrated this often.

D) **Correct.** Class A balances must be calibrated and certified every year.

39. A) Incorrect. The prefix *chlor–* means green.

B) Incorrect. The prefix *cyan–* refers to blue.

C) Incorrect. The prefix *eryth–* refers to red.

D) **Correct.** The prefix *cirrh–* means yellow.

40. A) Incorrect. Errors in amphotericin B products could result in renal failure, respiratory arrest, and even death.

B) **Correct.** Confusing clonidine and Klonopin may result in loss of seizure control, hypotension, or other serious consequences

C) Incorrect. Mixing up different forms of insulin may result in hypoglycemia or poor diabetes control.

D) Incorrect. Confusing the SALAD drugs tramadol, trazodone, and toradol may result in an inability to manage pain, abnormal psychiatric symptoms, or other serious consequences.

41. A) **Correct.** The Drug Price Competition and Patent Term Restoration Act of 1984 outlines the process for drug companies to file an abbreviated new drug application (ANDA).

B) Incorrect. The Health Insurance Portability and Accountability Act (HIPAA) of 1996 established protected health information and safeguards patient privacy.

C) Incorrect. The Patient Protection and Affordable Care Act of 2010 required individuals to have health insurance and required insurance companies to cover all individuals with new minimum standards in order to increase the quality and affordability of healthcare.

D) Incorrect. The Drug Listing Act implemented the national drug code number (NDC).

42. **A)** **Correct.** The doctor must approve a refill authorization.

B) Incorrect. Authorizations may not be approved for controlled substances due to federal or state laws.

C) Incorrect. Refill authorizations are called in by the doctor.

D) Incorrect. Refill authorizations may not be approved for short-term conditions.

43. **A)**
Break up the roman numeral.

MMMDCVI = MMM + D + C + V + I

Plug in the arabic numeral values.

MMMDCVI = 3000 + 500 + 100 + 5 + 1

= **3,606**

44. A) Incorrect. The suffix –*codone* refers to opioid narcotics.

B) **Correct.** The suffix –*praxole* refers to proton pump inhibitors.

C) Incorrect. The suffix –*pril* refers to ACE inhibitors.

D) Incorrect. The suffix –*pam* refers to benzodiazepines.

45. A) Incorrect. Over 100,000 people die in hospitals from medication errors every year.

B) **Correct.** Every year, 400,000 people die in hospitals due to medication errors alone.

C) Incorrect. More than 300,000 people die annually in hospitals from medication errors.

D) Incorrect. Less than 500,000 people die each year in hospitals from medication errors.

46. A) Incorrect. *ATC* means around the clock.

B) **Correct.** *ENDO* means endoscopy.

C) Incorrect. *STAT* means right away.

D) Incorrect. *TID* stands for three times daily.

47. A) Incorrect. An NDC number contains more than nine digits.

B) **Correct.** NDC numbers contain ten digits.

C) Incorrect. NDC numbers do not contain twelve digits.

D) Incorrect. NDC numbers contain more than eight digits.

48. A) Incorrect. Standard is a fee-for-service cost-sharing plan.

B) **Correct.** Extra is an HMO plan.

C) Incorrect. Prime is a PPO with a POS option.

D) Incorrect. Basic is not a plan at all under TRICARE.

49. A) Incorrect. Fungi can be transmitted during sterile compounding and can cause yeast and fungal infections in patients.

B) **Correct.** Amoebas are not found in pharmacy environments.

C) Incorrect. Bacteria can be transmitted by sterile compounding and cause pyrogens to enter the bloodstream if the technician does not comply with aseptic technique.

D) Incorrect. Viruses can be transmitted if the technician does not comply with aseptic technique.

50. A) Incorrect. Claim submission is the process of sending a claim to the third-party payer for reimbursement.

B) Incorrect. Co-insurance is the deductible.

C) **Correct.** Online adjudication is billing a third party for goods and services rendered.

D) Incorrect. Reimbursement is the compensation given to the pharmacy after collection of the patient's copay or deductible.

51. **B)**

Set up a proportion with grains on top and mg on the bottom. Recall that 1 grain ≈ 60 – 65 mg. Use 62 mg.

$$\frac{1 \text{ grain}}{62 \text{ mg}} = \frac{\frac{1}{4} \text{ grain}}{x \text{ mg}}$$

Cross-multiply and solve for x.

$$x = 62 \times \frac{1}{4}$$

$$x \approx \textbf{15 mgs}$$

Note: This can also be solved using Dimensional Analysis, multiplying by conversion ratios to cancel out units until finding the needed units:

$$\frac{1}{4} \text{ grain} \times \frac{62 \text{ mg}}{1 \text{ grain}} \approx 15 \text{ mgs}$$

52.
A) Incorrect. Poor diet can cause high cholesterol.

B) Incorrect. Smoking is a cause of high cholesterol.

C) Incorrect. Genetic factors may cause high cholesterol.

D) Correct. Exercise is not a cause of high cholesterol.

53.
A) Correct. Education and training prevent medication errors.

B) Incorrect. Failure to follow procedures can cause medication errors.

C) Incorrect. Poor performance is one cause of medication errors.

D) Incorrect. Many medication errors are caused by miscommunication.

54.
A) Incorrect. The pharmacist may monitor the medication.

B) Incorrect. The pharmacist may put restrictions on the medication.

C) Incorrect. The pharmacist may make sure the patient is complying with the directions for use.

D) Correct. The pharmacist would be violating HIPAA if she or he told a family member to monitor the patient without the patient's permission.

55. **D)**

Set up a proportion with g on top and mg on bottom. Use the fact that 1 g = 1000 mg.

$$\frac{1 \text{ g}}{1000 \text{ mg}} = \frac{5.8 \text{ g}}{x \text{ mg}}$$

Cross-multiply and solve for x.

$$x = \textbf{5800 mgs}$$

56.
A) Correct. The first five digits refer to the labeler code.

B) Incorrect. The second group of numbers refers to the drug code.

C) Incorrect. The last two digits refer to the package code.

D) Incorrect. The pharmacy is not identified on the package code.

57.
A) Incorrect. Social causes of medication errors are not due to metabolism problems in patients.

B) Incorrect. Calculation errors are not due to metabolism problems in patients.

C) Incorrect. Abbreviation errors are not due to metabolism problems in patients.

D) Correct. Physiological make up causes medication errors because of metabolism problems in patients.

58.
A) Correct. Hepatitis A is spread by contamination of food and water.

B) Incorrect. Hepatitis B can be spread by sexual contact.

C) Incorrect. Hepatitis C can be spread by sexual contact.

D) Incorrect. Hepatitis B and C can be transmitted through sexual contact.

59.
A) Incorrect. The Orphan Drug Act did not implement NDC numbers.

B) Incorrect. The FDA Modernization Act did not implement NDC numbers.

C) Incorrect. The Medicare Modernization Act did not implement NDC numbers.

D) Correct. The Drug Listing Act of 1972 implemented NDC numbers.

60.
A) Incorrect. Medicare Part A is not used for doctor's services.

B) Incorrect. Medicare Part A does not cover Medicare Advantage Plans.

C) Incorrect. Medicare Part A does not cover prescription drugs.

D) Correct. Medicare Part A is used for inpatient stays.

61.
A) Incorrect. QD is the sig code for every day.

B) Incorrect. The sig code for every other day is QOD.

C) **Correct.** QID means four times daily.

D) Incorrect. TID means three times daily.

62.
A) **Correct.** The faucet is located in the anteroom.

B) Incorrect. The laminar airflow workbench is where the technician prepares CSPs in the clean room.

C) Incorrect. Technicians use barrier isolators in the clean room as another safeguard against contamination so they can prepare CSPs in an aseptic box under the hood.

D) Incorrect. The buffer area is the area immediately next to the laminar airflow hood in the clean room.

63.
A) Incorrect. Drugs expiring within 1 month must be pulled from the shelves.

B) **Correct.** If a drug's expiration date states 6/19, the drug will indeed expire on 6/30/2019.

C) Incorrect. It is true that stock bottles should be marked accordingly to alert staff that the medication is expiring within the next 3 months.

D) Incorrect. Expired medications must be stored in a designated area away from regular stock.

64.
A) **Correct.** Another word for co-insurance is deductible.

B) Incorrect. Fee-for-service is not a deductible.

C) Incorrect. Retrospective payment is not a deductible.

D) Incorrect. Dispensing fee is not a deductible.

65.
A) Incorrect. A filter removes unwanted particles from a solution.

B) Incorrect. An adaptor is an attachment used for transferring medication from an IV bag to a vial (and vice versa).

C) **Correct.** The shaft is the long, narrow, hollow point of the needle.

D) Incorrect. The tip is a part of the syringe, not the needle. The needle is attached to the syringe at the tip.

66. **B)**

The least common denominator is the least common multiple of 8 and 5.

5: 5, 10, 15, 20, 25, 30, 35, **40**

8: 8, 16, 24, 32, **40**

67.
A) Incorrect. The prefix *endo–* means inner.

B) **Correct.** The prefix *peri–* means around.

C) Incorrect. The prefix *exo–* means out.

D) Incorrect. The prefix *sub–* means under.

68.
A) Incorrect. There is no Class IV listed in the Medical Device Amendment of 1976.

B) Incorrect. Class II devices are performance standard devices that are considered to pose moderate risks for human use.

C) **Correct.** Class I devices are general controlled devices that are low risk for human use.

D) Incorrect. Class III devices require premarket approval applications that are the equivalent to a new drug application.

69.
A) Incorrect. The elderly are not the most commonly population affected by calculation errors.

B) Incorrect. Women are not the group most commonly affected by calculation errors.

C) **Correct.** Children are most commonly affected by calculation errors.

D) Incorrect. Men are not as commonly affected by calculation errors as children are.

70.
A) Incorrect. The FDA does not have the complete authority to enforce the Resource Conservation and Recovery Act of 1976.

B) Incorrect. The DEA does not have the complete authority to enforce the

Resource Conservation and Recovery Act of 1976.

C) Incorrect. The CIA is not authorized to enforce the Resource Conservation and Recovery Act of 1976 and is not involved in such work.

D) Correct. The EPA has the complete authority to enforce the Resource Conservation and Recovery Act of 1976.

71. A) Incorrect. Medication error due to patient noncompliance with directions for medication use is not a result of the patient's physiological make up.

B) Incorrect. An abbreviation error would not result in a medication error due to intentional patient noncompliance with directions for medication use.

C) Incorrect. A calculation error would not result in a medication error due to intentional patient noncompliance with directions for medication use.

D) Correct. Patient noncompliance with directions for medication use is a medication error due to social causes.

72. A) Incorrect. TD50 is a dosage presented on a dose response curve.

B) Incorrect. LD50 is a dosage found on a dose response curve.

C) Correct. There is no RD50 dose on a dose response curve.

D) Incorrect. ED50 is a dosage presented on a dose response curve.

73. A) Incorrect. DAW 5 means that a brand name medication is dispensed at generic price. Substitution is allowed.

B) Incorrect. DAW 8 means the generic version of a drug is not available. Substitution is allowed.

C) Correct. DAW 1 indicates that substitutions are not allowed by the prescriber. This is used when the doctor deems the brand medication is medically necessary, and substitution is not allowed.

D) Incorrect. DAW 3 indicates that the pharmacist selected the brand name although substitution is allowed.

74. A) Incorrect. Taking another person's medication to avoid copays is being noncompliant.

B) Correct. If the patient is not taking a medication because the doctor discontinued the medication, the patient is still compliant.

C) Incorrect. Skipping doses means a patient is noncompliant.

D) Incorrect. A patient who stops taking medication altogether without the doctor's approval is noncompliant.

75. **A) Correct.** Child doses are calculated by weight and BSA.

B) Incorrect. Child doses are not calculated by height.

C) Incorrect. A child's age does not determine medication dosage.

D) Incorrect. A child's grade has no bearing on medication.

76. A) Incorrect. Shoe covers are required; they are the first PPE put on when garbing up.

B) Incorrect. Technicians use masks to avoid contaminating the clean room with body particulates.

C) Incorrect. Gloves are required in the clean room, so they are an important part of garbing up.

D) Correct. Although technicians and other workers should wear minimal or no make up in the clean room, they are not required to wash their faces while garbing up.

77. **C)**

Set up a proportion with ounces on top and drams on bottom. Recall that 1 fl.ounce = 8 drams.

$$\frac{1 \text{ fl.ounce}}{8 \text{ drams}} = \frac{4 \text{ fl.ounce}}{x \text{ drams}}$$

Cross-multiply and solve for x.

$x = $ **32 drams**

Note: This can also be solved using Dimensional Analysis, multiplying by conversion ratios to cancel out units until finding the needed units:

$4 \text{ fl.ounces} \times \frac{8 \text{ drams}}{1 \text{ fl.ounce}} = 32 \text{ drams}$

78.
A) Incorrect. Succinylcholine is not used to treat blood pressure.

B) Incorrect. Succinylcholine is not used for pain.

C) **Correct.** Succinylcholine is used as anesthesia and is a paralytic agent.

D) Incorrect. Succinylcholine is not an immunosuppressant.

79.
A) Incorrect. While more Americans than ever before are insured, this number is far too high.

B) Incorrect. More than 75% of Americans are insured, so this number is incorrect.

C) **Correct.** As of 2016, about 84% of Americans are insured.

D) Incorrect. This number is too low and therefore incorrect.

80. **D)**

Set up a proportion with mL on top and pints on the bottom. Recall that 480 mL = 1 pint.

$$\frac{480 \text{ mL}}{1 \text{ pint}} = \frac{480 \text{ mL}}{x \text{ pints}}$$

Cross-multiply and solve for x.

$$480x = 480$$

$$x = 1 \text{ pint}$$

Note: This can also be solved using Dimensional Analysis, multiplying by conversion ratios to cancel out units until finding the needed units:

$$480 \text{ mL} \times \frac{1 \text{ pint}}{480 \text{ mL}} = 1 \text{ pint}$$

81.
A) Incorrect. Metronidazole is not considered a high-alert medication.

B) **Correct.** Potassium chloride injections are considered high-alert.

C) Incorrect. Ketorolac is not high-alert medication.

D) Incorrect. Lisinopril is not considered a high-alert medication.

82.
A) **Correct.** Arteries carry blood away from the heart.

B) Incorrect. Veins carry blood to the heart.

C) Incorrect. Capillaries are the small vessels in tissue.

D) Incorrect. Thin-walled, valved structures that carry lymph are called lymph vessels.

83.
A) Incorrect. MTM is not necessarily intended to reduce costs.

B) Incorrect. While calling in refills to a doctor helps with patient compliance, it is not the main purpose of MTM.

C) Incorrect. Advising patients of delivery and mail-order options aids compliance, but it is not the purpose of MTM.

D) **Correct.** MTM is intended to improve patient compliance.

84.
A) Incorrect. Orphan drugs do not necessarily cure diseases; they only treat certain ones.

B) Incorrect. Orphan drugs are rarely used and are not intended for common diseases or conditions.

C) **Correct.** Orphan drugs are pharmaceuticals that are developed specifically for rare diseases.

D) Incorrect. Orphans drugs are not appropriate for all patients.

85.
A) Incorrect. 120/80 is considered normal blood pressure.

B) Incorrect. 100/70 is not considered high blood pressure.

C) **Correct.** A reading over 140/90 is considered high.

D) Incorrect. 110/60 would be low blood pressure.

86.
A) **Correct.** The physician's name is not required in the compounding log. It is required on the prescription label.

B) Incorrect. The lot number of the medication compounded is needed in order to refer back to the product for recall or other purposes as necessary.

C) Incorrect. The pharmacist initials the compound to show that he or she verified it.

D) Incorrect. The beyond-use date is required because once the medication is compounded, the expiration date is different from the date on the manufacturer's packaging.

87.
A) Incorrect. Benztropine does not treat Alzheimer's disease.

B) Correct. Benztropine is an anti-tremor medication.

C) Incorrect. Benztropine is not an anti-anxiety medicine.

D) Incorrect. Benztropine is not an anti-depressant.

88.
A) Incorrect. Allergy information is always included in the patient's profile.

B) Correct. Spousal information is not required for a patient profile.

C) Incorrect. The patient's date of birth is required on a patient's profile.

D) Incorrect. It is essential that a patient's insurance information be correctly entered on his or her profile.

89.
A) **Correct.** It is not realistic to avoid stocking SALAD drugs in the pharmacy.

B) Incorrect. Using Tallman lettering is one strategy to differentiate SALAD drugs from other drugs in the pharmacy.

C) Incorrect. Color-coding is a strategy to differentiate SALAD drugs from other drugs in the pharmacy.

D) Incorrect. Stocking SALAD drugs in a different area in the pharmacy away from the regular stock is one way to differentiate them from other drugs.

90. **C)**

Set up a proportion with mL on top and teaspoons on bottom. Recall that 5 mL = 1 teaspoon.

$$\frac{5 \text{ mL}}{1 \text{ teaspoon}} = \frac{x \text{ mL}}{2 \text{ teaspoons}}$$

Cross-multiply and solve for x.

$x =$ **10 mL**

Note: This can also be solved using Dimensional Analysis, multiplying by conversion ratios to cancel out units until finding the needed units:

$$2 \text{ teaspoons} \times \frac{5 \text{ mL}}{1 \text{ teaspoon}} = 10 \text{ mL}$$

Follow the link below to take your second Pharmacy Technician Certification Exam practice test and to access other online study resources:

www.ascenciatestprep.com/ptcb-online-resources